Worlds and Underworlds

Peter Vansittart

Worlds and Underworlds

ANGLO-EUROPEAN HISTORY THROUGH THE CENTURIES

PETER OWEN · LONDON

ISBN 0 7206 0452 4

To John Atkinson (1934–1973)

Best of pupils, gay and generous friend, wise man.

PETER OWEN LIMITED
20 Holland Park Avenue London W11 3QU

First British Commonwealth edition 1974
© Peter Vansittart 1974

Printed in Great Britain by
Bristol Typesetting Co Ltd
Barton Manor St Philips Bristol 2

Contents

Mysterious 'feelings' came upon him, that he wasn't used to; strange awarenesses of old, far-gone men, and other influences; men of Gaul, with big moustaches, who had been on his island, and had vanished from the face of it, but not out of the air at night. They were still there, hurtling their big, violent, unseen bodies through the night. And there were priests with a crucifix; then priests with murder on the sea. . . . He was uncannily aware, as he lay in the dark, that the blackthorn grove that seemed a bit uncanny even in the realm of space and day, at night was crying with old men of an invisible race, around the altar stone. What was a ruin under the hornbeam tree by day was a moaning of bloodstained priests with crucifixes, on the ineffable night.

D. H. Lawrence, *The Man who Loved Islands*

Author's Preface

I once walked five miles down a rough country road to visit friends. I arrived, knocked, saw a curtain twitch, heard a long extended moan, 'Oh *God*!'. Hastily, I withdrew, five miles. 'Oh *God*!' may await yet another generalized 'popular' English historical survey.

I have gambled on the existence of unacademic readers who, without wanting text-books or detailed theses, enjoy the English past and have some topical interest in some of the broader aspects of Anglo-Continental relations. To them I submit this book, as a footnote to, or preparation for, the great historians. From mingled affection and horror for Britain and Europe, the old wrongs, old tragedies, old ironies, old but not stale, I have attempted not to assert final truths – however peremptorily the text may read – but to recollect some clues. My own predilections or deficiencies make the emphasis more cultural than political and economic.

I enjoy acknowledging, with gratitude, the teachers, artists, classics, places and tales that have made me. There is scarcely a quotation here that does not still excite me. I am intrigued by Stonehenge being a circle, by an artist being the first casualty at Hastings, by pilgrims' graffiti in a lonely church, by Robespierre's awaiting 'the belated help of Time', by Zola's fascination with numbers. Even a historical trifle may reconcile us with the living or dead. I get unchauvinistic pleasure in reflecting that London knew Peter the Great, Mozart, Voltaire, Handel, Talleyrand, Van Gogh; sheltered Hallé, Louis Napoleon, Marx, Herzen, Lenin, Gandhi, Freud, Bor-Komorowski; was chosen by Conrad, Henry James, Eliot; survives so unforgettably in Doré, in Monet, and in James himself.

My bias is towards the stoical and sceptical. It is not original, but glumly true, that the self-consciously progressive tends to increase the area not only of popular participation but of capital punishment. 'To Utopia' and 'To the Guillotine' can be identical – a fact that I find, with increasing resentment, more obvious than it seemed in my youth.

I have tried to keep a balance between traditions and institutions obstinately British, and those symbols and obsessions that may be common to all peoples, of which religion and politics seem as much the result as the cause. Myth and ritual persist even within technology, which may indeed be silently reinvigorating them. I have given reminders that a child's game, music-hall song, folk tale, football hooliganism, may be as significant as treaties, battles, graphs, dates. Finally, I am interested in whether disillusionment with the past will devalue history as a relevant study : whether there is more freedom, happiness, perception in no longer knowing why a constellation is called Orion's belt; in no longer debating the origins of Pyramids, Reformation, Hitler.

I am grateful to Jenny Mussell for her hard labour on the manuscript.

Part One

1   A Britain of Gods

> And I know there are gods behind the gods,
> Gods that are best unsung.
>
> G. K. Chesterton

1

Everywhere, even behind apparent quiet, is incessant movement. Maritime magnetic surveys are suggesting that South America, Africa, India were once one, that Canada was joined to Europe. Sea fossils and forest remains lie in the Sahara, fish fossils on the Alps.

Opinions, too, are moods of time. Thirteenth-century Tibetans ate their parents as a mark of respect. Romans found sexual charm in the foot, Japanese in the back of the neck – as Gautier found in Venetian girls –, Victorians allegedly in the ankle. The *Beagle*'s crew gave trousers to naked Fuergans, who wore them as turbans. George IV used £20 worth of cosmetics a week. Lord Cornbury charged admission to dinners at which he wore his wife's clothes. Voltaire considered *Hamlet* the work of a drunken savage. Some Chinese consider it impious to live on dry land. For certain Eskimoes, to wear clothes indoors is disgusting. Brahmins find more virtue in starving than in growing their own vegetables.

Crossroads become markets, then towns which decline to outposts or rubble. A Blackfriars' house in Plymouth changed to a Debtors Prison, then to a centre for Plymouth Gin. In the Domesday village of Thakeham, a church memorial, once a stone face, has been worn to no more than a smile. Current practice dwindles to tradition, belief to hearsay or prejudice; marvellous gods end as decrepit warlocks or are buried in the days of the week. A Dover church is inscribed: 'Built 1910. Bombed 1917. Rebuilt 1920. Bombed 1941. Rebuilt 1949.'

Time moves fast; it also moves slowly. One can still meet Americans born of slaves, or those who have met Gladstone, Florence Nightingale, the Empress Eugenie, whose husband spoke to Napoleon I.

2

Pre-Celtic Britain is a detective story without hero or villain: witnesses are dumb; judges, though learned, are quarrelsome, the public credulous. No final verdict accompanies evidence and motives. The case is prehistoric, seen as if through a lens distorting and deceiving, yet it remains alive.

If no man is an island, an island is seldom wholly island. For perhaps 10,000 years Britain has been cut off from Europe by water but, in 200,000, has never been isolated. Between ice ages and floodings, men, plants and animals arrived from the East. Rhino, bear, tiger roamed a warmer Britain that later exported wine. At Wortwell were found, 1967, bones of an extinct species of elephant from over a million years ago. A Neolithic skeleton was exhumed, buried with an elephant's trunk, in South Wales.

Trade and immigration flowed through Neolithic Britain. Centuries before Stonehenge, Ireland and Spain were trading. English jet of 2500 BC is found in Spain; in Britain, Egyptian beads of 1300 BC. The island, rich in tin, gold, copper, jet, obsidian, in soil and navigable rivers, as Stone Age overlapped with Bronze, developed agriculture, mining, navigation, hunting, domestication of animals, slavery. War occurred : to cope with grosser human types, with climatic changes, restrictive markets, and the supernatural; for raw materials, for revenge. Major change was seldom genial. Until AD 1688 violence promoted each new dynasty save the Stuarts, who themselves succumbed to violence.

Incessant challenges intensified skills and developed both ritual and technology – axe, wheel, hammer, chisel, bow, control of fire. The New Stone Age, from about 2500 BC, made dramatic advances.

> A rural economy already containing the germ of ours today was suddenly imposed from without on a primitive society that had changed very little for some 20,000 years. This Neolithic settlement was, in fact, the first of a long series of contacts between Britain and the higher civilizations of the Mediterranean which have played so stimulating a part in the development of our culture. It ranked in importance beside such later influences as those of the Roman Empire, the Christian Church and the Renaissance.
>
> (J. and C. Hawkes, *Prehistoric Britain*, Pelican, 1943)

The Hunting and Farming Ages endured far longer than industrialism has yet done. Man retains residues of each, sometimes at odds with his present needs. By failing to cater for warrior adventure, fears of death and darkness, day-dreams of bright impossible distances, the City, disciplined and often inorganic, may impose complex, if indeterminate, strains.

By about 1900 BC, successive Bronze Age invaders, notably from
Spain, were ousting Stone Age rulers and bringing Britain into the
Mediterranean trade orbit. Sophisticated engineers erected Avebury,
the three Stonehenges, the 20,000 barrows and smaller stone circles
signalling to a sky thick with gods. Salisbury Plain was to be embossed with temples, palaces, sprayed with avenues and roads,
ritual as well as mercenary. A Neolithic, mile-long ceremonial avenue
with circular 'henges' (sanctuaries) is at Maxey. Silbury is the
largest artificial hill in Europe. Stonehenge may have been temple,
palace, observatory, even university : Inigo Jones, imagining that it
was Roman, delighted in its 'pure, harmonious proportions'.

Iberian Britons were adepts in enamel and bronze. Elaborate gold
and bronze work suggest a wealthy, perhaps sun-worshipping,
ruling caste sustained by international trade. Egyptian beads, Breton
daggers lay in Stonehenge barrows. Movement remained fluid and,
by 1000 BC, Asia Minor and Europe were being invaded by iron-
bearing Celts who by 600 had settled in Britain, lively and resource-
ful in art, manufacture, architecture, trade, war.

At Llongbroth I saw, hewing with steel,
Brave men of Arthur,
Emperor, director of toil.

Celtic Sussex exported iron; Celtic roads, perhaps strengthening
earlier thoroughfares, anticipated the Roman. In pottery, carving,
metal-work, Celtic design luxuriated in an exuberant mingling of
fancy and skill, echoed in Dark Age and medieval jewellery, English
and French. Celtic coinage was modelled on Greek. Later druids,
who might use Greek writing, studied what Caesar called 'enormous
quantities of sacred poetry', never written down, he believed,
partly to sustain the memory, partly to keep the knowledge secret,
a Mystery.

Less efficient was Celtic tribalism. Kings quarrelled. When Rome,
irritated by support given to continental Celts, invaded Britain,
some tribes supported the invader – naturally enough, for they
were not a single people and had not arrived simultaneously. Self-
interest ruled. Already analogies were found between Celtic and
Roman deities.

A grave for Gawayne of the Red Sword.
Concealed till Domesday the grave of Arthur.

Celtic gods haunted swamp and forest, cave and loch, rivers and
many-throated seas, gods matching the heights and depths within

the watcher. Ploughman's plain, hermit's crag knew the powers of spell and blade, dreams of initiation and transformation, in the wake of Bran, Nudens, Lear. Bel, sun-god, is recalled in 'Billingsgate', with Beltane his spring-feast. Lud, Lot, Lug, a light-god, fathered Gawayne ('the Spring'), named Lammas and, for some, London (Caer-Lud). Tin or Tan ('tinder'), Etruscan fire-god, seems to have been adopted as a Celtic god – 'San Tan' is Breton 'sacred fire', his many hills becoming 'St Anne's Hills'.

Arthur has associations with sun and fertility, wind and bear. In Cornwall the Great Bear is sometimes 'Arthur's Wain'. In Celtic verse he has magic powers and the morals of a cattle-rustler. Like Hercules he hunts supernatural monsters. His magic weapons are masterpieces of Gonfan the metal-god and Widea, son of Weland. Like Theseus, Ishtar, Orpheus, Hermodur, he raids the Underworld. There he steals a magic cauldron or grail, and one of his wives is abducted by the Dark King. He is sometimes depicted amongst zodiacal signs; sometimes too with goat and phallus-club, and is connected with Avalon, Isle of Apples. Goat and apples were part of Dionysian Mystery rites, the club is Herculean. Behind Arthur hovers Merlin, virgin-born, who like Joshua commanded the sun to obey him. Merlin drinks bull's blood before prophesying, his predictions including that of a virgin who would save France. He teaches that the universe was created from a divine egg, history beginning with the murder of a god disguised as an apple.

'In Bulls does the Earth-shaker delight.' Symbol of power, virility, earthquake, the bull fascinated men. To tame or kill him might promote vitality, restrain cataclysm. Lewis Spence claimed that a fertility bull was buried alive in Scotland, 1870. Men sought in animals what they themselves lacked : wisdom of serpent, valour of lion. They sat on dragon thrones, peacock thrones, flaunted heraldic eagles, boars, feathered snakes. The owl presaged sudden death : in South Italy it is still nailed over doors to exorcize ill-luck, as in Apuleius's *Golden Ass*.

A shadowy Britain lingers in children's tales and romance. There rules the Great Witch, Ceridwen the Mother, virgin source of wonder, song, inspiration, and Celtic princess seeking her lost cauldron. Idris the star-lover gives poetry, madness, death. Under Sewingshield Crags, Arthur and Guinevere sleep enchanted until the wanderer awakes them. In barren castle groans the King, sexually wounded like Adonis, healed by Peredur, Lord of the Cup, as, in Eliot's poem, the healing waters of generosity, sympathy and control will restore the Waste Land. Under Soar dwells Lear, a reputed father of Arthur, whose own father built Caer-Badin (Bath) for the owl-goddess and who flew aloft on artificial wings. At

Glastonbury, site of forgotten Mysteries, lurks Morgan, Fate God-dess, wife and sister of Arthur, Mother of the Betrayer. In Annyn, the Underworld, Prince Pwyll impersonates the Dark King. The sky is a great teacher.

Place-names tell of invading peoples and intrusive gods. Thundersley, Wednesbury, Carlisle, Tintagel, London, Avonmouth, Elephant and Castle, Wrexham, Leicester, Whitby – were created by beliefs, customs, events and language once foreign, and at times dreaded.

2 *Patterns*

I

Contrasts are endless, movement incessant, though the contrasts
are often superficial, the pace gradual and seldom assured. World-
wide habits of ritual, authority, mysticism hardened into patterns
thenceforward consistent, though the basic principles remain disputed. Konrad Lorenz and Robert Ardrey, researching amongst
animals, arouse popular interest and much critical dissent.

> I suggest that there are three beginnings . . . psychologically moti-
> vating the behaviour of all higher animals, including man. They
> are those same needs for identity, for stimulation, and for
> security . . . and security, normally, will be sacrificed for the
> other two. . . . Human war, for example, has been the most
> successful of all our cultural traditions because it satisfies all three
> basic needs.
>
> (R. Ardrey, *The Territorial Imperative*, Collins, 1967)

Primeval territorial needs, Ardrey finds, are dominant, expressed
in love, crime, deceit and aggression. 'Pain may be far more
stimulating than pleasure; death and disaster may present hypo-
dermic changes more potent than life at its fullest, success at its most
resounding.'

Man's freedom of will is a lengthy historical debate, but genetic
inheritances may well underlie religious and political movements,
national hysteria, the lure of dictators. Yet, though man may lack
profoundest freedom, may be determined by genes, environment or
class, his actual behaviour, ranging from Napoleon to Gandhi, en-
courages a fruitful illusion of personal will.

For early man, fate seemed controllable, by magic, by leadership.
Shamanism has continued, left over from peoples as unfamiliar as

16

the aurochs and bison they hunted. The philosopher-mathematician Pope Sylvester II became in medieval folk-lore a wizard alongside Virgil and Alexander and, like Garm the Good, Roger Bacon, Bishop Grosstête, signed a pact with the Devil in return for earthly power. Sylvester's remains lamented whenever a pope was endangered. Francis Drake became remembered as a magician with special powers over waters. In the eighteenth-century Enlightenment, Mesmer, Franklin, Priestley were denounced as occultists. New techniques would be feared, as Black Magic: the Indian telegraph helped precipitate the Mutiny.

2

Even Neanderthal Man seems to have conceived of an after-life. The soul, immortal human essence, is an antique conception, envisaged as flame, bird, butterfly, mouse, white dove, mannikin, gaseous envelope, 'flight without noise'. The Greeks symbolized it as a bean, Tertullian described it as bright blue. A contemporary African has seen spirits 'made of polished wood'. As the unconscious, the soul responds to older rhythms of bone, tree, sun; is enchanted by the art it provokes and is strangely troubled in the small hours. Rossetti believed his wife's soul became a chaffinch. Arthur in death was seen as a raven: medieval ravens were sometimes called 'Arthur'.

> His soul at last was still in him, his spirit was like a dim-lit cave under water, where strange sea-foliage expands upon the watery atmosphere, and scarcely sways, and a mute fish shadowly slips in and slips away again. All still and soft and uncrying, yet alive as rooted seaweed is alive.

(D. H. Lawrence, *The Man who Loved Islands*)

Inner Man is more than belly. Religions, including some early Christian sects, believed in transmigration of souls, reincarnation and *karma,* the effect of earthly behaviour on the soul's future. Contradictory impulses within the individual were explicable as several souls trapped in one body. Reincarnation had not been formally rejected by Christianity until 553. W. T. Stead, who helped to raise the Age of Consent, also to send Gordon to the Sudan, imagined himself a reincarnation of Charles II. George Patton, flamboyant American general, believed, like Ovid, that he had fought at Troy; also with Charles Edward in the '45.

Human culture is entangled with such beliefs. 'The chief doctrine of the Druids is that the soul does not perish, but at death passes

from one body to another.' (Caesar) Celts, Jews and Sioux often
associated soul with hair, symbol of virility and immortality. Llew
Llaw was unmanned by a woman robbing him of his hair. Scalping
added enemies' strength to one's own. Heroes might shave before
battle to avoid risking elemental powers. Cremation detached soul
from body. Early Christians believed the soul hovered three days
above the corpse. Yawners shielded the mouth to prevent the soul's
escape. Sneezing might expel it, so required a precautionary phrase.
Plato, Pythagoras and Hindu gurus produced intricate doctrines of
the soul. Black Magic imperilled it, water and mirrors could trap
it. Observers theorized from false premises : a man lay dead, a crow
sat on his face, therefore his soul was a crow. Bushmen fear the
camera, which can capture their souls. Hong-Kong fishermen
believe that sharks can kill them by devouring their souls, conceived
as shadows. For medievals :

> Instantaneous death occurs when the aerial spirit, escaping from
> the eyes of the sick man, strikes the eyes of a healthy person
> standing near and looking at the sick.

(Philip Ziegler, The Black Death, Collins, 1969)

Even the free-thinking Emperor Frederick II was reputed to have
encased a man in a tub, to see whether the soul could escape.

Dr John Dee, the Tudor mathematician and astrologer-royal,
credited spirits that spoke to him in the language of Adam and Eve,
which he did not understand. (His magic crystal is in the British
Museum.) W. B. Yeats, Ludendorff, Himmler believed in the literal
existence of good and evil spirits. Highlanders retain the notion
of soldiers' souls roaming the sky, whistling and fighting, dropping
blood, seeking expiation.

Esteban Montejo, a former slave in Cuba, over 100 years old in
1968, reflects :

> One thing that it is not given to us men to see is the soul. We
> cannot say whether it is such or such a colour. The soul is one
> of the greatest things in the world. Dreams are there to put us in
> touch with it. . . . Some people have only the magic sort of souls,
> while others have ordinary ones. But the ordinary ones are better,
> I think, because the others are in league with the Devil. It can
> happen that the soul leaves the body – when a person dies or
> sleeps – and joins the other souls wandering in space.

(The Autobiography of a Runaway Slave, Bodley Head, 1968)

An advertisement (*Daily Telegraph*, 13 July 1972) concerns

'Cosmic Consciousness, the experience of *momentary flights* of the soul, that is become *one with the universe*, and receive an influx of great understanding.'

Body-soul counterpoint became monopolized by professional priests, spiritual industrialists who projected long-lived speculations and rituals. For Leonardo, empirical and scientific, 'our body depends on heaven, heaven on the spirit.' Pope Leo X rejected the soul's immortality. In revenge for the Mutiny, the British blew Indians to pieces at the cannon's mouth, to destroy it. Tolstoy stated : 'To eat when one is hungry, drink water when one is thirsty : these are the great bodily pleasures : but to refuse food and drink and all bodily desires is more than a pleasure, it is the joy of the soul.' Platonic notions of the soul, divine intelligences and orders sustaining the universe, recur in Donne and in Yeats.

Mr James Field of Arizona left £125,000 for research into the soul. His will, confirmed July 1971, declared that it could be photographed leaving the body. Less explicitly, the soul the world over has been sensed as a compression of striving, soaring into incandescence with John Donne or St John of the Cross, a dynamic potential seeking to escape body, death, space, time, and achieve perfection. Twelfth-century Cathari held matter and body impure, imprisoning the soul that desperately needed release. In cathedral, palace, flag, military noise, sports team, was embalmed the soul of the people.

3

A vital principle was magic, the rituals necessitating delicate perception of natural rhythms, phases of sun and moon, night and sky, birth and death, and of animals.

Animal, hill, flame, man, possessed *mana*, magical spirit, stuff of the soul, rich with infinite possibilities of transcending the commonplace. Also *aura*, subtle atmosphere or personality, elusive and potent as scent, magnetic waves inducing nameless power. Minerals in soil and woods, and on hills, made holy certain 'magnetic' sites, for shrines and cemeteries. A twentieth-century German astrologer, Herr Volrath, wore a fez to restrain his aura (Howe). Experts manipulated these elements : priest-kings, alchemists, Black and White magicians. A tiny idol could radiate giant's force. Magnetic power seemed vehement mana. Fire hypnotized; fire-ceremonies – to purge, destroy, propitiate – bequeathed symbolic tales, myths, of world-destruction by fire which invaded Christianity, Mithraism, Islam and fascinated artists like Wagner, would-be artists like Hitler.

Imitation or resemblance represented reality. Magic lay in logical deductions from such unreal 'reality'. To eat a good book or good man would render one excellent. Bury a body, or doll, and the soil gained life. A Chinese sexual athlete would rub his penis with powdered deer-Horn, sea-cucumber, bull's genitals to increase his potency. Caxambia, the Brazilian footballer, ate cats to promote virility. At Wellington's funeral the Duke's horse carried his boots and a child asked whether all dead people got changed into boots.

The belief that human flesh-tallow gave light rendering the bearer invisible, lingered amongst French thieves who, under Louis XIV, carried a candle of human fat, for luck. A snail-shell resembled an ear, so cured ear-ache. Cowrie shells, fertility emblems, became coinage. Magic indeed promoted some trade and war. Gods might demand *Lebensraum*. Prisoners had to be sacrificed to impossible but indispensable deities. Victors drank victims' blood from their skulls to acquire their courage. *Skall*! War and hunting demanded rituals to ensure victory or explain defeat. Germanic tribes dyed their heads red, for martiality. Nineteenth-century Banyan Arabs, when sick, took strips of the Koran and drank them in water or wore them next to the afflicted part. War was made to capture prisoners for magic cannibalism, or to steal the minerals, plants, coloured stones needed for ritual : jet, amber, cornelian had special magnetic or occult force.

Untruth is not always lying, magic not necessarily gross superstition. To revere a tree can be more profitable than to squander it as timber. Mars and Venus may not exist, but passions can be tamed or venerated by ritual, domesticated as gods, outlawed as demons.

Climate, season, after-life were susceptible to rituals, which conditioned morality. Rites and adornments made authority supernatural. Kings were living idols, totems : kings who pretended never to eat, or to be their own fathers, to be animals or not to exist. Ancient Irish kings enacted sacred copulations with an Earth Goddess. The King of Swaziland annually rides a bull round his capital, Mbabana, during fertility rites. Kings could be sacrificed, for tribal health. Later, they might temporarily abdicate, replaced by a slave who after a brief mock-reign would be killed, sometimes after scourging, limb-breaking, anointment under a mock-crown. That a Great One should die for the people was a commonplace: the Bab, founder of Persian Babism, was martyred, AD 1850. Animal substitutes might appear. In Assam an ape was regularly crucified, a variation of the Jewish 'Scapegoat'. Jesus was sometimes 'Lamb', 'Fish', 'Panther'. In the early Passover the dead lamb was fixed on a cross. The cross was also a Buddhist emblem and, again, sacred to

Quetzalcoatl who, in some Aztec myths, was crucified. Kingship was not inevitable – the Kikuyu had none – but was usual.

The sacredness of royalty was never lost. Seven Christian emperors after Constantine wore Jupiter's oak leaves. Vespasian was credited with miraculous cures. The Japanese 'dynasty' is 'those who live above the clouds'. Remnants of royal or heroic sacrifice are embedded in Greek and Shakespearian drama. The Great One dies, so that the tribe can persist, sin be redeemed, the Curse lifted, the city endure. The death is not final. Dead Caesar remains a vital part of the play. Henry V repeats the lore of the sacrificial hero :

> Upon the King ! Let us our lives, our souls,
> Our debts, our careful wives,
> Our children, and our sins lay on the king :
> We must bear all.

Hamlet, Amlothi, 'the pure', suggests the legacy of a spring-god dying at each sowing, after a queen is drowned as a rain-charm. That the Chosen should die for others remains deep in the psyche, affecting not only kings but outstanding commoners, like the Irish rebel Pearse, shot in Dublin, 1916.

Kings must be superhuman. Awkward deportment might upset cosmic rhythms, so royal movements must be smooth and impassive. So potent was their mana that rulers might be forbidden to touch the ground – like the American flag – and were thus carried as, formally, the Pope still is. In early Christian North Africa even the newborn had, for a week, not to let bare feet contact earth.

Kingly and sacerdotal semen, dung, footprints, hair, clothes were rigorously protected from Black magicians, their persons allowed an aura deadly as electricity. A nineteenth-century Thai queen was accidentally drowned, none daring to rescue a body so sacred. A century after Sedgemoor, 1685, a silver buckle given to a boy by 'King' Monmouth was being used as a magic charm. Monmouth himself had 'touched for the evil'. Marc Bloch[1] finds Charles II 'touching' a hundred thousand people. A blood-stained Stuart hand-kerchief was still used as a healing talisman in Ireland, 1900. Pepys, ill in 1681, was urged to send his toe-nail clippings and three locks of hair to a local magus. Sixteenth-century Paracelsus held semen and faeces to be aphrodisiac. To spit on one's own body was a precaution against misfortune; Catholic priests at baptism still touch their fingers with saliva.

Tsar, Kaiser, Sultan, held sacred kingship to within the present century, until supplanted by the quasi-sacred Leader. Russian officialdom was still evoking, 1966, 'the sacred name of Lenin'.

4

Man demands answers, rating bad answers above silence. He
prefers what Gorky calls 'the enchanted lie' to bleak truths and
statistics; he readily translates the symbolic as literal. 'Fairy-tales'
recalled magical transformations. One could contrive one's own
luck. Marvellous lives in far-off realms were remembered or
induced by hypnosis, elixirs, drugs, sexual stimulants, lulling scents
and incantations, incredible colours, voices serene or manic, shapes
beautiful or monstrous. Dim apprehensions survive : of arrows shot
into the sky, and one falling, soaked in blood; of bull-men roaring
for victims; of a trumpet snarling from the ether at the start of a
new era.

Ritual enchantments, maenad laurel-chewing frenzies link Stone
Age treasure-seekers with our own drug-takers. Hashish, opium,
alcohol, cocaine, tobacco have for centuries been used as opiates for
pain, ill news, execution; or to create ecstasy. Robert Graves main-
tains that nectar and ambrosia were toxic mushrooms promoting
mindless riots, prophetic insights, demented orgies, intimations of
heaven and hell, transcendental visions in which death is resurrection.[2] Such narcotics still exist in Mexico, sacred to Tlaloc, Mushroom God. J. M. Allegro[3] has attempted to interpret Christianity as
a by-product of an orgiastic fertility cult, with Jesus a mushroom
symbol, whose seminal narcotic juices degenerated into bread and
wine.

To illiterates, everything is something else. History shows a
struggle to see things, memories, the body – live or dead – objectively. Symbolism was rampant. The Snake could stiffen, an
obvious sexual symbol; could flow, undulate, ripple, and was thus
associated with water. Aboriginal Australians revere the rain-serpent.
Weaving snake-dances in Wales, China, Mexico, and dragon-killing
rituals secured the rain, as circular dances flattered the sun. The
snake killed deviously, thus symbolizing the dark and vindictive,
yet its flexibility and skin-shedding linked it to time, to self-en-
lightenment.

> The principle of the imagination resembles the emblem of the
> serpent, by which the ancients typified wisdom and the universe,
> for ever varying and for ever flowing into itself – circular and
> without beginning or end.
>
>   (Coleridge)

This circularity was opposed by Christian finite time – Creation,

Incarnation, Judgment – though the Snake could be the symbol of St Mary of Antioch, as of Athens and the Cretan Great Goddess. Sacred snakes protected palace and temple. Snake and dragon were favourites of life-enhancing Dionysus. Popular magic demanded adder-eating, to regain lost youth. Snakes are not unknown in pictures of Mary. Anglo-Saxon stonework at St Nicholas's Church, Ipswich, shows Michael fighting a Wyvern (dragon) inscribed 'Her : Sct Michael Feht Vid Dan Draca.'

Medieval cabbalistic and devil-cults were vulgarly believed to adore snake and phallus, controlled by Jewish grand-masters. A Celtic snake-god, Hu Gadarn, was captured in Wales and burnt at Smithfield under Henry VIII. Durham was founded on a 'dragon-hill'. There are those who claim that Herefordshire Beacon and Glastonbury Tor have man-made grooves, to resemble coils. At Avebury Church a Gothic stone carving shows a Bishop fighting two dragons. In Britain and France, dragon emblems, effigies, masks were carried in Rogation processions, often in parish bound-beating, with particular care when approaching water.

Myth and ritual made man at one with the world. Sacrifice was universal, frequently of children, particularly orphans, who needed 'godfathers'. Rome killed children, in terror of Hannibal. Classical and biblical accounts of unusual deaths suggest sacrifice. Ritual deaths averted the anger or jealousy of gods, procured harvest, replenished the tribal soul, gave the abstruse satisfaction that accompanies the victimization of lover or hero. Man lives by shared ceremonies. Socrates' Athenians sacrificed against Plague. Sacrifice was Tragedy, charged, as in the bull-ring, with utmost tensions. Literally, 'Tragedy' was 'Goat-song', honouring Dionysus, with rituals that made suffering purposeful, ennobled inept or outrageous lives by teaching that failure can be success, death triumphant, with sacrifice the emotional pivot of life, enriching the world. In Britain, an Old Stone Age Derbyshire bone-engraving of a man wearing a horse's head hints at such rites. The Theatre long continued ritual castes and situations : single combat, elaborate killing, ceremonial prayer, wise old man, irreverent clown, simple or faultless victim.

Gods can be worshipped, abused, reproached. In the graveyard at Aberfan, where over a hundred children died in the 1967 disaster, is engraved : 'Why did you have to break our hearts to prove you need the best?' Sacrifice is never far distant from divinity. Human blood had powers craved by the dead, and by gods. At Cadbury, associated with Arthur, rubbish pits have revealed horse and ox-skulls, seemingly ritual. A human fertility emblem has been found at Grimes Graves, once sacred to Woden. Black bulls, black goats were sacrificed at midsummer under oaks. Red cats howled in Annyn. As

gods had created all, everything had divine *anima* which needed
refreshment: human blood fertilized a new building or bridge. A
man was supposedly sacrificed beneath the Tower of Babel. A
Bronze Age baby was found beneath Woodhenge, near Stonehenge.
Such a sacrifice occurred in North Germany, 1848. When Bishop
Latimer was burnt in 1554, onlookers remarked that, had this
occurred earlier, it might have saved the harvest. During the
Napoleonic Wars a London mob slaughtered a pig, yelling that it
was the Devil.

The dead could be contacted by spells, threats, promises, ghost-
dances. They protected the tribe, or had to be restrained by heavy
cairns. Pyramids cast long shadows. Death-cults required elaborate
ritual and architecture, eventually foaming into the profuse imagery
of renaissance tombs. Henry VIII abolished chantry and indulgence,
but ceremony survived, Victorian funerals and mourning making a
prolonged and satisfying ritual and festival industry, a soothing
comfort in poetry, prayer and ballad. 'Ring the bells softly, There's
crepe on the door.' Today, most of this is discarded, at whatever
cost, or none.

Hundreds of thousands of years I was flying to and fro,
Involuntary, like a mote in the air.
If I have forgotten that time and state, yet the migration
In sleep recalls it to my memory.

(Rumi, 1201–73)[4]

5

Flat Sumeria vividly exposed night skies. Star-clusters apparently
controlled the calendar: astral changes warned of floods, crops,
game, divine moods. The zodiac became compounded with ornate
hues, occult substances, intricate symbolism. Jupiter's moons suggested masculinity, the Evening Star femininity. Kings were
astronomers-royal, advised by astrological colleges. Blood and water
were, like tides, controlled by the heavens. Weather, months,
dreams, herbs, jewels, all Below, were enmeshed in all Above. The
Chinese believed that Nature was affected by music.

Cosmic webs were intricate. Zodiacal Virgo was simultaneously
September and Jasper; Leo, August and Ruby. Astrological values
retain meaning: 'martial', 'mercurial', 'jovial', 'saturnine'. Horoscope time was never quite superseded by Calendar time, magic by
reason. BC Athens had the complex 'Antikythera Computer' for
charting stellar positions. Mystery religions often postulated twelve

initiation stages related to zodiacal houses. Today, IQ tests and computers seem to be granted certain functions of the horoscope, supported by credulities often dangerous and sometimes grotesque.

Christianity scarcely touched astrology. Augustine experimented with it, Aquinas accepted it. It still attracts intellectuals provoked by discontents and too many calories. It can explain failure. Shakespeare's Antony laments : '. . . my good stars, that were my former guides,/ Have empty left their orbs, and shot their fires/ Into the abysm of hell.'

Henry Miller describes Madame Blavatsky as 'the Neptunian and the Uranian type combined.'[5] Nehru, Laval, Himmler, Hitler, Mussolini consulted such astrologers as Hanussen, Krafft, Feuchtinger. The Swede, Grünberger, foretold 1948 as Hitler's 'great year'. The astrologer Cheiro wrote of the future Edward VIII in 1931 that his peculiar planetary influences might well cause him 'to fall victim to a devastating love-affair. If he does, I predict that the Prince will renounce everything, even the chance of being crowned, rather than lose his friend.'

G. L. Nanda, in Nehru's Cabinet, believed in astrology and his friend, Professor Raman, foretold through horoscopes the murder of Gandhi and Kennedy. On astrological advice, Indian Independence, 1947, was postponed for one day. Jung would study patients' horoscopes. Electronic horoscopes, computer-fashioned, appeared after 1945, one of them retrospectively finding that Marcel Petiot, executed in 1946 for twenty-seven murders, would probably fall in love, 1972 : 'This Venusian person is bathed in oceanic sensitivity of infinite diffusion, agitated by universal love.' Certain Western capitalists use astrologers to help select personnel; universities are studying the effect of celestial movements on blood and water. Communist Czechoslovakia has established a department for astrological medicine. (*Guardian*, 27 April 1970). In 1972 the British Post Office, on a ten-year-old American precedent, briefly promoted 'Star-line', a fortune-telling telephone service. Following a scandal involving René Henaux, 'the Magus of Compiègne', 1969, a Paris court heard that the French spent £80 million a year on the occult. Also in 1969, Italian astrologers were demonstrating outside Parliament for recognition for their National Association. An astrologer at the Indian Embassy, Washington, predicted on 6 November 1972, an electoral victory for Senator McGovern !

6

For early man, vital sympathy existed between reality and its replica or substitute, fetish – expressed in art, idol, mime, parody. To

attract rain, Mexicans killed a victim with a shower of arrows
while priests imitated water-birds, flapping, screeching, pretending
to fly. Death-masks and effigies had magical properties. The 'genius'
of the Roman god-emperor inhabited his statue in the town centre.
Paintings had magic properties: only a few years ago, the Ikon of
Tenos was escorted to the mainland in a Greek cruiser, in hopes
that it would save the dying King Paul. Celtic tribes, medieval towns
might have guardian giants. Effigies of English kings, carried up-
right at their funerals, were placed in the national sanctuary,
Westminster Abbey.

Art – music, painting, dancing, ceremonial adornment, uniforms
– was not 'What I like' but 'What we need'. Magic, essential for
hunting, mating, war, the after-life and for authority, evoked the
excitement of a Mass during plague, of a political rally or pop
festival. Authority, Left or Right, considers itself sacred and
attempts to exploit art, resenting its bids for freedom. 'An art',
proclaimed Kaiser Wilhelm II in 1901, 'which transgresses the
laws and barriers outlined by Me, ceases to be an art.'

Imitation of totemic animals, gods, rhythms of earth and sky
increased man's subtlety, enlarged his sensual and linguistic range,
initiated patterns of imagery, ritual vision. Sexuality contained
supreme magic, naked orgies visibly replenishing the earth, assisting harvest, curing ills. Copulation on altars abashed the medieval
plague. Transcending class, time, possessions, earth itself, sex was
the one magic rite available to all.

Poets performed functions now left to priest, doctor, dictator,
entertainer, analyst. Skills in metaphor, incantation, verbal hypnosis
penetrated worlds hitherto inaccessible or unrecognized. People
endure through make-belief, which can reveal a higher truth. The
mind

> Has found form and colour and light,
> The cold glimmer of the ice-wrapped Poles;
> It has called a far-off glow Arcturus,
> And some pale weeds, lilies of the valley.

(W. J. Turner)

Poet, priest, clown negotiated with the unseen by re-arranging
words in startling relationships, as curse or blessing. In 1967 the
police were summoned to Addlestone by villagers frightened by a
gypsy's curse. Stones, colours, moon, sea, gods, beasts, demons, souls,
music, planets, the living and the dead were ultimately connected –
as late as *Macbeth*, royal murder, "gainst nature', could be presented as provoking earthquake, tempest, animal cannibalism. Words
could control fire, water, gods and kings. The medieval Mass of the

Holy Spirit enslaved God to the priest. Joke, obscenity, rhyme could, like music, change people by changing mood. Poets created agitation, the shocks of madness and tears. Druid poet-priests destroyed by satire, strengthened by eulogy, manipulated reputations. Their mysterious performance soothed and enchanted. Poetry and music wove spells, the more memorable, the more effective.

In the West, post-renaissance art became increasingly private and individualistic, though today, in street festivals and art-exhibitions, pub poetry-readings and general pop culture, this may be being modified. Dictatorships manufacture heroic public art and 'social realism', to enforce conformity. There are less forbidding instances. Rebecca West states that in the 1890s, Finance Ministers of Serbia and Bulgaria introduced budgets in blank verse.[6] W. S. M. Russell mentions Congolese coffee-labourers singing strike-threats in cantata form. (*The Listener*, 16 January 1964)

7

'The Sun is the mind of the Universe.' (Macrobius) Sun was health, fire purged. Dissenters were often burnt, to cleanse the air of noxious influences. Medieval Halloween torches expelling black spirits were a reminder of the 'Forlorn Fires', which had exorcized spells. Yellow-hammers, with obvious kinship with sun-worship, became linked with evil. In Scotland and Yorkshire the yellow-hammer is still reputed to drink a drop of the Devil's blood in May.

Flame, blood, lions, redness, gold, pale fires of mistletoe alike seemed related to the sun. Gold's blood-like hues summed up yet lay outside the primary colours, etherializing into profoundest mana, unimpoverished by its practical uses. Golden casques, diadems, ikons, crosses, talismans had glistening aura. Alchemists sought gold for coarse profit, elixirs, the dispersal of death-fears, gaining spiritual potency. Mystery religions, generating man's spiritual potential, used golden symbols.

As the body had soul, so all metal had 'spirit', which alchemy could transform into precious substance. Brandy was a by-product of alchemical research; strong drinks are still 'spirits'. Re-arrangement of basic components could, theoretically, transmute all. Moses and Aaron were legendary alchemists. Aristotle, the Arab Geber, Roger Bacon, Raymond Lully, Newton, Boyle, Dr Johnson, Leibnitz, Goethe dabbled in it. Experiments, sometimes hilarious, or glum – Lully tried to transmute the sea, Dr James Price, FRS, drank prussic acid – did assist chemical development. Dresden China and Mercury resulted from alchemical research, despite the chimeras of the Philosopher's Stone and Elixir of Immortality. The pursuit was unremitting. In 1938, Dunikovski was trying to distil gold from sand.[7] An Alchemy School at Salt Lake City, 'The Paracelsus Research Society', now offers a fortnight's course on the transmutation of lead to gold.

All metals had contagious powers. To kiss a sacred ring renewed life. Steal a man's amulet and you destroyed him. Celtic and Mediterranean smiths were reverenced; metal, Kipling's 'cold iron', had broken the Stone Age. Celts used swords as coinage; Scythians and Alans worshipped them; Teutons had trinities of sword-gods. The Crown, as St Joan realized, was more important than the King. Wagner's Rhinegold shatters social orders, ruins its owners, even the gods. African smiths were often chief 'Devils' of secret societies. Robert Graves[8] notes that Celtic smiths were assisted by music and poetry, the hammer ring helping develop Irish metre. The Habsburgs possessed the alleged sword with which Longinus pierced Jesus; its owner was in legend empowered to master the world. Supposedly, the relic was coveted by Hitler.

8

The humblest object – jug, door – had personality, mana. Places, shapes, acquired spirit. London is masculine, Paris feminine. Tsarist travellers would bow to 'Mother Volga'. Rome's patron was Jupiter, Athens's Athene. Mother Kiev contrasted with Lord Novgorod the Great. Moscow was Russia's head, Petersburg the heart.

Geometry excited perennial satisfactions. An Egyptian scribe, *c.* 1500 BC, considered that Art 'lies in the balance of straight lines and curves, cubes and cones.' The square was male, the triangle female, both imbued by Plato with mystical qualities. Magic squares were revered : a Greek philosopher envisaged God as a rectangle; Walt Whitman, a square. The pentacle was a universal magic symbol, the cross appeared in Hindu and Buddhist alchemy. Cross and circle were classic symbols of equilibrium, fusing in the circular Celtic cross, as at Porthilly, Cornwall. A protection against evil, the circle linked earth, sky, sea : birth, death, rebirth : universe, time, events. A Cornish stone circle is at Tregaseal, ('House of the Sun'), exposed like circular graveyards to an eye in the sky. The sixth-century Greek, Hercateus, reported Apollo visiting his circular temple in Britain every nineteen years for nocturnal music and dancing. Many Christian shrines are sited on pagan circles, healing wells, circular haunts of ghosts and sacred animals. Circular dances stimulated the source of life. The circle also had exorcist powers: Theophrastus advised that, when tearing out a mandrake, the performer should draw three circles round it with a sword. Mythology abounded with circular grails: renaissance thinkers connected the circle with God. Nazi Nuremburg Rallies bristled with magic shapes and talismans.

Similar was awe of numbers, entities bound to natural law yet susceptible to mysticism, as a cricketer craves 100 rather than 99. In Druidic Ireland, 3 was prominent in verse, religion, moral precepts. Creation flowered naturally into 3: man, woman, child; hypothesis, debate, resolution. Most religions worshipped trinities. For example, Woden was known as Warrior, Traveller and 'Third'. Messiahs mediated between man and God, darkness and light, completing the sacred triangle. Numbers seemed to have vitalities, rules, problems beyond human needs but susceptible to mysteries. In his Mysteries, Orpheus united Zeus-sky, Hades-underworld. The Great Goddess had 3 faces: virgin, mother, hag. Multiples of 3 strengthened the magic: 9 Buddhas, Queens of Avalon, Witches of Gloucester.

> The grave of Gawayne is at Pyton
> Where the ninth wave flows.

5 was expressed by the mystical pentagon, familiar amongst alchemists, Pythagoreans, magicians of all eras. There were 9 Toltec Princes, ranks of Angels, Valkyries; 9 absolutions are given to a dead pope. 12 was the splendid climax. Divine pantheons and retinues are usually 12. The dead Pharoah travelled through 12 stages of the Underworld.

The Etruscans believed that their destiny was 6,000 years of fortune, 6,000 of decline, the latter well advanced when Rome expelled her Etruscan kings. Roman oracles calculated, from the 12 and 6 vultures seen by Romulus and Remus, that Rome would endure 1,230 years. The date of the deposition of the last Emperor, Romulus Augustus, 476, did indeed tally with this.

The 6 points of the Star of David showed the days of Creation. Certain Gnostics taught that the soul was acquired only when the body was 7 years old: the 7 stones of the Prince of Wales's crown evoke the 7 sins and 7 divine gifts. 666 was interpreted as the sun, masculinity, Roman Emperor, Antichrist. The late Aleister Crowley, self-styled magician, claimed to incarnate 666. It has been, disputedly, related to the 'megalithic yard' (2.72 feet) allegedly used by the builders of Stonehenge and the Pyramids, the former 'laid out according to an ancient figure of natural magic, traditionally known as the magic squares of the sun. This consists of the first 36 numbers arranged in a block, so that each row, column and diagonal adds up to 111 and the total to 666.'⁹ Professor A. Thom sees prehistoric Britain achieving a synthesis of Pythagorean geometry, astronomy and mathematics.

Pythagoras, like Plato, was incorporated into Mysteries of magic numbers. Greek numbers were printed as letters, facilitating this degenerative process. Platonic idealism sought correspondences between reality and glamorous symmetries, unhelpful to classical science which, despite revival in Alexandria, became debased by numerical mysticism. Pythagoras particularly revered 7 and 10. 10 could be symbolized by a cross, in the Mysteries of Hinduism, Buddhism, Orphism, Mithraism and of Pythagoras himself; also at Eleusis, and amongst the Mexicans and Red Indians.

Man never quite loses the superstition of numbers. St Augustine believed in their magic. To Dr Dee, they were the live mystical principle of the universe. Numbers can overcome conscience: Maxim Gorky justified the ten million deaths from Stalin's collectivizations by references to the millions to be thereby enriched. For Richard Coe, Beckett 'like Joyce, is fascinated by numbers; but Beckett's calculations have none of that woolly-minded pseudo-mystical significance which Joyce attached, say, to the number 1132.'¹⁰

Freud was always perturbed by the effect on his life of 23, 28, 61, 62. Zola had

> a strong obsession with numbers, their relationships and the good auguries of certain primary numbers and their various multiplications. Such numerical and counting obsessions are familiar pathological features of nervous disorders. A supreme example of their control of a writer almost to the point of insanity is to be found in the work of the Marquis de Sade, and the effect upon his work is direct – each sexual exploit is repeated in a series in which progressive numbers of persons participate until the whole is reduced to a catalogue which can only be regarded as a written version of the repeated touching of objects for luck. One of Freud's examples of the pathology of everyday life.

(Angus Wilson, *Emile Zola*, Secker and Warburg, 1966)

Heroes of popular fiction may unconsciously fulfil these ancient and satisfying patterns. Buchan's Richard Hannay is almost a folk-hero : he arrives from the wilderness, hunts and is hunted, descends to the Underworld. By overcoming the hawk-like devil he saves the land and secures the chaste maiden. He is initiated into Mysteries, is involved with esoteric colours – Black Stone, Greenmantle – and numbers – 39 steps, 3 Hostages.

9

Names were more than tags. A taboo against naming the dead aloud might, as amongst certain Bantus, vitiate a sense of history. One's name had to be preserved from Black magicians. Gods cherished secret names : Ra's was captured by Isis, using witchcraft.

The Romans made a regular practice of discovering the secret names of enemy gods, and summoning them to Rome with seductive promises, a process technically known as 'Elicio'.

(Robert Graves, *The Crowning Privilege*, Cassell, 1955)

Jehovah's name was uttered only once a year, by the High Priest, overwhelmed by trumpets. Gipsies can still be given secret names, to confuse demons.

Names strengthened morale by identification with heroic ancestors, qualities or animals. Arthur ('Bear'), Harold ('Powerful General'), Bernard ('Bear-Brave'). To be nameless was to be naked. A name must be left behind, for the soul would suffer if forgotten in the bright world. It can express the barely expressible. A lover will crave to speak the beloved's name, even to his disadvantage. By assuming a name, stars, planets, woods, rivers, gained aura, were lustred with the divine.

Names attached man to externality. A peasant, a child, steals a tool, names it, is thus convinced that it is his own. Viking, Samurai, Saxon named his sword, which thereby became part of him. Medieval weapons were cut with runes and names : Charlemagne's sword was '*Joyeuse*'. Bells, pots, guns, fields had particular names and thus fragments of life. 'Arthur' remained powerful enough for the usurper, Henry VII, to give it to his heir, as a further rivet to his throne.

Whether social and religious change would escape these patterns, or whether they were endemic to the human structure, natural devices to adapt to Nature, must have concerned speculative minds in sixth-century India, Judea, Greece, and the growing commonwealth of Rome.

3 Rome

> They caught
> Luxury, like a syphilis, from their conquests.
> Then, feeling queer, they appointed one man
> to cure them
> And made a god of him.
>
> C. Day Lewis

> Rome began as a sacred grove, woodland, sanctuary for desperadoes and outlaws.
>
> F. M. Cornford

I

England has had constitutional links with Europe, as part of the Roman Empire, of Canute's Empire, of the Anglo-Norman monarchy, of the Angevin Empire. Henry VI was actually crowned in Paris as King of France, a title abandoned only by George III. Germans ruled both Britain and Hanover until 1837. Britain has five times organized continental coalitions against a dominating power.

The Roman occupation endured nearly four centuries, comparable to the span of British India. The expatriate governing class was similarly small, though its members intermarried with the natives. There were well-managed towns, luxurious villages, theatres, law-courts, efficient communications, hygiene. Roman Britain exported wine, tin, wool, oysters, pearls, grain, slaves, Cicero warning Atticus that the British made useless slaves. Several British-born leaders eventually tried to establish themselves in Europe as Roman Emperors, Magnus Maximus becoming a Celtic folk-hero. Tribal loyalties never quite died: increasingly, raids occurred from overseas and beyond Hadrian's Wall, at times seemingly with Celtic support.

The decline was slow, but continuous. British coinage is a significant graph, finely cut under the early emperors, increasingly poor from the second century. Lug, Arthur, Lear always hovered, old tongues and powers reviving as the cracks showed. Talk of atoms and rationalism vied with chatter about divination. Constantine the Great was born in York: legend identified his mother not

32

only with the Holy Cross Church, Jerusalem, but with the moon-goddess, Selene. Professor Jean-Jacques Hatt suggests that Constantine's monogram derived not from the Cross but from the Wheel of the Celtic god, Taranis, though his evidence is scarcely conclusive.[11]

The Empire could be tolerant, professional, unenthusiastic. Magnates usually accepted serious social responsibilities. Rome endowed British towns, established parish and diocese, the calendar. Remains of some 600 villas survive, particularly in the West of England. Tiles from a Roman hypocaust are embedded in an arch at Wenden's (Woden's) Ambo. St Alban's Cathedral contains hundreds of Roman bricks. Widford Church and Southwark Cathedral are on villa foundations. Aldborough Church superseded a temple to Mercury, whose statue remains in one wall. A mosaic floor at Fishbourne has checked borders enclosing medallions of sea-horses, sea-panthers, swirling round a winged boy astride a dolphin. The fourth-century mosaic at Hinton St Mary depicts the oldest British Christ.

These survived the Legions' departure in 410. Conquering barbarians avoided the mysterious towns and were baffled by Christianity, that had so obviously ruined the Empire.

Rome had employed 'barbarian' mercenaries in Britain, often unruly Teutons, though peaceful Teutonic settlements seem to have existed in Roman East Anglia. Tradition reported a post-Roman Celtic ruler, Vortigern, inviting in Teutons against the Picts – as Edward the Confessor relied on Normans and Bretons.

'Barbarian' often misleads. Theodoric, Bede, Alcuin, Alfred, Charlemagne, Canute were 'barbarians' – as were Gladstone and Chopin to the Chinese. Vizigothic jewellery, Ostrogothic government, the Gothic Codex Argenteus, Merovingian glass and pottery, Irish monasticism, Frankish craftsmanship, Viking decorative metal-work, Icelandic law, poetry and Great Assembly, Frankish churches and administration, Saxon architecture and literature, refute crude notions of barbarism, despite constant violence, migrations, confusion.[12] To the over-tired imperial sophisticates in Cavafy's poem, barbarians were 'a kind of solution', a sort of joy through strength.

2

Christianity was established in Roman Britain but, though the first Bishop of London was ordained in 314, the second followed only in 604. Nevertheless, the hedonistic monk, Pelagius, born before 370, was notorious in Christendom for denying the Original Sin

B

and Predestination maintained by Augustine of Hippo. Majority
man endlessly flops into Determinism : religious, political, astrological, biological, psychological. An early existentialist, Pelagius
held that man misbehaves through deliberate and preventable
choice, that Adam's sin hurt no one else. Fate is conditioned by Will.
This foreshadows Alberti, Renaissance Man. Declared heretic,
forgotten for centuries, Pelagius is the start of vigorous British
commonsense, a pragmatic measure preferable to the supernatural
energies of a dead god.

                                3

Greece helped fertilize Rome as Ireland did England. Greco-Roman
society often seems remarkably contemporary. 'The Spartans' official
formula for mobilization for aggression was "to declare a war of
defence".'[13] The later Empire shows familiar dilemmas, posing the
question whether, beyond some stage of sophistication, a community
is governable.

One sees in the later Empire imbalance between town and
country, with urban economic and political bewilderment, and
extravagance, sophisticated but unproductive – and a depopulated,
over-taxed, resentful and finally disloyal peasantry. Also, wasteful
agriculture; meaningless leisure inducing violence, apathy, sadistic
theatre; disease from pollution; religious intolerance and bewilderment; harsh colonialism; unemployment, with a choking, top-
heavy bureaucracy trying to peg prices and wages and make
unpopular jobs hereditary; corrupt politics, over-centralization,
vulgar millionaires rigging the market; conscienceless, myopic
speculators and contractors; erosion of soil and forest; economic
naïvety exporting too much silver to Asia; demagogues over-stimu-
lating dangerous slum-mobs; inflation sapping initiative and loyalty,
with too many in debt to the State, some of whom may have found
in the restless northern invaders a feasible alternative, which would
at least cancel unpaid taxes. It seemed that if the State was left to
do too much, public morale rotted, a lesson disregarded even by
such remarkable rulers as the medieval Emperor, Frederick II.
Human nature is opaque : people may search diligently for what
they do not always want to find. Whatever the truth here, the
Roman State and spirit became codified rather than adaptable.

The decline of slavery produced no contented working class.
Infanticide was common, with possible analogies with modern
legalized abortion. Magic and astrology flourished. The throne itself
was frequently up for sale or plunder by brutal and irresponsible
generals. From the Caesars stem, like radioactive heaps, the

unplumbed energies of secret police, inquisitors, general staffs, sup-
porting the ornate paint, scrollwork, and the fanciful protocol of
royal, papal and dictatorial courts.

4

Science had had tender beginnings in China, India, the Middle
East, continuing in the Classical World. Thales of Miletus calculated rather than prophesied the eclipse of 585 BC. Hippocrates
(d. 377 BC) studied not only the patient's symptoms but his general
background, omitting prayer, divination, sacrifice. The second-
century Ascelepiades of Alexandria diagnosed the emotional roots
of insanity, the body-mind dichotomy. Christianity did not much
build on this, tending to blame neurosis on demons, to be exorcized
by pain. Indian and Greek medical rationalism only briefly inter-
rupted shamanism and demonology. The Essenes, Jewish ascetic
and philosophic monastic set, which John the Baptist and Jesus
may for a time have joined, used magical healing formulae. An
ancient Egyptian prescribed : 'He who treats the sick must be
expert, learned in the proper incantations and know how to make
amulets.' Hippocrates himself allowed for astral influences. Cross-
roads, protected by Hermes, were long propitious for magic
cures.

In Greece and Alexandria, classical thought could interpret God
as the Unity of the Monad. Copernicus was anticipated, particularly
by Aristarchos of Samos, though on less thorough theoretical
grounds. Lucian perceived life as 'the fortuitous concurrence of
indefinite atoms'. Epicurus, Democrates, Lucretius conceived an
atomic universe. Lucretius denied the immortality of the soul, saw
atoms as the source of human behaviour, their unpredictability
allowing Free Will. Alexandria had state-endowed science, replacing
Greece as an intellectual power, for Platonic science had relapsed
into wishful thinking : of classical thinkers, only Archimedes impressed Leonardo. Later Roman education neglected science,
economics, human relations. These do not progress automatically.
The Babylonian decimal notation became forgotten. The classical
era experimented with steam, but did not develop it. Slavery
inhibits technical advance, by providing too easy power.

Islamic science was to far outstrip Greco-Roman and Byzantine,
whose education encouraged florid rhetoric, legal and philosophic
sophistry, adroit verbal games, imitative literature, clever but
academic, like crossword puzzles. Politics were authoritarian, assisted
by mobs clamouring for justice. Too much written history was
mere flattery of authority and abuse of its predecessors or, with Livy

and Plutarch, a compilation of elevating tales. (In Marxist states, it is now continuously re-written, the characters, as in a repertory company, forever exchanging roles.) That much classical art and education was provided by slaves is a significant comment. Terence was born an African slave.

The Empire was spendthrift with human life, slavery was commonplace though seldom melodramatic. Like Victorian Boer slaves, certain Roman slaves could trade, own land and other slaves. Horace was the son of an ex-slave who, as a landowner, sent him to study in Athens.

Slavery was reinforced by the Empire's collapse. Pope Gregory the Great (d. 604) confirmed slavery as an institution. 25,000 slaves are recorded in the Domesday Book, from a population of under two million. After the Plague of 1348, Florence imported slaves from Africa, the Balkans, the Black Sea, and Majorcan Jews sold Africans to Italian co-religionists. Christian churches and magnates enslaved in the New World. Virtual slavery built the spectacular Neapolitan baroque churches. The British Empire was long enriched by slave trading. 14,000 black slaves were owned by the West Indian Interest in Dr Johnson's England, bought or inherited like utensils, though sometimes freed, with property rights. Three centuries of slave-trade enriched Europe. The forms of twentieth-century slavery would have scandalized Cato and Pericles. About six million slaves were killed by Hitler. Stalin's slave camps are estimated to have contained eighteen million. UNO, in 1963, appointed an official to enquire into 'the growing problem of slavery and serfdom'. In 1967, twenty slave camps for canal digging were raided by the police in Multan Province, Pakistan. Slaves, whipped, sometimes killed, were being worked, chained, eighteen hours a day on public works at Sukhur, Pakistan, the contractor, Umar Shah, being sentenced to seventy-seven years' hard labour, October 1967. The same month saw an Albert Hall Rally of survivors from the slave camps of twenty countries, including North Korea, China, Russia, occupied Tibet and the occupied Baltic States. The Anti-Slavery Society, 1968, reported nearly thirty countries where slavery still exists. A Sultan of Muscat, deposed 1970, enforced silence on his slaves, so that they became mutes. 1971 saw reports of the castration of Afghan slaves.

The subject can attract whimsicality. Lord Halifax, a Foreign Secretary, Viceroy of India respected by Gandhi, visiting Virginia as Ambassador to America, wrote in his journal like a Roman patrician, or Dickens's Mr Skimpole:

I regret that there are no slaves; this would be my hour for visiting my slaves. I should talk affably with them. I should

visit the sick and aged and read the Bible to them, and when
gross impropriety or misconduct demanded it I should correct
them, and every now and then I should make them all sing
spirituals to me.

5

Rome's ruins, literal and metaphorical, haunted subsequent Europe,
through Romanesque Dark Age architecture, renaissance Classicism,
the Enlightenment. Half the words on this page are from Latin.
Roman Law and Christian Canon Law, dangerously interlocked,
were adopted by barbarian successor-states save in England and
Ireland. For a few years, Napoleon presided over a 'Roman' republic
of consuls, tribunate, senate. The classical metropolis of Alexandria
still excites a Cavafy, an E. M. Forster, a Lawrence Durrell. St
Paul's Cathedral, Peter the Great's St Petersburg, Lutyens's New
Delhi, the rotunda and colonnades at Jefferson's University of
Virginia, nineteenth-century banks, opera houses, department stores
are stupendously sham-classical. David, Poussin, Ingres, Canova,
Flaxman and Thorvaldsen were heirs to Greco-Rome. James I was
displayed on a coin as a Roman emperor: James II stands as another,
outside London's National Gallery. Rome provided what many still
expect of art, law, government, behaviour, establishing exceptional
moral standards, even though these were accepted more strictly from
literature than from history. Present discontents invent noble pasts.
Classicism survives, despite technology, illiteracy, irony, though only
a minority may understand 'Draconian', 'Socratic', 'hermetic',
'stentorian', 'Orphic', 'ill-starred', 'pander', 'Nemesis', 'hubris',
'chimera'.

Classical mythology was reinterpreted by anthropology and
psychology, with stock heroes presented as permanent symbols of
human urges, obsessions, adjustments. Generations of literary genius
prevented Odysseus from becoming a cliché. Jupiter, willing his
multiple transformations, was existentialist without knowing it.
Cicero's denunciation of Catiline is a lasting defence of the State
against anarchy. The indictment of Warren Hastings echoed that
of Verres. Horace invaded eighteenth-century French and English
verse. Ovid's fluid shuffling of image and personality in *Met-
amorphoses* ripples through Shakespeare, Botticelli, Ezra Pound.
Greek epigrams of love and death are carved upon European
sensibility. Livy and Plutarch informed Elizabethan drama and
French Revolutionary dreams. Queen Elizabeth I translated Horace
and Seneca. Plato influenced Thomas More, and his conception of

Idea gave unity to that dazzling exchange of music and words, colour and engineering, conceit and allegory – the Masque, of Ben Jonson and Inigo Jones.

Greek mythology pervades Romanticism, is stripped barer in Eliot's plays. Euripides remains dynamic enough for the Greek government to censor, 1967. The long howl of Oedipus has not been silenced by show-business. Theocritus long sustained the pastoral idyll untarnished by drudgery. Sexual insight, laconic, witty social comment make Ovid, Catullus, Propertius more modern than the Laureates Tennyson, Bridges and Masefield. Catullus mordantly countered the moral fables of Plutarch's heroes:

> Utter indifference to your welfare, Caesar,
> Is matched only by ignorance of who you are.

His verse, fragmented, non-linear, shifting time, place, sex, personality, like chessmen, is modernistic in mood and technique.

> Play out your love games
>   freely and swiftly
>   plant the new shoot
> an old name cannot lapse
>   you must make, in the one place, constant renewal. . . .

> Fold the doors softly,
>   bridesmaids,
>   feasting is over,
> let them ply arms and legs
>   in their love-games, the constant renewal.[14]

The religious art of Byzantium and Armenia fertilized European painting. Ciceronian prose-rhythms, verbal architecture, are caught in Gibbon, Johnson, Macaulay. Of Gibbon's style Bagehot remarked that, huge and imperial though it was, by ignoring the petty and vulgar it was unsuitable for truth-telling. Churchill's war-oratory, leavened by humour, has an orotund Roman ring.

6

Much Roman Law, centralized, patristic, was temporarily supplanted by Dark Age feudalism but survived in the Roman – though not the Celtic – Church, reviving in the Middle Ages. It was overhauled in detail but not in spirit by Napoleon, and remains in much of social democratic Europe, with some influence on Scottish Law. It provides solid implements requisite for business, property, universities, whatever organizes, builds, enlarges, from principles of efficiency.

The heritage of classical cities, postulating an aristocracy of mind, socially conscious, controlled, enquiring, humane, was absorbed by centuries of exceptional men and women. One was Milton, for whom the mingling of classical and biblical produced convictions magnificent and wide-reaching, though often violent and messianic.

Perhaps more sympathetic are the Socratic premises that tinged Enlightenment and Revolution: that institutions and codes will evoke virtue, that crime is due to ignorance, that men naturally desire the good. These became less axiomatic under Roman Christianity, which emphasized sin as much as love. Moral images abounded, still topical, as of Achilles preferring early heroic death to lengthy mediocrity, and Brutus and Cassius killing Caesar for the public good – paralleled by Pym's judicial murder of Strafford. These confirm Machiavelli's parable of The Fox and the Lion, teaching that one well-timed cruelty might avoid many prolonged cruelties.

Regulus, Gracchus, Agis, Cleomones risked or accepted death as social duty. Socrates and the Stoics, Seneca and Marcus Aurelius trivialized death-fears, are more contemporary than St Louis or William Rufus. Classical self-restraint, self-analysis, self-mastery, tolerance, intellectual and moral resolution armed Montaigne, who considered Socrates's mind 'the most perfect of which I have any knowledge', also, 'filling and emptying my mind incessantly in Plutarch and Seneca'.

The Stoics attracted eighteenth-century Augustans, and would have approved Burke, 1775: 'Magnanimity in politics is not seldom the highest wisdom; and a great empire and little minds go ill together.'

The Stoic – Seneca, Montaigne, E. M. Forster – wishes men well, rather than initiates policy: he does not blame, he endures with dignity: believes revolution more likely to produce scum than alter human nature. A Seneca will obey Nero, his intellectual and moral inferior. He is sceptical of extravagant possibility. Disinterested in public service, he sees beyond immediate party concerns and the mob to a universal society of like individuals. Impeccable in friendships, his maxims, sometimes sententious, of human brotherhood are liable to survive as literature rather than inspire as manifestoes. A refuge for those broken in falling empires, he has some responsibility for their falling, but his is not the greatest. He can be Olympian, sometimes a trifle silly. Honest, honourable, he does not disdain life's gifts but, like Montaigne, like Chekhov, does not expect them to solve the insoluble. His spirit enters Shaw: 'Like

Einstein, I am not happy and I do not want to be happy; I have
neither time nor taste for such comas.'

Like Christianity, like Marxism, like Rousseau and Nietzsche,
Rome was a blank cheque for subjective interpretations. Greek
Plethos (Fullness), Roman *Gravitas*, Aristotelian teleology, Platonic
idealism, beliefs that some races – 'them' – are natural slaves,
notions that the State exists to promote excellence or to discipline
mobs, can be concocted alike by the generous, the ruthless, the
academic, the cynical. Misunderstanding may have a generous part
in forming human outlooks. The present author, watching *Traviata*,
ignorant of Italian, imagined that, when Armand's father pleaded
with the prostitute to renounce his son, he was actually trying to
seduce her.

Dante evoked an empire vaster than the Roman, yet inconceivable without it. Caesar enflamed Napoleon, and Mussolini, a
political journalist of vivid, if shallow talents, in the tradition of
Greco-Roman rhetoric. Churchill's rhetoric, 1933, was far from
Propertius and Catallus.

The Roman genius expressed by Mussolini, the great lawgiver
among living men, has shown every nation that may be harried
by Socialism or Communism that there is a way out which
democracy is willing to follow, provided it is boldly led. I think
of Germany with its splendid clear-eyed youth marching every-
one along all the roads of the Reich, singing their ancient songs,
demanding to be conscripted into an army, eagerly seeking the
weapons of war and burning to suffer and die for their fatherland.

4 *Christianity*

> And one of them named Caiphas, being the High Priest that same year, said onto them, 'Ye know nothing at all, nor consider it is expedient for us, that one man should die for the people, and that the whole nation perish not.'
>
> St John

I

Myths expressed psychic insight, premonition, glamour; they exposed the forbidden, retained half-lost communal memories, were garbled interpretations of life, sanctifying custom, ritual, privilege. They were the graphic sum of human attempts to master existence, reducing the impossible to actuality, and redeeming the commonplace. Struggle, triumph, defeat sharpened into the Hero, the Villain, sometimes – such is human complexity – both in one. An Odysseus, remembered in tales, could, like Napoleon and Lenin, become stalwart realities in the huge world of myth, galvanizing or obstructing, endlessly altered by time. 'The great collective myths', Jung claimed, 'in some way represent the healing and formative work of Man's unconscious psychological process.'

How far religious, political and philosophical systems seeking to extend human possibilities and interpret life's purpose, were 'true' and different, and how far they were minor changes of emphasis, small shiftings of fairly constant social and psychic phenomena, would be a debate all but postponed until the eighteenth century. Whether Balder, Jesus, Mahomet, Lenin are genuinely autonomous or share a single psychological identity and dream-appeal still remains debatable, but certainly the area of dream is as significant as that of planning and judging. Dreams lure people into the archaic : to monster, magus, dwarf, fantastic plants and unfinished stairs. Loneliness develops bizarre caves and cathedrals. 'Force a child into a lonely bedroom at night,' Dickens spoke from his blood, 'and you'd better murder it.'

Greek speculation, Roman order, had not exorcized faith in sacrifice, idols, numinous shapes, redemption, personal immortality, though intellectuals could see Zeus the Lawgiver himself forced

to obey fundamental laws. Much of this lore was pessimistic.
Golden Ages never returned, empires failed, for no clear-cut
reason save divine wrath or capricious war. Gods themselves aged
or chilled, their rituals becoming mechanical. Orthodoxy required
periodic refreshment from warmer, more intimate 'sons of God' –
Mithras, Osiris, Adonis, Dionysus, Balder, Arthur, Pythagoras,
pillars in a fluid world; or from matriarchal avatars – the Great
Goddess, Isis, Persephone. All mediated between man and the
Absolute, through secret elitist Mysteries. Japanese, Persian, Chinese,
Greek, Roman, Celtic initiates became adepts through successive
rituals and doctrinal degrees. Mithras enjoined seven initiation
stages, analogous to the Platonic steps towards Truth, Perfection,
Light, the steps towards Absolute Beauty that Diotima taught
Socrates. The Red Indian Grain Dance was a Mystery, perhaps
akin to that of Persephone at Eleusis. Celtic Mysteries involved
labyrinthine spirals – so marked in Yeats's thought; a rock carving
at Tintagel resembles the labyrinth on a Cretan coin. English
country mazes and labyrinths – at Braemore, at Saffron Walden –
probably derive from classical games connected with Mysteries more
ancient, in which, in the exact centre, the fertility virgin awaits the
hero, wisdom awaits the candidate.[15] The ringed terraces at Glastonbury suggest to some, those of the Holy Mountain, Ceylon, a
Mystery site.

By enthusiasm, 'breath of gods', rather than passionless prayer
and passive ritual, pagan initiates sought illumination, personal,
democratic heavens, to quicken their divine seed. They 'died', with
resurrection of the spirit were 'reborn', amid bizarre sensations
were purged of sin and illusion, were baptized from magic grails.
Lulled by drugs, chants, lights, they watched sacred tableaux. After
physical death the adept travelled the 7 worlds of 7 planets, using
occult phrases, answering esoteric riddles, reaching towards fairy-
tale dimensions. In the Mysteries of Odin, as in Greek, Persian and
Brahmin, 9 and 12 were prominent.

> Nine homes I know, and branches nine,
> Growing from out of the stalwart tree
> Down in the deep abyss.

In *Corinthians*, Paul restates ancient notions of spiritual change.
Christ's warning to Nicodemus evoked Mystery. 'Except a
man be born again of water and of the spirit, he cannot enter
the Kingdom of God.' Resurrection could mean spiritual, not
physical rebirth. Fervour, not intellectualism, redeemed the common
life. Here was the urge of a D. H. Lawrence, a Henry Miller.

Some Mystery techniques seem postulated by contemporary Hartha-yoga: strict control of body and breath to overcome sickness, elevate to rare visions, proclaim new personality, the literal detach-ment of soul or mind from the body. Many included vision-inducing drugs, of which incense must be a very pallid echo.

From classical Mysteries to Mau Mau, secret societies secure omnipotence, sacred identity and redemption from insignificance – and appeal to deep-rooted snobbery.

There are some things that cannot be generally told – things that *you ought to know*. Great truths are dangerous to some – but factors for *personal power* and *accomplishment* in the hands of those who understand them. Behind the tales of the miracles and mysteries of the ancients lie centuries of their secret probing into nature's laws – their amazing discoveries of the *hidden processes of Man's mind* and *the Mastery of Man's problems* once shrouded in mystery to avoid their destruction by mass fear and ignorance.

(Advertisement in *The Observer*, 5 November 1967)

The promoters add that they,

an age-old brotherhood of learning, have preserved this Secret Wisdom in their archives. *They now invite you to share the practical helpfulness of their searchings.* Write today for a free copy. . . .

London advertisements for August 1972, include 'New Virgin stream of divine atomic consciousness from central sun plane', and 'a journey through Magic, Myth and Ritual to discover the roots of yourself'.

2

At Bethlehem ('House of Bread') had stood a temple to Adonis, 'The Lord', spring-god, mutilated, killed, reborn, renewing all life. Dionysus too, with his 'whirling maenads', was Lord not only of wine but of sap, impulse, inspiration: a jazz-god revoking logic, rules, privilege, intellectual discipline, civic virtue, doubts and loneliness. In dreams, the depths are simultaneously the heights.

Where are you, Dionysus? Leading your dancing bands
Over the mountain slopes past many a wild beast's lair,
Or upon rocky crags, maybe, of Olympus, where
Orpheus once gathered the trees and mountain beasts . . .

(Euripides, *The Bacchae*)[16]

Paganisms had evolved a common language of myth, ritual, saviour, kings, drama, sacrifice, hanging gods. Annunciation preceded Krishna, Buddha, Horus, Mithras. Many gods were stabbed, then eaten by ecstatic followers. Buddha, Plato, Pythagoras came to be held virgin-born. Egyptian and Syrian sun-worshippers intoned at the winter solstice: 'The Virgin has born fruit, the Light is waxing.' The constellation Cancer, prominent at midwinter, was also styled by the Greeks 'the Asses and the Manger'. Mithras too was born at the birth of the Unconquered Sun from new light striking dark rock, watched by shepherds. He killed the sacred bull and in his Mysteries the initiate, purged by bull's blood, aspired to the Seventh Heaven. Mithraic ritual and myth included the Chosen Twelve, baptism, last supper, fiery judgement. Puritan and masculine, in Persian tradition it denied the total supremacy of Light, preferring a constant but indecisive duel with Darkness. To assist the former, it rated right action higher than right belief. Outraging Judaism and proscribed by Christianity, this dualism reappeared amongst Dark Age Gnostics, medieval Cathari and the Assassins, who allegedly corrupted the Templars, and who may have appeared among the notorious Indian murder-gangs, the Thugs. A bull and fiery chariot, Mithraic symbols, reputedly haunt Godolphin House, Cornwall.

3

To a disputable degree, Christianity retained Mystery elements. 'He became Man that we might become divine,' declared St Athanasius. By faith, believers could be 'raised together' with Christ. 'Jesus has harrowed hell; he has led captivity captive; Darkness and chaos and death flee from the Light.' This, from Bishop Venantus Fortunatus (530–609) would have satisfied immemorial tradition. Whether Christianity is metaphor, simile or literal truth, whether it was merely the least tolerant and best-timed of rival cults, remains a lively issue, though not amongst humbler congregations, content with ritual and not confused by doctrine. An Italian woman at Catigliano, 1967, starved a boy to death then covered his body with gold leaf, believing him Jesus, herself chosen to sacrifice him for the world's sins. On her arrest, the Catholic villagers crucified a live owl on her door to neutralize her magic.

Allegedly more attractive to woman than Mithraism, Christianity possessed the Mystery combination of elitism and democracy. Its vision was that of Mysteries made public, a divine dream with inclinations towards nightmare. Angelic wings vied with dragons', seraphs with devils, radiant harmonies with scalding penalties.

Perhaps influenced by later Jewish doctrines of eternal punishment, and by the mystical Essenes and their shadowy 'Teacher of Right-eousness', Christianity while, like Orphism, promising paradise to initiates, solidified hell more emphatically than the Jewish Sheol, Celtic Annyn, Scandinavian Hel, Greco-Roman Hades.

Its mythology and ritual were eclectic. Transubstantiation recalled magic cannibalism. 'Crossing' and holy water had long expelled demons. Mithraic blood-lustrations expunged infantile sins and procured salvation : its exorcist rites included Bell, Book and Candle. In Spain, the connection between Mary and fertility was never lost. Exorcism remains. A Hampstead vicar, 1973, is a popular exorcist; Swindon Council, 1967, used the Churches Fellowship for Physical and Spiritual Studies to exorcize a haunted house; in April 1972, the Bishop of Peterborough appointed a diocesan exorcist.

The teachings and personality of Jesus were inexplicit, dependent on incomplete memories and variable translations. 'Let the dead bury their dead' can apparently be rendered, 'Let the villagers bury the dead.' 'The Virgin' can be 'Young Woman'.[17] 'The Kingdom of Heaven is *within* you' is currently offered as 'among you'. There is divergence between 'the poor' and the 'poor in spirit'. Jesus is evoked in unusual quarters. The ferocious Taiping Rebellion, headed by Hung Sui Ch'un, 'Younger Son of God' (1852), was loosely based on biblical texts and Methodist tracts.

'I am the Light of the World' was familiar imagery. The essence of the Sermon on the Mount was taught by Jesus's great contemporary, Rabbi Hillel. For St Paul, Jesus was the traditional Divine Victim, though conquering not barren soil or winter darkness but spiritual blankness. For some he is the crystallization of myth, one climax in a recurring pattern; for others, one of several similar teachers and healers, of sublime altruism – 'Love your enemies. Do good to those that hate you,' – in which sceptics might see a hint of craftiness, of victory through a form of irony or sarcasm.

The Gospels had promised an early Second Coming. 'A little while and ye shall see me.' Disappointed, the Church made scant break with old fears and remedies, though reinforcing the Judaistic mingling of tenderness and moral stringency. While it may have readjusted human goals, the fortunes of Poland, Spain, Ireland, Latin America suggest that it failed to readjust human nature. Majority morals seem to depend more on solvency and the rate of exchange. Baptism could scarcely eliminate the genetic and unconscious. The cool scepticism of *Ecclesiastes*, moreover, remained subordinate to jealous Jehovah and Jesus's impatient insistence on hell. Orthodox morality, if strictly enforced, is apt to produce domestic tyranny and Tyburn values. Religion seldom transcends nation, status, tradition : if one Christian or Jewish sect denounces apartheid, another defends it. Theologians, understandably but tragically, applied the rough and ready traditional concepts of justice and logic to the Divine Order. Evidence of the times was seen as evidence of all time. God was burdened with all too human, even too political a vocabulary of reward and punishment, heaven and hell, sin and redemption. The alleged divine inspiration of the Bible sanctioned apartheid, sanctimonious fraud, antinomianism, domestic cruelty, subservience to nonentities. Similarly, Marxist texts were to invite violence, heresy-hunts, credulous and conscienceless politics. Veneration easily congeals into superstition, unlike Common Law and parliamentary procedure, whose texts are continually challenged.

4

The Christian Emperor Theodosius forbade idolatry and divination, but vainly. Had not the Black Magus, Simon, flown in the air before Nero, until blasted by the White, St Peter? Suppressing a North African revolt, 398, Honorius's army was protected by the 'ghost of St Ambrose', akin to the 1914 'Angels of Mons'. Indulgences, miraculous relics, magic formulae remained. The Church had regularly to condemn Nature Worshp. Pagan magic was Black; Christian, White. A Black healing-well could be exorcized by a saint's touch, like Columba's in Scotland. Bede translated a book on divination from thunder. In 1268 Laodicean monks were imploring the phallic god, Priapus, to relieve cattle-disease and, as St Cosmo, he was worshipped in Bourbon Naples. At Vendôme a tear shed by Jesus over Lazarus was paraded against drought until the late eighteenth century, when Michelet mentions that French peasants took auguries and respected the Olympians. Frazer cites peasants at Eleusis blaming bad harvests on the removal of Demeter's statue to the Fitzwilliam Museum, Cambridge.

Human interests, practical and psychological, are conservative. Destruction of oracles, relics, sacred places would forfeit morale and revenue. Pope Gregory instructed the English to retain the temples, after purgation, and permit modified tree-worship and animal sacrifice.

Abstruse pre-Christian speculation survived in Gnosticism, encouraged by the mystical Gospel of St John, holding not to passive faith but to the secret knowledge of Mysteries. A paving-stone inscription to Abraxus, Gnostic God, lies at Brading.

Rome had been lush with gods, protecting even steps, doors,

privies. These now lapsed into demons or faded into Christian hierarchies. 'Every visible thing in this world', Augustine maintained, 'is put under an angel's charge.' St Jude was patron of lost causes, Oswyth helped women find keys, Blaise cured sore throats, Anthony guarded pigs, Giles (as at St Giles, Cripplegate) protected cripples, Cyprian sent rain and could become an animal. Gabriel was appointed archangel of radio, 1955, and television was entrusted to Clare of Assisi, for a thirteenth-century vision. (Craveri) St Bona is patron of air-hostesses, St Paul of under-water fishermen.

Holy hands were reverenced, with each priest consecrated by a bishop spiritually descended from the Apostles. A hand of St Teresa of Avila, believed to heal miraculously, is treasured by General Franco. The Gift of the Royal Miracle, the king's curing by touch, was physically transmitted by the dying French monarch to his successor by the contact of palms.[18]

Angels had Persian origins. Hermes, soul-guide and messenger, merged with Michael, guiding souls through Purgatory : as judge of the dead, balancing souls, like Anubis, he is carved on a Glastonbury church.

Apollo faded both into St Apollon and St John, with midsummer fire-festivals. Mother-goddesses could be adored as Virgin and Child. In popular legend, Virgin or saint, capricious, compassionate, whimsical or gullible, helped people escape hell – important, particularly after Augustine's assertion that dead children went there if unbaptized. The Roman greeting *'Perpetua felicitas'* was magnified into SS Perpetua and Felicity. Spanish Christopher borrowed something from Pan.

People demanded the specific. The Virgin was also Lady of Crops, dying on 13 August, the feast of Diana. In Rome, 15 August had been a holiday, for the defeat of Antony and Cleopatra; by the sixth century it was the Feast of the Assumption.

Names and numbers kept their allure. Christianity enjoined names of saints or archangels who thereby became part of the family. Michael, like Thor, protected in battle.

All the Heavenly Host is with us,
St Michael is our Field Marshal.

wrote Otto Kernstock, during World War I. To invoke Venus, as Tannhäuser discovered, endangered the soul. In William Gaddis's novel, *The Recognitions*, Brother Eulalio, for having all the vowels in his name, castigates his own pride.

The Bible emphasized such numbers as 7 and 12. 'Quarantine' derived from the biblical importance of 40. Masses for a late penitent

were often held on the third, seventh and thirtieth day after
death.

> The Number Eight singeth praise with us. Amen.
> The Number Twelve danceth on high. Amen.
>
> (*The Acts of St John*)

Christian images and ikons effected miracles, flew through the
air, aroused passions centuries later transferred to movie-stars – a
Valentino, a James Dean. Man fondles his imagination, treasures
his archetypes, so that for some months of 1936 Mrs Ernest Simpson
was rated a blacker threat to the Empire than was Hitler. The
Nazis organized 'resurrection cults' of early Party martyrs.

Vast staring eyes of Byzantine Christs in Majesty seemed inescapably live : the gentler Orpheus and Balder survived in the Good
Shepherd. Christ bearing the Cross echoed Hercules, sometimes
depicted as burdened with two crossed columns.

The Byzantine Roman Empire saw itself as the Platonic shadow
of Heaven, the Emperor reflecting God, the Cathedral the celestial
palace, the Court the celestial hierarchy. Such splendours apparently
persuaded Vladimir of Kiev to adopt Greek Christianity for Russia.
The Church could never forget such a vision, even using forgeries
to reinforce its imperial connections, until exposed by the renaissance
humanist, Valla.

Orthodox Christianity defined, more precisely, the 'sin', prevalent
in Orphism, and depressing the later Empire. It aggravated the intolerance of its Jewish antecedents, narrowing free thought. It
mistrusted the body, as prey to demons and though, by prayer, it
attempted mental disciplines, ignored the oriental correlation of
morality with right posture and breathing. It seemed to exhibit
salvation more as a final act than a continuous process. It was
like any other human church, whether religious or political,
executing and rehabilitating disciples with a monotony that startles.
Passive faith can be demanded more readily than busy curiosity.

Churches, however, are sub-divided. Whereas the Roman State
had *told* men how to behave, early Christian monasticism, with some
hints from the oriental, tried to *show* them, effectively reducing
Dark Age darkness. The monks worked as much as debated. Only
too well they knew that dogmatic evolution was not human
evolution, that the mind can be stationary. Montaigne saw a
village girl near Pisa, rough and hairy because her mother had
always slept beneath a painting of the hirsute Baptist. The young
Simenon carried a pencil, not for writing, but for 'touching wood'.

Anglican hymns repeat millennia of anthropomorphism. 'The Son of God goes forth to War. . . .'

'We brought nothing into this world,' states the Burial Service. Yet we bring the mass of world mythology. In 1972, Cardinal Ursi, Archbishop of Naples, was still combating paganism within Christianity. The Bishop of Peterborough, March 1971, warned against Black Magic and threats from poltergeists, manifestations of mischievous spirits, with features in common, 'intense cold, evil stench, and a pervading sense of terror'. And, on 1 November 1950, Pope Pius XII issued a Dogmatic Bull, defining the Assumption of the Blessed Virgin :

> Christ, indeed, overcame sin and death by His own death. Who-
> ever is born again to a new life through baptism has conquered sin
> and death through the same Christ. But God did not wish to
> confer upon the Just the full effect of the victory over death
> until the end of Time should come. The bodies of the Just,
> therefore, after death, return to dust. Only in the last day are
> they joined once more in glory to their souls. But God wished
> the Blessed Virgin Mary to be exempt from the general law. For
> she, by a singular privilege, had conquered sin through her
> immaculate conception and therefore she was not subject to the
> law of corruption in the grave. Nor did she need wait until the
> end of Time for the redemption of her body.

5

Christianity reinforced the oriental roots in the British imagination. The year itself had been a god : born, reigning, dying, returning. Easter, Rogation, All Souls, Harvest retained magic devices to embellish the common round, the calendar deriving from Celtic and Roman paganism. All Souls celebrated a ghost-cult. Thomas Hardy describes the Beltane Fires of the primeval New Year :

> Red suns and tufts of fire one by one began to arise, flecking the
> whole country around . . . it was as if these men and boys had
> suddenly dived into past ages, and fetched therefrom an hour and
> deed which had before been familiar with this spot. The ashes
> of the original British pyre that blazed from that summit lay
> fresh and undisturbed in the barrow beneath their tread. The
> flames from funeral piles long ago kindled there had shone down
> upon the lowlands as these were shining now. Festival fires to
> Thor and Woden had followed on the same ground and duly had
> their day. Indeed, it is pretty well known that such blazes as this

the heathmen were now enjoying are rather the lineal descendants from jumbled Druidical rites and Saxon ceremonies than the invention of popular feeling about Gunpowder Plot.

(*The Return of the Native*)

The tenth-century Saxon King Edgar complained that paganism was still the popular English religion. Canute, 1018, legislated against worship of sun, moon, trees, wells, stones. Pan, lawless, grinning, horned, or tusked Woden, were faces of the Devil, continuing the deep love-fear between man and beast and exciting the old fertility orgies, occult confessionals, circular dances, the glamour of the forbidden. Theodore, seventh-century Archbishop of Canterbury, denounced devil-dancers dressed as animals. The Inverkeithy priest, 1282, held a fertility dance; the Bishop of Coventry, 1303, was rebuked for animal-worship. A child witch-murder occurred at Tullieboolie, 1685. When Exeter Cathedral was bombed, dozens of small waxen figures were uncovered. In medieval Wales, salt was placed on a corpse: a 'sin-eater' dipped bread in it and ate it to absorb the departed's sins. At Lent, the Devil, in cat form, was expelled, or tortured or burnt. Hot cross buns had honoured Diana.

These little cakes have a long history, and seem to be descended from the wheaten cakes eaten at the Spring Festival alike by Greeks, Romans and Saxons. It is still believed that bread and buns baked on Good Friday never go mouldy and can be used as cures for various ailments.

(Christina Hole, *English Custom and Usage*, Batsford, 1941)

Burying the Sheaf, Black murder-magic performed in a church over a human-shaped straw-figure occurred in County Louth, 1893. In Saxon England a victim of snake-bite had to drink water touched by Irish books, as no snakes existed in Ireland. The Cornish Jesus, or Chalice Well, embalms a legend of Jesus and Joseph of Arimathea, on a tin-buying expedition, journeying to Glastonbury and miraculously creating fresh water by dropping the Grail into the well.

And did those feet in ancient time
Walk upon England's mountains green?

The churches at Wing, and Arminghall, which has remains of a Bronze Age oak temple, are held the oldest in Britain with foundations from 2500 BC, possibly sited for astrological observations, as continental cathedrals dedicated to Mary are alleged to relate to the zodiacal Virgo. Wing is held to derive from either 'Wiohtun's People' or 'Habitation of idols'.

The zodiac is cut on roundels at Canterbury Cathedral. Adam, Eve and Sagittarius adorn the font at Hook Norton, and that at Brookland has figures of months and the Zodiac. The Font itself has Mithraic memories like, perhaps, the Round Table, and also the Swastika, claimed to be a stylized sun. A Mithraic Lion (sun) and Griffin (wisdom) are carved on Wells Cathedral. North Cerney Church has a carved mantichora, a Persian monster with man's head and shoulders atop lion's body, subsisting on human brains. A mermaid is on Braybrook's font, a unicorn on the arm-rests at Tostock church; bench-ends at Ixworth Thorpe include griffin and unicorn; Wenhaston has a 'Wodehouse' – wild man, leafy, club-bearing satyr, wood-spirit, fertility symbol, cousin of Robin Hood, variously connected with Woden, witchcraft, with the Persian Rah-bin, 'Seeker of the Path' and with outlaw Pan-like freedoms. 'Robin' would have agreed with Brecht : 'What is robbing a bank compared with founding a bank?'

Churchyard yews suggest rites to forgotten gods. Henfield Church was begun about 770, reputedly on pagan ground. Old stones glimmer against smooth turf and tall, regular avenues of clipped yew, a still-life of formal greens and greys, solids and surfaces, flats and heights, where something of souls can be imagined.

5 Saxon England

Formerly men came from beyond our
borders, seeking wisdom in our own
land; now, if we are to have it at all
we must look for it abroad.

King Alfred

I

Under fifth-century invasions, Britain's Mediterranean trade,
Romano-Celtic villa life, organized Christianity and Law, communications and most towns dwindled or vanished, though London, York,
Winchester survived, sinister refuges for unlucky gods. Forest and
swamp revived. Rabbits, perhaps introduced by the Romans,
multiplied. Several centuries later, bears still existed in East Anglia,
Norwich annually supplying three for the royal bear-baiting.[19]
Some Celts put up periodic counter-attack, particularly in the
south-west. Others retreated to Wales, or Armorica (Brittany),
where Breton separatism still survives. Yet others may have remained, interbreeding or co-existing with the intruders. Much is still
being discovered. Conquest never extinguished the vital Welsh poetry,
associated with the great sixth-century bards, Taliesin and Aneirin.
Certainly, unlike the Gothic and Lombard conquerors of Italy,
the Teutons, like the Vandals, disdained Roman institutions and
glamour, for some generations debarring Britain from cosmopolitan
influences. The scene was one of confused violence: the Irish
pirating for slaves, Irish rule in Strathclyde, perhaps a brief Roman
return, Pictish invasions, Viking raids. York was successively ruled
by Celts, Romans, Teutons, a ninth-century pagan Dane (Halfdon)
a Danish-Irish king (Ragnold), by a Saxon earl, by the Normans.
Over a century of obscurity ended with some social and cultural
recovery. The new lords could be less outlandish than their names.
Raedwald's seventh-century burial-ship, disinterred at Sutton Hoo,
was eighty-two feet long, filled with Byzantine treasure, Gallic
coins, precious jewels and minerals.
Having mastered Celtic resistance, the Teutons revealed imaginative and political resources. Several kingdoms were maintained and

by the ninth century a precarious but acknowledged English throne
with secular ties with Europe had been established. Several Saxon
kings – as well as Macbeth – reputedly visited Rome. By the eighth
century, Britain was a greater international cultural force than she
had been under the Empire. Alfred had charitable contacts with
Jerusalem and, less historically, with Indian Christians. He used
Frisian shipwrights and such continental teachers as Plegmund.
Yet, despite Alfred's deprecation, the Saxons were not parasitical.
Alcuin of York (d. 804) tutored Charlemagne's nobility, sometimes
the Emperor himself, who kept his letters, some still extant. Viking-
Saxon England, 700–1066, received and exported, if few elaborate
ideas, at least books, mosaics, sacred vessels, engraved cups and
dishes, chessmen. Offa's dyke and ditch was a very considerable
engineering feat, 130 miles long. *Beowulf* is a masterpiece, at the
foundation of English literature. The Dark Ages produced fine
churches, monasteries, farm estates, water-clocks. Eighth-century
East Anglia enjoyed considerable art and learning, its religious art
showing Egyptian traces. Saxon coinage had no immediate superior,
Lewes possessing two mints. The silver sceat was particularly profuse
with lettering, ornamental designs of twists, circles, animals, including a porcupine. Saxon coins have been dug up as far distant
as Kiev. English books, jewellery, embroidery, metal-work, whale-
bone carving, notably sculpture – which survived the Conquest – are
found in France, Italy, Germany, Netherlands. Anglo-Saxon
embroidery was in rich demand, the 'Opus Anglicianum' was
respected throughout the Middle Ages, helping prepare for the
Stuart endowment of the Mortlake tapestry works.

Charlemagne's Empire, influenced in education by Britain,
affected, sometimes inspired English Illumination. This, once secured,
was, notably at Winchester, adorned, embellished, varied according
to regional tastes, mingling the golds and vermilions, the observed,
the fanciful, the fantastic, setting precise figures against intricate
foliage and lettering, often with huge or bizarre capitals and
sumptuous interlacings. The twelfth-century illuminated bibles at
Winchester, Lambeth and Cambridge had no superiors in Europe.

Though England remained aloof from Charlemagne's grandiose,
often bloody attempt to revive a Roman Empire, British movement
across Dark Age Europe was constant, from, Bede noticed, all
classes, despite weak or piratical rulers, bandits, obstinate pagans,
broken roads, disunity of law. Ethelred II's grandson went relatively
far, to marry a Hungarian princess.

Northerners possessed obstinate resolution undeterred by the
ultimate melancholy of long winters, forlorn uplands and tarns,
dank forests, tribal vendettas, harsh sea and fire, brief lives. Even

Woden, Thor, Balder, would die, unable to flee the eye of time
that all feared.

> Old walls stand, pulled by winds,
> Frost-draped, all buildings decayed :
> Wine halls dissolve, lords lie broken,
> Hearts in the dust, proud vassals
> Heaped by the wall. Battle took some,
> Leading them on lengthy paths : one the raven
> Bore high over waters : one the grey wolf devoured :
> A gloom-faced warrior hid yet another in the earth-pit.

2

There was much homely magic. Family troubles, confided to bees,
would expel the swarm. More important, Saxon and Viking had an
instinct for leadership tempered by dissent, by traditional popular
rights, by the responsibilities as well as the privileges of authority.
'Lord' means 'loaf-giver'. Saxon kings were expected to consult the
Witan. Alfred the Great was lawgiver as well as warrior, collecting
the laws of his predecessors, notably Offa. He delighted not in
laying down the law but in helping laws to be kept. Translator of
Bede, Orosius and, like Elizabeth I, of Boethius, also scholar,
inventor, administrator, ship-designer, his genius was comparable
to that of Trajan and Hadrian, and struggled against greater odds.
A passage from his Boethius was, one can imagine, worked out from
fullness of heart. 'He who would have full power must first strive
to get power over his own mind, and not be unduly subject to his
vices, and he must put away from him undue cares, and cease to
bewail his misery.' He founded hospitals and schools, assisted by
such thinkers as the Celt, Asser. His reign originated the Anglo-
Saxon Chronicle, unique in Europe. He is not to be judged by
liberal parliamentarianism : comparison seems more permissible
with the reforming, centralizing, educating Emperor of Ethiopia,
Haile Selassie. His prose – 'Power be not good unless he be good who
holds it' – plain, hard-hitting, has the clarity and strength of
copious feelings strictly controlled. Its strength descends through
Wycliffe, Tyndale, More, Cranmer, Raleigh, Francis Bacon,
Clarendon, Lilbourne, Cromwell, Milton, Swift, Cobbett, Hazlitt,
to Shaw, Russell, Priestley, Orwell : a style yielding forthright
sensations while remaining unsensational, eschewing Celtic exuberance and Romanesque tautology. 'Why not name the thing?'
Cobbett thundered at 'corporal infliction' used instead of 'flogging'.
It is style in which music must be balanced by meaning, with a

brushwork of moralizing easily accessible to humour. Stoic is
'The Wanderer' :

> The wise must be patient,
> Neither passionate nor in speech over-hasty,
> In battle neither rash nor irresolute;
> Not timid, nor prone to despair or greed,
> Should not boast before doing.

Severely existential, the North lacked omnipotent gods, a conviction that right action ensures solid rewards, in a landscape untrustworthy and violent. Gods were often bewildered and helpless against
the monstrous and elemental, as reason will quail before the
unconscious. Yet they were too human to be utterly relinquished.
The eight-century Franks Casket is covered with Christian and
pagan allusions. 'The Dream of the Rood' infuses into Christ's
passion a breath of tree-worship. Auden, like Kipling, refines Anglo-
Saxon themes and rhythms : 'Doom is dark and deeper than any
sea-dingle.' Britain has absorbed a sturdy northern conviction that
systematic philosophy is not irresistible. Unlike France and Germany, Rome's direct heirs, Britain has never pushed logic to
extremes. Dr Johnson, Tawney, are more typical than Marx,
Sartre. There is Hume instead of Hegel; instead of Nietzsche –
Carlyle, Shaw; instead of Goethe – Bede, H. G. Wells, Russell;
instead of Napoleon, Bismarck, de Gaulle, one must be content
with Pitt – and Churchill, whose philosophy would confuse the
most tidy-minded.

A British Prime Minister, C. R. Attlee, was to describe his
administration in the spirit of Offa and Alfred – of Burghley,
Burke, Peel, Gladstone, Disraeli, Salisbury, Balfour.

> It had always been our practice, in accord with the natural
> genius of the British people, to work empirically. We were not
> afraid of compromises and partial solutions. We knew that mis-
> takes would be made and that advances would be often by trial
> and error. We realized that the application of Socialist principles
> in a country such as Britain with a peculiar economic structure
> based on international trade required great flexibility.

Anglo-Saxon feeling for local rights was to become a distinctly
British system of unpaid local government and regional policing.
Pre-conquest England established a folklore of native freedoms,
shattered by the greedy and cruel Normans, in legends that were
known in Cromwell's army and amongst the Levellers, and survived into Chartist propaganda. Saxon and Viking parishes and

counties largely remain. Sheriff, Ealdorman, Reeve, Bishop, the Hundred, Shires and Manorial courts were retained by the Normans who, while dispossessing native landlords, needed an orderly people to rule, and to whom genocide was unthinkable. The manorial status of such a house as Wantley, Henfield, has been traced to Saxon times. The Saxon dane-geld, initiating national taxation, was extended by the Normans.

Coke, formidable Stuart Common Law jurist, pronounced that the English laws inherited by the Conqueror were 'good and ancient'. They were a mass of carefully guarded rights, never quite relinquished despite Enclosing, Centralization, State departments. They colour modern industrial relations with new vehemence. They presuppose that human relations are indeed human, lacking all-purpose generalizations. Common Law rose from witness, not theory, growing more from popular stubbornness than from the caprice of officialdom or ruler. Fines could compound many Saxon crimes, as among the African Masai, with whom forty-nine cows atone for murder. A Petition of Right, residue of King Edgar's legislation, was exercised in the High Court, May 1973, exactly a thousand years later.

Local courts, manors, strongholds were connected not by police but by oaths, perjury thus becoming deadly sin. Harold's reputed forswearing of William was more than breach of contract.

Saxon place-names are revealing. P. H. Reaney[20] shows women's names embedded in them, indicating female property-rights equal with male. On the morning after marriage a Saxon would give his wife a 'morgan-gift', land as personal property. Thus 'Moor Farm', 'Morris Farm', 'Murrain Wood'. These rights, mainly lost at the Conquest, were regained, and more fully, only after the Married Women's Property Act, 1882.

3

Vikings appalled. They sacked, burnt, looted. Vikings raided a Welsh monastery twenty-five years after Hastings. Nineteenth-century Coventry cathedral still exhibited a flayed Viking skin on the door. Yet, finally, they were more traders, settlers, organizers, than freebooting anarchists. If they wrecked Irish monastic brilliance, they founded Dublin, Wexford, Waterford. One-third of English place-names are Viking. 'Lord of the Isles' is a Viking title, as is 'Lady of Man', used by the Queen as Manx ruler. They were adept jewellers, carvers of complex decorations, boat-builders, chess-players. By the tenth century they had proved themselves worthy of their political autonomy. Oswald, Archbishop of York, was a Dane. Their tragic literature, laconic as axe-strokes, un-burdened by tired classicism, has Greek intensity, respects wisdom, sees life as small light wavering in huge darkness, though the light persists, illuminating sudden vistas, beautiful or intolerable, loving or baleful. Above magical clichés – the unburnable cloak, self-playing chess-set, inexhaustible drinking-horn – are deep-set human values and dilemmas: the temptations of power, gold, violence, the necessity of friendship, abhorrence of deceit and cowardice.

Vikings had the sailor's undogmatic character. The English Dane-Law discountenanced slavery. Briefly, England, with South Scotland and Northern France, was within Canute's Scandinavian Empire, his strong rule enforcing law and security, rebuilding religious houses, revitalizing London's trade. His death, 1036, restored the Saxon monarchy, though in the English language, and in folk-memory, the Viking lingered.

When the people of Hawick in Roxburghshire sing a song at the annual riding of their marches, the burden of which is:

'Teribus and Teri Odin
Sons of heroes slain at Flodden',

no argument will tempt me to think otherwise than that it en-shrines the memory of a much more ancient war-cry calling upon Scandinavian gods worshipped by the worthy burghers' distant ancestors. At least the memory of Tyr and Odin are obvious enough in this chorus which has been construed as

'Tyr habbe us, y Tyr y Odin',

which is as much as to say, 'Let Tyr (the Sword-god) have us in his keeping on the day of battle, both Tyr and Odin.'

(Lewis Spence, *Myth and Ritual in Dance, Game and Rhyme,*
Watts, 1947)

The Viking stone at Kirkby Stephen is carved with Loki's tor-ment. For causing Balder's death, Loki, Mischief-god, was tied beneath snake's fangs, his wife catching the poison in a cup. When this overflowed, earthquake occurred, as, August 1970, it did, at Kirkby Stephen. The Viking Flamborough Sword Dance is still performed at Bridlington.

4

Dark Age Christianity offered more than a theology, seldom pacific, often ferocious, of Fall, Atonement, Trinity, Grace. In an age requiring courage, it was a pioneering force against post-imperial apathy, galvanizing shrunken institutions and founding others, abashing barbarians, providing financial acumen, forbidding infanticide, organizing property and, as with the Benedictines, attracting specialists in agriculture, hygiene, architecture, education. It catered for man's hunger for status, more reliably than could transient kings. 'Let us', commanded the founders of Seville Cathedral, 'build a temple so grand that future men will remember us, if only as madmen.'

The Church, an aristocracy less of birth than of intelligence, law, possession, was long a tool as much for administration as morality. Beckett was not fully ordained, when appointed arch-bishop. Wolsey's illegitimate son, not in holy orders, was Dean of Wells. The seventeenth-century Cardinal de Guise was commanded to enter the priesthood or renounce the see of Rheims. The larger church interest was not in social justice or gospel other-wordliness but in material restoration. Rationalizing breakdown and shortages it held up promises of salvation which suffering and injustice might actually assist.

As a human institution its rhythms were worldly : dogmatic and experimental, idealistic and relapsing, tolerant and inquisitorial, energetic and torpid, confessional and bureaucratic – all overlapping. It exemplified an enduring historical lesson : that the more violent the revolutionary, the more urgently the revolution hastens to become amoral and static.

Forced, at best, to use political stratagems, the Church sustained man's appetite for power, aggression, mystery, through office, crusade, mysticism. Charlemagne's religious wars left hate and fear in Christ's name. Personal sanctity can itself be inhuman. Even Gandhi, humorous, wise, subtle, was angered when doctors relieved pain, thus interfering with divine Will.

The Church was scarcely concerned with providing a radical alternative to tradition. Capitalizing on its freehold as heir of Rome, it claimed monopoly of body and soul, and rejected its earlier pacificism and communalism, the assets of a despised or persecuted minority. 'Cursed be he who holds back his sword from the shedding of blood,' ordained Pope Gregory the Great. In crisis, Alfred might have agreed. Sacred texts, as in Marxism and Maoism, were used to justify extremes of behaviour, more damning than magnanimous.

Christian education was not unalloyed. The pagan library at Alexandria was burnt, perhaps with classics now permanently unknown. St Gregory punctiliously destroyed hundreds of godless manuscripts, which later ages would have revered as classics.

Monasticism discouraged but seldom utterly prohibited classical literature. Virgil began to be claimed as a shadowy prophet of Christianity, then as a White magician, builder of a miraculous glass bridge over Naples, itself protected by the poet's bones which, if exposed to the light, would cause tempest.

British post-Roman Christianity was divided between the centralizing, legalistic Roman version and the learned, more flexible, rowdier Celtic. The latter, from fifth-century Ireland, developed a monastic culture lively, imaginative, quarrelsome, sophisticated in arts, crafts, literacy, debate, rivalling Byzantium and Islam. The Ardagh Chalice, many-coloured, with lightly chiselled gold, silver and brass, was thought to be the Grail itself. Irish monasteries were minor universities which, more tolerant than many continental coevals, appreciated, while not imitating, pagan as well as orthodox texts. Irish poets are claimed to have known Arab Sufi literature. Irish scholars visited Charlemagne's court and schools, notably Columbanus and John Scotus. Madame de Stael's remark that paganism deified life, Christianity deified death, was inapplicable to such tyros, whose Dark Age Ireland, doubtless dramatic to the degree of danger, had an intellectual vigour superior to that of Tudor Ireland and comparable to Tudor England.

The Book of Kells, the Lindisfarne Bible, show that one of the oldest European literatures could be published with opulence of design and material. The Irish cultural effect on England, Scotland, Europe itself, was for a time as solid as the Byzantine. It owed much to Columba, the planner, the monastic quartermaster-general, to Ninian, Aiden, to Columbanus who founded nearly five score continental monasteries. Brendan Lehane[21] quotes M. Robert Schumann, at the establishment of the West European Iron and Steel Community, 1950, hailing St Columbanus as 'the patron saint of those who seek to construct a United Europe'.

Roman missionaries from Saxon England met distastefully, sometimes violently, Irish monks already established in Europe. Clinging to their headstrong, unsystematic Christianity, less dogmatic than Rome and Byzantium, bearded Irish zealots mapped with unseemly rage the nature of God, in resonant language accompanying inglorious recriminations. Finally condemned by Rome, Irish Christianity was abandoned by the English kings at Whitby, 665, a decision assisting the growth of Law, perhaps at the cost of intellectual dissent and clerical independence.

English Romanism was refounded by the sixth-century Augustine of Canterbury, Theodore of Tarsus, Hadrian of Africa. Augustine, landing 596, found a pagan Kentish king married to a Christian, and a Celtic Church in Wales established by Columba. London's

St Paul's dates from 604, on a hill once sacred to Diana. In East Anglia, where flourished the great ash-grey, red-capped crane, Christianity was, traditionally, revived in 630 by St Fursey from Ireland and St Felix from Burgundy, invited by the intellectual King Sigibert, who had been converted in Gaul.

Already the Church was not the sole patron of education. Sigibert himself founded a school and his courage has a flavour peculiar to this era:

> After reigning for some years he abandoned his life in the world, as many other kings and noblemen were to do in later years, and entered a monastery which he himself had founded. He had lived as a monk there for many years when Penda, King of the Mercians, invaded East Anglia and attempts were made to persuade him to leave his monastery and lead his soldiers into battle. Refusing to do so, he was led to the battlefield by force, and there, still refusing to violate his monastic vows, he was killed.

> (Peter Hunter Blair, *The World of Bede*, Secker and Warburg, 1970)

Such are time's tricks that Sigibert is more comprehensible today than he might have been to Lord Palmerston. Such behaviour, as from Thomas Beckett, forces reflection as to whether it is within genuine intellectual choice, or is a refinement of instinctive survival tactics, or brute obstinacy.

Ethelbert of Kent speaks a tongue still recognizable, and used as a preface by G. M. Young in *Today and Yesterday*.[22]

> 'I see you believe what you say, or you would not have come all this way to say it. But you must not expect me to give up all at once the customs which I and the people of England have followed from one generation to another. So – go on talking: no one shall interfere with you; and if you convince us, well, of course we shall be convinced.'

Britain was now to assert herself, culturally, if not militarily. Her missionaries embarked to Scandinavia, France, Germany. The Devonian St Boniface (660–754), the 'Apostle of Germany', was missionary and scholar, with works still surviving. As Bishop of Mainz he helped organize German ecclesiasticism. British missionaries became patron saints of Bremen, Münster, Deventer. A Saxon Bishop of York baptized the Swedish King. The bishopric of Utrecht was founded, 696, by the Englishman Willibrod. Here, in 697, was begun the Echternach monastery, home of the great MSS. bible, the Golden Gospels, illuminated, ivory-panelled, with jewelled and painted letters, pictures, reliefs.

The Saxon Church maintained considerable splendour and authority, through Dunstan, Osbert, Egbert, Ethelwald. It excluded European dancing from its rites but maintained Latin scholarship and increasingly encouraged English literature. Bede, Alcuin, Aldhelm had European intellectual fame, relatively as pronounced as that of Hume, Carlyle, Russell.

The Jarrow monk, Bede (673–735) is at the root of English intellectualism. 'Venerable' conceals his vivacious, Goethean curiosity. His international reputation, exceeding Pelagius's, has been compared to Gladstone's. He was a solid link with classical thought and the Christian Fathers. Nearly a thousand of his manuscripts survive in Europe, many still being published six centuries later. The only Englishman admitted to Dante's Paradise, within violence and uncertainty he sought truth, as teacher, theologian, moral philosopher, musician, natural scientist, hagiographer. Writing also on grammar, metre, cosmology, orthography, geography, chronology, his *History of the English Church* was the first major European work using BC/AD notation, misleading in its suggestion of moral progress.

Bede was no solitary landmark. There was Benedict Biscop (d. 689), founder of the Jarrow and Wearmouth monasteries that, like Whitby, Ripon, Hexham, were educational power-houses, exchanging learning with Rome, Seville, Vivarium, and with Ireland, though perhaps more in touch with Europe. The script and decoration of the Codex Amiatinus imitated the Italian. Charles Thomas[23] mentions the 'splendour of Hexham, a Mediterranean basilica implanted in the water-meads of the Tyne.' Biscop, of South European and North African culture, visited Rome six times, returning with scholars, musicologists, books, craftsmen. Like Bede, he looked outwards to Europe, not inwards to Ireland. Such native adventurousness survived the Conquest: the eleventh-century pilgrim, Ansgot of Burwell, travelled to Compostela with English companions. Under Henry I, the Saxon Adelard of Bath, classical and Islamic scholar, translator of Euclid, travelled in Asia minor, North Africa, South-East Europe. A few generations later the French abbey of Cluny helped generate a Western monastic revival, not least in Britain, where a considerable scholastic, religious and administrative achievement was led by such kings as Edgar, Offa, Athelstan, and the churchmen Ethelwold and Dunstan.

The cosmopolitan court of the last Saxon kings was to founder under the Normans, 1066. The anonymous chronicler writes:

Then Duke William sailed from Normandy into Pevensey. When King Harold was informed of this he gathered together a great host and came to oppose him at the gray apple tree, and William came upon him unexpectedly before his army was set in order.

Yet Saxon administrative organization was confirmed, though more thoroughly, the great King demanding above all order, in a world still intemperate.

Part Two

6 Feudal Europe

> Yesterday the abolition of fairies and giants:
> The fortress like a motionless eagle eyeing the valley,
>   the chapel built in the forest:
> Yesterday the carving of angels and of frightening
>   gargoyles.
>
> W. H. Auden

> Up to a certain time Life was con-
> ceived as a Dance, and after that time
> Life was conceived as a race . . . one
> is rhythmic and recurrent movement,
> because there is a known centre; while
> the other is precipitate or progres-
> sive movement, because there is an
> unknown goal. The latter has pro-
> duced all that we call progress; the
> former produced what the medievals
> meant by Order; but it was the lively
> order of the Dance.
>
> G. K. Chesterton

I

Generalizations deceive. Like childhood, the 'Middle Ages' ebbed
and flowed with possibilities, false starts, continuations, variations
on antique themes. It can be claimed that eleventh-century Europe
enjoyed some practical international structure, through pilgrimages,
fairs, conferences of kings, priests, masons, guildsmen, reinforced
by Christian ideology and organization: Canon Law, liturgy,
hierarchy, control of monasteries, Latin – used in the Hungarian
Diet as late as 1843. Fourteenth-century Hungary was ruled by a
Frenchman, Poland by a Hungarian. Ethiopian Coptic monasteries
sent delegates to Italy, where black African slaves were used. The
Pope suspended Bishop Grosstête, prodigious English intellectual,
for refusing a rich Lincolnshire living to a non-English-speaking
Italian. Many English ecclesiastics were absentee foreigners, while
a Hertfordshire monk could become an abbot in France, archbishop in Norway, finally Pope, Hadrian IV (1154). Like nineteenth-
century Welsh Methodism, the medieval Church gave the poor a

C

chance to rise. He, Grosstête, Archbishops Walden and Chicheley were alike of poor parentage. Richard the Canon, of twelfth-century Warwick, granted tithes in Warmington, Arlescot and Shotswell to the Norman abbey of Préaux, where he was probably abbot.

Necessarily, the Church's concerns were more practical than ethical. Survival was paramount. It had outpaced Mithras and Woden by purposeful contempt for pacificism and tolerance. Weeds were to be ejected, tares burnt. The harvest was more important than the individual grain. A loving Father may yet be a flogging Father. 'Whoever places himself outside the Church will be doomed to eternal torture, even if he allows himself to go to the fire, alive, for Christ's sake.' (Augustine) St Bernard added zest to the Crusades. 'In the death of the pagan the Christian is glorified because Christ is glorified.' The Church readily accepted Christ's fury against the Jews : 'Ye are of your father, the Devil,' a text helping to sanctify centuries of anti-Semitism. A pope sanctioned William's invasion as a Crusade, drenched Catharist Provence with blood, applauded the Bishop of Norwich's savage suppression of the 1381 rebels, the Bishop later commanding, worthlessly, in Flanders. A mild echo of this militancy occurred, 30 July 1972, with the Rev. Hugh Eylon-Jones preaching at Cowes on 'British naval sea-power decisive in recent wars' !

Latin services were frequently incomprehensible even to the priest. Children might be placed at birth in religious houses by parents devout, superstitious or crafty. Though poverty and sickness might be relieved, the Church frequently broke its own laws, enforcing labour on holy-days, neglecting preaching and parish work, maintaining slavery.

> Wherever we are able to examine the relation between clergy and parishioners, we are forced to the conclusion that most of the ordinary parish clergy were inefficient, ill-educated and undistinguished men.
>
> (H. S. Bennett, *Life on the English Manor (1400)*, Cambridge, 1937)

Credulity pervaded king and serf alike. One can imagine a humble girl alone in an ornate side-chapel, shyly offering Jesus her one treasure, her breast. The authorities could have punished her, both for immorality and for doubting the Saviour's ability to see through her gown.

With huge territorial empires, the Church was entwined with the feudalism of kings, seigneurs, universities, guilds : an Archbishop of Bordeaux might be vassal to the English King, himself liege to the French. Espousing both Caesar and God, Rome, while claiming to transcend feudalism – throughout one has the sensation of exceptional men like spires, straining to soar – ruthlessly demanded feudal privileges. The early Spanish Church was subsidised by wholesale slavery.

Man's instinct to form churches, hierarchies, parties, closed shops, has qualities of bitter competition. O and A, Light and Dark. Like fire, it flickers towards both destruction and creation, arousing dreams of the imprecise but fateful, the sinister and the charitable. Like fairy-tale, opera, like a fair, country house or college, the medieval Church reflected the multitudinous processes of being alive : the gropings, feuds, misunderstandings and verdicts. Its graphic art and its preaching gave it one of the world's most powerful propaganda processes, with effects not yet dead, even for many atheists. Its lights, images, processions reflected basic impulses, exploited by the Inquisition, reaching forward to the dictators. Most animals seek status : hierarchies change little more than their names.

English and continental monarchs, savagely or diplomatically, disputed clerical legal privileges, doubtless with some popular support, despite the tragedy of Becket. The privileges could appear exorbitant. A rector of Nelson's village, Burnham Thorpe, arrested for piracy, successfully pleaded Benefit of Clergy, leaving his two accomplices to be hanged for 'duress de mayhem'.

Periodic international congresses to reform the Church were abortive. The personnel, lay and clerical, were conservative and sexually exclusive. Top-heavy with male politicians, Europe was enfiefed to male Pope, Emperor, kings, male God, male Devil, only partially mitigated by a Mother-Goddess revival, Isis Stella Maris becoming the mediating Virgin. In palace and hovel too many women were objects. Ethics were conditioned by local needs. An eleventh-century French serf was valued at thirty-eight sous, a horse at a hundred. Serfdom remained legal in Prussia until 1807, in Russia until 1861.

The Saint, in politics, was unwelcome. When Pope Celestine V (1294), model of uprightness, attempted to take the Sermon on the Mount as a literal administrative programme – refusing to bless wars, continue clerical frauds, accept brothel profits, treat with criminal despots, countenance slavery, Church landlordism and profiteering – he dislocated within weeks the entire Papal mechanism and made governments throughout Europe realize what nuisances a Jesus, a Francis, really were. Though canonized (1313) Celestine was ejected after five months, though less drastically than the saintly Henry VI of England. Like Gandhi, both Celestine and

Henry believed in apostolic poverty, legality of example, in absolute
goodness as a form of persuasion, of moral blackmail. Both ultimately
betrayed or disappointed their supporters. Philip the Fair, Henry
II, were worse men, better rulers.

2

The Holy Roman Emperor claimed the prerogatives of the Sacred
King to preserve Christendom, but usually only as Austrian ruler
was his authority more than nominal. Regional kings were gradually freeing themselves of powerful vassals, though still having to
rely more on their personality than on law. Philip the Fair,
Frederick II, Edward I, maintained their grip, their sons failed.

Christianity, like Islam, was a useful source of intelligent energies,
and king and priest had perforce to be not only rivals but allies,
quarrelling over land, law-courts, investitures, but long mutually
dependent, particularly when nascent capitalism disclosed alarming
forces based on money and free thought. Spengler saw conflict
between castle (Fact) and Cathedral (Truth), the noble a symbol of
time, the priest a symbol of space, but the priest could himself be
a noble and to the lowly watchers the quarrel was more over
spoils than principle.

Unprotected by regular police, stable frontiers, national law,
reliable gods, authority still had to rely on make-belief: fetish,
ritual, names, supernatural sanctions. Warningly, a central boss at
Bovey Tracey church has four heads – Bishop, Pope, King, Baron
– sprouting from a single neck. At Long Burton the Royal Arms are
carved over the church porch, with 'Curse not the King. Noe, not
in thy Thought.' When Amin of Uganda, August 1972, demanded
the expulsion of Asians, on orders from God in a dream, he was
using a well-tried medieval technique. Philip the Fair would have
approved the broadcast on Radio Uganda, 7 September, 1972 :

> President Amin this morning received the Rev. John Obiri
> Yeboka. . . . the Reverend told the President that he should not
> worry at all. He said nobody is going to kill him because he is
> in the right direction of God. . . . Rev. John will bring [to an
> official Lunch] some of the people whom he has risen from the
> dead since he came to Uganda. They will include a person who
> died yesterday at 4 pm and after prayers rose at 7 pm.

Names, titles, linked all history, rolled it up, were encrusted with
gold, had roar of lions, strength of Alps, radiance of sun. The
Ancient Greek medical guild comprised 'Sons of Aesculapius'

Jewish holy men were 'Sons of God'. (The late Prince Chichibu of
Japan was formally entitled 'Son of God'. On his enrolment at
Magdalen, Oxford, the President, Herbert Warren, observed that
the college was accustomed to the sons of important personages.)
To illiterates, titles reverberate like majestic gongs or the mating of
whales. 'Sapor, King of Kings, and Brother of the Sun and Moon.'
'Ivan, by God's grace, Great Lord, Emperor and Grand Duke of
all the Russias, of Vododamur, Moscovia, Novgorod, Emperor of
Kazan, Tiversky, Vgorsky, Bulgaria and all Siberland, Great
Commander of the Northern Ports.' 'Supreme Pontiff.' 'Apostolic
King.' 'Bearer of the Golden Rose.' They storm life and death by
the grandeur of sheer sound, or the opulence of colossal fraud,
'Plenary Indulgence', 'Republic One and Indivisible', 'Will of the
People', 'The Revolution', alike containing the logic, unprovable
but irrefutable, of a Mystery.

All that peoples could enforce on their rulers, short of desertion
or rebellion, was in bestowing names: Wryneck, Blue Tooth,
Broadfoot, Sluggard, Lion, Fine Scholar, Fat, Bold, Intolerable.

Statues of gods, Madonnas, saints, rulers, retained mana. Philip
the Fair had life-sized statues of his predecessors erected in his
palace, awing by their solemnity. Gibbon was to notice at Burgos
a medieval Jesus with its hair cut monthly.

3

The Knights were the supreme masculine authority, rising against
Moors, Vikings, Mongols, Turks, Slavs. All Europe had seemed
menaced by eighth-century Islam. They began as a line of defence,
counter-attacked in crusades against pagan and heretic, then,
superannuated, were largely eliminated as public pests, hurling
themselves against authority and each other, and became a sort of
anthem. Military orders evolved, like the Templars and Hospitallers,
with specific codes and duties, though the codes remained ideals
and the duties eventually lapsed. 'They feast every day splendidly,'
grumbled John of Salisbury, 'but they shun labour or exercise,
like a dog or snake.'

From a distance, Knights are fairy-tale heirs not of Christ but
Rome. Bohemund, el Cid, du Guesclin, Chandos – knights, beaked
like iron cruel birds, sealed and plated like dragons, starry, emblazoned, feathered, gilded, daubed with myth, creations of
heaven and hell, perched like live forts on gigantic horses, and
swollen with pictorial, cosmopolitan language. Heraldry resembles
old cricket scores, almost meaningless yet lulling, touched with
poetry. Behind 'Grace, caught Flowers, bowled Midwinter' glints

'Fesse Vaire between Three Fleurs de Lys, Argent Fess Gules with Molet Gules in the quarter.' One can day-dream of Black Knights, awed by their Honour, defending solitary standard on hopeless field, White Knights lamenting the Lady they did not always want. Knights battering for plunder, or undying name, lying bleached in Spain, Prussia, Palestine, or at a bend of the Avon, aimlessly drinking in damp strongholds, hawking and raping, preferring death to boredom or ridicule, conceiving unbroken honour incompatible with unbroken bones, their descendants deeming it dishonourable to cheat at cards, but not dishonourable to bilk tradesmen. Knights . . . foul-mouthed about ague and girls, thrashing wives and servants, robbing the poor, recklessly hunting even when there was nothing left to hunt, wrecking the peasants' corn, over-eating, cajoling and threatening God simultaneously and, like the tempestuous Angevins, undecided whether to be noble saint or uproarious sinner. Knights . . . planting hatred and fear as others plant beans, ordering heroic poems about themselves which they swiftly believed.

Romance is the music of distance. Malory wrote his haunting Arthur, Guinevere, Lancelot – 'And it befell upon a day' – in prison, apparently for thievish, selfish brutality.

Like Hitler and Mussolini the Knights could hack out their identities only by incessant activity. Better act, crassly, grossly, uselessly, than do nothing and remain supine and unreal, in a contemptible world. Only occasionally their hooliganism seems redeemed by magnanimity, respect for oaths, the unfortunate, for enemies, the fallen, for life, if not for lives. They remain at their best in defeat. 'By Saint James', de Montfort allegedly cried as the royal forces closed in at Evesham, 'they come on in good order and it was from me they learnt it. Let us commend our souls to God, for our bodies are Prince Edward's.' Coeur de Lion's pardoning his slayer is recalled more readily than his massacre of Saracen families at Acre.

Richard loved language, could be lordly and petty, disdained costs, acted with unusual courage. His voice, from a Danubian jail, is individual when chivalric verse was often monotonously formal.

My men and barons
From England, Normandy, Poitou and Gascony,
Know that, had I a friend,
I'd not leave him in prison, however humble he be,
If it were just a question of cash.
I say this, not as reproach, but
Still in prison do I lie.

As if staring deep into tapestry, scarlet and black, the imagination hears the Black Prince weeping before battle, for doomed youth, yet perpetrating an atrocious massacre; Templars howling at the stake, French lords slaughtered at Agincourt, Charles the Bold eaten by wolves, English Knights terrorizing juries, evading taxes, hustled to the block after Wakefield and Towton; Richard III declaiming 'I am myself alone.' Knights, 'the fools of Time, which die for goodness, who have liv'd in crime.'

Chivalry long transcended nationality. Troubadour poetry passed from court to court. Tournaments, denounced by the Church that may have scented a pagan rivalry of mock-sacrifice, heroic tragedy, were, from York to Naples, promoted as prize-fights : the English William the Marshal was offered a £500 transfer fee by tournament backers and, in international combines, Knights insured themselves against injury, capture or death, champions pledging themselves against fighting each other.[23]

The most spectacular tournament was in crusades, already common to Islam, though commercial classes won the best prizes. Brilliant, quarrelsome, greedy, the Knights co-operated badly. Carving out personal fiefs, they abused ideology, their kingdom undermined as much from within as without. Templars and Hospitallers, to safeguard their gains, made some accommodation with Islam, even with the Mongols, encouraged in the last by Edward I. As in the 1821 Greek War of Independence, 'patriots' made advantageous pacts with the Turks. As for the crusaders, for all their cultural effects, they were immediately associated with massacres of Jews, inter-Christian hatreds and betrayals, and naked conquest.

4

It has been maintained that hierarchical society demands aggression as a basis for its economics, as well as a salve for drudgery and emotional frustration. The crusades substantiated some of this, with their variety of motives. Immediate issues may be the stimulus but are seldom the profoundest causes of war. Men are not all of a piece. In 1914, even the mild intellectual, Stefan Zweig, confessed that his greatest happiness would be to ride as an officer against a civilized enemy, particularly France, 'the France that one must chastise because one loves her.' One doubts if individual crusaders brooded very deeply about spice-markets, pilgrim-traffic, infidel blasphemy, Christ's tomb. Beyond territorial ambitions, the motives of many may have been vague, though the commercial impulse was sufficiently imperative. Economics may not have total say, but say

they undeniably do have. Spanish New World settlers energetically
bought African slaves from the heretic English, in defiance of their
own laws. Notoriously, despite Napoleon's blockade his armies
fought the English in British-made boots and cloaks.

The international trade guilds, monopolists demanding high
standards and privileges, were conservative : in thirteenth-century
Italy they banned an early spinning-jenny – but the oriental spice
trade was essential for ill-fed, badly nourished Europe, in which
sixty French famines are recorded, 970–1100, and opportunities
were limitless. Conditioned by church, manor, family, men must
have found crusades not only a pretentious property-grab but a
militant pilgrimage to realize spiritual assets; also a chance for
freedom, space, light, and the lure of the gamble. Households
were enriched by several centuries of crusades, which, stupendously
profitable to Italian urban middlemen, established a storehouse
of ill-will still alive in Moslem folk-memory. To Moslems, as to
Byzantines, the 'Franks' were the new barbarians. Frankish massacres of Jerusalem Moslems, and the burning alive of Jews, 1099,
were in appalling contrast to the magnanimity of Caliph Omar
when capturing Jerusalem, 638, and provided a comment both on
crowd-hysteria and the nature of institutions. Goodwill may be
humanity's ultimate saving grace but cruelty is the more immediately infectious, and the Jerusalem blood-lust joined the Albigensian
Crusade, Cromwell's 'Hell in Connaught', French September
Massacres, as permanent black lines across history.

Islamic intellectual, military and hedonistic versatility must have
disturbed   the   unhygienic   crusaders   and   their   intolerant
priests. The very cult of chivalry had Islamic antecedents. At their
most creative, 750–830, the Arabs had preserved some Greek knowledge at universities in Egypt, Syria, Spain. By fusing 'Indian'
numerals with Alexandrine science they facilitated technological
advance. The ninth-century Baghdad University included a
translation bureau. Al-Razi and Ibn Sina (Avicenna) scientifically
diagnosed disease. Adept in maths, chemistry, astronomy, anatomy,
physics, history, horticulture, domestically opulent, the early Arabs,
while still free from later Islamic puritanism and Turkish overlordship, profoundly affected the versatile, hedonistic Emperor
Frederick II (1194–1250), who founded the University of Naples,
enriched that of Salerno, and whose Sicily enabled an East-West
cultural exchange far exceeding that of the crusaders' Kingdom of
Jerusalem, though perhaps exaggerated or misunderstood by his
admirers, Hegel and Nietzsche.

Moorish Spain flaunted hospitals, baths and libraries, schools
and gardens, a richness of glass, silk, flower barely envisaged by

Christendom which lacked public libraries until 1440, in Florence, and where baths were synonymous with brothels. 'Don't wash,' wrote Michelangelo's father, 'don't wash,' advice which would have shocked Frederick II. Cairo, a university city, was comparable to Platonic Athens.

Militarily unsuccessful, the Crusades stimulated North Italian capital, helped rip down mental parochialism. Novel luxuries appeared. Wines, paper, jewels, apricots, metal-work streamed in from Spain and the Near East and, by the fourteenth century, silks from China, Persia. The rich began washing; enlarging gardens, vocabularies, menus; dressing more elaborately; evoking more fantastic heraldic images; paving their cities; wearing clear-cut beards; sleeping between sheets; widening markets. Marseilles, Venice, Genoa particularly benefited. A French interest was begun in North Africa, ending only in the bloodshed and terrorism of the Oil Age. Saracen musical instruments – lute, shawm, naker – were adopted. The patterns and colours of Islamic textiles, painting, pottery, calligraphy, entered the Western imagination, influenced Romanesque design, are still apparent in Matisse, Klee, Miro, Hartung.

In return, Europe could offer silver, but by the fifteenth century her mines were decaying.

Her ideological concepts were unhealthy. Anti-Catharist crusades wrecked the intriguing Provençal civilization and effected the supremacy of Paris over the South. Pope Boniface VIII's family feud with the Colonna was awarded crusading status. Pointed arch, flying buttress, epic verse evolve or dwindle, but the ominous 'Deus Vult' remains fixed as Chartres, not only amongst Christians. British and French in eighteenth-century Canada slew each other with rival crusading fervour, to be continued by Jacobins, by atheist Marxists, Maoists and Fascists. Dr Goebbels assured war-time Germans that they were 'like crusaders for God'. Pakistan proclaimed the *Jehad* (Holy War) against India and Bangladesh, 1971.

A suave middle-aged Colonel, irritated by questions about casualties at previous meetings, suddenly said, almost shouted, 'I do not believe that anyone killed in a Jehad really dies. Anyone who lays down his life in a Jehad does not die. As far as I am concerned he lives for ever.'

(*Guardian*, 9 December 1971)

5

Failing in Palestine, successful in Prussia, Spain, Provence, the
Crusades helped build the secular national state, particularly in
France and England, at cost to Knights and Papacy. Symptomatic
was the Templar frame-up, as spectacular as Hitler's butchery
of the SA, Stalin's extermination of kulaks. By the final Christian
collapse in Palestine, 1291, the Templars had lost their original
crusading function. Great Gothic builders, they had accumulated
almost 10,000 European estates, and an immense banking
organization. 'Sums could be transferred by payment at one
Templar preceptory, and the issue of a letter authorizing withdrawal elsewhere.' (Barber) The Knights were now defending not
faith but capital, and thus became vulnerable to new ambitious
classes. Building on the work of Philip Augustus (1165–1223),
Philip the Fair (1268–1314) was using bourgeois assemblies against
feudal barons, exploiting novel taxations, centralizing the administration, coercing the Pope. Needing money, supported by the rival
Dominicans, Philip led the assault on the Temple. Throughout
England and Europe, save Spain, the Templars were arrested,
accused of idolatry, sexual perversion, Black Magic, garbled echoes
of pagan Mysteries, and of Islamic Assassin dualism that anticipated
Nietzsche's 'Since God is dead, all is permitted.' They were imprisoned, tortured, burnt in hundreds. In curious appendix, a skull
claimed to be that of de Molay, last Templar Grand Master,
burnt alive outside Notre Dame, was used by a nineteenth-century
American Devil-cult, the Palladistes.

Accusations of blasphemy and witchcraft were normal weapons
against minorities. Eleventh-century Frieslanders had maintained
a self-governing republic against landowners and bishops who broke
them in a bloodily successful crusade. Similarly, early Christians
had been accused of Black Magic to explain the defeat of the
Roman gods. Alice Perrers, Edward III's hated mistress who climbed
up beside judges and interfered with the law, was denounced
as a witch in the Commons, as was the wife of the powerful
Humphrey of Gloucester. The wife and sister-in-law of the French
Minister, Marigny, were likewise accused, like Joan, two centuries
later, like James I's hated favourites, the Somersets.

The Church too used spiritual powers against weaker political
rivals. The Inquisition was established, to follow up the Albigensian
Crusade. Against Napoleon and Hitler, the Vatican remained
officially inactive, but in Britain Cardinal Bourne arraigned the
General Strike, 1926, as 'a sin against Almighty God', and in 1960

the Church denied the Sacraments to members of the Maltese Labour Party.

The unity of Christendom, as of Islam, can be exaggerated. While proposing eternal values the Church lacked eternal respect for free speech and social justice. Moral values were largely conditioned by self-interest. This is recognized today as much by 'socialist' regimes as by Christians. On 15 September 1972, Red Russia signed a trade treaty with Franco's Spain. Christian Naples helped Arabs capture Messina, 843. The Cid overcame Valencia with Moslem help, 1089. Commercial Venice, unhampered by feudal oaths and religious obligation, diverted the Fourth Crusade to a naked conquest of Christian Byzantium, destroying and looting nine centuries of art and literature. The Horses of St Mark were stolen by the 'crusaders'. Like Genoa, Venice had deplored the early crusaders as endangering her Moslem trade-interest. There are Islamic tinges in Venetian art. Venetian-Genoese rivalry obstructed the Christian resistance to the Ottomans, Venice allying herself to Islam after 1453. Routed by Charles V, Francis I besought Turkish aid against fellow Catholic Habsburgs. Cypriots preferred Turks to Venetians; Dominicans hated first the Templars, then the Jesuits. Christian merchants of Marseilles sold child-crusaders to Moslem slave-markets. Frankish Knights flourished ostrich plumes exchanged by Egypt for Spanish timber. Sixteenth-century Christian Maltese pirates were as brutal as the Barbary.

Religious dissent remained. The Church still crassly neglected the education and sustenance of its ground-root, the parish priest. It was easy, it still is easy, for the written word to be admired, not for what it said, but for the fact that it was written. For the rich, the revival of towns meant enlargement of status, the quest for salvation being often postponed until the death-bed. For many, Orthodoxy had lost Mystery, this element surviving in proscribed cults in which, Gnostic-wise, the Gospel was only allegory : the raising of Lazarus symbolized redemption from spiritual ignorance. With sexuality identified with sin, personal hygiene often suspect as self-love, public nakedness, with its latent thrills, though condemned, strove to reappear in secret societies and occult sabbats – as it was to in renaissance paintings and, by proxy, in the homely codpiece. There were rumours of debased dances and rites, honouring the Devil, whose sperm was ice-cold – as today the touch of certain 'faith-healers' is reported very cold or very warm. In southern France, Roman, Mithraic and Druidical survivals, reinforced by Arab teachings and trade links with the East, entered the Catharist Albigensian notions of the Devil, co-equal with God, creating the

world, fathering Adam and Eve, contaminating all matter and life.
That the Cathari, in their lives, and in treatment of women, were
often more compassionate and austere than the northern Orthodox,
did not prevent their ruin. In England a shadowy 'Great Society'
of discontented peasants, Lollards, priests, petty tradesmen, even
guildsmen, seems to have gathered in surreptitious social protest,
though hopelessly dispersed after the rising of 1381.

In contrast were those 'above the Law', worshipping animals,
the Devil, each other, or proclaiming themselves divine, playing
upon St Bernard's words which, in Mystery spirit, declared that
whoever loved God in his inmost soul, transformed himself into
God. The Brothers and Sisters of the Free Spirit, and kindred cults,
juggled with ancient beliefs of a charlatan God winning power
by fraud, and man winning immortality by revolt, freedom,
irresponsibility. If God had created Nature, then let Nature be
fulfilled to its limit. Society was evil, the Free Spirit good. Sexuality, Nature at its most natural, was expressly stimulated.
'And if one brother desires to commit sodomy with a male
he should do so, without let or hindrance and without any
feeling of sin. as otherwise he would not be a Brother of the
Free Spirit.'[24]

This would have appealed to the twentieth-century antinomianist,
Aleister Crowley, who was hailed, if only by himself, as representing
the Celestial Spirit Aciwaz, superior to all human laws and
morals.

Like many revolutionary Mysteries, the Free Spirit, while holding
that heaven and hell could be reached on earth, divided humanity
into crude majority and subtle elite. From similar premises the
the Church condemned Waldensians and Wycliffite Lollards for
preaching apostolic poverty and translating the Bible. For within
the Church too, by the fourteenth century, were urgent leaders of
reform. John Ball, the English peasant-leader, was a priest, as was
Wycliffe. Wycliffe (1324–84) and the Bohemian Hus (1369–1415)
attacked indulgences, relics, simony, rich clerical politicians, demanding 'dominion founded on grace'.

Francis's more devoted followers were castigated for the rather
too pointed applications of early Christian simplicity by the saint,
compassionate, gracious, humanistic, to whom all office and offices
were hateful. It remains a valid issue whether society can afford
a loving but irresponsible and extremist Francis. His rejection by
the Church was unfortunate but not criminal and, for many,
justifiable. Francis, like Celestine, was responsible only to himself
and Jesus : in workaday society it may be insufficient.

6

'Without contraries', Blake wrote, 'there is no progression.' Muscles, physical and intellectual, need use. 'I have loved justice and hated wickedness,' lamented Pope Gregory VII, 'therefore I die in exile.'

The mind personalizes opposites, so that Good becomes a radiant hero, Evil a twisted dwarf, reptile, dark prince. The Virgin counters Hecate with her owls and spells. From dream, instinct, frustration, poverty, class-hatred, malnutrition, loneliness, old age, the Witch and the Devil beckoned. As learning became distorted, human rights rudimentary, nature remaining dangerous, so colours, shapes, rhymes, prayers, crafts acquired emotional momentum. In a violent world of sparse literacy, lives were instinctive, craving symbols. Art and craft had not only to pass time, kill time, but make time less painful. The forbidden had glamour, dissolving patterns which had become too solid. Belief in the Devil was ordained an Article of Faith, 1233. The fourteenth-century Bishop of Cahors was beaten to death for practising Black Magic. A French archbishop was accused, 1347, of planning ritual murder by waxen models, as in Hardy's *The Return of the Native*. A Cardinal's nephew was executed, 1623, for a similar attempt against Pope Urban VIII, as was a Frenchman in the 1820s, for stabbing a waxen image of Charles X.

William de Lines was executed, 1453, for selling his soul to the Devil, to whom Madrid has a monument. On the Hell-Window at Fairford Church, Flemish-influenced, Satan rears his long scaly tail and fishy head, swallowing sinners and leaving others to be ground in a mill.

People, not always under torture, confessed to witchcraft and impossible crimes, as they still do. Witches were not exclusively female but traditions of evil crone and unscrupulous siren suggest masculine jealousies. Orthodox religions everywhere resented women in public life, perhaps in unacknowledged apprehension of Spengler's view that man *makes* history, woman *is* history. A certain uncanniness seemed to pervade the female body and principle. A medieval lawyer, Jean Bodin, asserted: 'Women are particularly prone to sorcery and witchcraft, being liars, having larger intestines than man, and being half-way between men and wild beasts.'[25]

Early Christian thinkers, all male, held labour-pains as Eve's punishment. Michelet, in nineteenth-century France, suggested: 'the Black Mass in its primary aspects would seem to be the redemption of Eve from the Curse laid on her by Christianity. At the Witches' Sabbat women fulfils every office. She is priest and altar

and consecrated Host whereof the people communicate. In the
last resort is she not the very God of the sacrifice as well?' A woman
might be literally used as an altar, as Madame de Montespan was
said to have been, in Black child-murder. In 1967 a Mr Raymond
was married in San Francisco under Satanist rites with a witch,
Lois Morgenstrum, sprawling naked on the altar.

There is no convincing proof of diabolism as an organized counter-
church, despite many colourful or perplexing manuscripts. 'He lies
like an eye-witness' runs a Russian proverb. The medieval air sometimes seems dense with witches' breath. French legal parchments
attest a devil disguised as a toad rushing in open court from a
defendant's body. Devils were formally indicted, speaking bad
Latin. The Archbishop of Rouen had a personal devil, 'Little Thor'.
Bells could not only assist harvest but exorcize devils – so that
clowns, mediating between 'genius' and common-sense, sometimes
wore them. At Trèves, around 1510, bells were rung all night to
force down flying witches. A soldier was seen at Bordeaux, 1610,
fighting winged devils like a demented sword-dancer. A French
nun was deemed possessed of 6,500 devils. The Devil bit the
Blessed Christina of Strommhelm and broke the arm of the formidable St Teresa of Avila. At Wurzburg 900 witches are
quoted burnt in one week, including a boy of ten who had sung
a song about the Devil (1628). Fifteen children and seventy women
were burnt at Mopra, Sweden, 1699, 1,000 victims suffered at Lake
Como, 1524.

One remembers the French countryside convulsed, 1789, by
'brigands' who did not exist; and the imaginary Russian troops
in England, 1914.

Certainly the Devil was real enough to the unlettered, but the
simple annals of the poor are seldom written by the poor themselves.
A vision rises of sullen shapes doubled over harsh and darkening
fields. What are they thinking? We do not know. A flame momentarily lights the averted heads. Then blackness.

The medieval Church matched Black Magic with White, using
Roman precision. St Dominic produced the Virgin and two
archangels to effect a cure. Gustav Davidson[26] cites 3,400 angels
from a total that, by the fourteenth century, was 301,656,722.
Satan himself was a fallen angel, of whom the medieval counted
133,306,668; one, Penemue, taught man the dangerous craft of
writing. Lutherans were to postulate ten billion devils. To accept
such proportions is like dancing to Indian music; possible but not
easy.

The Church condemned gambling, but unrealistically in a
gambler's world. People pitted themselves against fate or submitted

to the idle play of the universe under Aclahaye, bringer of luck. God, like a telephone, might ring, or remain darkly silent. The soul was an acre preyed upon by the unseen, by prayer, by enchantment. The wicked rich apparently prospered more than the virtuous poor but certainty was never absolute.

Cathedral, castle, palace, guildhall misled by their solidity. Ground conditions continued harsh. Of the average English medieval village, H. S. Bennett concludes, 'The loss by death was so severe that it took over two years to add one new individual.' He finds that, about 1300, more than a half of all Englishmen were still serfs. Two centuries later, only one of Montaigne's six children survived infancy. Gibbon was born 1737, his parents lost all six subsequent infants. Only one of Goya's many children survived.

Plague, fastings, lack of Vitamin C, craving for sugar, could produce hallucinations, neurosis, skin-disease, 'Devil's work'. In St James's Palace courtyard an inscription marks 'the leprous virgin' buried beneath. Baldwin IV of Jerusalem died of leprosy, and so, some said, did Henry IV of England. Cannibalism was known in the Highlands. Tentative speculations connect St Joan with *tintinnus*, which causes ringing in the ears, flashing lights and colours.[27] Toxaemia, from bad diets, induced miscarriages. Centuries would pass before the threat of famine receded. A particularly gruesome French famine occurred, 1709, over a century before the Irish horrors.

Crowd madness was regular. Dance-mania could be fatal, as in Germany, 1374, and Wales, 1740, and even in France after World War II. Terror of plague, hell, Christ's sufferings, Jews, monsters, mingled in abstruse mental tableaux or unwholsome action. Jews were periodically butchered, as at Lionheart's coronation. The tower of St Nicholas's Church, Yarmouth, was left unfinished, through plague : St Mary's, Ashwell, has a 1350 plague inscription : 'Wretched Terrible Destructive Year –The Remnants of the People alone Remain.' A king of Portugal, and Holbein, died of plague which, as in London, 1592, could decimate whole populations in a single summer. One third of Europe and England is said to have perished during 1348. Plague helped promote children's mass self-flagellation at Speyer and, at Erfurt, 1237, a children's pilgrimage, dancing and hopping, many said 'to have remained sickly afterwards, and to have suffered particularly from tremors in their limbs and even from fits.' (Nöhl) Medieval Basques reported an epidemic of flying children. St Joseph of Cupertino (1603–63) allegedly levitated eighty yards, watched by the Spanish Ambassador. His contemporary, Magdalena Crucia, Abbess of Cordova, later a self-confessed witch, levitated several yards and induced her hair to grow, and shriek at will. V. Sackville-West[28] writes of St Teresa's frequent levitations that 'The Bishop of Avila was probably not surprised when he saw Teresa lifted into the air during Mass, but to Teresa herself it was one of the greatest shames and inconveniences she had to suffer.'

These tales are not irredeemably antique. In June, 1871, a Mrs Guppy, 'one of the stoutest women in London', was described as levitating three miles unconscious, from Highbury Hill Park to Lamb's Conduit Street – arriving on a table during a seance despite closed doors and windows!

Chartres, Westminster Hall, Brussels Guildhall, must be seen against general squalor recalling the slums of Imperial Rome or Victorian Coketown. At the Paris Churchyard of the Innocents, 'skulls and bones were heaped up in charnel-houses along the cloisters enclosing the ground on three sides, and lay there open to the eye by thousands, preaching to all the lesson of equality.'

7

Despite frequent set-backs, and periodic Magyar, Mongol, and Turkish terror, masterpieces too familiar to detail were achieved. Failures of Pope and Emperor could not fail to provoke theological moral and political speculation. Revived interest in Roman Law assisted reason, if not continuous good-will. Stimulated by an Arabic version of Aristotle, Aquinas strove to fuse classical reason and teleology with Christian time, space and learning – 'An arrogant fool,' Colet considered. Frederick II encouraged medicine and law, the latter perhaps too much. He wrote a treatise on birds, not as symbols but as creatures; examined religion as phenomenon, not revelation; was an authority on Italian vernacular poetry. He commissioned a book from the Briton, Michael Scott, Greco-Arabic scholar, relating character to physiognomy.

Medievals could profit not only from cathedrals but the tapestries of Arras and Tournai; the schools of miniatures, those delicately rich blues, golds, vernal greens, evolving with Jean Fouquet at Tours, and the Limbourgs at Berry; the tender colours and deep observation of Robert Campion and Roger van der Weyden; the songs of Thibaut de Navarre, Guiot de Dijon, Bernard de Ventadorn; the court music of Dufay; the splendid materialism of French and Burgundian courts – Orleans, Berry, Dijon, Paris, papal Avignon, Toulouse – the universities, cathedrals, monasteries. A personal, human voice sings down the ages. A *trouvère* laments : 'I sing of a comely girl who has taken my heart. If only that cuckold of a

husband would get his arms broken, I might find favour with her!'
Music, like wine, suggested paradisial delights: in song was spiritual
and earthly brotherhood. Secular poetry was spread lavishly by de
Machaut, Villon, Chaucer, together with the more sombre moralities
of Langland. Charles of Orleans created a lyric style while in
knightly captivity in English manors.

To ensure survival, human ecology requires idealism, perversity,
anger, dissent. The intellectual rigour and passions of Abelard
clashed with St Bernard, creating shocks not yet quite stilled.
Beneath, the old dances and songs persisted, ever-renewed.

> She stood in her scarlet gown.
>   If any touched her,
>   The gown rustled.
> Eia!
>
> She stood in her scarlet gown,
>   Her face like a rose,
>   And her mouth like a flower.
> Eia!

(Carmina Burana)[30]

Yet the most trained minds, wrangling over Realism and Nomina-
lism, experimenting with optics, building Chartres, were not
immune from superstition. Words collect dead matter, the imagination culls strange properties from the air. Even in palaces and
universities the dying sucked a unicorn's horn dipped in wine. The
after-life was perhaps treated more seriously than in Periclean
Greece: a Macclesfield brass states: 'The pardon for saying 5
Paternosters and 5 Aves and a Credo is 26,000 years and 26 days
of Pardon.' Arab science was in decline after the thirteenth century.

Surviving works of Plato and Aristotle tended to sacrifice experiment for considerations of harmony, shape, beauty. Universities
still required astronomy for a degree. In 1467 a celebrated mathematician was asked to select, by horoscope, a date favourable for
the foundation of the University of Pressburg, which he did,
with unsatisfactory results. White Magic was still publicly taught
in sixteenth-century Cracow.

Preoccupation with numbers was not subverted by the retreat of
the Mongols and the revival of lay institutions. Within the Church,
Father (pope, hierarchy, convention) struggled with Son (non-
conforming saints like Francis, Celestine, Wycliffe) and Holy Ghost
(the Mystics). Joachim of Flora, a monk (d. 1202), taught that
history was divided into the successive reigns of Father, Son, Holy
Ghost, the last already ending. These represented ascending stages

of human evolution: serve Hebraic Law, Gospel and Promise, joyful Liberation. They are also seen in

> . . . the Joachite phantasy of the three ages that reappeared in, for instance, the theories of historical evolution expounded by the German idealistic philosophers, Lessing, Schelling, Fichte and to some extent Hegel; in August Comte's idea of history as an ascent from the theological through the metaphysical up to the scientific phase; and again in the Marxian dialectic of the three stages of primitive communism, class society and a final communism in which the State will have withered away. And it is no less true . . . that the phrase 'The Third Reich', first coined in 1923 by the publicist Moeller van den Bruck, and later adopted as a name for that 'new order' which was supposed to last a thousand years would have had but little emotional significance if the phantasy of a third and most glorious dispensation had not, over the centuries, entered into the common stock of European social mythology.
>
> (Cohn)

Though even the Church had never lacked such scientists as Roger Bacon (*c.* 1214–94), these were usually opposed by the prelates, and the Middle Ages showed scant fundamental advance of popular thought. Trial by Ordeal, in which God, invisible King, was invited to judge disputes, was legal until 1215, reminiscent of Lutembe, the sacred crocodile at Entebbe, seen by Julian Huxley,[31] who judged thieves, either by biting the accused's left arm, or rejecting it. As plague-remedies, sick rooms were draped in red, red banners were waved, images of St Roth brandished, mirrors hung to scare disease by its own ugliness. Dried bats and toads were laid on boils, charms recited, saffron and snake's bones used in magic rituals, guns fired at the festering East, milk laid out to suck in plague-demons, mermaid-scales recommended as medicine which, until the seventeenth century, was largely a branch of astrology, with herbs taken in certain astral and lunar phases.

Louis XI (1423–83), a most astute ruler, was addicted to miraculous relics and morbid death-fears, presenting Paris with an entire Holy Innocent, in crystal. To such a man, a candle symbolized Christ, the flame his divinity, its extinction his death, its relighting his resurrection. Earl Tiptoft of Worcester, brutal renaissance soldier and bibliophile, had himself beheaded in three strokes, to honour the Trinity. Personality was conditioned by the Four Humours, a determinism as pronounced as that of later doctrines of psychological and glandular types.

Symbolic assimilation is often only based on an equality of

number. . . . Thus the twelve months signified the apostles, the four seasons the evangelists, the year, Christ. A regular cluster was formed by systems of Seven. With the seven virtues correspond the seven supplications of the Lord's Prayer, the seven gifts of the Holy Spirit, the seven beatitudes and the seven penitential psalms. All these groups of seven are again connected with the seven moments of the Passion and the seven Sacraments. Each of them is opposed to one of the seven deadly sins, which are represented by seven animals and are often followed by seven diseases.

(Huizinga)

Colour retained symbolism. Black was generally death, evil, lies, Saturn, sometimes rebirth. Sometimes forgotten lore makes one want to weep. 'Black is the badge of hell,' the king says, or quotes, in *Love's Labour's Lost*. Blue signified holiness, immortality, virginity, Jupiter; Yellow – gold, sun, with sulphur-yellow the Devil; Green – youth, joy, victory, resurrection, fertility, Venus; Purple – justice, kings, Mercury; Red – war, virility, Mars, demons – Thor and Judas having red hair. White could be purity, innocence, moon, Diana. Christianity extended this. Priests wore blacks, scarlets, whites, violets, purples : black for austerity and Good Friday; blue for faith, loyalty, divine generosity; purple for Ash Wednesday; red for martyrs.

The Knights attempted to disguise their own decline with explosions of colour, dazzling though less violent tournaments, inflated notions of honour. Outdated by artillery, armour grew superbly pictorial, embossed with renaissance gods and tritons, satyrs, unicorns, gorgons, medusas, cyclops. Golden helmets were topped with live linnets in golden, bejewelled cages, gemmed casques flaunted yard-high plumes. Damascened, fluted, emblazoned, etched, scalloped, body armour imitated the fantastic convolutions of court attire, joining the wearer to classical epics : to Hercules, Jason and Hector. Equally magnificent, if less obtrusive, were the ledgers of the Fuggers of Brussels, first of the millionaire international lay bankers, prop of the Habsburgs, more powerful than all Knights and many monarchs.

8

The majority of medievals were illiterate, not in itself contemptible. 'I turn in upon myself and find a world.' Goethe's words apply to any dispensation. One of the most musical medieval poets, Wolfram von Eschenbach was, Thomas Mann observed, illiterate. Reading partially replaces one sort of memory by another, the peasant by the clerkish. It can destroy deep communal rhythms and huge vocabularies. Hebridean islanders were still making 'instant poetry' over events of World War II : Greek peasants chant wild, flowing poetry at funeral wakes. Jim Phelan[32] writes of mountains :

> 'You can see them coming in, and hear them whispering.' That is not my line, but a quote from my mother. She was almost illiterate, peasant stolid in demeanour, knew nothing of fiction, or of poetry except ancient ballads. But that is her line.

Higher education eliminates the Mrs Phelans, not inevitably for the better. For H. G. Wells, education should build up the imagination. Frequently it impoverishes it. 'Educated men bleach the meaning out of words, there is no colour left.' (Patrick White) This gives some point to Lord Melbourne's remark : 'I do not know why there is all this fuss about education, none of the Paget family can read or write and they do very well.'

A university itself can display cant or intolerance. Oxford supported Wycliffe, then abandoned him when he lost baronial support by attacking Transubstantiation. The Sorbonne supported the burning of Joan. German and Russian universities were obsequious to Hitler and Stalin.

Medievals shared organic myths displayed in cathedral, ritual, and chivalric status symbols. The benefits, psychic and social, though often praised, are disputable, as were the heroes and symbols themselves. God, Jesus, Satan had various faces, healing or threatening. If there was much integration, there was also resentment, bewilderment, savage heresies, brutal ripostes.

The mind learnt not from books, but from chiliastic art, sermons, old wives' tales; was dense with monsters, eerie whispers, omens, ghostly depths. The Wakes – funeral plays, dances, games, to quicken the dead – expanded into great fairs. Practical needs were entwined with false comparisons. Frederick II doubtless spoke with feeling, 'Our job is to show things as they are.'

The sword's two edges could denote right and wrong. The aspen quivered from nausea engendered from having supplied the Cross; elders were unlucky, having been Judas's gallows. One magpie foretold sorrow, two joy. A raven's feather in the wind, twists of a flame on the hearth, were omens. In thunder, plague, and famine was the direct voice of God. Celts ate hazel nuts to induce prophecy. St John's Wort expelled the foul fiend. A virgin's dream of daffodils warned her against entering a lonely place with her lover. Violets symbolized Christ's sufferings. To ensure a daughter, a rose was plucked : for a son, a lily. The lily, in Central Europe, represented

the soul. The rose was light, rebirth, love, female sexuality; haw-
thorn was delight; the cherry, love. Joseph, in the ballad, harshly
rebukes Mary, 'Let the father of thy baby gather cherries for thee.'
Whitethorn, fertility symbol, was sacred to Frig, and Mary.

In the last harvest sheaf might lurk some quivering animal, clearly
the field spirit. Irish pilgrims still climb Croag Patrick Hill with
figurines made of harvest corn. Dead babies were needed for magic
oils.

Finger of birth-strangled babe,
Ditch-delivered by a drab.

Witches sterilized cows by ointments from unbaptized children.
To spit beans exorcized ghosts, rowan affrighted witches. The
mandrake, 'insane root that takes the reason prisoner', shrieking
when torn from the earth, cured insomnia and gout. St Joan was
held to secrete one beneath her armour, as a talisman; publicly
burnt in Rome by priests as warning against superstition, 'man-
drakes' are said still to be used in Kent, against sterility. Witchcraft
superstitions were being denounced, 1973, in Russia, where a Party
card, no. 0000001 is still issued to Lenin.

Ritual sacrifice continued, with elaborate beheadings of richly-
clad noblemen, on decorated scaffolds and with emphatic panoply of
exhortation, music, prayer, procession. Also with burnings of witch
and heretic, starkly menacing yet, like hell, perhaps abstrusely
satisfying.

Cats were burnt at midsummer. Witches were prone to transformation into cats, and hares, which fishermen feared to mention
aloud. Hares, said to gather in circles of thirteen, were favourites
of love-goddesses and of Mary: alive with bounce and movement
they symbolized sacrifice and rebirth. Buddha and the corn-spirit
were alike reborn as hares. Pepys carried a hare's foot as a medieval
talisman.

In Britain, badger's grease is still sold for magic and aphrodisiacs.
The wren was particularly sacred, as disguised spirit or fairy, the
incarnation of a king or his soul. As 'King of the Birds' he was
alternately protected or killed, like early kings themselves. 'Hunting
the Wren' was popular in Ireland, legend placing a tiny gold crown
on its head: in one tale, Robin Hood was killed by a wren, seen
by A. L. Lloyd, the authority on British folk songs, both as a
survival of pre-Christian sacrificial rites and as connected with
subversive political societies. 'The tyrant wren had become a symbol
for baronial prosperity.'

In Pictish and Celtic Scotland, horse-cults had had leaders called 'devils' : everywhere the Devil disguised himself as rat, fox, hare, goat . . . live reminders of spiritual backsliding.

> I have seen the Wolf, the Fox and the Hare,
> I have joined in the dance of the Wolf, the Fox and the Hare,
> Lord have mercy on me.

Two men were burnt as wer-wolves, at Besançon 1521.

Mana remained live in fetish and totem – crown, banner, sword, relic – possession of which increased local prosperity. Viviedo owned the Virgin's milk and one of Judas's pence; Venice and Padua both exhibited St Luke's body; Charing, Kent, had the Baptist's heading block. The bones of St Germain, Bishop of Paris, defeated the Vikings, 885. The shin-bone of St Mammas cured skin disease. Rome revered a jar of breath from the beasts at the Manger. 'At Minorca, the relics of St Stephen converted in eight days 540 Jews; with the help, indeed, of some wholesome severities, such as burning the synagogue, driving the obstinate infidels to starve among the rocks.' (Gibbon) Emperor Sigismund gave Henry V the heart of St George, one of whose legs was bought by the otherwise shrewd Henry VII. A French count discovered, 1279, the body of Mary Magdalene, a white spot on her forehead showing where Jesus had kissed her. She was later canonized a saint of France.

Alfonso I of Aragon cherished Livy's arm. Tobosa still exhibits Dulcinea's hair. At Pontefract, the belt of the rough Earl Thomas of Lancaster was a holy relic. (Centuries later a smelly old lady was found keeping, against her skin, remains of a cigar dropped by Liszt.) The execution-place of the child-murderer, Gille de Rais, 'Bluebeard', was a healing shrine. Gallows-rope had contagious curative powers, on the same principle that snake-serum cures snake-bite. Osbert Sitwell's mother kept a piece of such rope at her bed-head.

> Grease, that's sweaten from the murderer's gibbet
> Throw into the flame.

Sterile women would pray or enact magic under a gibbet. The tongue of a man hanged on Friday raised the Devil. In Hardy's *Wessex Tales*, a woman finds that the ancient cure for a withered arm is to let it touch the neck of a recently hanged man.

Henry VIII treasured Jesus's tear, and sweat shed by Archangel Michael. At her wedding, 1853, Eugénie was given by Napoleon III a reliquary holding two fragments of the Cross. Chelsea children,

1950, were shown the crown of Blessed Cuthbert's skull, St Ethelreda's hand, Venerable Sutton's thumb, blood-drenched linen of Blessed Henry Morse, part of the rope that hanged Blessed David Lewis, and Thomas More's vertebra. Plenary Indulgence could be earned, 1221–1969, by walking through the Porticincala Door, Assissi. Henry VII, often thought of as chilly and ironic, ordered 10,000 masses for his soul.

Fairies are universal : Japanese *onis*, Arab *djinn*, German *nixies*, Irish *leprechauns*, are variously explained as aboriginal survivals, souls of the dead, hallucinations. The wailing *banshee* was the residue of primitive Irish gods seeking revenge on the Celts. Manx women still prepare milk for the Little People. Mrs Cleary was burnt in Ireland, 1894, by her family, who avowed that she had been replaced by an evil fairy who suffered in her stead. W. B. Yeats accepted fairies. In the early 1960s, Irish workmen building a nuclear plant near Sizewell, Suffolk, struck, because one saw a fairy.

9

The Jews held that God had planted in Adam's soul the *yebzer hara*, spirit of mischief. Laughter reduced king to serf, refuted logic and scholasticism, broke the world's limits, miraculously facilitated the impossible. Zyto, at the fourteenth-century Bohemian court, was both jester and magician, mascot against evil eye, humbling pretentiousness. Here is the indispensable catalyst. Ribald songs and caricatures preceded and accompanied the Reformation. Chinese emperors, arrogant or unrealistic, had been tamed 'by a discreet use of humour'. (Lo Siang-lin, 1971) Lenin confessed that Chaplin was the one man in the world he wanted to meet. The symbolic connection between laughter and healing was recognized when Henry I's jester, Rahere, founded St Bartholomew's hospital. He can still be seen in Michelangelo's 'Last Judgement'.

The medieval Devil, antithesis of stern God was 'the Merry Old Gentleman', a soubriquet not lost on Dickens. In the round of semi-pagan Christian festivals, merriment kept alive the spirit threatened by drudgery, injustice, poll-tax, hunger, hell-fire. Church art showed amusing imps alongside the austere and retributive. The future could beckon, tragically or comically. Authority too can have its play. When the late Pope John was asked how many people worked in the Vatican, he replied, 'About half'.

7 Medieval England and Europe

> Englishmen are destined by law, moral
> and natural, to be subject to French-
> men, and not the reverse.
>
> Abbot Suger

I

Like 'Conversion', the 'Conquest' was less final than it seemed.
Church and State were controlled more thoroughly, sometimes more
savagely, but Saxon institutions and laws were reinforced rather
than overthrown. With some understanding of finance and land-
management, William disliked the exceptional, disorderly, awry.
Having to rely on native support against anarchic vassals, he and
his sons avoided the grandiose. Not until Richard Lion Heart did
England do much more than help finance the crusades. Financing
other people's armies was to become a permanent English tactic, for
survival, for expansion.

'Foreign' had other meanings when even neighbouring villages
were divided by custom, dialect, loyalty. Yet scholars, artists, craftsmen organized internationally, and young guildsmen were forbidden
initial practice in their native town. By the thirteenth century,
universities at Salerno, Salamanca, Montpellier, Orleans, Oxford,
Cambridge, Prague, Lisbon, Cracow, Buda, Cologne were as firmly
set as Paris, Bologna and Pavia, which claimed foundation by
Charlemagne, 774. Disdaining feudal frontiers, scholars strode all
roads, bellowing indecent songs, robbing pilgrims, fighting over
Duns Scotus and Aquinas. It is suggested that medieval students
formed a larger proportion of the population than at any time until
today.

Culture deepens with cross-currents. International fairs were held
at Winchester, Troyes, Leipzig, Novgorod—English alabaster reached
Poland; Gascon vintners, Italian builders, plied trade in England
where, until the thirteenth century, the French-speaking kings
built castles of French design. Archbishops Anselm, Lanfranc,
Boniface were prelates and civil servants from abroad. Irish monks
still staffed the twelfth-century Abbey school at Chartres. Byzantium and Sicily were sophisticated, multi-racial societies. Matthew
Paris of St Albans painted in Scandinavia.

Until, perhaps, Edward III, continentals must have regarded England as a poor relation exporting Cotswold and Yorkshire wool, Nottingham alabaster, and tall stories; also as a useful market for wine and financiers. Until the Yorkist Navigation Acts, Germans and Italians monopolized the English carrying trade. Yet much was shared : images, values, memories of bright gods gone to seed. Villon's catalogues – Elisha, Helen, Abelard, Heloise, Charlemagne, Joan, Blanche – were as familiar to the courtly and monastic public in England, as were Arthur, Tristan, the Homeric heroes and the Tales of Boccaccio. Peasants everywhere felt awe of kings and relics, mistrust of parchments, cravings for the Virgin and for others' lands, ambiguous attitudes towards priests, God and Satan, 'The Wronged One'. A solid world of fancy enveloped all Gothic Europe, a missal-world in which the allegorical mural at Widford, showing three dead kings accosting three live ones, was everywhere recognizable. Craftsmen's imaginations bubbled over with pasts cosmopolitan as ghost, centaur, unicorn, phoenix, salamander, giant. Nameless artists, with half-heard snatches of old songs, worked from hints of the monstrous and tremendous : the ginger-bread house, the satyr, the Swan-redeemer. Norwich cloisters are carved with dragons, vines, acrobats, fiery martyrdoms, Julian the Apostate. Ripon's misericords show a griffin eating a human leg, dragons fighting, mermaid, pig playing bagpipes for two pig dancers. Reynard the Fox is carved at Bristol. The thirteenth-century painted Doom at Chaldon has Asiatic motifs : sinners boiling in a cauldron, the Devil gripping a bridge of spikes on which quiver other unfortunates, while a usurer vomits gold; Christ purges hell but an angel turns the key on the Lost. Gargoyles were international, as racial or religious caricature or uninhibited fancy. Those at Chetnole have human heads for eyes.

Politically, twelfth-century England was within the Angevin Empire of Henry II, no Pitt, more a Churchill: restless, interfering, masterful, intelligent, with a flair for bad judgment; difficult, unlovable, pugnacious; alternating between the dark and the full-blooded, the generous and vindictive. He began the depressing conquest of Ireland with papal approval, his quarrel with Becket is world-famous. His rule, over England, Normandy, Anjou, Aquitaine, Brittany enabled vigorous cultural interactions, and perhaps gave the English dreams of Rome, certainly of Troy, with Geoffrey of Monmouth's concocted British epic, *Historia Britonum*.

For a century and a half, French influence was necessarily dominant, from fashions to sport. The Hundred Years War may have been partly a protest against this. Northern cathedrals soared from moulds largely French. Then Henry II's quarrel with France

brought English students back from Paris to Oxford, which borrowed the Sorbonne system of studies and degrees. Scotland,
independent until 1603, had kept up a 'special relationship' with
France, often hostile to England.

As in Tsarist Russia, French was long the tongue of the Anglo-
European elite, with Latin preserved for the clergy, civil servants,
scholars, monkish scribes, and amongst poets, particularly in northern and western England, reaching a climax with Langland
(*c.* 1332–*c.* 1400), more insular, Christian, class conscious and traditional than Chaucer, who had travelled in Italy and France and
knew their contemporary literature as he did Virgil and Ovid.
Chaucer's *Book of the Duchess* had French prototypes, his *Troylus
and Crysede*, Italian. French Romance gave graces to earnest,
sturdy, observant and elegiac English literature, its gifts of the
delicate and lyrical, erotic and allegorical emerging from the
manners and learning of its numerous courts, and universities.

A more specialized French import was Royal Tennis. On a tomb
at Elford is a boy holding a tennis-ball, accidentally killed at play,
1470.

From Burgundy, often an ally against France, would come
musical counterpoint, sculpture of Klaus Sluter, oil-paintings of
the Van Eycks, Campion, Van der Weyden, Flemish tapestries.
Also, emblazoned reports of ducal splendours : extravagant mechanical wonders, an orchestra of twenty-eight within a pie, a glittering
table-decoration forty-six feet high containing more than forty
people, with boars blowing trumpets, goats singing a motet, wolves
playing the flute, live birds flying out of a dragon felled by Hercules.
(Huizinga)

2

Nine thousand English medieval churches are strewn with clues to
outside cultures. Gothicism owes little to classicism, more to Islam.
The Pointed Arch is Arabic. Bodmin has traces of Arab technique
surviving in stone, as 'Admiral' ('Emir') survives in language. The
very stone was often from Normandy, notably Caen. Swalcliffe has
Saxon foundations, Norman arches, English Perpendicular screen,
Tudor and Stuart monuments. Roman foundations, Celtic scrollwork, Saxon pillars may reinforce a Norman church. Arches at
Cookham have bas-reliefs borrowed from the Byzantine or Greek by
the English. Flemish influence is marked in East Anglia where
fourteenth-century immigrants fled from feudal pressures. A Flemish
weavers' church stands at Saffron Walden. Sixteenth-century
carved bench-ends at Hilfield – St Peter, Cock, Keys, Serpent – are

Dutch or German. Pilgrims' graffiti survive at Bosham, a church on Roman and British foundations, with a daughter of Canute traditionally buried in the crypt.

The Christ in Majesty at St Thomas's Hospital, Canterbury, is held to be the start of an authentic English design. Specific English developments were in the Fan and Skeleton Vault, powerful but graceful, in the Curvilinear and Perpendicular, making new and thrilling skies above savage shanty-towns, though the style was seldom or never exported. Norman, Early English, Perpendicular, Decorated, can merge in a single church, as at Wiggenton. William of Sens and William the Englishman worked on Canterbury Cathedral.

Only with the final loss of French possessions could the aristocracy become recognizably English, and the island acquire tough, insular self-confidence, reinforced by spectacular though misleading military triumphs. Henry III's French favourites were condemned as 'foreigners'. Edward I spoke English. The rectors of a normal East Anglian parish, Robert de Oysterne, Johannes de Greneford, Gregorius de Wasing, were changing by 1350 to a Thomas Preston and a Johannes Bacon. By 1362, English had replaced French in schools and law-courts, and by Chaucer's death, 1400, in Parliament. The *Morte d'Arthur* and Froissart's *Chronicles* appeared in translation in 1405 and 1523 respectively. Henceforth, the national language, still evolving from Teutonic and Romance tongues, would be more flexible. The Privileges of the Cinque Ports had included such words as 'Outfangentheof'. The pace of change was, of course, slower outside London. At least one religious house (Laycock Abbey) was still speaking Norman French at the Dissolution. (Young)

Italy, talented, legendary, was inescapable, a centre of banking, literature – Dante, Petrarch, Boccaccio – and of music, Landino dying 1397. Until the Reformation, indeed, the English seem to have been as emotional, violent and operatic as the Italians. Much English silver, 'Peter's Pence', went to support the Papacy. The French themselves were indebted to Italy. Chaucer visited Italy on public service, and many of his tales were taken from Boccaccio. Italian bankers from Lombard Street teaching rudimentary economics – only in 1494 did Pacioli invent double-entry book-keeping – sustained the early Plantagenets. Their coinage notation, Librae, Solidi, Denarii, contracted to LSD.

Lanfranc of Padua, Archbishop of Canterbury (*c.* 1005–89), founder of an international school in Normandy, had had to enforce Gregory VII's decree of clerical celibacy. In 1213, King John, muddled by feudal wars and ritual curse – Excommunication and

Interdict – formally surrendered England as fief to the Pope, an action more strategic than real, yet the most signal claim from Rome until the Pope deposed Elizabeth, 1570. Less successfully, the barons too appealed to the Pope against the gifted, wily and luckless King John.

Continental scholars – Bernard, Aquinas, Abelard – provoked passions in England and Scotland. Dominican and Franciscan friars founded and staffed colleges at Oxford from 1231, Alexander of Hales, in a gesture seldom associated with senior common rooms, renouncing his Chair in their honour.

Franciscan intellectualism, making Oxford a rival to Paris, owed little to Francis himself who, in a grasping, competitive world, was still concerned more with fruitful ignorance, the simplicities of love, beauty, and the praise of God, narrowly escaping episcopal condemnation.

3

Medieval England was, nevertheless, no passive recipient of continental favours. She could adapt as well as learn – the English sonnet could be more fluid than the Italian – and offer her own challenge through scholars and craftsmen acknowledged abroad. Foremost were Hales, Duns Scotus who opposed Aquinas, the rivalry between Thomists and 'Dunces' striking off international heat; Grosstête, English scholar, first lecturer to the English Franciscans; Abbot Hardinge, Walter Map, Matthew Paris; John of Salisbury, moralist who became Bishop of Chartres; William of Occam, political adviser with Marsilio of Padua to Dante's hero, Emperor Henry VII. Occam was celebrated for attempting to detach philosophy from theology. 'Things not known to exist should not, unless it is absolutely necessary, be postulated as existing.' The qualification already seems very English.

Wycliffe's heresies reverberated as far as Bohemia, from whence came Richard II's queen, and helped harden orthodox intolerance. His plea that rulers, lay or priestly, by losing moral authority thereby forfeited political authority seemed more incisive than Jesus's adroit but blanket injunction to render unto Caesar, without inspecting Caesar's credentials. Wycliffe was no demagogic storm-trooper. His Lollards rather anticipated the Quakers in their pacificism, rejection of capital punishment, ignorance, simony, papalism and episcopacy, celibacy, pilgrimages, slovenly work; their opposition to wealth and elaborate clothing, and to Mystery and White magical elements in religion – the Latin bible, indulgencies, relics, transubstantiation, image-worship, the confessional.

Roger Bacon (*c.* 1214–94), a Franciscan, was an empirical scientist, with aspects of Faust, Prospero, Leonardo, H. G. Wells : chemist, inventor, alchemist, mathematician, pioneer of scientific method for whom tradition and wishful thinking were no substitutes for experiment, analysis, research and proof. Here was a secular Wycliffe, with an honourable place in temperate dissent. 'Authority may impel belief but cannot enlighten the understanding.' He too found flaws in Aquinas, was open to Arab teaching. His geographical speculations interested Columbus.

English early renaissance music had lasting excellence even to Burgundian ears, and the great works of John Dunstable (1380–1453) survive chiefly in continental MSS. The French admired the English musicians brought to Agincourt by Henry V, himself a gifted composer. Though her painting was in decline, twelfth-century English embroidery, Cistercian illumination, stone and alabaster sculpture were in demand abroad. The Romanesque 'Raising of Lazarus' in Chichester Cathedral is as graphic and unsentimental as any in medieval Europe, vying in range and vitality with the more widespread French schools. Lynsted Church has monuments by Epiphanus Evesham, first English individual celebrity in European art. Walter Oakeshott[33] suggests that British illuminators of the Winchester Bible also worked at Sigena, Spain, on 'the greatest series of early thirteenth-century Romanesque frescoes anywhere in Europe.' John Harvey[34] writes :

Yevele and the carpenter Hugh Herland renewed the Great Hall at Westminster in 1394–1400 where Herland's oak roof remains as the greatest single work of art of the European Middle Ages. No such combined achievement in the fields of mechanics and aesthetics remains elsewhere, nor is there any evidence for such a feat having ever existed. This amazing work owes its existence to the taste and cultural energy of the King, Richard II, for whom the contemporary Wilton Diptych was painted, while Geoffrey Chaucer wrote his Canterbury Tales.

4

Anglo-continental relations were often violent, notoriously but not exclusively in the Hundred Years War. Germans, French, Flemings and English helped capture Lisbon from the Moors, 1147. Crusades and feudal wars enriched the professional classes and, through many feudal bankruptcies, helped endow civic liberties. Yet, like Rome, England, after final defeat in France, 1453 – as after

Waterloo, 1815 – had to cope with dangerous, unemployed ex-soldiers, fodder for the Roses Wars.

Medieval wars are now interesting not for the dividends they procured, the bridgeheads they established, but for the questions they provoke. How much did they appeal, not only to dynasty and cartel, but human nature itself? Were they solutions to boredom, sexual shame, repressed aggression, local tyranny – as more recent wars were, for many, a deliverance from landlord and factory? There is no answer : none can tell what the medieval soldier thought. Centuries later, Cobbett met a veteran of the Battle of Talavera, 1809, who never knew who had won. For Bernard Shaw, a soldier was to be 'a cheap object who has but to obey orders, charge with the bayonet at men with whom he has no quarrel, shoot and be shot at, and give three cheers when titled persons inspect his buttons.'

Anglo-European economic links were solid. Cash-bond and legal quire depended on Gascon wine, oriental spice, Flemish cloth made from English wool. Cotswold sheep had been fostered since the Romans. Sheep and cask were the realities behind leopards and lilies, maintaining throne, guildhall, law-court, chapter-house against unruly castle. Not until Queen Victoria did Australian merino and man-made fibres finally undermine the English raw wool. Low Country ports and markets had to be kept open at any cost.

The decline of fifteenth-century North German trading cities, long dominant in England's economy, allowed the growth of East Anglian ports. England's monopoly of her own sea-trade, four centuries of commercial and naval power, sustained conflicts with mainland nations. English commercial leaders would assert themselves, usually with royal backing – the Throne's fortunes rose and fell with customs duties – tonnage and poundage – against conservative nobles and prelates.

Not only the rich crossed the Channel. As feudal conscripts, as pilgrims, humble folk might travel, not only to Canterbury and Walsingham, but to Rome, Jerusalem, Compostella. Pilgrims, like crusaders, were not necessarily devout : they might be law-breakers or simple adventurers. Licensed as 'pilgrims', British settlers helped repopulate Spanish towns captured from the Moors.[35] English were with the early Portuguese explorers of Africa. An alliance with Portugal, 1373, remains extant : by it, Britain was granted access to the Azores, 1943, during World War II.

Fourteenth-century England saw more internal mobility. Manorial serfs escaped to towns, or to earn cash on distant farms, particularly after the plague disasters. Immigrants increased : from Dublin, from Lille, presumably attracted by the expanding cloth trade.

Flemings, as farmers and craftsmen, had settled in East Anglia soon after the Conquest. Many fourteenth-century Flemings, capitalist clothiers, industrious journeymen, quarrelling with their Duke, fled to England, bringing advanced techniques that helped compensate for the loss of Jews expelled by Edward I. This fusion increased England's vital search for markets, less for raw wool than for woven cloth.

As with most refugees, their industry was matched by their unpopularity. The Peasants' Revolt, 1381, found time for massacres of Flemings. These were not only clothiers but land-experts, brass-engravers, builders, artists. A linoleum palimpsest at Ewelme Church shows a lady plucking lute or dulcimer. Venetian and Flemish merchants were assaulted in Tudor London. Nevertheless, Dutch settlers built Reedham Church, land-reclaimers – Vermurden, Van Cropenbrough – began draining the Fens. A renewed intake of Low Country refugees, from Spanish terrorism, into Tudor England, reinforced by German immigrant miners and specialists in zinc and brass, assisted early industrialization, England swiftly leading the world in coal production, under Elizabeth. Around 4,000 Flemings and Walloons were living in Norwich, 1570. French and Dutch engravers brought Stuart coinage to finer pitch. From sixteenth-century Flemings came the musical madrigal. An eighteenth-century London Fleming, Hermann Tabel, established a type of harpsichord that long dominated English key-music. His pupils, Kirckman and Shudi, the latter in partnership with the Englishman, Broadwood, for many years monopolized the production of harpsichords and grand pianos. The great economist David Ricardo, MP (1772–1823), as much as Marx the father of socialist economics, was son of a Dutch Jew.

Huguenots, fleeing from the Catholic persecutor, Louis XIV, brought progressive methods of finance and industry, particularly in silks and silverware. 80,000 arrived in one influx, absorbed into a population of about six million. Walter de la Mare was of Huguenot descent. More Dutch, arriving with William III, reinvigorated the wool trade. Refugees from the French Revolution enlivened fashion and journalism. Hanoverian Germans initiated Norfolk cabinet-making. Over 200,000 Poles from World War II were living in England, 1974.

Cromwell's Republic, by-word for intolerance – though it introduced port wine, permitted an unusually free press and saw the beginnings of opera – restored the Jews, with incalculable effect on the City, on imperial policy and culture. British science has vastly benefited from a Brunner, a Mond. Victorian prosperity was assured by two sons of French immigrants, Brunel, the engineer, and Bessemer, with his process for converting iron to cheap steel, 1856. Banking was enriched by alien expertise; a Rothschild, having helped finance Wellington in Spain, became chief banker to the government. Parliament is more colourful for a Disraeli, a Shinwell. German Jews subscribed much to the artistic life of London and the urban north. Culture has consistently been broadened by a Hallé, Engels, Delius, Vinogradoff, Belloc, Barbirolli. Chaim Weizmann's scientific work for Britain during World War I, particularly in high explosives, won official, if ambiguous British interest for a Jewish National Home in Palestine. A new wave of Jews, from Nazi Europe, occurred during the 1930s. These were usually richer, more sophisticated than their predecessors from Poland and Russia but their welcome was not uproarious, despite skills as doctors, dentists, scientists, chemists, psychologists, musicians.

Flight was not always one-way. After the 1688 revolution, thousands of Irish Catholics and Scottish Jacobites emigrated to France, becoming dockers, ship-builders, sailors, soldiers of fortune. Napoleon's Marshal Macdonald had Scottish blood. Of Irish lineage. Marshal MacMahon became President of France, 1873. The Austrian army and navy owed much to Irish adventurers, as did South American independence.

8   *English Institutions*

> Tradition means giving votes to the
> most obscure of all classes – our an-
> cestors. It is the democracy of the
> dead. Tradition refuses to submit to
> the small and arrogant oligarchy of
> those who merely happen to be walk-
> ing around.
>
> G. K. Chesterton

I

A certain sense of responsibility informs English history, amongst a
people potentially unruly, compelled by law to own arms, and,
chroniclers complained, disinclined to work hard, though with an
appetite for pleasure. This is expressed in capacity for local government and, until recently, a reluctance – or inability – to push crisis
to its limits, together with a dislike of over-explicit social formulae.

The Monarchy itself was regulated more by circumstances than
by precise definitions. The Stuarts ruined themselves attempting
to control changing circumstances by legalizing powers previously
explicit in personality and occasion.

Medieval France and England produced shrewd, centralizing
kings, aware of Shakespearian truth :

Our remedies oft in ourselves do lie
Which we ascribe to heaven. The fated sky
Gives us free scope : only doth backward pull
Our slow designs when we ourselves are dull.

The Norman monarchy was doughtily conservative, solid, un-
idealistic. William I, personally devout, forbade unlicensed communications with the Papacy, and established the Throne on 1,400
strategic manors.

Few kings attempted to fulfill their coronation oaths to the letter.
Their duty was to govern, if possible govern well. Unscrupulous
Philip the Fair was reckoned successful; mild Stephen, pious Henry
VI, were not. None of Henry's 150 miracles affected politics or
war. Dr Rowse comments :

D   97

When he had to don his robes of state for some State occasion,
he atoned for the sin by wearing a hair-shirt underneath. He
was too good for this world; in the end he was put out of it.

(Bosworth Field, Macmillan, 1966)

Happy is the country that can afford good men royal!

Lacking police, reliable communications, predictable finances,
medieval government was, at best, harsh. 'When will you learn',
demands King John in John Arden's play, *Left-Handed Liberty,*
'that a straightforward King is a dead King?' Even the Tudors
at their most full-blooded had no standing army; the Stuarts failed
precisely when they tried to establish one. Halifax the Trimmer
considered dissimulation a jewel in the Crown. Rulers seldom
represented Camus's notion of charm : a way of getting the answer
Yes without having asked any clear question.

The English King had one immutable asset : republicanism was
unknown; was contrary to religion, psychology, common-sense.
Baronial rebels against John merely called in the French King's son,
on promise of the Crown, blithely abandoning him on John's
dramatic death, 1216.

The English Monarchy was distinctive. To the kings of England
and Jerusalem alone was homage done irrespective of all other
feudal ties. (Barber) Though the difficulties of grappling with
changing land and money values was seldom understood, pre-
Stuart financial acumen was considerable. Some expectation of
taxation had been current since the Saxon Danegeld. Later rulers
extended this. For war needs, the Saladin Tithe was enforced not
only on land but goods, requiring King and Council to apply
periodically to a new institution, Parliament. ' Adapt, Adapt, and,
once again, Adapt,' could have been the English slogan. Regular
taxation evoked grumbles but maintained relative stability. When
overdone, 1381, the protest was bloody yet, if immediately useless,
ultimately forced authority to reconsider. When Charles I found
adaptation impossible, civil war passed tax-control from King and
Council to Parliament and King. Solvency secured national prowess
and, by the eighteenth century, sufficient surplus to protect exports,
secure colonies, finance change in manufacture, agriculture, transport, thereby stimulating a British world-supremacy.

All classes were liable to taxation. Church and aristocracy could
not, as abroad, remain aloof. The principle of no taxation without
some measure of consent was early established. Though, like the
law, it was not always more than a principle, a principle is, nevertheless, more effective than no principle, as Hampden, Pym – and

Washington – were to demonstrate. It helped modify fanaticism, affected political theory. Bracton, medieval jurist, wrote in a manner unappealing to Philip the Fair, Frederick II, Genghis Khan, Saladin :

> The King is under God and the Law; for the Law makes the King, and without the Law there is no King.

There were always those remembering this, even from disgusting motives and with deplorable results. Only Richard II actually denied the theoretical supremacy of Law.

The medieval Monarchy could lead social change, conquering Wales, partially conquering Ireland, failing in Scotland; establishing judicial and political institutions, new towns, new markets, new fashions; patronizing the arts. It restored buildings, as Henry II did Glastonbury, probably unaware of its associations with sun-worship and Annyn. It debarred the Inquisition, though allowing the occasional burning of heretics, Henry IV's heir, in person, vainly urging one heretic, Sawtre, to repent.

The courts of Henry III and Richard II, political failures, were cosmopolitan. Richard II, forced from power as an irresponsible and immoderate public nuisance, ended in horror : a perplexing man, perhaps over-civilized in an age politically brutal, socially crude. Sacheverell Sitwell[35] describes him in a 'dress of white satin embroidered with leeches, water and rocks, hung with fifteen silver-gilt mussels, and fifteen cockles of white silver, doublet embroidered with gold orange trees on which were set a hundred silver-gilt oranges.' Yet his failure was not total. Time alters the past, tricks the future. Crowded with political enormities, his reign was spectacular in ways only clarified after the passions, tantrums, injustices and betrayals had subsided. His original Irish policy was more generously imaginative than any until Gladstone's. A pacific 'Good European', he shared, if with weaker moral fibre, some of the enlarged, if selfish, vision of a Frederick II, a Francis I.

He was the patron of Chaucer, of Gower, of Froissart, and we have Froissart's word that he was a charming conversationalist in perfect French. He was the employer of Henry Yevele, the greatest of English medieval architects; his reign is the golden age of the brass-engraver, the mural painter and the sculptor of effigies in the round. . . . Richard was the first King of England to sign his own letters. He was probably the inventor of the handkerchief, and the first English cookery book was especially compiled for him. But the finest testimonies to Richard's love of the arts are still at Westminster. In the Abbey is the superb tomb he ordered for himself and his first wife, and across the way is the great roof of his Westminster Hall.

(Harold F. Hutchinson, *The Hollow Crown*, Eyre and Spottiswoode, 1961)

For all his failings he was the opposite of him who, Wilde said, knows the price of everything and the value of nothing. His pre-occupation with the handkerchief has the fastidiousness of Beau Brummell, who made fashionable cleanliness, and trousers. Greater men are remembered for less.

Personal rule demands high splendour or awesome austerity, though the Plantagenet court scarcely rivalled those of Burgundy, Milan, Ferrara, Naples. Few of Richard's subjects were grateful for his opulence. The poor, disarmed, then rejected by the boy-king, 1381, who had to think with their knees and back-joints, the lords and merchants who lost heads or purses, and the man who eventually finished him, had grimmer concerns.

Man be ware and be no fool,
Think upon the axe and the stool!
The axe was sharp, the stool was hard,
The thirteenth year of King Richard.

2

Later medieval England had increasing wealth to be taxed. Exports, including iron, and maritime power increased, at the expense of the Germans, Flemings, Venetians, Genoese, French. Edward III, 1327, enchartered the Merchant Taylors, first of the great Companies that transformed Britain from a provincial outpost to a world power. The Merchants of the Staple set up a wool-exchange in Calais; the rival Merchant Adventurers established themselves at Bruges and Antwerp, the dominating financial and manufacturing powers until Spanish mismanagement helped bring supersession by London. And the colonial Empire had begun, inauspiciously, in Ireland – source of cheap food, land, labour, prestige, but to this day disturbing, like a sacrificial skull planted beneath a resplendent city and never quite exorcized.

Save in London, the restrictive guilds declined as individualistic capitalists and traders replaced the privileged combinations of craftsmen and journeymen. Such figures as Whittington, Lyon, de la Pole, Canynges, sitting in the Commons, often allied to great feudalists like John of Gaunt, were fourteenth-century but not specifically 'medieval' and wanted grosser profits than the old guilds and notions of the 'just price' had envisaged. The Church was losing its monopoly of education. Richard Whittington endowed libraries. Blundells School was founded by a clothier, Harrow by a merchant, Aldenham by a brewer, Walthamstow by a draper.

Unlike the peers in France, Germany, Spain, the more far-sighted English noblemen did not disdain trade, or inter-marriage with anti-feudal legal and financial classes. Early governors of the Hudson Bay Company, Stuart monopolists in skins and tobacco, were Prince Rupert, James of York, John Churchill.

The medieval English Crown preferred to appease, not oppose these classes, to assist their progress and share the rewards. It was abroad that the new men remained unprivileged, socially eventually drastically subordinate. Movement between English classes was sanctioned by money, not blocked by immovable status. Impoverished by primogeniture (though younger sons did occasionally inherit), noble cadets married money as much as property. Serfs could purchase freedom were money to hand which, before the fourteenth century, it usually was not. Richard II, Henry V, made financial or political pacts with non-feudalists – Brembre, de la Pole, Whittington – a process continuous, if resented by older castes. Shakespeare's Crookback sneers :

> The world has grown so bad
> That wrens make prey where eagles do not perch;
> Since every Jack became a gentleman
> There's many a gentle person made a Jack.

Such must have been felt by later aristocrats towards the Disraelis, Rothschilds, Barings, Northcliffes, Beaverbrooks.

Aristocratic survivals of the Roses holocaust – which, to the masses, seems to have provided only incidental nuisances during rising prosperity – hastened to marry into the upstart but rich Howards, Seymours, Cavendishes, Pagets, Dudleys, preserving their name, that shield against time. The new men could gain titles – Northumberland, Leicester – more ancient than their pedigrees. Titles modified class-hatreds into snobbery : aristocracy did not solidify into an exclusive sect.

Husks of nobility remain. At a dinner of the Scriveners' Company, April 1965, were present a former Queen's Remembrancer, Portcullis Pursuivant of Arms, Norry and Ulster King of Arms, and Mr Sam Toppin.

Abroad, the Knights, unchallenged until the thirteenth century, were increasingly outmoded and dangerously isolated. In England,

less exclusive, they accepted social responsibilities in Parliament and
as Knights of the Shire. Later, tamed into country gentry, they
filled the very British position of Justice of the Peace. (Barber.
Wood)

Until the nineteenth century, aristocracy and gentry virtually
monopolized Parliament, Church, Bench, officered the army, navy,
militia, grandly patronized architects, controlled local church and
local franchise, served as Lords Lieutenant dominating Assembly
Rooms and sporting occasions, particularly the Hunt. Until Reform,
1832, many parliamentary seats, like church livings, were in their
gift, as Rotten or Pocket boroughs, the former losing territorial
significance as populations swelled or even vanished. Gladstone's
first seat was 'given' him by the Duke of Newcastle, 1831, following
his Oxford Union speech attacking Reform. Reform deprived the
magnates of direct control of boroughs but they remained influential, against increasing opposition. In the age of Cecil Rhodes and
Bernard Shaw, a Cecil peer could still be Premier, a Northumberland, Derby, Devonshire hold high office.

This social fluidity, an irritant to doctrinaire exponents of class-
war, was hastened by the modernizing Yorkists and Tudors, with
unusual gifts for choosing efficient ministers, then discarding them
when no longer essential. Empson was son of a sieve-maker. Dudley
– father of Northumberland, virtual ruler of England, 1549–53,
grandfather of Elizabeth's Leicester – was perhaps the son of a
carpenter, Wolsey of a master-butcher, Cromwell of a taverner-
blacksmith. Nobility, Burghley observes, is but wealth grown old.

By the fifteenth century, lawyers were freely prospering from the
headlong baronial follies and civil wars. Until the Stuarts they,
particularly the judges, usually supported the Crown, though seldom
mere hacks or parliamentary place-men. More, Cromwell, Bacon
were lawyers. Already they knew how to prolong their clients'
difficulties, one case lasting 1410–1604, yet the profession created
more than it might seem. The Inns of Court were to subsidize poetry
and drama as the Chapel Royal did music. Not untypical was the
Tudor, William Death, Principal of Staple Inn, Attorney of Common Pleas, founder of Dartmouth Grammar School.

3

Britain has never shared the continental reverence for the State:
Holy Russia, Fatherland, La Nation, the Reich. The British State
is generally held to be little more than the faulty elements that
compose it, used but not loved. Even the Empire inspired more
affection than awe and, as often, indifference.

Meanwhile, the Crown prudently invited other classes to help shoulder responsibilities, most significantly, not in Council but in Parliament.

The English Parliament was not unique. In Iceland – where, W. H. Auden writes, a bishop was put in a bag – the Althing dates from 930. The Manx Tynwald pre-dates Westminster. Yet the English Parliament proved more enduring and resilient than Philip the Fair's bourgeois Assemblies, the French Estates-General, Spanish Cortes, or the German Free Cities.

De Montfort's Parliament, 1265, working from tentative precedents, brought in representatives from Knights and Towns as auxiliaries in his quarrel with the Crown. More exactly organized by Edward I, it became a royal device to facilitate taxation and irregular supplies though, under weak kings, claiming some political rights. It acquired judicial powers, watchful of the Council, in time bringing down royal ministers and favourites by Impeachment, Show Trial, or by Attainder, mere declaration of guilt by parliamentary vote, a procedure imitated throughout the world by subsequent revolutionaries. Churchill, 1945, ever susceptible to resonant archaism, suggested in Cabinet a Bill of Attainder against the Nazi leaders, though America and Russia insisted on regular public trial.

Parliament, not Council, was manipulated into offering Richard II's crown to Henry IV. He would have taken it anyway, supported by his archers, but the precedent was important. Parliament could be bullied by feudal lords or by powerful rulers, as in Africa today, but never quite succumbed, accumulating still further precedents, and under Henry IV initiating legislation.

Like Magna Carta, Parliament was not an instrument for majority rule but a protection against it. Throughout history, it has been a compromise between the elites, the Interests and the masses. Between 1429 and 1832, franchise and membership were restricted to a small, propertied minority – Disraeli lost his first election, 1832, by twenty votes to twelve – a jealous association of pressure-groups, coalescing and dissolving according to needs. Obscurer loyalties, religious and feudal abounded; conditions of agriculture, trade, brewing, shipbuilding, priestcraft, conditioned much policy. Clans were more important than rigid class. For centuries, faction outbid Party. Lines still remained fluid : Gladstone began as a Conservative; Churchill's party changes were notorious, or admirable; Palmerston, the Whig, was invited into a Tory Cabinet. Coalitions could occur as late as 1931–45.

Parliament was usually more than the toy of economics though sometimes not much more. The flexible English class-structure

allowed lesser lords, gentry, burghers, lawyers – town, country,
university – to sit together in the 'Communities', the Commons.
This never meant the common people. Disraeli could refer, 1852,
to 'our popular, though not democratic institutions', and the distinction remains pointedly valid. Parliament, nevertheless, could
broadly coincide, if not always with popular support, at least with
some degree of national interest. Drawn by law (1429) from the
propertied classes, unpaid until 1911 – thus disqualifying poorer
aspirants – members were still more socially varied than in continental assemblies, and tended to be the more respected. Paid or
unpaid, they are not regarded as financially squeamish. Scandals
have been unendingly rumoured or exposed. The 1852 Parliament
was lampooned as 'the Bribery Parliament'. The Corrupt Practices
Bill, 1868, has not proved final.

Usually aware of popular feelings, Parliament has seldom considered them paramount. Either independently, or coerced by the
Crown, it might flagrantly disregard them. Indeed, dissolution of
the monasteries, the Reformation Settlement, the executions of
Protector Somerset, Charles I, Monmouth, the appointment of
Cromwell's major-generals, the abdication of Edward VIII, the
Suez Affair (1956), mass immigration, the abolition of capital
punishment, EEC entry, were royal, parliamentary or Cabinet
decisions with unproven popular support. A sensible balance
between factional leaders, between Interests, and the exceptional
concept of a legal, eventually paid Opposition, has avoided any
significant revolt since 1688. The Commons strenuously preserve
rights to question the Prime Minister twice a week, and all Ministers
at any time.

The Interests did not always scruple to exceed constitutionalism.
Medieval lords – Gaunt, Bolingbroke, Warwick – retained private
armies until emasculated by the Tudors. They could overawe
neighbours, juries, sheriffs and, until 1745, rebellion could threaten
the Crown itself. Until a century ago, another Interest, the under-
nourished, illiterate, superstitious, often under-employed streets,
while lacking the vote, could drastically intervene, forcing, with
parliamentary support, Charles I into condemning Strafford.
Precedents existed for 1783, when 'a combination of City interests,
country Tories, and opposition Whigs compelled the Pelham
Ministry, by means of a nation-wide agitation, and the threat of
London riots, to defeat its own Bill for the easier nationalization
of alien Jews.'[36] From medieval times, mass petitions and marches
to local and central authorities could ensure some success.

Parliament has excited the imagination of the world, though the
world has in large rejected it. Nevertheless, first exported to

Virginia, 1619, the Mace was, in various forms and with various, sometimes unwholesome results, adopted by most of the British Empire and its successor-states. Representative assemblies in British India were the first in Asia.

4

Parliament itself is but one of many institutions which, while it sustains them, is also sustained by them. The medieval king was the 'Fount of Justice'. Sale of justice strengthened royal finances and, in the early Middle Ages, the feudal lords. By the fourteenth century the King was claiming or reclaiming many manorial rights. A strong monarchy could support popular liberties against church and manorial courts, and the English was the toughest in Europe. This support was crystallized, centuries later, by the young, enigmatic Elizabeth I's instructions to the judges :

Have a care to my people. You have my people – do you what I ought to do. Every man oppresseth and spoileth them without mercy. They cannot avenge themselves, nor help themselves. See unto them – see unto them, for they are my charge. I care not for myself, my life is not dear to me. My care is for my people.

She added with unconscious insight, 'I pray God whosoever succeteth me, be as careful to them as I am.'

The Crown's temptations could have been to forgo Common for Roman Law, legacy of despotic emperors administering vast territories, handy for property-owning hierarchies to whom popular liberties were as tiresome as a right-of-way across the nobleman's lawn. Protected, however, by sea-power and strong local traditions, England retained Common Law, not seriously threatened until the Tudors and Stuarts.

The essence of Common Law was not legal theory stemming from an arbitrary executive, but in human precedent and custom operating through local and royal courts assisted, from the twelfth century, by Juries. With dim Frankish origins, jury-service, then as now, was resented, but could fitfully resist, sometimes from very resentment, the caprice of lord, steward or spiteful neighbour, though until 1972, juries were restricted to the propertied.

Three intruding continental aristocracies – Saxon, Viking, Norman – thus evolved England's characteristic legal style. The King was encouraged to organize, interpret and enforce Law, but not, like a Roman Emperor or dictator, to invent it. From 1166 to 1972, when permanent Crown Courts were established locally, Royal

Assize Judges travelled on circuit, linking Crown and provinces, saving litigants from chasing the King's itinerant court. They reminded feudal lords that a less partial authority existed, if sometimes weakly; they could assess the private interests of witnesses, jurors, plaintiff, defendant.

The system was, perforce, imperfect. Lawyers have never ingratiated themselves into popularity. The theatrical or bullying talents of Counsel could blur truth. Juries could be bribed or bullied: be gullible, prejudiced, perverse, stupid or lazy. The judge's summing-up from an impressive position in formidable disguise, could confuse, enlighten, mislead, rebuke. The brilliant Jeffries was to show that the distinction between judge and prosecutor could be inexact. Edgar Lustgarten[37] describes a jury enduring almost two days of a diseased judge trying Florence Maybrick for her life, and (1889) inflicting such dicta as: 'You are apt to assume a connection between the thing which is a proof in the result of which you are to arrive – because it is put before you – and in that way you may be led to do a greater or less degree of injustice according to the state of the case.'

Yet, all in all, the system, in its rough way, was tolerated by the citizenry, profoundly impressed Voltaire and the Enlightenment, the French and Russian constitutionalists and, until he finally visited Britain, Marat. A British attempt to introduce the Jury to Corsica foundered on the vendetta, but Common Law was introduced throughout much of the Empire, remains the basis of Dominion Law, and of American, save in Louisiana. At the inauguration of Pakistan, 1947, the intractable Mr Jinnah acknowledged British Law as 'one of the greatest bulwarks and safeguards of popular liberties'. British Criminal Law was retained by India, the West Indies, and, more subjectively, by much of Africa.

Equality before the Law was a staple English axiom. If not always strictly enforced, sometimes officially rejected – against seventeenth-century Catholics, victims of Attainder, and dissenters – it was in general accepted as the pious norm. Lord Suffolk, 1498, was at least arraigned before King's Bench for killing 'a mean person', though eventually pardoned. Lord Ferrers was actually hanged, 1760, for killing his steward. Political Interests, as over slavery, property and during the Civil War, preferred to manipulate the Law rather than expressly deny it. Habeas Corpus from 1679, though liable to be suspended in crisis – 'I like the Habeas Corpus, when we've got it' (Byron) – provided the world with a simple precaution against irresponsible arrest, though it did not apply to black slaves. Often reproached as impersonal, dilatory and cumbersome, Common Law tends to prove less corrupt than systems more personal or glamorous, in which justice is rather bargained for than administered. It has helped fertilize a British liberal tradition which, despite complacency, running injustices, cruelties, cannot lose by comparison with Shakespearian drama, English novel, British medicine and physics.

Traditional and informality have extended to British agricultural and industrial relations, often to the economic advantage of the weaker sections. Such relations were left largely unregulated until the 1971 Act, itself more resembling Roman Law in being ordained from above, not developed on the shop-floor. Objectors maintain that work relations, like love relations, succeed least within legal covenants and penalties, a view at odds with that of 'Socialist' governments in Russia, China, Cuba, and with procedures in Canada, America, Sweden. But the British tradition, thus violated, was centuries old : each farm and factory had been virtually autonomous, like the medieval manor it replaced, without a national framework of written contracts but with each having its peculiar atmosphere of discipline, grievance, pay or lack of pay.

One need not sentimentalize English Law. People traditionally distrust all Law, Common or Roman, which tends to become a Mystery. 'Justice', Voltaire stated, 'was invented to ruin the innocent.' For Burke, 'There is no greater injustice than that perpetrated in the name of the Law.' For Brecht :

The men who lead the State over a cliff
Call government too hard work
For the ordinary man.

Yet, as against the Mystery of High Court professionalism, the bulk of English Law was enforced by unpaid amateur magistrates as the medieval Lord declined, and local gentry replaced the Norman sheriff. These were naturally conservative : fixing local wages from 1389, enforcing church attendance and game laws, suppressing unions, generally conserving their own interests yet also preserving regional independence. 90 per cent of all British crime, 1972, was, uniquely, being handled by 20,000 lay Magistrates. The system does allow initiative from below. It can be modified and peacefully redefined by such courageous figures as Granville Sharpe (1735-1813), champion of negro rights and, in defiance of the Interests, helping the abolition of black slavery in Britain. Conan Doyle's almost single-handed fight against Home Office officialdom, on behalf of a single victimized Indian (1907), Mr Edalji, helped the establishment of the Court of Criminal Appeal.

As a sombre appendix one must add that slavery was legal in

Worlds and Underworlds

the Middle Ages, slumping not through legislation but from economic developments. Laws regulating slavery were left unrepealed,
and, from the introduction of black slaves in Tudor England,
provided a theoretical justification for renewed serfdom, despite
some adverse judicial comment. Often, though not invariably, slaves
were regarded not as humans but as goods, until at least the Somer-
sett case, 1772, though this, as Walvin shows, only jolted and
publicized the system, rather than finished it. Legislation continued
to be flouted until Abolition, 1833.

5

English feudalism was probably less exacting than continental:
taxes less onerous and unpredictable, villages less impoverished,
justice more equitable. Serfs had more obligations than rights but
some rights they did have: of property, of protection, and with
serfdom itself declining more rapidly here than abroad.

There was always much irregularity. 'Freedom under the Law',
'Prohibition of Torture', 'Abolition of Slavery' were frequently
tendencies rather than facts. Under Henry VI, private armies
coerced courts and juries, though without actually denying their
validity, thus necessitating tough Royal Prerogative Courts – the
Star Chamber, and the Council of the North – to restore centralized
order. Torture was never recognized by Statute or Common Law
but was long exercised in private. Philip the Fair's client, Pope
Clement V, on Christmas Eve, 1310, rebuked Edward II for in-
sufficiently torturing the Templars. Rack, thumbscrew, 'Little Ease',
are part of British folk-lore. The Crown protected itself by extra-
constitutional Treason Laws, countenancing show trial, casuistry,
moral hooliganism, mutilation, torture. Henry VIII's Lord Chancellor and Solicitor-General racked Anne Askew; King and Council
'examined' Guy Fawkes. Tudor England allowed the boiling alive
of poisoners. Children could, in law, be burnt. Hanoverian accused
who refused to plead could be 'pressed', with water and stones,
sometimes fatally. The Empire always carried reports and rumours
of illegal oppression. An ex-Black and Tan officer confided to
Mosley:

The account which most remains in my memory was the use of
thin rods to beat the victim into unconsciousness, when they
were revived with eggs boiled until they were placed under their
armpits; this was stated to be a Chinese form of persuasion.

(Sir Oswald Mosley, *My Life*, Nelson, 1970)

Ireland, 1972, was resounding with accusations of torture against suspected terrorists imprisoned under suspension of Habeas Corpus. The use of noise-machines to promote sleeplessness was officially forbidden, March 1972. Abroad, torture was being alleged in Greece and Turkey, 1973.

Only in Cromwellian England was there any genuine revolutionary threat to traditional institutions, from religious and political zealots. In general, the English Channel protected national institutions from the threat of foreign kings. English Jacobins, Luddites, Chartists could provoke riots and savage repressions, but with small possibilities of success, and were as much reformist as revolutionary. Yet Dickens perceived gaps between official claims and dehumanized, bureaucratic facts. In 1855 he was considering, perhaps unfairly on the eve of very considerable reforms, that 'representative government is become altogether a failure with us, that the English gentilities and subserviences render the people unfit for it, and that the whole thing has broken down since that great seventeenth-century time, and has no hope in it.' Fabian socialism and trade unionism, unlike Marxism, by deciding to use constitutional institutions, renewed their vitality. Only recently have doubts been proclaimed, from conflicting quarters. Fears were being uttered in Parliament, after 1970 that Parliamentary authority could be altered at will by the EEC. If so, Parliament itself has succeeded where the Pope, Napoleon, Hitler failed. Mr Peter Shore, opposing the Common Market Bill, 13 July 1972, claimed that for the first time since the Stuarts the British were to be taxed without Parliamentary consent.

Thus, save in Ireland, Britain has hitherto remained stolidly faithful to her institutions. For all its virtues, and virtue, the Republic was brief, its major-generals execrated. The only successful rebellions since 1485 had majority Commons support. Dilke's and Chamberlain's republicanism faded. Stafford Cripps momentarily envisaged (1931) an authoritarian socialist republic but lived to enter a conformist Cabinet and advocate Christian austerity from the pulpit of St Paul's. (It is true that, on 16 November 1948, still a minister, he meditated upon steel nationalization by violence, if the government failed to achieve it 'by legal means'.) Traditions, however, need continuous inspection. 'There was nothing,' wrote Cranmer, 'by the wit of man so well devised, or so sure established, which in the continuance of time hath not been corrupted.'

New, perhaps torrid debates may now be approaching.

There are those who see human institutions as dykes canalising a raw, viable, morally ambiguous human potential into the fructifying ways of civilization, and those who see those institutions as barriers to a flood of abounding creativity.

(David Martin in *The New Left*, ed. Maurice Cranston, Bodley Head, 1970)

6

Beneath the Balance of Power, the rise of bougeoisie and grammar school, the popular imagination remained, with its secrets, fears, myths, laughter.

Words have depth, riddles become light, names contain tales. 'Oulchester', Roman fort haunted by owls. 'Lundy', Norse for Puffin. 'Aintree', Lonely Tree.

White Colne was Colum de Miblanc in 1163 and owes its attribute to an under-tenant who held land there in 1086. His nickname, *Demiblanc*, a small coin, was contracted first to *Miblanc*, then to *Blanc*, and was finally translated into English, White.

(Reaney)

Breton names in Essex recall French Celts fighting at Hastings. Farms are named: 'Labour in Vain', 'Golly Nap'; even the fields: 'Misery Mount', 'Cow's Leaze'. 'Soho', Monmouth's battle-cry at Sedgmoor, was a hare-coursing call.

Social history makes man at home in a single world of all wrongs, griefs, hopes. At the George and Dragon Inn, Dragon's Green, is a garden stone: 'In loving memory of Walter, the Albino Son of Alfred and Charlotte Bull. Born February 12, 1867. Died February 18, 1893. May God forgive those who forgot their duty to him who was just and afflicted.'

To stand alone in a church, within multitudes of the dead, may induce sensations of invisible witnesses.

The weariness of long-forgotten races
I cannot brush off my eyelids.

(Hugo von Hofmannsthal)

Silence of ruined castles and abbeys, abandoned chapels, can revive monsters, lost ambitions, the singular, like the human-faced bat carved on a choir-stall at Wells Cathedral, seeming to mock the giant effort towards immortality.

A church may be scorned, avoided, ripe for demolition, yet

remain more than damp stone, stale air, fading languages. Philip
Larkin wonders, in his poem 'Church Going', 'What remains when
disbelief has gone?' Church services may pronounce sententious
platitudes, or the strange, challenging and perplexing :

For in much wisdom is much grief and he that increaseth
knowledge increaseth sorrow.

The past revives in Bramfield church. Its first rector was Becket.
The font surmounts a Saxon well which, at his canonization, began
miraculous cures, originating a pilgrimage. And a Hampton
epitaph reads :

Beyond the Prophet's settled term of age
Wither'd and dry I then dropt off ye stage.

Once, a church was used for prayer, sacraments, admonition,
propaganda : as armoury, sanctuary, market, pigsty, stable, gossipery,
art-gallery, concert hall. A bishop described St Paul's, 1561, as
harbouring 'all kinds of bargains, meetings, brawling, murders, conspiracies.' Halstead Church has an inscription which reconciles
the centuries : 'John Worth, let be your nyce legs.' With its statues,
symbols, frescoed dooms, allegorical windows, gaudy stone and wood,
glimmering brass and alabaster, candle-flames and shadows, magical
stoup and font, sumptuous altars, bloody crucifixes, sacred vessels;
its thrusting heights and eerie depths with souls glistening above
the worm-racked dead, the church, like a movie, assaulted mind,
eye and ear simultaneously : reason and unreason. Church art was
White Magic, soaring in spires, haloes, blessings, flames, crowns,
trumpets; the angel was soul as winged spirit; candles echoed
fire-worship, the Cross, tree-worship. Pillars, darknesses, clearings
may have reminded men of forests from which issued so much
enchantment and profundity. Here was a disturbing dream scattered
with truths, lies, threats, demands for cash and privilege, linking
three worlds in a knot of stone and glass, ancient stillness, grey
dusk, painting shafts of light dense with forebodings, tenderness, the
gentle, the monstrous, as near and inescapable as dry rot or sudden
love.

Now sinks the sun beneath the wood.
    (Mary, I pity your lovely face.)
Now sinks the sun beneath the Rood.
    (Mary, I pity your son and you.)[38]

From the fourteenth century, biblical translations were giving British Christianity new edge. Wycliffe, then Tyndale, Coverdale, and the King James translators, gave the imagination deep and sonorous rhythms and images. These were supplemented by the sententious devotion, finely-pointed phrasing of Cranmer's Book of Common Prayer. 'A broken and a contrite heart thou shalt not despise.' 'Accompany me with a pure heart and humble voice unto the Throne of the heavenly grace.' All this, together with the emotional drive of a multitude of anthemists, hymn-writers and psalmists. 'Lift up your heads, ye everlasting gates, that the King of Glory may come in.' Tudor and Stuart sermons, profound or strident, magnificent or banal, were entertainments as popular as cock-fighting or the play.

The surge of words had confusing effects, incalculable as from Shakespeare and Dickens. The imagery was didactic, muddled, raving, bellicose, tender; it contained Jewish exclusiveness, righteousness, hankerings for Judgment; also Hellenic clarity and reason; the Mysteries' quest for Light by discipline, fraternity, or hocus-pocus. At best, a stark lapidatory command establishes a splendid commonplace on which to establish charity and order. 'Hate evil and love good,' Amos enjoined, 'and establish judgement in the gate.' Nevertheless, precise definitions are often lacking – goodness is easier to affirm than to define – and in much dispute was much bloodshed. With even the priests now able to understand the Bible, many might feel that too much miscellaneous scripture was made canonical, establishing contradictory conclusions, dark injunctions. 'Suffer not a witch to live,' 'Compel them to come in,' were scarcely compatible with 'Love one another as I have loved you.' Texts for retribution, through some bias flowing from animal nature, human organization, or both, tend to countermand those of forgiveness and detachment. Texts were profitably manipulated by priest and ruler. The Confucian *Analects*, the *Koran, Capital, Mein Kampf* make uneasy companions but their teachings are unambiguous. Nobly written, the Bible's profundities were easily disguised or corrupted by metaphor. The conception of God as King or Father vulgarized divinity, surrendered infinite compassion to dogma and inquisition. 'There shall be wailing and gnashing of teeth.'

Christianity, like all institutions, could be dynamic, intolerant, vicious, even murderous. Yet Machiavelli, like Nietzsche, could find evidence to arraign it for rejecting the pagan exaltation of physical strength and action, for humility and contemplation. 'This manner of life seems to have weakened the world and surrendered it as prey to the wicked, who can deal with it as they like, unpunished,

seeing that the generality of men, to gain Paradise, think more how
to endure wrongs than how to avenge them.'

Christianity made small effort to realign the appeal of hierarchy,
power, even slavery. James Walvin[39] cites a prayer designed
especially for eighteenth-century blacks : 'O merciful God, grant
that I may perform my duty this day faithfully and cheerfully;
and that I may never murmur, be uneasy, or impatient under any
of the troubles of this life.'

7

Magic persisted. Bungay, colleague of Bacon, was credited with
raising the fog that destroyed the King-maker at Barnet (1461).
'Wind-changing Warwick now can change no more.' *Sir Gawayne
and the Greene Knight,* fourteenth-century Middle English masterpiece, most eerie of Arthurian romances, entwines Christian and
pagan, White and Black Magic, together with visual beauties and
psychological realism. Godiva was perhaps Godda, heroine of a
lost fertility rite. At Copford Church, on the pagan zodiac, Virgo
is correctly stationed, but with Christian embellishments,
an effort to make respectable the ancient patterns, as in *Sir
Gawayne,* where fertility-sacrifice is transported to a Christian
setting or allegory.

Today, behind Christmas tinsel, venal or profound, still lurks
some wistful heritage from the dark time of the year, when men
danced, chanted, implored and perhaps slew, seeking safety from
each other, and from what could not be precisely named.

Parsley sown on Good Friday assured joy, fortune, and cured
sick fish. To sleep above yarrow gathered on St Swithin's Day
increased sexual virility. Undertones of ritual hunt and animal
sacrifice remained. The leader in Yule sword-dances wore a fox-
skin; at Abbot's Bromley a Wake-day Procession, with Fool, Hobby
Horse, Robin Hood, Marion, still includes Horn Dancers wearing
reindeer horns. Devil-cult leaders were reputed to don horns and tail.

Fame of Black witches exceeds that of White, the White
'Cunning Man', medicine-man, using magic to find stolen goods,
bless ploughs, counter Black arts, heal.[40] He anticipated the psychia-
trist in tracing sickness to a social and emotional disorder rather
than to sin, and to God's Will.

Macfarlane finds the last Essex 'Cunning Man' dying 1860,
and shows English witchcraft differing from Scottish, continental
and African, virtually lacking orgies, aerial fantasies, sexual
antagonisms and perversions. Hanging, not burning, was the particular English penalty.

Black witches bewitched horses, killed infants, caused blight, excited demons 'like black frogges'. The loud-mouthed, importunate, eccentric and original were suspect. Wide-spread persecutions accompanied the progress of Stuart science. Macfarlane and Professor Lyn Thorndyke interpret this as the witch becoming scapegoat for post-Reformation decline of political freedom and public charity. Macfarlane sees the weakening of manorial organization, the new divisions between richer and poorer villagers, the loss of Catholic rituals against misfortune, all increasing the need for confidants, healers, Black scapegoats. History is a search for someone to blame. With the rich now shedding responsibilities for the less fortunate, sublimation of guilt may have led to accusations of witchcraft against those whom suffering or resentment may have provoked into suspicious behaviour.

> The Reformation discarded visible duties (Mass, Confession, Rosaries . . .) but substituted stricter intellectual duties. The Priest had been the visible link with the Infinite : now man was left to face by himself the Devil and Witch. Over a million witches were burnt in Europe and America in the seventeenth century.
>
>   (Spengler)

Macfarlane cites prosperous, advanced Essex as having the most prosecutions, 1560–1680. These prosecutions were 5 per cent of all criminal proceedings. Unlike France and Germany, England lacked a sadistic clergy, though in court alibis were useless, commonsense irrelevant, children could accuse their parents or be accused. Those who prefer public opinion to Common Law might ponder these trials. 'From a certain point of view . . .' Macfarlane concludes, 'Witchcraft prosecutions may be seen as a means of effecting a deep social change; a change from a 'neighbourly', highly integrated and mutually independent village society to a more individualistic one.'

Pylons and computers do not extinguish, may even enlarge, cravings for witchcraft. Winston Churchill's war memoirs (Volume V) contain a telegram :

> *Prime Minister to Home Secretary.* Let me have a report on why the Witchcraft Act, 1735, was used in a modern court of justice. What was the cost of this trial to the State? – observing that witnesses were brought from Portsmouth and maintained here in this crowded London for a fortnight, and the Recorder kept busy with all this obsolete tomfoolery, to the detriment of necessary work in this country.

Yet in 1946, a Rev. Burns was advertizing that he could remove 'witchcraft, spells, crossings'. At the Old Bailey, 1968, a Yugoslav, denying breach of promise, declared that he had been bewitched. Two months earlier, the court had sentenced a Jamaican who had charged £880 to exorcize two Indian ghosts from the house gates and another from a car, £746 18s 0¼d to remove six ghosts from the house, £112 for a magic ring, £956 0s 0½d as a fine for the wickedness of removing the ring from the finger and examining it, £298 for replacing the ring, £205 for a magic necklace, £425 to change the 'personal ghost' in a car. The Nottingham Civic Festival, July 1971, paid £100 to Lee Petulengro for 'keeping the city rainless for more than a fortnight. Casting spells from London, he was one of fifty applicants.' The *Aquarian Guide to Occult, Religious and Mystical London and Around* (1971) lists over three hundred clairvoyants, witchcraft and Flying Saucer groups.

8

The older Britain still flickered and glowed unaffected by Assizes and ceremonial business, entangled in a population grappling with enclosures, new art, religion and science, disturbing versions of the Bible, reports of vast landscapes overseas, a Britain compounded of hearsay, tradition, ritual, dreams and nonsense. Off Pembroke, sea-nymphs tolled Garen's Bell, mermaids haunted Solway. Under the Black Mountains, cattle walked the surface of the Van Pool within which the goddess awaited her human lover. At Stiperstone, Wild Edric and green-clad Godda ranged the hard hills together when danger leaned over the sea, and in Bramere Pool lurked a fish-god girt with Edric's sword, while a Roman ghost rowed above. At Belbroughton a ghostly funeral procession paced the fields with dog and headless Norman. Troy remained fresh as yesterday, so that Geoffrey of Monmouth had to produce 'Breta' as Britain's Trojan founder. In woods still wandered the antlered Herne who, like Odin, Herla, Gwyn ap Nudd, Little John, led the Wild Hunt over the night sky. Robin 'sprouted in the April woods'. When Ned Ludd, or whoever organized the Luddite riots, established himself in Sherwood Forest, whether or not by design he could stir the folk-memories and loyalties kept alive by popular plays, ballads, jingles and old sayings. Black hounds haunted grey shrunken trees at Wistman's Wood, Dartmoor; Arthur hunted the supernatural water-snake at Llyn Barfog; Gawyne's skull lay at Dover. By the sign of the Cross, St Columba saved a companion from a monster in Loch Ness. At Ray Island a Roman centurion walked under the moon. By Stanton Drew the Devil piped dancers into stones and skeletons. Bird and animal avoided the mermaid at the Black Mere, Leek. Dragons had roamed Ludlow, Horsham, Burford, Cleveland. 'Hope Mansen' was Hope Mal Oysel, 'place of the ill-omened bird'. At Glastonbury, each Christmas, blossomed the staff planted by Joseph of Arimathea.

Part Three

9 Newfoundlands

> When the Lord thy God shall bring
> thee into the land whither thou goest
> to possess it, and hath cast out many
> nations before thee . . . and when the
> Lord thy God shall deliver them
> before thee, thou shalt smite them and
> utterly destroy them; thou shalt not
> covenant with them nor show mercy
> unto them.
>
>   Moses

I

Medieval Europe – Bruges, Ghent, Brussels, Venice excepted – had
been abashed by the splendours of Islam and reports of Marco Polo's
Cathay. Though Africa was their chief gold supplier, whites knew
little of her until fifteenth-century changes demanded seawards
expansion. Silver mines were declining. There was need to by-pass
the Turks, overwhelming Byzantium, 1453, besieging Vienna,
1529, and again, 1683 (encouraged by Louis XIV), complicating
traditional trade-patterns. Increased populations, higher domestic
standards required more varied foods and goods – cotton-yarn, silks,
peppers, sugar. Natural curiosity too must have been demanding
an outlet.

Novel maritime technology and design encouraged riskier enterprises; improved maps, compasses, clocks and mathematics. The
Cape route excluded greedy Venetian middlemen. Challenges and
responses were alike extraordinary. The great travellers and sailors
created the future: early spacemen, they handed out new worlds.
By 1415, the Portuguese had a foothold in Morocco; in 1487
visited Ethiopia; by 1557 were established in Asia, at Macaw, from
which streamed Chinese silks, tea, porcelain. The Tudor, Anthony
Jenkinson, reached Bokhara. Captain Chancellor was in Moscow,
1553.

'The sea', says Euripides, 'washes away the evils of men.' A
landlubber's remark. For three centuries, ships were packed with
vermin, scurvy, rheumatics; manned by criminals, adventurers,
misfits, press-gang victims, suffering frost-bite, wreckage, marooning,
keel-hauling, torture, killings, starvation, mutiny. Beating, Buggery,

Brandy constituted for Churchill the 'naval tradition'. Yet Magellan
sailed 14,460 leagues in thirty-seven months in a hundred-tonner,
as Drake did the world. Cape Horn remains an image of pain. Of
2,000 men in Anson's famous voyage, 145 returned, with £480,000
treasure.[42] One realizes the relativity of nautical progress, the vital
human factor. To sail under Magellan, da Gama, Drake, Pinta,
Cook, Anson, could have been safer than to do so under Captain
Smith of the *Titanic*. Polynesian canoes navigated the Pacific better
than did the Europeans with their maps, compasses, astrolabes,
quadrants.

The Discoveries arouse questions of human fortitude and endurance: whether, without these, civilization is significantly impoverished; whether crime, cruelty, dictatorship can be forms of
protest against physical inertia, over-developed cerebration, purpose-
less, standardized, boring cities. There is also Chesterton's belief
that nothing is boring, there are only bores.

2

Spain and Portugal were first in America; Holland and Portugal
in Asia; Portugal in Africa, perhaps home of earliest Homo Sapiens,
planner and inventor, and, historically, of Bushmen, Pygmies,
Hamites, Berbers, also of the Negroes, and the eighth-century
Arabs. Her history, distinct from Egypt and the Mediterranean
littoral, had been considerable.[43] A central Nigerian Nok civilization
existed around 500 BC. By AD 400, negroid Ghana was farming, and
trading in gold, glass, pottery, scissors, until disrupted by the
Arabs. Between King Alfred and Luther, the literate, iron-using,
musical West African empires of Ghana, Songhi, Mali produced
sculpture, jewellery, original costume-design, poetry, Mali exporting
gold to Europe.

Copper was mined in eighth-century Katanga. Medieval Central
African ivory and gold reached China, with whom Islamic kingdoms also traded. Ancient African sculpture, ironwork, bronzes,
ivories – Kuba carving, Kushite iron, gold, ebony – were to influence
Braque, Picasso, Gaudier-Brzeska. African skills in metal-work survived transplantation by whites to the New World. Nigerian brass
could be austere, intricate, then almost baroque. Golden head-
dresses glamorized statues. The thirteenth-century Hausa 'Lion
King' of Mali, Mansa Musa, visited Mecca, 1324: his cities were
prosperous, orderly, cultured, luxurious, with considerable women's
rights. Social responsibilities were shared, feudal-wise, amongst
almost all classes in Ghana and Mali. Mali's law was admired
beyond Africa. Interchanges were constant: salt, cattle, horses,

shells, ornaments, coinage, ideas. Ibn Battuta, Arab historian, reported 12,000 camels annually using one route alone. Fifteenth-
century Songhai, long peaceful, had efficient agriculture, finance,
justice, a university at Timbuktu, financed by exporting gold, slaves,
ivory, ostrich feathers, camel-cloth across the Sahara, in exchange
for metals, salt, European swords. Empires rose, declined. The
Congolese Yoruba, known for their woodwork and metallurgy and
legal systems, had walled cities by 1300 – Ife, Benin – one with a
main street four miles long, and an Alfred-like ruler, Shamba
Bolongongo. Contemporary with Edward III, tightly-organized
Karanga cities of Zimbabwe (later S. Rhodesia and N. Transvaal)
exported gold and ivory. Ugandan states developed independent
of Islam, and the Portuguese found East African city-states of culture
and technology; trade in gold, palm-oil, ivory, cocoa, the supposedly aphrodisiac rhino-horn; stone houses, maps, nautical instruments, harbours; remains of Greco-Roman contacts. Skins, gold,
ivory, spices, pearls, sugar, ginger, held ominous attractions.

3

In America, seeking Mexican silver at Zacatecas, Peruvian at Potosi,
the Iberians invaded empires of social and religious complexity
which yet lacked iron, wheel, plough, domestic animals, most
grains, though maize had been cultivated by perhaps 3,000 BC. These
deficiencies enabled, or necessitated, powerful control, by Throne
and Altar, of land, water, food, the building of roads, towns, buildings, the elaboration of mass ceremonies.[44] At peak around AD 700,
the Central American Mayans were a sophisticated society of
temples, roads, pyramids, writing, mathematics. Mayan cities,
Uxmel (960), Labna, Mayapan, could vie with any in Europe. Like
the Etruscans, the Mayans were obsessed with numbers, particularly chronology, correctly establishing, without telescopes, a date
of 400 million years ago. Independent of the Hindus, they had
discovered zero. Some American Indians still conceive the universe
as a square, symbolized by Four. The Aztecs saw themselves as
under the Fifth Sun in the Fifth Cycle: man having been successively eaten by jaguars, transformed to monkeys, threatened by
fire, overwhelmed by flood. The Fifth Age would end mysteriously.
Montezuma's capital was larger, more sanitary, than Madrid,
Lisbon, London. Though notorious for bloody mass-sacrifices, the
tyranny was not simple. As in Europe, the sky was populated with
the unseen. As land was an earth-goddess, it was reserved for the
sacred King and priests. Absolute private real-estate, as in Peru –
and ancient Sumeria – was forbidden.[45] Ultimately the State was

owned by the gods, supported by an income of human blood, including that of an annual ritual king. Jung met Pueblo Indians still convinced that their rituals alone sustained the sun for all mankind. The Aztecs, only recent conquerors, had developed this native belief, taking hundreds of war-prisoners for sun-sacrifice, and thus, like Carthage, unable to rely on help from vassals in crisis.

The whites must have been astonished at the cities, roads, pyramids : the splendours, nakedness, public ownership, sacrifices. Nakedness, to many whites everywhere, was apparently more disturbing than erotic. The familiar – tree, animal, food, armour, field – existed, yet at angles subtly altered : as for the child who described a cow as 'an animal with legs all the way down to the ground'. Much was repulsive. At the Aztec festival of Tozoztontli, the first-fruits were offered.

Until they had made offerings at the temple in this festival, nobody would think of smelling a flower. Flowers were believed to attract spirits as well as butterflies, and the smelling of a flower was very often thought of as a sharing of some beauty, some quality of scented breath with one's ancestors. The festival at the beginning of this period was in honour of the Rain God, Tlaloc. There were tearful sacrifices of children at this time.

(Burland)

The Christian Europeans could have benefited from some pagan values. The technically inferior might be culturally, sexually, morally enlightened. Certain Eskimoes were found who, benefiting by small populations inhabiting endless space, were disconcertingly peaceful, generous, amiable, uninterested in property rights and without religions of heaven and hell. American Indians permitted the *Besdache*, the homosexual dressing and behaving like a woman, without ridicule. C. P. Mountford[46] considered the Stone-Age Australians unselfish, uncompetitive, gentle, intelligent, at one with their surroundings, skilled with hand and body. The brief pugnacities of primitives and animals can be contrasted with the cold, planned excesses of civilized war. The Indian institution, the *Ghotul*, a community of children and adolescents allowing complete sexual freedom, seemed to produce adults free of nervous tension.[47] Malinowski claimed that the absence of murder, theft, neurosis amongst Pacific Trobrianders was due to sexual freedom and lack of the authoritarian father.

4

Later Europeans charted mental processes common to all lands. In Java, the novelist Bernice Rubens found a 'Cunning Man' supplementing traditional lore with modern methods. 'Amuck' is Javanese, and he claimed to cure madness.

> I asked him how he did it. He showed me herbs and described his herb massage and then he said, 'I talk to them.' 'What do you say?' He gave me a whole system of Freudian analysis, how he talked about their mothers and fathers, what they remembered of their childhood. I asked him did the name Freud mean anything to him. 'Does he live in Jakarta?' he asked.

Man endures through symbols that escape time and politics. Only through time, writes Eliot, is time conquered. Chronological time becomes time suspended. Today we see 'primitives' more clearly than did Cortez, Magellan, even Raleigh. All societies cherish totem, fetish, taboo : regimental eagles, colours, mummified leaders, uniforms, crowns, maces, sacraments, sacred texts, relics, idols, mysteries. Graham Greene[48] saw a devil-dance in Liberia :

> It was the blacksmith of Mosan Bolahun then who now swayed forward, a heavy blanket robe and long raffia mane and raffia skirts. The big drum beat, the heels stamped and the gourds rattled, and the devil sank to the dust. . . . I remember a Jack-in-the-Green I had seen when I was four years old, quite covered except for his face in leaves, wearing a kind of diving-suit of leaves and twirling round and round at a country cross-roads, far from any village with only a little knot of attendants and a few bicyclists to watch him. That as late as the ninth century in England had religious significance, the dance was part of the rites celebrating the death of winter and the return of spring, and here in Liberia again and again one caught hints of what it was we had developed from. It wasn't so alien to us, this masked dance (in England too there was a time when men dressed as animals and danced), any more than the cross and pagan emblems were alien. One had the sensation of having come home, for here one was finding association with a personal and racial childhood, one was being scared by the same old witches.

Margaret Mead has indicated the relation of racial differences to tradition and environment. To Eskimoes, all flowers are identical, all snows are different. Differences can be more apparent than fundamental. Cannibalism can arise from lust, greed, magic or, as

with Maoris, shortage of meat. In north India, polyandry safeguards property and is rated less selfish than monogamy. Kamchat-
kans gave men the domestic functions while women administered;
Dahomey Kings had fierce female guards, contemptuous of men;
in Assam, men could be legally inferior to women; Russian women
fighter-pilots served against Hitler and Israeli women are trained
to fight.

Erudition does not of itself exorcize the primitive. In his
autobiography[49] Leonard Woolf writes of his wife, the novelist:

> I could never quite understand Virginia's feeling about her books
> and their reputation in the world. She seemed to feel their fate
> to be almost physically and mentally part of her fate. I do not
> think that she had any belief in life after death but she appeared
> to feel that somehow or other she was involved in their life after
> her death. Being so intimately a part of herself, a hurt to them
> was felt as a hurt to her, and their mortality or immortality was
> part of her mortality or immortality.

All continents revealed similar sky-symbols and myths. For all,
opposites – Ahab and Moby Dick, *Yin* and *Yang*, God and Devil –
prevented social stagnation. The Mexican god, Yipe Totec, skinned
himself alive, perhaps expressing man's brooding self-doubts and
need for dynamic shock, akin to Odin hanging himself for nine
days. Aztec sacred god-eating seemed to parallel the Christian
Eucharist: the kindly Quetzalcoatl, Feathered Serpent (one of whose
emblems was a lamb on a cross) was frustrated by Tezcatipoca, god
of magic, night, death, as Balder was by Loki. Quetzalcoatl, virgin-
born, descended to the Dead, rose after nine days and departed,
promising that on a certain year bright-haired strangers, bearded
like himself, would come from the sea to restore the land. By
fateful fluke, Cortez arrived on the date foretold, with Venus in
the promised position. The father of the Peruvian Inca, Atahualpa,
foretold that his son would lose his throne to strangers.

The Europeans were so used to their own symbols that they were
blind to the incongruity of condemning others', which at best
seemed to them a barbarous or blasphemous parody of Christianity.
This persisted. The Victorian British Governor Hodgson ignorantly
mistook the Ashanti totem, the Gold Stool, for a mere throne, and
its concealment led to further misunderstandings, killings, annexa-
tion. Seventeenth-century invaders, themselves adept in idolatry,
drunkenness, bloodshed, ceremony, must nevertheless have felt
virtuous horror at the 'barbarian' temptations and Mysteries:
astrological ball-games, magic, narcotic mushrooms and herbs. A
Spanish friar, 1529, wrote:

They eat the mushroom with honey – when they begin to be excited they start dancing, singing, weeping. Some see themselves dying in a vision, others as being eaten by a wild beast, others imagine that they are capturing prisoners of war, are rich, possess many slaves, have committed adultery and are to have their heads crushed for that offense.

(Quoted by R. E. Schulles in UN *Bulletin of Narcotics,* 1969)

Drug-cults still prosper. 'Pot is the magic drug because it can transcend the generation gap.'[50]

A modern traveller in Mexico attests to the permanent, subterranean images. Eating the psilocybe mushroom, he saw a tall Chinese dragon black all over and outlined in vivid green, nameless calms, convulsions, a brilliant white ball without heat or glare.

The denial of the ultimate truth was itself the ultimate truth. . . . I felt like a prophet, a figure from Blake with a long white beard. I put out my hand to touch my knee, but it was a hundred yards away and my arm stretched a hundred yards to reach it. I thought of a Chinese jade which I had not even seen, found by a man whose name I had not heard mentioned for twenty years, and the jade became a symbol of ultimate truth. Soon my intellect seemed to be working on a dozen different levels of consciousness at once and I was chasing ultimate truths like rats in a haystack.

(John Lincoln, *One Man's Mexico,* Bodley Head, 1967)

5

While humanist scholars were discovering, or rediscovering, moral and scientific evidence for the unities of men and nature, the *conquistadores,* priests and knights alike, were shattering them. Anthropology was not a European motive. In India and Africa, the Portuguese were implacably resolved to oust Arab traders. The slave trade, 1441, with captured Africans presented to the Portuguese Prince Henry the Navigator, was ratified by Papal Bull, 1481, which gave Africa to Portugal and insisted on the compulsory baptism of slaves. Towns like Mombasa were destroyed, Fort Jesus built to cow survivors. The introduction of maize was belated recompense. The Portuguese indeed have remained as inflexible as the Boers in their racial attitudes. In 1954, the present (1973) Portuguese Prime Minister stated that Portuguese-Africans 'are to be regarded as productive elements organized, or to be organized,

in an economy directed by whites.' The English Royal African
Company was granted monopoly, 1672, of the Atlantic slave-trade.
Islam was as cruel as Christianity, coastal kings raiding inland for
slaves to exchange for iron, copper, tin, linen, fire-arms, spirits.
For three centuries slavery enriched the English economy, particu-
larly Bristol, Liverpool, the Baptist Church, the Great Western
Railway. Nine million slaves perished in British, Dutch, French,
Portuguese, and Italian ships. Until 1772, blacks could legally be
shipped from Britain at their master's will.

The crusaders had not despised Saracen and Moor. The renaissance *conquistadore* knew of Aristotelian theories of inferior races,
despised the American Indians and, in return for syphilis, spread
smallpox, bullets, Roman Christianity, the last, already threatened
by Lutheranism, in a nervous, persecuting, degenerate phase. Only
the paternalist Jesuits, in Canada and Paraguay, used welfare,
trade, music, propaganda, alienating the regular clergy who finally
incited the Spanish King to expel them from Paraguay, 1767. A
Las Casas, a William Penn, treating the Indians as civilized equals
– which was reciprocated – were few enough to be gratefully
remembered.

Iberian militarists and priests, desperate for land, gold and con-
versions, enslaved, declassed or exterminated several million Mexicans, a million Haitians. Christianity, with its promises, could have
been welcomed by Aztec victims but, 'not a hundred yards from
the site of the sacrificial pyramid and skull-racks of the Aztecs, the
Inquisition erected its stakes and scaffolds. Whereas the pagan
priests drugged their victims before cutting out their hearts with
a single blow, their Christian counterparts made sure that the
wretches they condemned were fully conscious and suffered as
lingering an agony as could be contrived.' (Lincoln)

Mr Lincoln adds that what really horrified the Indians, though
accustomed to Aztec holocausts, was

the sadistic cruelty with which the Spaniards punished the most
trivial misdemeanours, ecclesiastical or secular. It was the policy
of the friars to introduce their religion by the mildest means
possible but their example was not followed by all the clergy.
In the auto-da-fé conducted by Bishop Landa in Yucatan, three
hundred and fifty-nine men and women were tortured and a
further six thousand, three hundred and thirty were flogged, shorn
and fined. Among the tortures listed are the following : binding
arms and thighs and twisting the cords tight with rods; filling the
victim's belly to bursting point with water and then trampling
on him till water and blood gushed out of his ears and nostrils;
hanging by the wrists with heavy stones attached to the feet;

scorching the tenderest parts of the body with wax tapers or scalding them with boiling water.

Such atrocities were perpetuated. Prisoners in the South American Wars of Independence were sewn together, had hands severed, eyes gouged, Fra de Coronil vainly demanding the killing of every Venezuelan over seven. In Australasia, blacks suffered genocide, by shooting, hanging, poison, beating, from representatives of Augustan England. Virginian slaves could be punished by hanging, burning, castration. For President Theodore Roosevelt, the Red Indians were 'squalid savages', and, with these, no treaty was ever respected by the whites. In Pacific and Caribbean, Europeans tended to cheat islanders initially friendly. The Brazilian authorities officially admitted, 1968, that Patacho Indians had been methodically infected with smallpox, several million such people having in recent decades been exterminated by eviction, forced labour, dynamite, bullet and poisoned wells.

Racial tolerance was not a Jewish or Christian virtue, since the Divine injunctions to destroy the Philistines, Amelekites, sons of Cain, and their beliefs. The anthropologist W. H. R. Rivers noted how missionaries, eager to uproot pagan customs, broke the native zest for life, ensuring decline, even extinction. 'Ye shall burn their graven images with fire.'

Man is adroit at finding pretentious reasons for aggression. Slave-owners held that conversion justified slavery. Franz Stangl, Nazi commandant at Treblinka death-camp, 1942–3, explained (1971) that he had had to 'compartmentalize' his thinking :

Perhaps the Jews were meant to have this enormous jolt to pull them together; to create a people; to identify themselves with each other.

He suggested that God too was good and bad.

My conscience is clear about what I did, myself. I have never intentionally hurt anyone. But I was there. So yes, in reality, I share the guilt.

More genuine misunderstandings throve. Whites and natives could understand no property-values other than their own. That theft was not necessarily immoral or malicious was unbelievable to Europeans.

Red Indians had no conception of land being alienated, any more

than sunlight, air, water – so could not credit their chiefs'
signing away immemorial territories to the invader.

(C. E. Carrington, *The British Overseas*, Cambridge, 1968)

Travellers' tales provoked beliefs of Africans interbreeding with
apes. South African racialists still reject miscegenation by appealing
to *Exodus* : 'A man may not mix his seed with that of the animal.'
Edward Long, in his *History of Jamaica* (1774), felt that Africans
were closer to monkeys than to men.

Christianity, under strange suns, had novel offshoots. Jesus,
Mary, mingled with Mexican gods and carnivals, Voodoo blood-
rites, ghost-dances, animal sacrifices; the Brazilian festival, *Um-
bando*, merged African gods with saints, particularly St George,
and rich Brazilian Catholics still propitiate spirits with wine, food,
candles. The Ku Klux Klan used Christian terminology.

Such appetites are unrestricted by time and place.

The outbreak of Voodoo in New York as a cult followed by
thousands of half-believers is difficult to explain, for it appeals
to people of all economic and educational levels. Not long ago
a Manhattan Court granted a divorce to a woman who had
claimed that her husband tried to poison her by sprinkling
graveyard dust in her salad dressing. More recently the president
of a newly-opened advertising agency in Fifth Avenue was
caught taking part in a pre-dawn ceremony to ward off the
Evil Eye and to attract new accounts. Surrounding him in his
marble and glass penthouse, decorated with paintings by Jackson
Pollock and de Kooning, were phials of dragon's blood, tufts
of elephants' hair, three iron magnets and a large salt cellar
of all-purpose Jinx-chasing spray useful for victims of satanic
influence 'and to repel outside influences'.

(*Daily Telegraph*, 15 October 1968)

6

The challenge to England was inescapable. Foreign markets and
sources were in her blood. Already, some thirteenth-century English
coins were of Malinese gold. The Discoveries offered the chance to
outgrow Venice, Portugal and the Low Countries, to consolidate
growing naval power. More practical than Spanish hidalgoes, to
whom treasure was more important for itself than for what it
could buy, the English wanted lands for trade and investment.
The Royal Exchange and Drake's cannon were interdependent.

The Italian, Cabot, sailed from Bristol to Newfoundland, 1497. 'Indians' arrived in Bristol, 1502. Frobisher brought Eskimoes to London, 1577. Theoretically debarred from the New World by the Pope, Tudor Protestants sold slaves to Catholic Hispaniola, were colonizing in America, reaching Russia, Persia, India, China, in search of spices, drugs, ores, jewels, slaves, pepper, potatoes, chocolate, sugar, cloves, turkeys, which were exchanged for cloth, weapons, gunpowder, brass, tin, and trousers for those who did not want them. Pepper Standard rivalled Gold Standard. Calais had gone, but there would be Virginia, Jamaica, Madras. The accompanying sea-power must have extracted new national spirit, finally overcoming awe of foreigners, adding zest to insularity, arrogance, fearlessness, ambition.

The Crown itself invested in new joint-stock companies, imperial foundations, to include the Levant, Turkey, Muscovy, Hudson Bay. It also helped finance African slavery, particularly through the Company of Royal Adventurers to Africa (1163) and the Royal African Company (1672).

The pioneers, Chancellor, Drake, Hawkins, were resolutely followed by such magnates as the 'Turkey Merchant', John Eldred, last sailing East aged eighty, reputed to have voyaged to Aleppo, through a week of storms heaved up by witches. The *Tygger* sailed to Aleppo, 1583. 'Her husband's to Aleppo gone, Master o' the Tiger.' Five leading merchants were aboard, determined to smash Portuguese monopoly of Indian routes. From Syria they travelled overland towards India, were captured by Portuguese, though Eldred escaped to become founder-member of the East India Company. To the resplendent Mogul, Jehangir, the Company offered 'virgins, a cornet, Burgundy wine, mastiffs, cloth.' (Carrington) In Great Saxham survives Eldred's Thorn, his favourite tree.

Hey diddle dinkety poppety pet
The merchants of London they wear scarlet :
Silk in the collar and gold in the hem,
So merrily march the merchant men.

Contemporary British racial tensions derive from 1555, when John Lok imported from Guinea ivory, spices and 'certaine black slaves'. These were used as domestics amongst many social classes, particularly in London. They did not inevitably remain slaves. Some actually flourished in freedom. Blacks built themselves a London house, 1597, 'contrary to building regulations'. (Walvin) Elizabeth tried several times to legislate against a colour problem magnified by ignorance, superstition, fears of cheap labour. She

E

sought, vainly, to shift the newcomers overseas. The expansion of West Indian sugar multiplied the slave trade itself, and the wealth of British America.

7

The Discoveries jolted European imagination, and economics. In a century and a half of inflation, from the effect of American metals, those who plied most gaudily might achieve least. Aristocratic Spain disdained economics, unaware that her true interests were less overseas than in the wealthy Low Countries. These she lost, by cruelty, stupidity, obscurantism, watching with supine aloofness her grandeur crippled by rising prices and greedy competitors. 'The opening up of the ocean as a high road precipitated the Reformation and built up Antwerp while in the end it ruined Spain.' (Brooks Adams)

British political enterprise was partly a reflex of her commercial vigour. Pym and Hampden were not only landowners but directors of the Providence Island Adventurers. Geography demanded the English foreign policy of Balance of Power between weighty neighbours, involving immense wars against Spain, Holland, France, Germany, which gathered in French India and Canada, Dutch South Africa and Australasia, Spanish Gibraltar. Antwerp itself, embryo of a World Bank, was eventually entangled in Spanish wars, leaving the market-prizes open to London. England, Spain, Holland, France, Portugal, would grapple in Caribbean sugar imperialism, Britain and Holland compete for West Africa, the East Indies.

The new vistas were not only economic. One sees their effect on More, Montaigne and Shakespeare, who read Hakluyt and, perhaps, Pory's translation of Leo Africanus's *History and Description of Africa*. Caliban became a reproachful menace never quite exorcized. Roe's description of Jehangir's court was the basis of Milton's Satan enthroned. Flamboyant words, images, luxuries created landscapes solid as Dante's hell or Homer's Troy: El Dorado, Pontick Sea, the Propontic and the Hellespont, dazzling Cathay and the Lands of Prester John and of the Golden Horde.

. . . antres vast and desarts idle,
Rough quarries, rocks and hills whose heads touch heaven . . .
And of the Cannibals that each other eat,
The Anthropophagi, and men whose heads
Do grow beneath their shoulders . . .

The Discoveries shifted the pilgrimage from an interim solution to the ideal of final escape to a western Eden. More subtle conquests, opportunities, associations were perceived by Donne.

Licence my roving hands, and let them go
Before, behind, between, above, below,
O my America, my new-found-land,
My kingdom, safeliest when with one man mann'd.

Caliban, priapian, simple, with the dark attractions of monstrosity, would become over-reverenced by those repelled by rootless, over-cerebrated urbanization, to whom blood-sacrifice was preferable to boredom, inertia, injustice. Intellectuals and visionaries would seek ideal sunlit communities under a benevolent Quetzalcoatl.

The demolition of vast empires by a few bigots and pirates could also induce total pessimism about human purpose, divine design. Sixteenth-century explorers also revealed Europe as but a fragment of a lavishly endowed world, while, simultaneously, telescope and microscope demonstrated that Earth itself was not the centre of God's universe, not necessarily the centre of God's thought.

For some, here was a challenge to justify existence in a more thrilling world; to others, a lonelier, more fearful plight, with God harsher, or abandoning man altogether to the cruelties of Nature or Society, resistance requiring extremes of docility or aggression. Of early renaissance Europe, Deschamps lamented:

Time of Mourning and Temptation, Age of Tears and of Envy, and Torment, Time of Langor and Damnation, Age of Decline approaching the end – Time filled with Horror.

> Love your enemy, bless your haters, said the
>   Greatest of the Great;
> Christian love among the Churches look'd the
>   twin of human hate.
> From the golden alms of Blessings Man had
>   coined himself a curse:
> Rome of Caesar, Rome of Peter, which was
>   crueller, which was worse?
>
>   Tennyson

I

History stimulates, because human motivation is seldom precise. Loyalty, snobbery, nationalism, neurosis, the barely conscious, can at times outbid even money. Charles V, Richelieu, Cromwell – Robespierre, Hitler, Stalin – were animated by more than cash. Conversely, bribery sometimes purchased empire and papacy. Policies and concepts, however vivid, are usually muddled. At the mercy of time and interpreters, they are as if pollarded. Private enterprise can express itself in slavery, or cancer research; public enterprise in the guillotine or a hospital; a church may be a sanctuary or Samuel Butler's 'musical bank'. Elizabeth could show that duplicity was more socially useful than honesty, Charles I could not. Royal domestic virtues could be national disasters.

Renaissance and Reformation were not clear-cut revolutions but an interplay of trends, moving at different speeds and in different directions according to locale, tradition, circumstance.

Superficially, sixteenth-century Europe seemed propitious. Despite Turkish advance, trade and security were reviving on a Roman scale. Plague still stalked, now joined by syphilis, but famine, rape, private war were, at the cost of local freedoms, being countered by further centralization under educated laymen. In England, Tudor manor-house was replacing the castle. Greenwich Observatory was the first state-supported scientific institution. A free public library was opened in Lambeth Palace, 1610. The Elizabethan, Dr Gilbert, experimented with electricity[51].

Choices seemed possible between the well-tempered international humanism of More, Erasmus; the generous eclecticism of Cosimo di Medici, uproarious hedonism of Rabelais, restrained comprehension of Shakespeare and Montaigne. There was the tolerant, searching, educational genius of da Feltre, Commenius, Colet; the analytical objectivity, 'scientific attitude' of Linnaeus, Copernicus, Galileo, Francis Bacon, Servetus, Harvey, substituting the authority of experiment for that of classical text and Catholic dogma . . . against the heady, nationalistic fanaticism of Luther, Calvin, Knox. There was also the amorality of leaders, Catholic and Protestant alike : Mary Tudor, Alva, the Borgia Popes and princes, Henry VIII, Philip, and the Pope who held Te Deum for the St Bartholo-mew Massacre. As now, 'Reasons of State' justified all crimes.

Co-operative pacifist, educationalist experiments were attempted by the Moravian Brothers. The printing press, academies, new schools and universities promised onslaught on exhausted schol-asticism. Modern textual criticism was incipient in Petrarch, Valla and Montaigne. Philology became a serious study[52]. At St Paul's, from 1509, Colet and Lilly had taught not only classics but English, Colet's talk reminding Erasmus of Plato. Michelangelo, Cellini, Leonardo, Cosimo and Lorenzo, the Tudor monarchs, Alberti and Raleigh, could indulge in combinations of physics, music, mathe-matics, poetry, medicine, astronomy, law, classics, painting, em-broidery, education, sport, philosophy, drama, history and engineer-ing, loves, friendships, hatreds. Inigo Jones was engineer, archaeologist, numismatist, architect, theatrical designer, writer, scholar, Platonist philosopher. Pico knew twenty-two languages. Enthralling plastic and graphic arts tilted the mind. The Ren-aissance produced a popular theatre, disrespectful and profound; ironic epics; a concept of International Law; the rise of legal and commercial classes who could surely promote tolerance, ease, pacific common-sense.

Yet, throughout most of Europe, much of the new spirit was once again to be diverted into magic, dogma, state-worship. A Pascal even a Newton, would largely relinquish science for religion or mysticism. The promise of 1500 dissolved in generations of religious and civil wars, mass-killings of peasants, heretics, witches.

Perhaps the choices had been illusory, each historical cell containing its opposite, progress merely small shifts within a genetic inheritance virtually unchanging, despite extravagant extremes, not of human nature but human behaviour. Free thought, moreover, requires free time, and counter-trends were already reducing the little that the common lot had ever enjoyed. Puritanism, revolting against renaissance body-cults, was demanding, often with brutal vehemence, whether life was duty or pleasure. Only the moderates could conceive it being both.

2

'We carry within us,' wrote Sir Thomas Browne, 'the wonders we seek without us; there is all Africa and her prodigies in us.'

With vigour renewed, renaissance Europe debated the body, reviling it through Savonarola, glorifying it through Michelangelo, dissecting it through Leonardo; exercising it in war, hunt, dance; displaying it in drama, decorating it, lamenting its decay.

Throughout history the body had either been God's putty, brief house of the soul, or the only source of gods and angels. It could be illuminated as radiant Apollo, degraded to charred sinner, bartered for goods or dowries. Medievals had oscillated – fasting, then over-eating, St Dominic lashing himself furiously while reciting a psalm. It could be shaved, bearded for abstruse doctrines; castrated for Attis, Sultan, papal choir or opera; crucified, burnt, circumcised, sold as meat in Berlin, 1945, conveyed for lust, jerked by torture, deployed as cannon-fodder, foot-bound by Chinese matriarchs, flogged for poverty; be wigged, laurelled, crowned, haloed; be analysed into water, carbon, magnesium, genes, glands, chromosomes. It controlled roads, it polluted rivers, moaned for whores and saviours, deserts and banquets; was stupefied or galvanized by drugs, glorified on mountains, chastened or enflamed by the Abstract. It plans Jerusalem, beats drums, waves flags, plays in quartets, gapes at Picasso, queues for permission to queue, slips into ghosts and werewolves when listening alone to the tick of the years, ebbs and flows at whim of officials : sent to capture a railway station, Berlin Reds, 1918, retreated, for lack of platform tickets! Controlled by instinct or custom it bolts the bathroom in an empty house; is visionary before a fire; is plumed, veiled, elongated; defiant, exalted by Florentine art not into empty, heroic Ajax but by what Lord Clark calls Michelangelo's deepest preoccupation, the struggle of the soul to free itself from matter.

Until Darwin, Marx, Freud, Renaissance Man could consistently believe that the body, freed from Gothic and Byzantine distortions and Christian sin, could set proportions to the universe, be manipulated by will and knowledge, revolution, legislation.

All bodily potential was exploited by humanistic versatility. Wren was architect, astronomer, mathematician, pioneer of innoculation and blood-transfusion. The body dominates *Hamlet*, whose hero is a compound – reflective, courtly, ultimately deadly – of lust, sloth, anger, activity, wit, spiritual nakedness.

Individualism too could be naked. 'I glory that I call this act my own,' rings from the savagery of Webster's *The White Devil*.

'I am myself alone,' Richard III smiles. Autobiography, portrait, diary became typical. The Renaissance had consciously celebrated the naked and physical. Classical athletics were revived in new Italian schools. The heroic forms of David, Apollo, Achilles, draped only in the glow of pristine Platonic or Homeric myth, however ideal or monumental, tried to create a realistic unity of past and present, between Arcadia and Europe, Troy and Italy, Olympus and Heaven. Florence founded a Platonic academy; Ficino sought correspondences between Platonism and Christianity, with life seen in capital letters, but with grace and damnation less desirable than the revelation of truth through beauty. Man had aspired to become angel, now let angel become man. For Sir Philip Sidney, learning must 'lead and draw us to as high a perfection as our degenerate souls made worse by their clayey lodgings can be capable of.' Yet the unconscious would remain, still hankering for vulgar hells and Mysteries, filled with strange anecdotes; with urges not only to love but to betray and execute one's lovers, rout enemies unseen and perhaps imaginary. Darkness spotted the glitter. Akin to Dürer's 'Melancholia', Hamlet's exordium of man ends with 'a vile and pestilential congregation of vapours.'

3

The Renaissance was no dramatic expulsion of medieval nonsense, a curtain rising on naked heroes, or free-thinking Bacchantes staging a come-back. Novelty is rare, the unique never happens, few revivals are genuine. Many medievals – Roger Bacon, Richard II, Frederick II in Palermo scoffing at Moses, Jesus, Mahomet, and himself the friend of Averroes – had been only nominally medieval. Frederick's kingdom, overloaded with bureaucrats, lawyers, police and censors, was, for all its brilliance, unpleasantly modern in its despotism and caprices. Francis, Dante, Cimabue, Wycliffe, Pisano were dead by 1400. The medieval John of Salisbury had justified tyrannicide as heartily as any renaissance Jesuit. Plato and Aristotle had been studied at Chartres, where sculptors seem to have imitated Greek antiques.[53] Usury, often associated with Protestant capitalism, was older than Rome. Templars, Lombards, Bruges, Antwerp, Sienna, had not prospered upon charity. The compassionate medieval St Bernardino had preached what casuistry could abuse : that usury is lawfully exacted from God's enemies because their goods are morally not their own, and because the motive is brotherly love, weakening the enemies so that they might return to God.

'New Ages' magnify existing tendencies, propose solutions for changing situations, but never wholly shed the past. Neither

Reformation nor Renaissance meant absolute advance; both spawned glib definitions of progress and had roots in an imaginary Golden Age. Renaissance symbolism could be as abstruse as the medieval.

With Galileo, with Francis Bacon, direct connection between the universe and human behaviour – that incest and crime could provoke earthquake, magic convulse Saturn – could no longer be officially maintained. Bacon (1561–1625) knew of Democritus's notions of atomic reality. Rabelais (*c.* 1490–1553) searched for truth as much in depths as in heights though, physician and philosopher, he would have rejected such concepts, knowing that bodily excesses were trivial beside spiritual enormity. The lens of Bourne, of Tycho Brahe, revealed worlds more precise and outstanding than those of astrology, narcotics, or Dante. The Royal Society – which one day would include Freud – the Florentine Society, the Paris Academy of Sciences, Gresham's College, were cathedrals probing not soul but matter. An oriental god and devil, mystical or capricious, could be seen as impersonal energies, creative or destructive. The intoxicating Platonism, poetry of shapes and ideals, could not seriously affect Leibnitz, Napier, Descartes, Locke. Galileo trained his telescope on the moon, 1610, and found no Diana. Pomponazzo, 1516, denied the immortality of the soul. Objects could be stripped of demons and angels yet become universes dense with invisible properties : an altar was wood, fibres, molecules, atoms, electrons.

Systematic research was overtaking intuition, invading political and moral philosophy. Hobbes conceived the world merely as matter and motion, thought and feeling reflecting the mechanical play of atoms : ideas of soul, sin, innate morality were only self-induced, with man needing control from above as strict as that of gravity or magnetism. Paré, Servetus, Harvey in medicine, Steno in geology, Linnaeus and Turner in botany, knew something of man's animal inheritance, though this was long left undeveloped. Bacon promulgated 'scientific method' which reaches general truths by meticulous experiment, testing, checking of particular cases. This was extended by Newton (1642–1727) whose insights penetrated sky and ocean, numbers and physics, the densities of time and space. It enabled a busy, enquiring, self-confident technological society, on intellectual bases scarcely challenged until Einstein and Popper.

Archaeology (Poggio, Circaco), astronomy (Kepler, Brahe), geometry (Descartes, Pascal) assumed modern significance. Napier produced logarithms, Leibnitz and Newton the differential calculus. Brahe's fellow-Dane, Romer, estimated with fair accuracy the speed of light. Jesuits studied advanced physics and mathematics.

This ferment was international. Cross-culture made Flemish painters fascinated by Venetian art. Florentine savants argued with those from Cambridge. Francis I patronized Leonardo, Bronzino, Cellini; for his School of Fontainebleau, assisted by other Italians, Rossi and Primaticcio, he acquired works by Perugino, Raphael, Piombo, del Sarto. The Venetian *canzone* descended from the French *chanson*. Linnaeus, the Swede, was classifying plants, stabilizing botany.

Porta, Cardau, de Caux, Lord Worcester pioneered steam-power. Thomas Savery's steam engine appeared, 1698. Gilbert of Chichester experimented with electro-magnetics, Boyle detached chemistry and physics from astrology. Medicine too transcended frontiers, with the French physician, Paré (1509–1590), the Italian, Baglivi (1668–1706), the Spaniard, Servetus (1511–53), the Englishmen, Harvey (1578–1657), Sydenham (1624–89), Willis (1621–75) and the medical statistician, Graunt (1620–74). By 1625, Sanctorius's thermometer was available to Europe.

Archives began replacing legend and allegory – Truth, Jane Austen wrote, aged fifteen, is very excusable in a historian – producing Machiavelli's and Bruni's histories of Florence, Clarendon's *History of the Rebellion*, Sleidan's *History of the Reformation*. Leland and Camden were lively historians, accurate cartographers. Bruno's theories of cosmic unity, reinforced by observations of man and geography, informed Joyce's *Ulysses*, as Vico's historical cycles did *Finnegan's Wake*. (The theosophist, Annie Besant, 1847–1933, saw herself as a reincarnation of Bruno!) Historians, nevertheless, were slow to discard Byron's assessment of the virtues of the historian – Learning, Diligence, Wrath and Partiality. Impartiality is rare, not always admirable. To discuss Belsen, Katyn, or Hiroshima in the same tone as Gladstone's household accounts or the Gross National Product, suggests perhaps a fine historian but a curious fellow-citizen.

There was also much wishful thinking, men imagining a past that might exist only in a remote or ideal future.

Life was enhanced by mirrors, print, word, opera, by the truthful, unallegorical portrait of a Holbein, a Samuel Cooper. French was replacing Latin for the educated European. Guided by a Montaigne, Commenius, More, Ascham, education could be more humane, extending even to women, themselves entering more freely into politics, art, discussion. Savaged by Knox, they were defended by Castiglione. A Philip II, Charles V, Francis I, could not have coerced Isabelle and Beatrice d'Este, Elizabeth Tudor, Bess of Hardwicke, Vitorria Colonna, Margaret of Habsburg, chilly Jane Grey – or their Shakespearian counterparts, Beatrice and

Rosalind. The educational system of Vittorino da Feltre (1378–
1446) postulated elites not of birth but of learning, simple, profound,
versatile, responsible, magnanimous, tolerant; equipped for leisure
as much as labour; through synthesis of classics and mathematics,
music, athletics and 'character forming'. Colet wished the Bible to
be read through reason, not through the magic that had deified
Plato, Pythogoras, Hippocrates. 'I see the cause is not in God but
in man's folly, that his people live in misery throughout the world,'
wrote the Polish educationalist, Samuel Hartlib.

4

Nevertheless, scientists and their clients too could compartmentalize
their minds, the telescope both impair and strengthen the astrological society. Sir Thomas Browne, humanistic physician, assisted
in prosecuting witches. Lady Hatton, wife of Elizabeth's Chancellor,
was feared as a witch, her heart reputedly ripped out by the Devil,
in Bleeding Heart Yard, Hatton Garden. James I, busy intellectual,
forced through a Witchcraft Act, 1604 and, in *Demonology*, affirmed
that to spare a witch was not only unlawful but doubtless as great
a sin as Saul's sparing of Agag. Wesley credited witchcraft. Frederick II himself, for all his scientific and humanistic intellectualism,
had retained astrological credulity.

Brahe believed in astrology, as did John Dee, foremost mathematician, secret agent of Elizabeth I (signing himself 007). Dee, like
Ludendorff and Himmler, believed in good and evil spirits. Together
with Brahe, Bruno, Kepler, he was encouraged by the Habsburg
emperor Rudolf II (1576–1612) whose mind was crammed with the
scientific and occult.

Kepler had been astrologer to the warrior, Wallenstein. Machiavelli, to whom greed and fear were more evident than virtue and
self-reliance, respected auguries and astrology. Shakespeare's sonnet
marks the world as 'this huge stage', which 'presenteth nought but
shows Whereon the stars in secret influence comment.' The chemist
Nicholas Culpeper (1616–54) was also astrologer and alchemist.
Kenelm Digby (1603–68) of the Royal Society dabbled in magic,
tending to anoint not only the injured part, but whatever had
caused the injury.

The Swiss chemist, metallurgist, mineralogist, Paracelsus (1493–
1541) believed that stars fixed their signs on plants, so that one
resembling a bodily part could help cure that part, a daisy thus
producing an eye-drug, a theory that interested Jung. Pope Paul III
delayed a treaty, to consult the stars. English priests were penalized
(1561) for casting the horoscopes of Leicester and Elizabeth. A

planetary wheel, drawn for Monmouth's horoscope by Pregnani, is in the British Museum. Aenius Sylvius, later Pope Pius II, wrote in *De Liberorum Educatione* : 'A Prince must not be ignorant of astronomy, which unfolds the skies and by that means interprets Heaven's secrets to men.' Renaissance art with its colour symbols and allusions cannot be fully appreciated without some astrological understanding. G. R. Potter[54] reproduces a painting by Martin Schnaffer, of intricate symbolism : Mars is Tuesday, Arithmetic, Strength, Red, Copper.

Nor were devotees unsustained by evidence. The Cheshire astrologist, Robert Nixon, correctly foretold his own death by starvation at Henry VII's court. A violent change was foretold for France, 1789, by Cardinal D'Ailly (1414) and, a century later, by Turrel. Muller (1476) predicted it for 1788. Nostradamus (1503–66), court physician, successful against plague, named significant details : 'Varennes', 'Elected Capet', 'bloodshed'.

Scientific attitudes did not excite the streets, which remained indifferent, sceptical or hostile. A German crowd murdered Moll, inventor of the modern loom, 1682. Post-Reformation Europe was haunted by Faustus, symbol of scientific man's greed for knowledge at all costs. In Britain, despite stupendous scientists and Scottish engineering genius, people have generally been more concerned that a thing should work than to know how it works. Science too can entail its own superstition. Dr Keith Robertson, at Warminster, 1966, announced that the Star of Bethlehem had been a Flying Saucer!

A Leonardo, Bacon, Newton, Faraday, Rutherford, Pasteur scarcely eliminates national mummery, chatter of the heart linked to the Sun, brain with the Moon, kidneys with Venus. Gods still lingered, often harmless, some agreeable. Montaigne observed :

Where I now live, the married women twist their kerchiefs into the form of one [phallus] projecting from their foreheads, thereby boasting of the enjoyment they receive from the genuine article. When they become widows they turn it round to the back, hiding it under their coifs. The wisest and most respectable matrons in ancient Rome felt it honourable to offer flowers and garlands to the god Priapus, and when they married, young virgins were made to sit on his more unseemly parts. Nor am I sure but that in my own time I have not seen glimpses of a like devotion.

Though Linacre, fervid Greek scholar (1460–1524) had founded the Royal College of Physicians, Tudor children's lives were precarious. Even in eighteenth-century France, sickness claimed three Dauphins in eighteen months.

New ideas were in the air, the ferment of the Renaissance was
making itself felt in every branch of Western life. But medicine
was still permeated with medieval practices and superstitions.
Belief in the curative properties of precious and semi-precious
stones was firmly held ... among the many remedies for teething
troubles was the tooth of a male viper enclosed in gold and silver
and hung round the child's neck ... another remedy was to rub
the gums of the teething baby with a finger moistened with fresh
butter and the milk of a bitch mingled with the brains of a pig.

(Magdalen King-Hall, *The Story of the Nursery*, Routledge,
1958)

5

Classical lore, particularly in literature, had never been quite
subdued. Guillaume de Machaut (1300–77) could include Theseus,
Hercules, Jason, Absalom, Ulysses, Delilah, Argus in the same love
poem. Social and technical changes now sent the imagination
scuttling backwards even while experimenting adventurously. The
Aldine Press, and Erasmus, printed classical texts for an international public excited by neo-Platonism, though this was often not
much more than emphasis, superficial but delightful – particularly
for the North – on Mediterranean warmth, light, eloquence, movement, nakedness. Long-buried sculpture, half-forgotten tragedies,
resonant argument enthralled the artists, dilettantes, patrons and
rulers who, even if they were popes, could be scarcely disguised
pagans, connecting sin not with Adam but with faulty artistic
design, failed metre, inharmonious translation. Cardinal Sadoleto
was called, in wonder, 'The Christian'. The search for truth might
not always have been thorough, but the surfaces intoxicated.

Until about 1500, literary developments were the most prominent.
Rediscovery of ancient manuscripts together with cheaper distribu-
tion stimulated not only classical philosophy and history but Judaic,
Greek, Egyptian occultism. The god Thoth, 'Hermes Trismegistus',
reputed founder of Egyptian astrology, appeared in a mosaic in
Sienna Cathedral. Pico della Mirandola claimed Christian evidence
from Jewish and Egyptian astrology and alchemy. Milton's mind
was stocked with the antique and contemporary, pagan and Christian, existing simultaneously. Buried Greek and Philistine gods,
spoilt oriental and African shrines, add a vivid, proscribed glamour
to Milton's 'Ode on the Morning of Christ's Nativity'. 'In vain
the Tyrian Maids their wounded Thammuz mourn.' The Mysteries
revived, adventures and initiations of the soul now streaming
through poetic and philosophic speculations or games. Bruno

attempted to restore an esoteric Isis cult. Neo-Platonist discoveries or inventions supplemented or travestied Christ. 'Hellenistic form and Christian sentiment met in Michelangelo,'[55] Classical symposia were re-enacted beneath Plato's bust. The Classical Trinities were restored in the Three Graces. Orpheus, Dionysus, were hailed as forerunners of Christ or as naked and glorious pagan absolutes. Malatesta charged Alberti to build an Olympian temple at Rimini. Edgar Wind[56] suggests that Botticelli's 'Birth of Venus' was an attempt to recapture a lost classical painting by Apelles. Michelangelo passed off one painting as an original classic. Raphael's fresco of Apollo and Marsyas 'transformed a gruesome tale into a Socratic metaphor.'

Yet the Renaissance had at first accelerated tendencies already existing, rather than directly imitating classical models. Donatello saw antique art as a source of ideas to be used with extreme freedom and inventiveness.

Much neo-Platonism would have startled Plato. More literal explorations and imitations came later, though never dominating the genuine masters, and the models were generally of the later, 'decadent' Empire : the proportions of Michelangelo's David are far from classically Greek. Indeed, the entire era is controversial; Spengler, derided but often suggestive, maintained :

The Renaissance never even touched the real classical, let alone understood it or 'revived' it. There is not a single one of their [the Florentines] great works that the contemporaries of Pericles or even those of Caesar would not have rejected as utterly alien. Their palace courtyards are Moorish courtyards, and their round arches on slender pillars are of Syrian origin. Cimabue taught his century to imitate with the brush the art of Byzantine mosaic . . . the domed Cathedral of Florence is a masterpiece of late Gothic, and St Peter's is one of early Baroque.

Original impetus is hard to sustain. Literature, particularly, was at the mercy of too much minor scholarship, pedantry and cliché. Quite as typical as Michelangelo and Leonardo was

Winter departs : the forest is dressed again with shining
Leaves and white Flora leads the dances.
The North Wind yields to the West. Now, Amaryllis,
We can pasture our flocks in the secluded wood and
Gather the secret pleasures of Aphrodite.
Honour the goddess, deck her with new garlands,
And let a lamb soak her holy altars.

(Marc-Antonio Flaminio, 1495–1550)

Men and women adepts, nevertheless, were concerned not only
with plastic and graphic art but with renewed cults of friendship
and physical perfection, with the moral lessons to be found in
Homer, Livy, Plutarch, Plato, and from Socrates. Romanticism
drew breath from classical legends, magic, ruins. Dramatic tragedy,
usually of Roman pattern, could replace tournament, Mass, miracle
and mystery-play.

6

Despite politics, religion and war, Anglo-continental ties were
pulled tighter through trade and learning. Bruni and Ficino powerfully affected fifteenth-century London intellectuals, particularly
the Platonist, John Doget, Richard III's chaplain. More and Colet
were in regular contact with Italian scholarship. Lord Oxford,
Philip Sidney, Donne, Inigo Jones, would know and love Italy –
like Wordsworth, Shelley, Byron, the Brownings, Landor, Turner,
Ruskin. William Dobson (1610–46), finest of Charles I's English
portraitists, owed much to Tintoretto. Milton's Latin Poems (1645)
were appreciated by Italian *litterati*. Continental oil-painting and
perspective altered English vision : by perspective and mechanical
marvels, Inigo Jones made court theatre a sensation for the eye as
much as the ear.

Caxton learnt his art in Germany and Bruges; Holbein, a Swiss,
worked for Henry VIII; Erasmus of Rotterdam lectured on Greek
at Cambridge. Henry VII's new Nonesuch Palace was vividly
French, influenced by Fontainebleau. Montaigne's essays, detached,
amusing, probing, gently speculative, knowledgeable without being
knowing, were absorbed by Shakespeare and developed by Bacon,
Browne, Swift, Sterne, Johnson, Goldsmith, Locke, Dryden, by Mill,
Huxley, Russell, Chesterton, Orwell, helping train the British mind
in knowledge, criticism, order.

Not all was light. There was a Spanish image, sinister and
haunting, of dark, ruffed tyrants, lit by Inquisitorial fires, looming
too close – a few generations later the Spanish Ambassador, regarded
as Raleigh's killer, was howled at as 'The Devil in a dog-cart'.
Monolithic Spain, however, also typified the passionate mysticism
of St Teresa, St John of the Cross, which Donne and the English
metaphysicals must have pondered; the picaresque humanity of
Cervantes and de Vega; the fantasies of the Baroque, 'synthesis of
extremes' in which the soul was explored as thoroughly as the
Atlantic. Something Spanish is perhaps discernible in Spain's great
enemy, Raleigh, in his harsh wit and spiritual autonomy, his
spectacular dress and inordinate dreams, in his austere writings so

far from the carnivalism of London slums – writings witty, unencumbered by flamboyant or empty conceits, with leaping passions controlled, yet sometimes overwhelming in tenderness, the tenderness of the love-poems cut from his solitary pride the more convincing because of that pride. Emperor Charles, King Philip, would have appreciated Raleigh's laconic thrust: 'Only, we die in earnest, that's no jest.'

Spanish Habsburgs held to medieval moral absolutes, political rigidity, Catholic piety, in contrast to Henry VIII and Elizabeth; to Henry IV, born a Protestant but who became a Catholic, 1572, after the St Bartholomew Massacre, rejoined Protestantism, 1576, and, for the French Crown, resumed Catholicism, 1593.

Spain was the political and religious enemy of Reformation England, but – as with modern Germany – the emotional attitude was more complex. France was the old, the genuine enemy, however alliances might ebb and flow. Spanish taste, humour, painting, literature, the grave Spanish decorum, the unsettling Spanish mysticism evoked an English response, ambiguous, but seldom wholly unsympathetic, as much to be reckoned with as the talk of Spanish cruelty, persecutors, naval hatreds. There is nothing anti-Spanish in Shakespeare. From the first, Don Quixote was popular in England: while unmistakably Spanish, he was not wholly un-English. If King Philip was the monstrous threat, Katherine of Aragon was the wronged and beloved queen, whose tragedy inspired one of Shakespeare's most poignant scenes, and whose ghost haunted Kimbolton Castle.

> The queen of Castille has a daughter
> Who won't come home again,
> She lies in the grey cathedral
> Under the arms of Spain.
> O the queen of Castille has a daughter
> Torn out by the roots,
> Her lovely breast in a cold stone chest
> Under the farmers' boots.
>
> (Charles Causley)

Only Spain and England at this time had popular theatres.

Italy, above all Italy, both of the lost, almost mythical Empire and of Petrarch, Tasso, Ariosto, was still tutoring France and England, evinced in the School of Fontainebleau, the Louvre, Whitehall Palace, Somerset House, and in manners, diplomacy, fashion, thought, whether of Petrarch, Latini, or 'the murderous Machiavell', whose writings, free of feudal or religious commitments, have a modern ring, stimulating or ominous. Exuberant Italian decoration was adapted by Williams at Longleat and Hardwicke. The great and mysterious Inigo Jones learnt from Alberti, from Palladio. Wyatt and Surrey embellished the sonnets of Dante and Petrarch. Castiglione's *Courtier* helped transition from Knight to Gentleman. Englishmen attended Poliziano's Greek lectures in Florence. Shakespeare's Gaunt complains of

> Fond lascivious metres, to whose venom sound
> The open ear of youth doth always listen :
> Report of fashion in proud Italy,
> Whose manners still our tardy apish nation
> Limps after in base imitation.

English Perpendicular had, as at King's College Chapel, completed native Gothicism, which did not tamely surrender to the Italians, themselves more often extending than destroying the past, even though the domes and columns, ordered space and mathematical symmetries of Wren so effectively oppose the sprawling, evolving mass of the Gothic. Torrigiano's tomb for Henry VII at Westminster 'combines Gothic linear precision with classical restraint'. (Joel Hurstfield)

Italian pressures in England and Germany could be at second-hand through the Dutch, Burgundian, and especially the Flemish, themselves creating schools of landscape and portrait which, through Holbein, Van Dyck, Lely, Kneller, were to lead towards Gainsborough, Reynolds, Romney, Lawrence and the water-colourists unmistakably English : Blake, Palmer, Cotman, Cozens, Bewick.

Bruno himself visited England, dedicating a book to Philip Sidney. Italian journeys by John Shute and Inigo Jones tapped the genius of Alberti, Vitruvius, Scamozzi and Palladio. English architects ceased to be lackeys of builders and surveyors, and their work flowered into such achievements as the Whitehall Banqueting House, Greenwich Palace, the double cube room at Wilton, and Osterley Park. The taste of Charles I, unsurpassed in Europe, further encouraged the Italianate, though the genius of Inigo Jones was never that of a fulsome imitator. Furthermore, his elaborate scenic effects for Jonson's masques transformed court theatrical design. Jonson himself imitated the theatre of Seneca and Plautus, and, like Shakespeare and many successors, used heroic or satirical classical themes, enthused with new style and bias. Webster and Tourneur presented lurid contemporary Italian courts, in which dukes and cardinals, like Jewish usurers, were grandiosely contemptible and with a tendency to defraud or poison. Charles I's court was an ordered, civilized centre of international art, employing such sculptors as Fanelli and le Sueur, painters like Van Dyck, Dobson, Mytens, Gentileschi and, briefly, Rubens. At the centre was the Royal Surveyor, Inigo Jones himself and the superb royal collections included masterpieces of Titian and Tintoretto. First for the King of Denmark, then for Charles I, worked John Dowland, finest lutanist in Europe.

Monteverdi's Venice opened the first public opera house, 1637 and, from Venice, Florence, Mantua, Italian opera crossed to London and Dublin. Italian, Flemish, and English – Morley, Weelkes, Wilbye – perfected the madrigal. With Byrd, Tallis, Gibbons, English church music achieved an excellence never since surpassed. Purcell learnt much not only from his compatriot, John Blow, but from the Italian Lully. Amongst Tudor court musicians were the famous Bassanos from Venice, and Laniers from Rouen.

Rivalling the Bible and Plutarch was Homer. Like Antwerp and Venice, London became an outstanding printing-centre, and Caxton's first publication was *Histories of Troye*. Chapman's translation of Homer magnified a world of bloodshed and defiance, beauty and resignation, with sudden asides compassionate or sardonic. Ulysses moves from barbarism to vision; man, in all but physique, outmatches the gods. Of superior moral temper, scourged by mortality, he must grasp the hurrying moment more quickly, more fully, than any deity. Apollo, god of poetry, was not himself a poet; by metaphor, simile, reflection, deed, by his supreme power of enriching the commonplace, humanity cut steps into the universe. A lowering plume scaring a child, a dog dying, elderly men watching cold beauty, 'Let her go back to the Ships', illuminated all life by their very brevity. And a name could be seized to conquer Death : some reputation for magnanimity, fortitude, wisdom, which Zeus himself never wholly commanded.

Mediterranean humanism, graceful or powerful, ordered or ruggedly searching, remained, through Goethe, through Flaubert, largely unquestioned until the present century, when dictatorships ordained the heroic, archaic, monumental aspects of the Renaissance, and everywhere new psychology, technology and social attitudes disputed the assumptions of Michelangelo, Titian, Montaigne, Rabelais, Erasmus.

7

Shakespeare, restricted by no classical doctrine though retaining and exploiting traditional beliefs, had absorbed Ovid and Plutarch, also borrowing from Boccaccio. The blazing mass of Falstaff is Rabelaisian, recalling the boastful, aggressive, imaginative Cellini and, Edith Sichell tentatively suggests, the Venetian humanist Pietro Aretino, racy, coarse and witty, who traditionally died 'while laughing at an indecent joke'.

Like Bacon, Shakespeare read Montaigne, Pliny, probably Virgil, perhaps Villon. Into the apparatus of magic, anthropomorphic religion, feudal chronicle, classical legend and stock tale, the ancient elements, humours, saws and cosmic dance, he injected not only the modern but the urgent. Between the melodramatic opening and the tender finish of *Hamlet* is an anthology of stale beliefs, popular songs and prejudices. Yet simultaneously they relate to personal responsibility, the role of the individual in society, the nature of power, the brutalities of obsession, fears of death, the hazards and effects of immoderate passion, conceptions of destiny which contain the interlocking of chance and tendency. An approach so universal, and, like the universe, at first glance shapeless, was not universally appreciated. 'It seems', Voltaire complained, 'as if Nature had amused itself by assembling in Shakespeare's head the greatest imaginable power and grandeur and the lowest and most detestable form of witless vulgarity.'

A running existentialism added a bracing challenge when much hitherto accepted or cherished was toppling.

> The fault, dear Brutus, lies not in our stars
> But in ourselves . . .

Wits from the Inns of Court could sharpen themselves on metaphysical play and swift imageries. The broader audience, still rooted in Catholic England and the mythical Beyond – where flowers have symbolical qualities, a ghost struggles, without incongruity, for revenge, and stones have been known to speak – indulged in homely allusions, protective bawdiness, liberating horseplay, plucking at satisfactions not always articulate.

> King Stephen was a worthy peer,
> His breeches cost him but a crown.

'The social student', wrote Virginia Woolf, 'can pick up hardly any facts about social life from Shakespeare's plays.' Maybe, but from *Henry IV* he can at least observe the long continuity of English society. Falstaff's London protrudes into the brutal, insolent, roaring world of Dickens and Mayhew, contains the social assumptions of the Edwardian music-hall. 'We want work – and Not Much of it!' Through the centuries runs noisy patriotism, unaccompanied by desire to enlist; mistrust of the Law as a confidence trick played on the poor, conviction that lords are no real good, together with reluctance to reject them wholly. Also, the ability to mitigate war, fraud, politicians, by a joke.

Charlie Parnell's naughty shape
Went stealing down the fire escape.

Henry IV shows a total society, where sin, irrationality, the dead can upset the daily order as harshly as rebellion, proclamation, a warrant. Even Rumour has a speaking part. The past is not only political. When Silence breathes out 'And Robin Hood, Scarlet and John', one feels the vivid powers of old tales, akin to the 'strange potency of cheap music'. Falstaff continues the tradition of the jester, whose off-beat wisdom averted ill-luck from rulers. The play has further revelations, showing the inexorable tightening of London's grip on the provinces, through violence, deceit and the axe. Also the struggle of imagination – Richard II, Hotspur, Falstaff, attractive but limited, often irresponsibly cruel – against ruthless yet responsible champions of law and order. Constant references, sombre or jocular, to gallows, disease, death, are reminders of the nature of kingdoms.

Elsewhere, Claudius, Banquo, Othello are mixtures of observation, empathy, shrewdness, the realization that personality is not unity but discordance, a casket of potential seldom fully opened, circumstance pillaging it ruthlessly but not totally. Like Rabelais, the Englishman saw people not as astrological ciphers, classical effigies, moralistic abstractions, but as the generous play of contradictions : public and private, will and irresolution, reason and intuition. All fluctuate imprecisely but tellingly. Falstaffian extravagance encloses a moderation – 'Can honour set a leg?' – exploding the lofty maxims of a Hotspur, even of a Macbeth and Anthony. Man is neither absolutely free nor implacably conditioned. Nothing is finalized, though Shakespeare knew all recesses of the body, the black behind the gold. Freudian is :

In men, as in a rough-grown grove, remain
Cave-keeping evils that obscurely sleep.

His comments on the everyday have laconic deadliness.

Our own Love, waking, cries to see what's done,
While shameful hate sleeps out the afternoon.

Significant detail, of colour, gesture – Lear's button – reconciles the watcher to life, though death is immanent, progress negligible, miracles seldom happen, prayers are answered but often ironically, cruelty is rampant and common decency not always eager to leave its corner, and bitterness and spite may in an instant nudge aside valour and magnanimity. Yet, in extremity, the deposed and absurd can still utter 'Ripeness is all.' In the condemned cell, wayward Richard II finds compassion and understanding.

Witness to the ornate griefs, hidden lusts, slippery language of high politics, Shakespeare knew, with a tragic sense that Leonardo would have acknowledged, the horrors of loneliness and frustration.

War is no strife
To the dark house and the detested wife.

Fair is foul. Nothing is but what is not. A golden crown may melt to poison, the relentless hero prove more feminine than his mate. Idealism and rhetoric whip up groundling applause but pay no bills. Cleopatra's desolation has a sort of triumph. Falstaff's jocularity has kinship with 'the Merry Old Gentleman', with Fagin. The villains are not demonic and unreal but criminal victims of human agencies, often of goodness gone askew. Hamlet startles with moral ambiguities, tangled motives, sadistic refinements, poetic radiance, ironic secrets, forbidding wit, within a cause of debatable righteousness. Would Hamlet have been a useful ruler? Shakespeare makes no direct comment but is liberal with clues. He is 'committed', but to more than sects. 'Whether we like it or not,' Rebecca West has said, 'we must admit that there is very little in Shakespeare that can be used as propaganda for adult suffrage.'

The effect is of understanding, perhaps stoic acceptance. Free Will often appears deceiving or absent, yet resolute pessimism props up a world less chaotic than it seems. Without some bias towards order, responsibility, symbolized by monarchy, aristocracy, individual goodness and obstinacy, society would not have survived. Music, loyalty, laughter are persistent brakes upon anarchy, despair, inordinate lust. Extremes are penetrated but few victors are extremists. Even Iago is afflicted not by enthusiasm, divine or satanic, but by mediocrity. Issues are complex, metaphors compel profundity, yet the conclusion is the reverse of what Goethe called the German destiny of making everything difficult.

8

Any spasmodic drift towards tolerance and reason was not hastened by the Renaissance, whose gifts – wise teachers, harmonious friendships, intellectual good-cheer, artists and scientists dedicated not only to fame but to truth – were too often accompanied by curses.

Humanism could entail inhumanity, that of a Cesare Borgia or Cortez, as much as the tolerant geniality of Duke Frederigo of Urbino, ruler, patron, scholar, a political da Feltre. A plea by the Bohemian George Prodiebrad, for European federalism, scandalized renaissance popes and kings. No sensational connection occurred between accurate clocks, maps, pumps – and charity, social consciousness, the wider intelligence. Tiptoft, Borgia, Malatesta, Henry VIII refuted any classical belief that fine learning of itself makes fine people. Duke Heinrich Julius of Brunswick, playwright and scholar, consistently burnt witches. Triumphant individualism could disdain conscience. 'Richard loves Richard,' declaims the murderous, fabulous Crookback.

Roman Law, freshly studied, assisted absolutism, especially in Germany. Classical eloquence could easily foam into classical rhetoric, distorting thought, enraging politics, renewing superstition. 'O God of Battles, steel my soldiers' hearts,' has an operatic tinge. That science mitigates aggression is never axiomatic. A Speer, a von Braun, is a perennial reminder of the limitations of sheer intelligence. Intellectual inroads into traditional Christianity and the astrological universe were detached from political morality.

Modern artillery and conscription were beginning in Prussia and Sweden; aggressive nationalism was thriving in the Counter-Reformation, while Europeans were spreading over the world not in unison but rivalry.

Invention facilitates wickedness. European guns, exported to Morocco, wrecked the flourishing Songhai Empire, 1589. 'Fire-arms', Montaigne wrote, 'have such little effect, except upon the eardrums, that their use has been abandoned.' He was wrong. Guns spoke incessantly, usually on ignoble issues. Similarly, it proved easier to have a press than a free press. Pamphlet and printed sermon excited controversy but also hatred. For four centuries the printed book was unrivalled as a swift and economical medium. 'The Book', Kafka wrote, 'must be an ice-axe to break the sea frozen within us.' For Gorky, 'When I hold in my hand a new book I feel something alive and miraculous has entered my life.' But what book? What life? Like the texts of Rousseau, Marx, Freud, Lenin, Mao, the vernacular Bible would, initiates claimed, justify all : the burning of witches in Geneva, the killing of Servetus, the beating of children, subjection of women, Cromwell's Irish massacres, the slave trade. That Oath on the Bible replaced Oath on the Relic was in itself no progress, the Bible too often the inspiration not of wisdom and delight but punishment, and tedium.

Renaissance love of art had distressing by-products, men now

speaking of 'the art of war'. (Field-Marshal Wavell was to declare
that war was no art but a game, and a very dirty game.) Michelangelo and Leonardo were military engineers. Voltaire noted
Spanish battles preceded by violin music, another operatic
detail. Artists and intellectuals, indeed, while not always com-
batants, are seldom pacifists. 'You cannot imagine the thrill it
gives one to get behind a machine-gun and blaze away,' Malraux
wrote to Saint-Exupéry. Baiting of lunatics and blinded animals
was undisturbed by the new learning : Pepys and Evelyn watched
cruelty with the attention of connoisseurs. Stimulated by Livy and
Plutarch as well as the New Science, political thought harshened.
Like Marx after him, Machiavelli believed compulsion was necessary for progress – unlike Montaigne, Gandhi, A. S. Neill.

Classical sexual tolerance was eagerly imbibed by renaissance
courts and popes; no direct Christian convention inhibited the
sonnets of Shakespeare and Michelangelo or the live nakedness
of the new Graces, Venus, Adonis, Diana. Protestantism, however,
supplied a rival, narrower ethic.

Built as a fortress against Death, Christianity too easily could
imprison life. 'Compel them to come in.' Reformation implied
return : to patriarchal austerities, Judaistic monotheism, rule by
the Elect. Warned by Adam's fate, the Reformers mistrusted, not
revered the body, re-encrusting it with original sin, though this,
after Hitler and Stalin, was less obviously deniable than it may
have seemed to Federigo, Aretino, Rabelais.

Luther, Calvin, Zwingli, Munzer fought vulgar hermeticism,
idolatry, indulgences, fraudulent miracles, simony, clerical celibacy,
monasticism. Extreme Protestants – Anabaptists, Fifth Monarchy
Men, Levellers – denounced private property, government by moral
delinquents, all government save that of the Elect. In general,
Protestantism challenged not the reality of the soul and immortality
but the priest's White magical powers over both. It deepened the
blackness of Hell and Devil, but tended to replace idol-worship
and Madonna cults with word-worship, through Bible and Sermon.
Sermonizing could be a dangerous posture, a spiritual arrogance
frequently merging into political arrogance. The pulpit symbolised
not only protection, instruction, inspiration, but inviolate supremacy,
male absolutism. While strengthening personal religious fervour,
'enthusiasm', it drastically narrowed the future life into stark
alternatives of damnation or salvation, without the old intermedi-
ate stage of purgatory.

Luther was more violently medieval than Erasmus and More.
Vehement believer in witches, he also claimed to have fought with
devils. 'The air all about us is filled with demons.' More considered

him 'a vile and pestilential buffoon'. Far from condemning war, bigotry, despotism, Lutheranism merely shifted their bases.

Though Luther identified money with the Devil – renaissance popes seemed more interested in raising capital for art, building, war, than in care of souls. Protestantism is often identified as the ideal ethic for capitalistic and nationalistic advance, praising hard work, concentration, economy, obedience, self-discipline, useful in mining and manufacturing towns and in the rising sea-ports, destructive of restrictive internationalism and prohibitions, encouraging the ruthless individual to be responsible to no one but himself. Or,

> Calvin's predestination was the religious expression of the fact that in the commercial world, success or failure does not depend upon a man's activity or cleverness, but upon circumstances uncontrollable by him.
>
> (Engels)

At bottom, leadership in all ages is secular, conditioned by secular problems. If a Frederick II, Edward IV, Stalin ignore God's Will, an Innocent III, King Philip, Pius XII, Franco will manipulate, assert, twist, forge or usurp it. Venice, Genoa, Florence, Bruges, Antwerp, had, generations before Bristol and La Rochelle, been managed by professional, literate capitalists and money-conscious nobles, yet, like ambitious Portugal, remaining 'Catholic'. The relation between commerce and ideology is unlikely to be precise : the stereotype of a young, rational, liberating Protestantism combating superstitious, tyrannical, archaic Rome is unrealistic; the moral gains of the Reformation were questionable.

9

The Protestant virtues – self-reliance, respect for legality, faith in Providence – could be exploited by *laissez-faire* which, while changing the world and accumulating fortunes – visible evidence of God's approval – also connived at drudgery, prostitution, poverty, famine, slavery. Though continuously inspiring reformers and evangelists – Penn, Owen, Shaftesbury, Fry, Nightingale, Schweitzer – it also strenuously raked in authority to justify the static and unwholesome, over-revering Jesus's 'The poor are always with you.' Poverty was to imply failure, even sin. Puritanism sought to improve people, but at the cost of their cruder joys. It was easily affronted by others' appearance. Thomas Cromwell imprisoned a man for wearing hair to his shoulders : 'Deformed and unseemly manner'.

Witness of savage German wars, futile episcopacies, mechanical religious rituals, Luther in reaction was darkly pessimistic, trusting to Faith and the strong arm. With Machiavelli, with Hobbes, he came to believe that eradicable human faults demanded lay despotism to control them, in imitation of the universe controlled by God whose decisions, whose being, were unaffected by sacraments and popes. Heaven itself required despotism. Human faults derived not from faulty social arrangements but from inherited Sin and the roaming Devil, which rendered rebellion not only foolish but wicked.

> Let all who can cut them down, slaughter and stab them without mercy, openly or secretly, as one must a mad dog, and remember that there is nothing more poisonous, noxious and utterly diabolical than a rebel.

So Luther castigated the peasants who, mistaking spiritual freedom for political freedom, had earlier hailed him as their messiah. That very genuine dilemmas of law and policy should evoke such ferocity needs the scholarship of a von Ranke, imagination of a Breughel and Dürer, wholly to understand, together with a glance at biblical passages approving killings and damnation. Luther was in contrast to the peasant leader, Munzer, himself a tempestuous warrior, but whose ideals of international brotherhood extended even to Islam; who hated property and lords, mistrusted beliefs in literal immortality and to whom – as to Schweitzer – Jesus was less an historical figure than a creative archetype reborn in every mind and, as in the Mysteries, to be quickened by spiritual illumination. Likewise the Devil was not, as for Luther, a tangible species, but the sum of human weaknesses. Racked and beheaded after defeat by the lords, 1525, Munzer was never quite forgotten.

Luther in triumph did not mellow. For him, the anarchic incompetence of the German Empire necessitated despotic national princes and invulnerable private property. 'God would prefer the State to exist, no matter how evil, rather than permit the mob to riot, no matter how justified it is in so doing.'

Nor must the Protestant assault on priestcraft be exaggerated. Protest is usually selective, not total. 'Man and God', Luther declared, 'need a third party as go-between no more than do two lovers.' This is typically vivid, but misleading. The Catholic puritans, Dominic, Savonarola, Loyola, the Lutheran pastors, Calvin's elders, Non-Conformist public opinion, were all inquisitorial, totalitarian. Fervid Protestantism was as intolerant as Rome over free speech, free thought, and more so over sexuality and laziness. Slavery was preferable to idleness, a sin to which the poor and the blacks were held to be consistently, even inherently, prone. Reformers spoke reassuringly of God's protection, Grace, fatherhood; harshly of sin, punishment, hell. They could say in effect, 'Cheer up, or I'll beat you.' Idealist determinists, Calvin and Knox, moral dictators, promoted early polit-bureaux, intolerant of dissent, sexuality, even reasonable discussion. For Knox, 'Jacob have I loved but Esau have I hated' was a text increasingly handy. Protestant and Catholic slogans, as in the Crusades, were in the spirit not of the seer but of the sergeant-major and press-gang.

Of the Kirk Ministers – fearful of Dionysus, Venus, Apollo – John Buchan, himself neither Catholic nor atheist, and whose grandfather insisted that on Saturday, Sunday and Monday only religious books be read, wrote :

> If they gave manhood and liberty to Scotland, they did much to sap the first and shackle the second. Condemning natural pleasures and affections, they drew a dark pall over the old merry Scottish world, the world of the ballads, and the songs, of frolics and mummings and 'blithesome bridals', and, since human nature will not be denied, drove men and women to sinister and perverted outlets.
>
> (*Montrose*, Hodder and Stoughton, 1949)

Robert Burns, as much as Hume, was to be a reminder of the virtues of sanity.

Despite the Protector's love of music, the English Republic remains synonymous with sanctimonious repression. Throughout Europe, Spring had throbbed with frolic song and uncouth disturbance, but,

> May-day is a festival of purely pagan origin, a simple and spontaneous expression of joy at the beginning of true summer. In the Church's calendar it is the Feast of St Philip and St James but these saints have little connection with the traditional ceremonies . . . the garlands still carried by the children, the maypole itself, at once the symbol of the flowering tree and of fertility, the old bonfires, the carols sung on towers and high places, and the now almost forgotten custom of spending the night in the woods and bringing back branches in the morning, were all intended to mark the return of the summer. It was because the Puritans, nearer in time and thought to their primitive origins than we are, recognized many of these customs for the fertility rites that they actually were, that they hated them so bitterly, and put them down wherever they could.
>
> (Hole)

Domestic sternness, backed with divine sanctions, remained paramount for two centuries. As *The Children's Friend* put it (1868):

> No worse sign of a child's character can appear than a readiness
> to speak lightly of a parent's authority. The great God who made
> heaven and earth, and can make good all He says, looks upon
> disobedience to parents as one of the most grievous sins a
> child can commit, and pronounces a dreadful curse upon it.

Such dogmatism has proved tough as a pick-axe, and light-years
away from St Francis. The voice of the Puritan divine sounds
through such moralizing, complacent tyrants as Podsnap, Gradgrind, Murdstone; through Tolstoy:

> Women have only two emotions: love of their husbands and
> love of their children, and, as a result, love of dress, for the
> husband, and of money, for the children. The rest is only artifice,
> imitation of men, tools for seduction, coquetry, fashion.

Gandhi, a Hindu Puritan, was callous towards what Westerners
would consider his wife's well-being. The sect of Exclusive Brethren
decreed, 1965, that no woman should reject a Brother's proposal,
whatever her inclination. There are those who feel that absolute
sainthood is the best method yet known for getting one's own way
the entire time.

Sanctioned by the fierce Old Testament God, the Protestant
State became a mystery powerful as Eleusis or Vatican. Indeed, by
the late eighteenth century the Inquisition was eclipsed but the
State, whatever its nominal religion, retained inquisitorial brain-
washings, secret tribunals, judicial purges, censorships. The
Reformation had other alarming symptoms. Like Taoists, Vikings,
early Christians and Marxists, Luther believed that society must
worsen before redemption, a conviction confirmed by the Thirty
Years War. Jehovah too had his 'Chosen', and Calvinists were
now announcing that at Creation the Lord had doomed the majority
to hell. Here was determinism more implacable than astrology,
Catholicism, than Darwin, Freud, Marx, more akin to Hitler's
master and slave racialism. Influenced by the *Book of Revelations*
and the magic of numbers, some maintained that only 440,000 could
be saved. This division between Elect and Damned could not but
inspire self-satisfaction, self-righteousness, envy, suspicion, harshness.
In England, the Westminster Confession of the Presbyterians,
1646 explained:

The rest of mankind God was pleased, according to the unspeakable council of His own Will, whereby He extendeth or withholdeth Mercy as He pleaseth, for the Glory of the Sovereign Power, to pass by; or to ordain them to Dishonour and Wrath, for their Sin, to the praise of His glorious Justice.

Like religion itself, like dictatorship, Protestantism helped people endure worlds partly of its own making. Biblical heroes and imagery – Solomon, Joseph, Judas, Job, Golden Calf, Whore of Babylon – now in resonant translation, were as dramatic as the Homeric. Hating the Theatre, Protestantism made drama out of soul. The Pilgrimage was once more a crusade, internal, individual, against giants and sirens and the merely mistaken.

He who would valiant be
　'gainst all disaster,
Let him in constancy
　Follow the Master.

Puritan militant self-confidence was enviable to the restless and improvident. Predestination assures that if one side must lose, the other must win. 'Keep in the midst of the path,' Bunyan promised, 'and no hurt shall come unto thee.'

In Old World and New, seldom for long distinguishing between sublime nonsense and ignoble rubbish, haggling over God like politicians over inflation, Catholics and Protestants hated, or were made to hate each other, as strenuously as Jesus did the Pharisees. Before being burnt, Bruno made retort to his Catholic judges (1600), still hideously topical : 'This Sentence, delivered in the name of a God of Mercy, is perhaps more a cause of fear to you than to me.' Luther, coarse, courageous, with a racy, thrilling gift of tongues, was no less a pillar of European cruelties :

Since we punish thieves with the halter, murderers with the sword, and heretics with fire, why do we not turn on all these evil teachers of perdition, those popes and cardinals and bishops, and the entire swarm of the Roman Sodom with arms in hand, and wash our hands in their blood?

Religion, like all else, is manipulated by time and chance. Dominicans staffed the Inquisition : today they form revolutionary cells in Brazil. For generations, however, the Counter-Reformation was far from genial. The Spanish preserved Naples through three centuries of poverty, Inquisition, censorship. In Richelieu's France the Inquisition forbade chocolate as a dangerous drug. In Spain,

witnesses of a burning could earn forty days' indulgence. Pius V
commanded death for whoever disclosed what the Inquisition had
inflicted on him.

Renaissance and Reformation contained modernists like Henri
IV, Walsingham, and Elizabeth who feared old age more than
God – 'God's Death' was her noisy oath; also Montaigne, a quiet
voice amid barbarism, reflecting :

> There is a certain consideration, and a general duty of humanity,
> that binds us not only to the animals, which have life and feeling,
> but even to the trees and plants. We owe justice to men, and
> kindness and benevolence to all creatures who may be sus-
> ceptible of it. There is some intercourse between them and us,
> and some mutual obligation. I am not ashamed to admit to so
> childishly tender a nature that I cannot easily refuse my dog when
> he offers to play with me or asks me to play with him at an
> inopportune moment.
>
> (Essays)[57]

But a Socrates, St Francis, Rabelais, a Montaigne, Voltaire,
E. M. Forster, while they may flourish in an institution – in a
court, college, club – are not obedient party-members or hired
hacks, and their larger influence is diffuse or postponed. Montaigne
was on the Index by 1676.

The Jesuits hated the Inquisition but, master-minding the
Counter-Reformation, concurred with its premises, Leninist premises, that worthwhile ends justify atrocities. The Papal Secretary
of State wrote of Queen Elizabeth, 1588 :

> Considering that this woman has caused the loss of so many
> millions of souls to the Faith, it is beyond doubt that whoever
> may despatch her from this world with the pious intention of
> serving God, not only will be sinless but will acquire merit.

10

The Thirty Years War, ostensibly the climax of religious fury,
exterminated actual millions of Germans and Bohemians.

> There is something to be savoured in the situation of the founder
> of international Law (Grotius) and a Cardinal of the Church
> (Richelieu) engaged in ruthless bargaining to extend a war which
> had already magnified without parallel every human depravity,
> cannibalism not excluded.

> (D. P. O'Connell, *Richelieu*, Weidenfeld and Nicolson, 1968)

Like other sagas, from Palestine to Ireland, its religiosity was little more than an aid to recruiting. Catholic France allied herself to Protestant Sweden and Islamic Turkey against Catholic Austria.

From the perennial Bourbon-Habsburg vendetta, Swedish and Teutonic land-hunger and Richelieu's obsession with French grandeur, ensued a Mongol ferocity from which plundered, typhus-ridden Germany perhaps never quite recovered. A peace of exhaustion, 1648, left each region with a faith selected by its ruler, freed from any ideal of international Christendom.

In the British religious struggles, the victims were few enough to be individually recorded, with martyrdoms divided evenly enough between both sides. Some were memorable. When the Rector of Hadleigh, Dr Taylor, was bound to the stake, a Mr Warwick threw a log into his face. 'Oh friend,' Taylor reproached him, 'I have harm enough, what needed that?' Before the flames were lit for the rite that flayed Europe as if from hell, he added to a bystander words that St Joan might not have disdained: 'Joyce, I pray thee come and pull off my boots, and take them for thy labour. Thou hast long looked for them, now take them!'

The English Reformation was not designed by proletarian weavers, chiliastic prophets, far-sighted capitalists planning world-development. Lollardry had never been a mass-movement. The impulse was primarily that of a strong monarchy that abolished papal power, nationalized the Church and, on monastic lands, endowed new ruling classes, schools, estates. Catholics too joined in the plunder and, even in the Marian counter-attack, refused to disgorge it. Erasmus, himself a Catholic, had considered the monks obscurantists and the friars racketeers. The Dissolution released one-sixth of English cultivatable land for more active development, not by Crown or People but by the most purposeful of the old and new aristocracies. Protestantism, too, save for Primitive Anabaptists, did not envisage Franciscan holy poverty. 'Money', Wesley said, 'is unspeakably precious.'

Accidents of individual personality – Luther, Lenin, Eden and Nasser in 1956 – do not invent history but can give tendencies an individual jolt and flavour. Henry VIII, inwardly as much medieval as renaissance, no Protestant but a spendthrift, neurotic, nationalistic, became his own pope, with consequences he never foresaw.

The face of popular life changed. Cathedrals had evolved slowly, varying styles achieving complex unity, adding new lights to the old shadows huddled in strange corners, carved with furtive, grinning devils. Protestant churches and chapels were now to be tidier, unpainted, austere, shying away from the lavish, seething,

yearning, Counter-Reformation Baroque, operatic and propagandic.
The sprawling Catholic mythology reminded Protestants of Smithfield, Inquisition, Armada. Iconography affronted Puritanism as it
had Islam. The Mass narrowed to Sermon, Psalm, Hymn, sometimes richly glowing – Byrd, Handel – sometimes banal.

> Let us with a gladsome mind
> Praise the Lord for He is kind.

Changes could be cruel. The wilderness must be sown and
reaped; Canaanites be eliminated on the way. The Puritan re-
former, Dowsing, of no generous vision, was one of those who grasp
some fragment of life, expand it and thrust it on others as God's
Will, encouraging what Dickens called 'the national dread of
colour', at their worst resembling the Thugs who combined private
respectability with ritual strangling of strangers. Dowsing injured
East Anglia more than bombers, in 1664 alone smashing 841
painted windows. He records:

> At Clare, 6 January. We broke down 1000 superstitious pictures.
> I broke down 200, 4 of God the Father and 3 of Christ and the
> Holy Lamb, and 3 of the Holy Ghost like a Dove, with a whip;
> and the 12 Apostles were carved in wood on the top of the
> roof, which I gave orders to be taken down, and 20 cherubims
> to be taken down, and the Sun and the Moon in the East
> Window to be taken down.

English Protestantism identified Catholic Europe with absolutism,
corruption, censorship, bigotry, persecution surmounted by vicious
splendour. The Pope had deposed Elizabeth, 1570. Gunpowder
Plot, Great Fire, Popish Plot roused credulous, chauvinist mobs
and unscrupulous intriguers against Catholics – as Plague had
against Jews – to riot, blackmail, lynching, repeated in the Gordon
Riots, 1780, when looting unemployed howled against Irish Catholic
immigrants. Catholic queen-consorts were natural scapegoats for
unpopular policies.

Lunatic frenzies had some justification in that Charles II became a secret Catholic, accepting money from the Catholic aggres-
sor, Louis XIV, to outmanoeuvre a Paliament tinged with republicanism. His successor, James II, against advice from the Vatican
and Versailles, attempted almost single-handed a Catholic despotism, ensuring actual revolution, 1688.

Later prejudices must have responded complacently to Hogarth's
'Calais Gate', with its greedy, greasy priest. Penal Laws, 1695–
1829, limited Catholic rights in property, politics, education.

Moderate Tory Protestantism, prospering on commerce and empire, was content with the old alliance of Throne and Church, somewhat modified to include Parliament. Not so the poorer and more militant, to whom bishops were tools of Crown and Property and the rich were minions of Satan. 'Right Prelating is busy Labouring and not Lording,' Latimer had preached.

Puritanism had many sinews, temporarily united in the Civil War but, at the killing of Charles I, dissolving into angry sects competing under the more broadly-based Cromwell government. Roundhead leaders, Hampden, Pym, Fairfax, Manchester, Cromwell, the wealthy, God-fearing squires, merchants, sea-captains, would scarcely abolish private property and privilege at the behest of visionaries, humourless preachers, discontented soldiery, a few saints and serious political theorists : the Levellers, Anabaptists, Quakers, Ranters, Fifth Monarchists, who saw sober England in terms of Jewish history and the Apocalypse. Property, by imposing responsibility, seemed a form of Grace, entitling its owners to earthly privilege. Equality existed within sight of God but, in the World, hierarchy was necessary for men, for animals. Equality could not manage a ship, company, nation. Belief in God as personal arbiter of human destinies long survived. During the American Civil War, Lincoln considered, 1862,

By His mere great power on the minds of the now contestants, He could have destroyed the Union without a human contest. Yet the contest began, and, having begun, He could give the final victory to either side any day.

Puritanism could derive not from self-confidence but from fear : fear of the body, of disorder, poverty, the Devil. From the unconscious erupted demons, temptations, appetites, condemned by the Will, ascribed to Satan. One did not have to be a Knox or Calvin to share Robespierre's revulsion at Danton's definition of virtue, as what he practised nightly with his wife. From the Reformation can be discerned early lineaments of Tennyson's 'British goddess, sleek respectability'.

Blanket definitions and prejudices cannot cover the many-ranging effects of the British non-conformist conscience. Sensations of sin, sexual guilt, vague oppression, can stimulate a social awareness. After civil war and persecution, Dissent distrusted lay government while continuing to promulgate the despotic pulpits, and paternal authority, against sin, against laziness.

Dissenters – and Catholics – were excluded from public office until 1829, practising Jews until 1858. Only after 1871 could they teach at Oxford and Cambridge. Their busy energies would be expertly channelled, not only into capitalism, but into crusades for reform, humanitarianism, social justice, free trade. Puritanism implies concentration. Clarkson, Gurney, Wilberforce, Zachary Macaulay, often opposed by many Anglican bishops, successfully attacked slavery. Unitarians, like the scientist, Priestley, welcomed the principles of the French Revolution. Nonconformists were active amongst the first trade-unions, co-operatives, Free Traders, the early Labour Party : they were foremost in missionary enterprise overseas, proselytising, doctoring and denouncing. Descendants from those fleeing north of London after the Restoration became prominent in industry, utilitarianism, invention. British banking, including Barclay's, owed much to Quakers, one of whom, William Tuke, built Britain's first humane lunatic asylum, the York Retreat, 1796.

Like Mormons, the Quakers proved the practical advantages of virtue, enterprise, hard work, leading to the good things of God's earth. The religious have never been backward in equating worldly success with heavenly grace. 'God gave me my money,' said the oil millionaire, Rockefeller.

Cromwell himself was more enthusiastic about education than many Augustans. Puritan Dissent helped found Church schools, Sunday Schools, Working Men's Colleges, University College, London, the Universities of Durham and Manchester. Dissent had an ethos of moral and political usefulness, self-righteous participation. Inclined to bully, it was thrusting, competitive, industrious; mistrustful of the body, eroticism, physical beauty, eccentricity; at best reforming, through a Lloyd George, at worst, nosy. 'He who hates vice, hates men,' Danton gibed at Robespierre. Its social conscience and moral vigour infused much English art, through Blake, Hogarth, Fielding, Defoe, Thackeray, Dickens, George Eliot, D. H. Lawrence, Wells, and Orwell. As an apologia for reform, not revolution, English Dissent was the despair of Marx and Lenin.

> Lord, I ascribe it to thy Grace
>   And not to chance as others do,
> That I was born of Christian race
>   And not a heathen or a Jew.

(Dr Watts, 1715)

11 Monarchy

Royalty is government in which the
attention of the nation is concentrated
on one person doing interesting things.

Bagehot

I

Monarchy is a vital emotional drive though it takes devious forms,
not least in republics and soviets. The Crown compromised between
reason and magic. It was simultaneously a Department of State and
national fetish, the depth of the one usually in inverse proportion
to that of the other. 'Royalty', Bagehot considered, 'will be strong
because it appeals to diffused feelings. Its mystery is its hope.'

However feeble a feudal monarch, he did not invalidate Monarchy, the personal summary of government, the primitive sacra-
ment binding society. It can still convince without formal evidence :
the Webbs revering Stalin; Lindbergh praising Hitler.

The Tudor monarchy combined efficiency with mystery, in
glamour still unfaded. For nearly a century it remained resolutely,
even excitingly, in control, curbing the armed aristocracy – Warwick
the King-maker and his 7,000 retainers – freeing trade from
foreigners, encouraging and co-profiting with the City, consolidating
overseas enterprise, effecting religious settlement, patronizing the
arts, directing the nation with acumen and economy. The Crown
was like Brechtian drama : pageantry, debate, instruction, 'a basis
for action'.

The most successful administrators and theorists – Alfred,
Canute, the Conqueror, Elizabeth, Burghley, Hooker, Walpole,
Chatham, Hume, Locke, Burke, Mill, Bentham, Lloyd George,
Attlee, were never utopianists. The failures, Mary, James II, saw
abstract impossibilities instead of diagnosing actual circumstances
or regarding real people. Some, like Charles I and Strafford, were
forced to extremes by extreme situations. Some, like Ramsay
MacDonald, mistook eloquence for leadership. The high-minded
Mary Tudor could have profited from Melbourne's causticism :
'Things are coming to a pretty pass when religion is allowed to
invade private life.'

Chance could interfere : Henry VIII's lack of male heir, Edward VI's ill-health; but three exceptional monarchs maintained stable policies with gifted authoritarian ministers – Dudley, Wolsey, Cromwell, Northumberland, Burghley – and officials, always dependent on the Crown. Lack of pedigree obstructed neither advancement nor degradation. Royal favour, monastic loot, outright purchase, endowed the Cecils, Seymours, Cavendishes, Courtenays, Villiers, Pagets, Russells, Herberts, so dominant in public life for three centuries. The Tudors were of the European Renaissance, pragmatic, politically amoral, fitfully cruel, connoisseurs of art, language, sensation. Only Mary was fanatical. Despite individual enormities there would be no English St Bartholomew Massacre, burning of Magdeburg, or Revocation of the Edict of Nantes.

2

Self-confidence assists art, particularly the art of government, which needs charm, patience, responsible selfishness, executive flair, and, as the Tudors recognized, a signal mingling of sensitivity and aloofness. This was personal performance afterwards misunderstood by all save Charles II. Tudor success was that of recognizing that, for a small country on bad terms even with Scotland, sea-power and adroit diplomacy were essential for initial survival, then for advance. They knew that ideology enflames emotions but only rarely – under a King Philip, a Hitler – does it condition policy. With a Crown acquired by violence and – unlike the French – without a regular army, the Crown ruled by splendour, but not by splendour alone. Never despising trade, it built ships, leased them to merchants, stimulated the planting of overseas depots that would become colonies, grateful, or forced to be grateful, for English trade and protection. The Board of Trade and Plantations, from 1969, was to wield powers greater than those of many European governments. For the Stuart plantation of Ulster by Scottish Protestants, few today are probably grateful.

Foreign policy was unromantic, seldom tempted, like Henry VIII, towards arbitrary extravagant gestures, though Wolsey momentarily dreamed of an England pronouncing decisions between Bourbon France and Habsburg Spain – of a Pope Wolsey, an Emperor Henry. *Festina lente* was a favourite renaissance motto, elasticity of conduct a renaissance strategy of life, in which one could be plunderer and killer, poet and musician, Defender of the Faith, head of Christ's Church in England, zealous womanizer and reproachful husband.

Consolidating order after the feudal Roses turmoil, the Crown simplified power, centralizing to an uncommon degree, not only through Parliament, Common Law, JPs, but through the prerogative Courts, more inclined towards Roman Law, judging without jury, enforcing decrees from London and York against feudalists too independent, and cavalier towards courts more traditional. Magistrates and JPs fixed prices and wages. The Crown attempted, often vainly, to protect the poor against exploitation and irresponsible enclosing.

The Monarchy continued the medieval indifference to nationality: legally, the Monarch himself could be Welsh, Scottish, Dutch, German. The Welsh Tudors preserved the institutions: Council, Parliament, Parish, Episcopacy. Henry VIII, spreading the responsibility, used Parliament to push through the abolition of Papal power, dissolution of the monasteries, seizure of Roman tithes. Thereafter, the State appointed bishops, for long exponents of docility, conservatism, even conformist propaganda.

Protests were feeble, amongst the ruling classes. An occasional More recoiled, and suffered. Only when threats from the feudal North, from the Counter-Reformation, from Spain, diminished would Parliament shed obsequiousness.

Tudor contrasts are too spectacular for comfort. The aura was glowing yet disquieting. Despair and stricken nerves were never far from the jewels and lutes, the virginals, galliards and marchpane. The great rulers must have been more nervous than they seemed. A lonely, inherited chill seems huddled within their slow, resplendent forms. Henry VII, with his triumph and calculations, Henry VIII with anthems and madrigals, wives and secrets . . . one recalls young Edward VI's hard, unyouthful observations, Mary's frustrated agonies and atrocious epithet, and the tensions that would have stopped a weaker heart than that of the shrewd, dramatic, intellectual Elizabeth. Lesser figures, Pole, Jane Grey, the Norfolks, do not evoke gaiety. 'After darkness, I hope for light,' Jane wrote at the end. The leading career politicians, from Dudley to Essex, seem wearing skins of armour, gleaming, but cold to touch. Only More, even on the scaffold, reminds one of generosity, humour, good manners.

Yet human touches pierce the stiff, brocade-like atmosphere. Henry VII's accounts included 'To the children playing in the garden, 9/4d.' 'To beer drunken at the farmer's house, 1/–.' 'To a fellow for eating coals, 5/–.' Elizabeth, ever afraid of death, kept at her bed-head, a locked casket. At the end they found inside it 'his last letter', sent by the dying, enigmatic Leicester. Her father's court was a congress of learning, art, jocularity, of ceremony, processions, music, the ruler exchanging 'Your Grace' for

'Your Majesty'. The next dynast, James, typically overdid it, demanding 'Your Sacred Majesty'. But imaginary children dogged these versatile, capable monarchs, and the courtiers who had lost so many relatives. 'My son will rule,' Anne Boleyn said. She was not alone in being drastically mistaken.

The Crown used axe and stake, torture, mutilation, attainder, violation of safe-conducts, against dissent, treason, heresy, recusancy. Also, secret police, with their half-promises, hidden examinations, torture. The bias of Tudor show trials long survived: it was not wholly lacking as late as the Casement trial, 1916.

The court had periodic savage reminders from ulcerous, accomplished Henry VIII that ministerial powers could lapse bloodily. Howards, Seymours, Dudleys were always at hand, ambitious and unscrupulous, with Cromwells and Cecils in their train. Lyric and madrigal encircled the block; syphilis blackened love. Whitehall, Nonesuch, held glittering shadows, epitomized by the operatic Anne Boleyn, who ravaged Henry's wilful passions until the moment she accepted him, and incited his poetry.

> O my hart and o my hart,
>   My hart it is so sore.
> Sense I must nedys from my love depart,
>   And know no cause wherefore.

Restless, moody, black-haired, black-eyed, 'Nan Bullen', Queen of England, was to be arraigned at a public Show Trial of treason, incest, adultery, at which her own father hastened to affirm belief in her guilt and approve her sentence. Elizabeth's mother was beheaded by the sword of a masked 'master-craftsman' from Calais, at the cost of £23 6s 8d. 'It is a very little neck,' she had said, as always wavering between mirthless laughter, and tears never wholly miserable. In the Tower she was said to have composed 'O Death, rock me asleep'. The scene seems specifically Tudor: the song, the sword hidden under straw, to spare her feelings but not her body. Her life was hysterical, her death had the dignity that the scaffold rites – so much black velvet, so many soundless, frozen figures, such distorted areas of blessing, exhortation, salutation, curses, secret fears and hopes, and the thudding farewell – called from so many sufferers . . . Dudley, Empson, Buckingham, More, Cromwell, Somerset, Northumberland: and Mary Stuart 'apparralled in a kind of joye', then lying headless under a billiard cloth, her dog creeping from beneath her skirts; then Norfolk, Essex, Raleigh, Strafford, King Charles, Russell, Monmouth, some of whom found in death the resolution not given in life.

Ruined by her ambitions, appalled by her triumph, not recognizably guilty nor perhaps quite innocent. Anne, fairy-tale princess
pursued by an evil spell in an unreal kingdom, survived in country
lore, seen as a ghost driving a coach, or as a hare, her father's
spectre chased across Norfolk by infernal dogs, the Gabriel Hounds
carved, with the Wild Huntsman, at Stoke Gabriel Church.

Tudor and Stuart Courts were graced by Erasmus, Linacre,
More, Cranmer, Holbein, Pole, Philip Sidney, Spenser, Hooker,
Parker, Raleigh, John Harrington, Byrd, Bacon, Ben Jonson, Inigo
Jones, Van Dyck, Kneller, Harvey, Prince Rupert, Pepys, Dowland,
none of whom was a narrow specialist. 'No slug, Raleigh,' Aubrey
commented. Women developed apace with men. In her teens,
Lady Jane Grey was not exceptional in knowing Italian, Hebrew,
French, Greek and Latin.

To minds less lettered there were other preoccupations. Since
Katherine of Aragon, England had been within the Spanish orbit
and, with the marriage of Philip and Mary, Englishmen feared
that they would soon be within the Spanish Empire, soon to be
pirated so zestfully by the Devonian seamen.

> Flower of England, Fruit of Spain,
> Met together in a shower of Rain.

The shower put out no heresy-fires and, not for the last time,
the London government was hooted at for policies hateful to public
opinion. The Prince of Spain seemed Prince of Darkness, the Pope
Bishop of Hell, Bloody Mary the luckless witch, and Elizabeth
Gloriana, the golden fairy. Yet the black was inextricably en-
grained within the gold.

Catering for all human contraries, the Elizabethan monarchy
was a dazzling display of paradox, the brutal and enslaving entwined with the tender and exquisite. The Queen herself was a
theatrical, a painfully-held balance of Boleyn and Tudor, of
indecision and ruthlessness, morbidity and luminous energy, of
culture and undisclosed appetites, with radiance and self-doubts
close to Hamlet's. She could watch animal torture; her successor,
human torture. She presided over and perhaps inspired national
achievement: Protestant sea-power, the commercial enterprises
of Gresham, the good sense of Hooker, the paintings of Hilliard,
polyphony of Tallis, Weelkes, Byrd, poetry of Jonson and Shakespeare, Spenser and Donne. Yet exactions were sore. Lawlessness
and suspicion were everywhere, making *laissez-faire* unthinkable.
The State was ruler: sanctuary rights had been abolished, men
directly faced the Monarch or his representative.

England itself was changing. Shakespeare could have seen old, dispossessed monks, newly enclosed fields, mechanized draining, blast furnaces, novel Sheffield steel, the production of soap, coal, lead, iron, glass, copper and brass.[58]

London's interference was stricter than under many of the Hanoverians, attempting to order how people should worship, dress, work, fight, play, marry, beg, trade. The printing press facilitated effective power. Tillage Acts against inefficient farmers pre-viewed modern socialist measures. A 1545 law on credit legislation is still unrepealed. 'One is oppressed, one is almost stifled, by the completeness and intimacy of the controls.' (Rowse) The Queen did not aspire to dictatorship but she wanted order, protection from Spain and Scotland, also to have her own way, at least among her immediates. Like all Tudors she could be neglectful of Common Law, arbitrarily excluding Raleigh from public service and despatching him to the Tower for marrying; also Peter Wentworth, for too plain a demand in the Commons for free speech. 'Your privilege', she told Parliament in after years, 'Is aye or no.' Already restive, Parliament was to seek further privilege : when a Stuart imprisoned Sir John Eliot or attempted to silence Members, protests were more ominous. Meanwhile, Topcliffe's Elizabethan secret police and spies were everywhere. A Cambridge friend of Marlowe's was burnt for atheism. Merchants, shipwrights, mayors had to be tolerably respected by the Crown but Kyd's lines were not incongruous despite Elizabethan wonders.

> O eyes, no eyes but fountains fraught with tears,
> O life, no life but lively form of death,
> O world, no world, but mass of public wrongs.

Tragedy was the age's profoundest imaginative achievement but

> Goodnight, sweet Prince,
> And flights of angels sing thee to thy rest.

was uttered, even shouted, to audiences equally attuned to blood-drenched cockpits and scaffolds. Countrymen could be no less callous. Evelyn Hardy[59] shows Irish refusing to rescue drowning Spanish co-religionists, believing, like African peasants today, that by depriving it of lawful prizes they would offend the sea.

Public life seemed to pace the Queen's ageing. In the tragic fall of Essex, even of Mary, inescapable Death gibed at renaissance colour, juggled with the grim follies and ironic tricks of existence which could identify love with disease and ruin, self-discovery with

hell, knowledge with Faust's reward. 'In greatness is no trust,'
Beaumont mused over royal tombs at Westminster; 'though gods
they were, as men they died.' The Reformation made many dread
Death more than they trusted in God. An upsurge of sombre
Puritan preachers, distasteful to the Queen, saw life as Death's ante-
room. 'The bright day is done, and we are for the dark.'

3

Hindsight shows the Monarchy more questioned from about 1590,
with the Commons, the lawyers, merchants, country gentry, many
of them Puritan, nagging at the old Queen's prerogatives, commerce
discontented with capricious royal monopolies, Puritanism assault-
ing the Anglican hierarchy. The City, always a rival and jealous
community, was more radical against an arbitrary Crown than
against a corrupt and unrepresentative parliament. Though papal
threats had receded, Spain seemed still disappointingly powerful.
The Stuarts had, with inferior talents, to cope with much not of
their own making: inflation, dissent, dissatisfaction not with
Monarchy but with royal rights long accepted, though some minds
must have pondered the Dutch Hague Abjuration of 1581 against
Philip, that the King had broken his contract and was to be
dismissed like any other unfaithful servant.

Feudal dangers had ended with the beheadings of Norfolk and
Mary. Cecils, Howards, Villiers sat secure on monastery lands. No
Catholic would, it seemed, reign in Whitehall. Imperial currents
were flowing. Formerly so paternalist and progressive, the Crown
could now appear wilful and obstructionist. Intellectual and artistic,
the Stuarts lacked flair. Also, they were foreign. Pepys's opinion
was common : 'The truth is, there is so universal a rooted nastiness
about the person of every Scot (man and woman) that renders the
finest show they can make nauseous, even amongst those of the
finest quality.' Court favouritism and monopolies excusable by
Elizabeth, was increasingly resented. James I lacked dignity. His
Court had sinister Tudor elements but without the majesty : was
corrupt and sensational rather than awesome. Carr and Villiers
were mediocre, even silly beside Raleigh, whose killing, reputedly
to appease Spain, was reckoned a national disgrace. That friendship
with Spain had advantages was noisily unappreciated by Elizabethan
survivors, though senior ministers took Spanish cash.

Inflation was corroding the royal income, while royal responsibilities increased. New or revived taxations by James and Charles
were denounced as illegal and tyrannical, lawyers exhuming Magna
Carta of which, in *King John*, Shakespeare seems not to have

heard. Such powerful lawyers as Coke would not have forgotten Bracton's belief that the Crown must give as well as take. Royal theorizing aggravated the tensions.

The early Stuarts, also, were uneasy outside their splendid palaces, so alive with taste and wit, spectacle, intrigue and resentment. The family had already suffered regicide, from an English queen, wholly supported by an English mob. James I was terrified of assassination. Charles I perhaps would sink into melancholy fantasy, into the glowing depths of his masques, curios, books, paintings, the sumptuous harvest of his taste which ranged freely amongst the masterpieces of Europe and England : Rubens, Van Dyck, Shakespeare, Jonson, Dobson.

Grand trappings often conceal precarious power or weaken power hitherto accepted. Napoleon's stolen crowns made his family ridiculous. James' 'Divine Right' was an uneasy appeal not to Law or personal prestige, but to magic, inappropriate to an ungainly, unusually fallible homosexual in padded clothes seated on Elizabeth's throne, unsuited to an age that would know Hume and Locke, and particularly dangerous in London. London was the largest, most turbulent city in Europe, without general franchise but loving political quarrels, the abuse and acclamations of a Raleigh, Essex, Buckingham, Laud, Clarendon, Shaftesbury, howling for Strafford's head and for 'King Pym' as, a century later, they would for 'Wilkes and Liberty'. Squirearchy and commerce were becoming loyal to the Crown, no longer as leader or defender, but as symbol.

Royal attempts to rely on Council and Church, against Parliament, were seldom illegal, but unrealistic, continually foundering on insolvency. Episcopal aggression evoked counter-aggression. Puritans were prosecuted, evicted, mutilated : a Headmaster of Westminster was condemned, though vainly, to have his ears nailed to a post, before his own pupils. No Stuart possessed a quorum of what Elizabeth counted as royal virtues : 'Justice, Temper, Magnanimity, Judgement'.

English defence costs proved as dire to Charles I as American did to George III. Inevitable disputes about control of taxation broadened to acrimony about control of soldiers. The government's sensible decision for an unheroic part in the Thirty Years War left militancy free for internal violence, with 'the Interests' – Shipping, Printing, Cloth, the City and Law-Courts resolutely Parliamentarian. Yet civil war opened tentatively, with less excitement than the latter-day struggles over Reform, Corn-Laws, and the Parliament Act of 1911. To rejoice at Buckingham's murder, Strafford's execution, to insult Laud, was easier than to fight an anointed King. Direct action evokes unsuspected loyalties and dilemmas. Only Munich (1938) and Suez (1956) divided the nation more thoroughly than the public beheading of the dignified but morally unreliable Charles, whose 'tyranny' became mild and constitutional compared to that of Cromwell, Richelieu, and the Puritan colonial governors. After the public execution of a king, loyalty to the throne, though it may increase in fervour, must be more self-conscious, a political and emotional decision, defensive or challenging. No longer a primitive, sacramental matter of choice.

4

In the Republic (1649–1660), Protector, 'Rump', Army, Presbyterian Preachers, finally Cromwell alone, imposed one law throughout the island, as harsh towards revolutionary extremists as towards royalists. Illiberal towards gross popular pleasures, it permitted controversial, even extravagant pamphleteering, a rare toleration for Catholics, the return of Jews. Witches were energetically prosecuted, Matthew Hopkins, 'Witchfinder-in-chief', student of James I's *Demonology*, causing several hundred East Anglian floggings, imprisonments, executions.

Though, briefly, brains and talent now counted more than birth, generous republican aspirations mostly failed : proposals for women's suffrage, secret ballot, national schools. From the Putney debates, 1647, amongst Cromwell's soldiers, came the basis of the first draft of the American Constitution. The Rump Parliament became unworkable, buzzing with too-noisy sectaries. Like love, political audacity thrives on frustration : once enthroned, it tends to dissolve. Levellers, Cromwellians began hating each other more than the royalists. Cromwell was forced to substitute major-generals for Members and Lords-Lieutenant, presbyters for Church, finally himself for King. He hardened London's grip. Simultaneously he was fighting a Dutch war, a Spanish war, acquiring Jamaica and invading the Mediterranean. His England became a leading power in a Europe still awash with the blood of the Thirty Years War. Blake and Cromwell, men of conscience, nevertheless realized that not English morality but English ships would promote influence abroad, a conviction discarded only after 1945.

At his best, Oliver Cromwell, opposing his military and religious militants, was an English radical, opportunist, concerned less with things than with people, less with committees than with direct action, impatient with muddle, fractiousness, petty or vindictive obstruction, liable more to anger than hysteria, accepting personal responsibility – though with a grievous habit of covering, say, an Irish massacre with divine sanction. Freud was to name a son after him.

He maintained or transformed more institutions than he destroyed. C. V. Wedgewood[60] finds him virtual founder of the Civil Service where 'the sense of public duty' supersedes traits more subjective. Britain's only dictator, he differed from Lenin and Hitler, who wanted not a better society but the Perfect State, rejecting all long-standing institutions – independent juries, judges, press, church – save the most primitive – the army and police – and the most obstinate – the bureaucracy.

That, with his personal God, he also had dark limitations is still remembered in Ireland, where his savagery outmatched the Tudor. Confiscating over half the country, dispossessing 6,000 landlords, responsible for a notorious massacre, transporting hundreds to the Caribbean, setting up ugly camps for Catholic priests on Arran, he succumbed to the vicious Anglo-Irish madness. The Irish, of rich personalities, language, potentials, were for generations liable to eviction by absentee landlords, taxed to support an alien religion, periodically afflicted with famine, their protests pitilessly suppressed. Penal Laws, denounced by Burke, to whom governors should be not lords but trustees, forbade the Catholic majority to hold office, inherit land, and virtually deprived them of franchise, education, freedom of worship.

In England, the generals were bullying and small-minded, and have never significantly returned to politics. The Republic, a minority solution, now depended on Cromwell alone, who refused to admit the supernatural appeal of more traditional monarchy. Reluctance to support the Crown totally changed to reluctance to reject it totally. The sub-divided English class-pattern, unaltered by the Republic, allowed much freedom of action by the Interests, who generally sought some popular assent, 'a defence of liberties'. The Monarchy was restored, on probation. No Divine Right but a profitable peace policy allowed Charles II, in his last years, relative freedom from Parliament, in which the Interests began converging in a loose but discernible dual-party system, with passionate, sometimes bloody, struggles about Liberty.

'Liberty' did not mean liberal democracy. Its most brilliant leader and agitator, Shaftesbury, owned slave-interests. He wanted an England uncluttered by the hazards of royalty and the dangerous importunities of the poor. The under-privileged were not to demand privileges, and were seldom to be granted them. The rational temper of a propertied elite would guarantee social stability.

In general, Whig pragmatism never regarded reason, order,

system, responsibility, so essential to a trading society, as latent in the mob. That liberty could co-exist with poverty and injustice did not yet seem incongruous. 'Liberty' defended property, sometimes by bloodshed, against irresponsible, frivolous or feeble executives, against unacceptable royal taxes, against Catholicism. It did not seek to exemplify selflessness or even probity. Speaker Lenthall, who defied Charles I, also paid his fellow-members lavishly to prevent prosecution for embezzlement. The history of Parliament suggests some truth in Herr Settembrini's remark, in *The Magic Mountain*, that malice is the animating spirit of criticism, and criticism is the beginning of progress and enlightenment.

There was something of both in Stuart England: the Royal Society; the writings of Clarendon, Halifax, Dryden, Rochester; Restoration Comedy; the extension of trade and settlement in India, America, Africa. Habeas Corpus was enacted, though both in England and America it is never irrevocable. Lincoln suspended it during civil war, 1864. Britain suspended it during both World Wars, and in Northern Ireland, 1971.

Sea-power still fluctuated. Under the early Stuarts, Barbary pirates had slave-raided in British waters. Cromwell successfully counter-attacked. Charles II's Dutch wars saw the burning of Chatham but the capture of New Amsterdam (New York) in America and the final seizure of the British colonial carrying trade from Dutch shipping. Also:

The elevation of Pepys at the age of forty by the royal brothers, to the secretaryship of the Admiralty, though little noticed at the time, produced results which affected not England alone but the whole world. By his precept and example he created the modern Civil Service, and transformed a muddled, extravagant and inefficient naval organization into the most lasting and powerful instrument of force since Rome.

(Arthur Bryant, *Samuel Pepys: The Years of Peril*, Collins, 1935)

Charles II died, 1685. Bishop Burnet wrote:

The King's body was very indecently neglected. Some parts of his inards and some pieces of the fat were left in the water in which they were washed: all which were so carelessly looked after, that the water being poured out at a scullery hole that went to a drain in the mouth of which a grate lay, these were seen lying in the grate many days after.

The English had always refused a regular army controlled by a King, who could legally recruit wild Irish and Scottish. The papist,

James II (1685–88) attempted a personal Catholic absolutism supported by a standing army, the more justified by Monmouth's hapless attempt on the Crown. The Interests rallied against James, on the principle that the Law was superior to the King: class-interest and national interest were superior to royal interest. Courageously refusing at the cost of his office a command royal but illegal to admit a Catholic monk to Magdalen, Dr Peachell, the Vice-Chancellor – of whose red nose Pepys wrote that it 'makes me ashamed to be seen with him, though otherwise a good-natured man' – confided to the Secretary: 'the laws of the land and the oaths we lie under are the fences of God's church and religion, and I cannot suffer myself to be made an instrument to pull down those fences.'

Like Vortigern, the Interests summoned aid from overseas, replacing James by his Dutch son-in-law, though on definite terms, A proved warrior against aggressive France, William could be relied upon to do duty as national saviour and, as joint-sovereign with Mary, not to overdo it. In Holland he had been no absolute monarch, but merely First Magistrate and military commander of a turbulent republic. He could thus fit in, occasionally impatiently, with English compromises and cabals and help them to work.

The 1688 settlement ended personal rule through Privy Council and Prerogative. Thereafter, troops, taxation, policy were controlled by regular Parliaments. Trade was now too complex and wide-ranging to depend on royal caprice. Henceforward it was the responsibility of experts, long unconcerned with much social conscience. A sense of the absolute rights of property and money prevailed. Significantly, the leading philosopher of the age, Locke, also helped reform the coinage. There also evolved that signal conception of the Legal Opposition, vehemently rejected by Lenin, by which failed Ministers no longer forfeited liberty, even life. Liable to petty vote-catching explosiveness, it proved a workable outlet for vigours dangerous when blocked. The theories of Locke dismissed magic from British government as those of Newton did from matter, though more devious irrationalism lingered on, like garbled recollections of human sacrifice secreted in a nursery-rhyme.

The Monarch was now tamed by the Interests, their terms more severe as Cabinet government solidified and the Empire widened. The brief reign of Edward VIII (1936) showed how severe. ('Hark the Herald Angels sing, Mrs Simpson's pinched our King,' the children sang.) Yet the Crown remained more than a cipher. For centuries it retained important areas of patronage. George III attempted some parliamentary manipulation, not through Divine

Right but as a politician influencing his fellows. The extent of his personal ambitions is still disputed. Informed interference was characteristic of Victoria. Edward VII had some, though exaggerated, diplomatic role.

> There'll be no war
> 'Long as we've a King like Good King Edward,
> For he hates that sort of thing.

Bagehot's definition of constitutional monarchy's three inalienable rights, 'To be consulted, to encourage, to warn', has been preserved, not least by George VI in relations with Attlee; also in some private yearnings for a Crown safeguarding popular feeling and by-passing the Party elite. There is a story that his father, George V, holding himself judging public opinion more correctly, employed the long disused royal prerogative and countermanded a Cabinet decision permitting his cousin, the deposed Tsar, to enter Britain as an exile, though anyone wishing to pursue this at the Windsor archives will not find himself encouraged. The Crown drains off emotions that might otherwise crystallize around politicians. 'A Royal Family', Bagehot continued, 'sweetens politics by the seasonable addition of nice and pretty events. It introduces irrelevant facts into the business of government, but they are facts which "speak to men's bosoms" and employ their thoughts.' Bagehot's view was confirmed as recently as 1973, when, in a month of political sex-scandals, a royal romance 'spoke to men's bosoms'.

Conceivably, if Parliament finds itself on the defensive, against the EEC, supranational corporations, powerful trade unions, regional separatism, government departments ruling by decree, police assisted by too many ununiformed 'law enforcement officers', together with popular cynicism, people's thoughts may stray from nice and pretty events, in directions not at the moment clear.

5

Abroad, monarchy had fortunes more dynamic. Charles V had seemed a true Roman Emperor, or Charlemagne, ruling (1530) in Austria, Germany, Hungary, Spain, Bohemia, the Low Countries, much of Italy, North Africa, Central America, the Pacific. Yet his effort for European unity failed, harassed by revolts and Reformation. God too seemed like an author who has disowned his book, and Vatican pretentions had largely dwindled into one more European throne. Subsequently, the Thirty Years War strengthened the thrusting national monarchies to whom continental unity was displeasing even as an ideal. The war prolonged feudal privileges, ruined thousands of villages and cities – Nuremburg males were licensed, 1650, to take two wives each for ten years to repair war-casualties, difficult to envisage in London or Bristol – and impeded middle-class liberties. Christian Russia, Prussia, Austria united only to eliminate Christian Poland. To these, as to Spain, England, Bavaria, France was the most dangerous, notoriously in the Pala-tinate devastations, 1674 and 1689. From then until Waterloo, 1815, France regularly invaded German states, a fact largely forgotten in the twentieth century by all save Germans.

Unlike the Germans, the French were traditionally difficult to rule, provinces and corporations jealously guarding ancient rights even against the Crown, which had thus to glitter more fiercely. The Estates-General pronounced, 1614, 'The King is Sovereign in France; he holds his throne from God alone, and there is no power on earth, whatever it may be, spiritual or temporal, which has any right in respect of his realm, which can deprive the King's sacred person of it, or dispense or absolve his subjects from their loyalty and obedience which they owe him, for any cause or on any pretext whatsoever.' Though withdrawn, its sentiments were not forgotten, particularly by Richelieu and Louis XIV.

Like Bismarck, Richelieu demanded social discipline strict as Palladian designs, thereby creating a throne too large for those likely to sit on it. The reaction, 1792, had its own sinister grandeur. The Cardinal, subtle, logical, cultivated, yet resembled Luther in mistrust of other people. An all-powerful throne and church were essential to preserve not individual rights but national security, national myth. The Estates-General, which had affinities with the English Parliament, he ignored, fatefully. Like Lenin he subor-dinated justice, morality, belief to this end. 'In State affairs, justice does not demand authentic proof.' He was closer to Robespierre than either would have welcomed.

Recovering from war-atrocities, European monarchy easily imi-tated France. The State of Tsar or King was now a religion. 'One Faith, One Law, One King.' Louis XIV's dictum has since grown tediously familiar, as have his wars for 'the liberation of minorities', even 'the incorporation of racial comrades'. Moral and practical counter-attack would swiftly emerge. 'Teutonic super-iority over all other forms of civilization is firmly established, quite apart from its military power, which assures it of victory.' (Fichte, 1762–1814) Erasmus might have lived in vain. One sighs for Mon-taigne, detached, gently amused, concerned, despising nothing but humbug, serene amongst the dangers and frenzies of Counter-Reformation.

Uniformed seventeenth-century armies were drilling on Roman scale under untrustworthy despots. Swedish conscription and regular pay were soon copied by Prussia, the New Sparta, barren, envious of more prosperous neighbours, particularly under the ambitious Frederick the Great (1712–86) whose father declared : 'Desertion is from Hell, the work of the Devil's spawn.' Frederick, in triumphant vainglory, spent two-thirds of the national income on the army.

War can simplify labour relations, restore purpose to blighted lives. Eighteenth-century wars stimulated science and machinery for mass-production. Other ways were available, 'Fighting,' Frederick, admirer of Voltaire, patron of Bach, remarked, 'there must be more fighting. You ask why? Merely to make a name for us!' Voltaire might have relished more the King's definition of a crown as 'just a hat that lets in water'.

Even courts for whose patronage of minority tastes and philosophies posterity is grateful, flourished at exorbitant public cost. Cromwell had sold Charles I's famous paintings, to restock the Treasury. 1,400 Versailles fountains used more water than was allowed all Paris. The building of Versailles, like that of St Petersburg, cost hundreds of lives, and its routine annually cost France a quarter of her Budget. Foreign policy tended to be ludicrous or malicious : to steal a neighbour's country was less immoral than to steal a neighbour's wife.

Large continental armies needed swollen bureaucracies, a process largely avoided by Britain who, relying on savagely recruited and ill-paid sea-power, would postpone wholesale war for as long as possible. She preferred to supply temporary allies with money and equipment rather than men.

That the 'Enlightened Despots' preferred Law as decree rather than as a live, evolving organism, did not deprive them of all enlightenment. Habsburgs – Maria Theresa, Joseph II, Leopold II – effected major reforms in taxation, health, the army, land, serfdom, education. Voltaire and Mirabeau admired the Prussian Civil Code. Peace treaties, save towards Poles, were relatively civilized, re-arranging overseas possessions and frontier fortresses, seeking indemnities, but without question of genocide. The monarchs could at times choose sensible Ministers, a Pombal, a Colbert. They regarded their countries as personal estates, to be improved but only by royal benevolence. 'Argue as much as you like', Frederick the Great said, 'but obey'. They could imprison without trial. Their silence was alternately the silence of loaded guns and the silence of books. Catherine deposed, perhaps killed, her degenerate husband. They could be minor artists, forerunners of those Romantics who regarded themselves as more important than their art. Their courts, stifled by etiquette, were often bizarre, unreal. Grand Duke Peter Romanov court-martialled and hanged a rat. Frederick William I of Prussia was obsessed with tall soldiers, for decoration, not battle. Too much power operated in too small a space, sometimes, as in Spain, Russia, Bavaria, from rulers of precarious sanity. C. D. Darlington[61] suggests that by narrowing their bridal range, Reformation and Turkish conquests weakened the dynasties by depriving them of more varied genetic strains.

The most influential was Louis XIV, exemplifying monarchical ritual, industry, bigotry, self-advertisement. 'He guided his people towards bankruptcy through the complications of a spirited foreign policy with an elaborate dignity that still compels our admiration.' (H. G. Wells) By expelling the Huguenots, Louis, like Hitler, deprived the nation of specialized skills and intelligence. His expensive and useless wars ultimately helped ruin the monarchy he had raised so high.

European Crowns never quite escaped Louis XIV. The aura of Divine Right outlived Revolution and Commune. The last French King claiming Divine Right abdicated as late as 1830. Until 1918 European emperors saw themselves as exalted colleagues of God, the conditioned reflexes of royalty too long unquestioned. In 1914, they still had personal powers over armies, over choice of Chancellor, were still tribal totems embalmed in resounding names: 'All-Highest', 'Supreme War-Lord', 'Apostolic King', pronouncing on all subjects to a world only slowly ceasing to listen.

The common belief in an Empire
which casually grew without direction
is quite unjustified. Almost every
British colony was deliberately founded
by a formed body of settlers according to a preconceived plan and, generally speaking, the more complete
the plan the more successful the
colony.

C. E. Carrington

I

Wars, however expensive for the community, frequently profit the
few. Wealth unprecedented, though unequally distributed, shone
through Augustan England : brazen wealth from determined,
often callous trade monopolies, including those of opium and slaves.
Hudson Bay, East India, Guinea, South Sea, Royal Africa Companies existed not to spread philanthropy, culture or gospel, but
to promote wealth. Pepys, inspecting a merchantman, had walked
'above the knee' in cloves and nutmegs. Until 1813, the East
India Company tried to exclude missionaries. Carrington notes
'loot' as one of the earliest words adopted from Hindustani. Politics and money were active colleagues. Edward Wortley Montague
was both Ambassador to Turkey and representative of the Levant
Company.

Parliament, public, economists, had long periods of hostility or
indifference to the colonies, which nevertheless supplied various
uses. They were obvious outlets for young male adventurousness
and aggression, for the missionary, for the debt-ridden and criminal,
for surplus populations, for difficult children, and were useful too
for novelists anxious to shed a character. Dickens employed them
for the last two. They were not expected to yield cultural assets,
although in 1902 General Brabazon was recommending the toma-
hawk to the committee of Imperial Defence. Primarily, they existed
for commerce on one-sided premises, bound to trade only with
Britain, export only through British ports. They trebled the national
income, although, by taxing Irish and American exports, London

fanned a momentous ill-will that, by losing America, forced greater
reliance on India. Colonial industry was discouraged, colonies regarded as investment areas rather than human communities. Irish
cloth and cattle trades were destroyed; Irish wheat was to be
ruined by the repeal of the Corn Laws. Disraeli, 1844, summarized
Ireland as 'a starving population, an absentee aristocracy, an alien
church, and, in addition, the weakest executive in the world.' The
Irish rich, too, greedily took advantage of the distress after the
Famines.

The early West Indian colonies gave small reason for pride.
Criminals, deserters, diseased failures, wretched indentured lab-
ourers, were overworked first for tobacco, then for sugar. These
were reinforced by African slaves, treated with a savagery not yet
forgiven.

In Polynesia, Captain Cook, questing, observant – he watched
a human sacrifice with anthropological curiosity – wrote of the
whites that they had introduced to the natives 'wants and diseases
which they never knew and which serve only to disturb that happy
tranquillity they and their fathers enjoyed.'[62]

Profits were stupendous. From Africa, ivory, gold, diamonds,
slaves, cloves; from Canada, fur, timber, fish; from the Caribbean,
sugar, rum, raw cotton; from America, tobacco, to be re-exported
to India from where, above all, flowed the profits – from spices,
saltpetre, tea, rice, calico, silks, sugar – that built Blenheim, Nash
terraces, financed industrial and technological revolution. Chatham's father was a formidable East Indian trader, 'Diamond Pitt'.

Reproached for being the most insular save the Swiss, Tibetans,
Nepalese, Britain accumulated the largest empire yet known, to rivals
an unendearing feat. Like Rome, she found that the need to
defend frontiers, to forestall competitors, to gain cheap labour,
harbour rights and suburban territory, entailed local alliances and
interferences, thus further frontiers, involvements, diplomacies,
or collision with another great power whose defeat led to responsibilities and annexations that were becoming imperial. Afghan
Wars were waged less against Afghans than against Russia.
Independent-minded governors and generals, too, might cross
frontiers without London's permission, confident that, for prestige
reasons, they would be officially supported. A consul could rather
too easily become proconsul, particularly after a discovery of gold,
diamonds, oil. Native ill-treatment of minorities provided further
excuses for interference. Motives were not pure, methods were
brusque, results not inevitably extortionate. The British built a
mosque in Singapore, increased Malayan trade, security, population, eliminated piracy. In Singapore, Raffles (1781–1826) 'set

himself to mitigate the harshness of British rule. He was a linguist, a student of oriental life devoted to the Malayan hopes . . . he prohibited the slave trade, regulated the conditions of slavery, abolished forced labour and the legal use of torture and mutilation.' (Carrington) Sir Charles Napier's famous 'We have no right to seize Scinde, yet we shall do so, and a very advantageous, useful and humane piece of rascality it will be,' could, perhaps, be justified, though only an occasional colony, like Pennsylvania, showed positive good-will towards the natives, whom the English too often treated worse than did the French.

Protests abounded in Britain herself. Liberal or envious politicians attacked the systematic plunder of Bengal, the bribes, the mass-famines assisted by millionaire speculations in rice, the disregard of native custom, the beatings and slavery. Burke, 1783, lashed the East India Company for taking much, giving nothing. Pitt defended the American rebels in Parliament. 'Will you punish them for the madness which you have occasioned?' A Clive, a Hastings, was embarrassingly vulnerable.

Yet the greatest critics, Burke, Fox, Adam Smith, Cobbett, were stay-at-homes, often ill-informed. Few would have lived comfortably under the Mongol Empire, some would not have lived at all. No Indian Pitt or Burke offered themselves to Indian electors. Burke wielded memorable general principles as if they could instantly be applied to India, of which he knew little : principles wholly at odds with Bengali traditions. India was raddled with caste, apathy, exclusive male rights, too costly festivals, poverty. Thugs were as typical as gurus. The decrepit Mongol Crown, no more substantial than the moribund Holy Roman Empire, was a vacuum of civil war, terrorism, usury, anarchy, the nominal rulers as alien as the British and French. 'There were no nations in India and, except for the penniless exile Shah Allum, nothing left in existence whose title went back much over fifty years.'[63]

Profits of trade, then of administration, were undeniably huge, even after parliamentary interference, 1767. Yet man is seldom conditioned for money alone : status may appeal as much; furthermore, from abstruse or inaccessible motives, he may combat poverty, waste, inefficiency. He may have humane curiosity. He may vote for a rise in his rates. Cobden and Bright roused Lancashire cotton to refuse, against immediate interests, to sell to the American Confederates, unemployed workers subscribing to Northern funds.

A Wellesley, Cornwallis, Hastings, compares reasonably with Louis, Frederick, Catherine, even Maria Theresa, let alone Robespierre and Napoleon. For India, the alternative was not the Great Mogul but the ruthless Maratha freebooters, destroyers of Indian

unity, giving in return not even frontier defence. The East India
Company, after victories over France, 1760, supplied internal
peace, regular for capricious taxation. The reviled Hastings,
certainly lax about money, 'set himself to cure Mongol corruption,
banditry, fiscal chaos, peasant oppression.' White intruders could
love and respect India. Great scholars and orientalists like William
Erskine (1773–1852), Richard Benton (1821–90) and Brian Hodgson
excavated or translated local histories, religions, ethnologies, customs, not only for the West but for Asia herself. Civil Servant
Charles Frederick Usborne became a noted Punjabi savant. This
interest did not lapse. Francis Younghusband, leader of the morally
dubious expedition to Tibet (1903–4) – which excited more indignation in Britain than the total conquest of that buffer-country by
Mao's China – was not only administrator and soldier, but an
author, authority on Indian thought and beliefs, promoter of
congresses on world religions, President of the Royal Geographical
Society. Chief Justice Jones of Bengal explored and published
Sanskrit. The missionary, William Carey, taught Sanskrit and translated Hindu scripture into Bengali. Ancient India was redis-
covered. Hastings 'recommended Sanskrit, not for utility, but as a
key to "rich stores of knowledge" which must "excite in the breast
of the English student a respect and benevolence" for the Indians.'
Naïve in party tactics, he had no petty vision. Repelled by ignorance,
squalor, disease, like a Stoic senator he blamed them not on racial
and religious shortcomings but on human failure. Like Kipling, he
could see British and Anglican narrowness, greed, intrigue and
snobbery. He encouraged the study of old Indian law and founded,
1784, the Bengal Asiatic Society. Fieling continues :

> Amid dubious experiments and inconceivable obstructions he
> persisted in his ideal of restoring the best in Indian custom. Ten
> leading Brahmin pundits were called to Calcutta, to codify in
> Sanskrit their legal principles, thence to be translated into
> Persian, and then into English. . . . He referred with alarm to
> persistent reports of 'an unadvised system' of law for Bengal being
> compiled at home. The way 'to rule these people with ease and
> moderation' was to leave them what 'time and religion have
> rendered familiar to their understandings and sacred to their
> affections'. This was the right of 'a great nation', not only
> 'superior wisdom' imposed from outside.

This view did not prevail. The subsequent, and remarkable,
Indian Civil Service was confident in its own superior wisdom,
ignoring what Indian customs it could not control or subvert, upon

precedents of Common Law and common-sense, both alien to and often outrageous to Indian affections.

White mortality in India and the Caribbean was heavy. Individual survivors could prosper, on behalf of their opulent London directors but, like Roman proconsuls, had eventually to return, facing clamour for retribution from the public-spirited or malicious.

Joseph Wall, for all his fine connections, was hanged at Newgate in front of a cheering mob for having, twenty years before, while Governor of Gorce, sentenced a mutinous sergeant to an unlawful flogging that caused death.

(Arthur Bryant, *Years of Endurance*, Collins, 1942)

Balance of Power strategy, the need for markets, interrelated developments in mines, transport, steam-power, agriculture, population-growth, communications, furthered immense eighteenth-century British wars, increasingly savage, mainly against France, often in alliance with Holland, Austria, finally Prussia, now beginning to be a Great Power. The loss of the American colonies did not impair the course of British manufacturing and colonizing.

By the Treaties of Utrecht (1713) – ending what Churchill called the First World War – Aix-la-Chapelle (1748), Paris (1763), French imperial ambitions were dispersed until Napoleon, together with threats to the Low Countries, the Rhine, British exports. Britain secured the West Indian sugar trade, French Canada and India, Spanish Gibraltar, Minorca, undisputed access to all seas, monopoly of the Spanish-American slave-markets. Slave trade was still unaffected by the Enlightenment. 'We cannot allow the Colonies', declared a Minister, Lord Dartmouth, 1775, 'to check or discourage in any degree a traffic so beneficial to the nation.' 'Natives' tended to be dismissed as naturally inferior. Hume himself declared in the *Gentlemen's Magazine* : 'There was never a civilized nation of any other complexion than white,' a view confirmed by the *Encyclopaedia Britannicas* of 1810 and 1884. (Walvin) This helped 'excuse slavery', though opposed by the Enlightenment, Wesley, Paine, Wedgewood, Sharpe, Wilberforce.

Her gigantic losses would not be forgotten by France, who aided the American rebels and would sustain a twenty years' war against the old, predatory, shrewd but perhaps still assailable rival. But meanwhile, like Spain, she was eclipsed.

The Seven Years War raised the glory of British arms higher than ever before or since. The four central years of the War, 1757–61, when Pitt was in high office, form the only period in British history when national policy has been systematically directed to imperial ends, and when combined operations have been based on a true strategic initiative. Neither Cromwell nor Marlborough nor William Pitt the Younger nor Lloyd George has had the will and the power and the strategic insight and the understanding of imperial necessities as the governments of France in the eighteenth century and of Germany in the twentieth century have planned and fought. The elder Pitt is the only British Statesman who has made war an instrument of policy, almost the only 'imperialist' premier in British history, using that word in its derogatory sense.

(Carrington)

British profiteering, however, was not wholly violent or territorial. Since the Tudors, the City had traded with Russia. Peter the Great (1682–1725) was helped by the Swiss, Lefort, and the Scot, Patrick Gordon, in centralizing the Tsardom, reforming the army, building fleets. He spent three months in England, 1698, studying ship-building, commerce, coinage, astronomy, surgery, anatomy, military science, geography, natural philosophy. Evelyn rented him a house, unwisely, for the royal followers were aptly known as 'unbaptized bears'. He left with 500 British craftsmen, gunners, builders, canal engineers, artillery experts, pilots, mathematicians. British, Dutch, Germans, Italians, French raised from the swamps sham-classical St Petersburg where the Irishman, John Field, evolved the poignant nocturne, perfected by Chopin. Alexander I visited London, as a victorious ally against Napoleon.

Much tentative Anglo-Russian goodwill was to be dissipated by Russian intrigues in the Turkish Balkans, by British fears for India; by the Crimean War, by unimaginative or desperate British politics, 1917–1939, by the leaden Russian bureaucratic despotism left unchanged by the Revolution. That Russia three times helped to rescue the West from French or Teutonic overlordship was remembered more by the public than by the politicians though, to deal with Stalin, more than politics was needed. The answer was never discovered.

2

Such was the relative tolerance of the Grand Epoque that her aggressions did not prevent France from being the chief foreign cultural influence in England. She was not alone. The German, Zoffany, having studied in Rome, settled in England, 1758, and painted London celebrities. British pottery schools at Derby, at

Chelsea, had intricate relations with Dresden and Sèvres. Taste was influenced not only by Pompeii but by Palmyra, Baalbek, the Far East. An Indian palace, with ornate writhings, swellings, taperings, arose at Sezincote. British painters still paid tribute to the monumental powers of Michelangelo. Italy remained inescapable : in opera, the testimonies of innumerable excited travellers, and the limitless fascinations of ancient Rome. English gentlemen collected busts of Trajan and Augustus, quoted Roman precepts and epigrams in Parliament, posed as Cato or Cicero, imitated Roman prose-rhythms. Rubens felt himself a Senecan Stoic; young Europe sought the public-spirited heroes and martyrs of Plutarch and Livy. 'I've often cursed my fate,' Beethoven was to say of his deafness, 'but Plutarch taught me resignation.' Once he compared himself to Hercules at the cross-roads. Danton was a fine classical scholar. Dr Johnson's statue in St Paul's was draped in a toga, like Charles James Fox in Bloomsbury Square. Nash's terraces echoed Diocletian's Adriatic palace. For Christ Church, Spitalfields, Wren joined Gothic spire to a Doric portico, as Gibbs did at St Martin-in-the-Fields. Neo-classical façades appeared in Glasgow, Edinburgh, Brighton, Bath, Cheltenham. The romantic classicism of Goethe and Winkelmann flowed through Canova and Flaxman, to Byron, Keats, Shelley, to Browning, Landor, Turner. The Elgin Marbles, rescued from the Turks – or stolen from the Greeks – inspired multitudinous imitations.

The results were not universally acclaimed. Horace Walpole compared Vanbrugh's meticulously formal Blenheim to the palace of an auctioneer chosen King of Portugal.

France, however, the France of Descartes, Boileau, Bossuet, Corneille, Racine, Molière, was the most prestigious state in Europe. Charles II was half-French, many Cavalier poets had known French exile, Pope and Dryden learnt from French techniques and criticism, notably from Boileau. In the next century the debonair waves and curves of French rococo were reproduced in English domestic furnishings : mirrors, curtains, porcelain, table legs, metal fittings. The Prince Regent was a prodigious patron of French *cuisine*, becoming the satirist's 'Prince of Whales' in the process. Only the masses remained stolidly unimpressed by 'Louis Baboon', perhaps more convinced of his cruelties and bigotry than thrilled by his glamour.

The elite shared a European style, expressing itself in French. High life was not profound, more the shapely cult of a veneer : of mannered decorum, adroit or hypocritical restraint, highly trained mediocrity, but creating conditions in which genius could generally work. Conversation was laced with wit, allusion, malice, repartee brilliant as a carillon. Society embraced Catherine the Great and Potemkin, Frederick the Great, Maria Theresa, Voltaire, La Rochefoucauld, Goethe, Hume, Leibnitz, Schiller, Pombal. The Knight had lapsed into the Courtier, the soul was a perfunctory exclamation or poetic image. Here, in a caste polite, permissive, self-indulgent, Method governed literature, drama, marriage, sport, diplomacy, war. 'Gentlemen of the French Guard, you fire first,' Lord George Hay invited the enemy, at Fontenoy. Opposing generals, even in early revolutionary days, exchanged gifts. Until Napoleon, foreign wartime tourists and savants could travel in enemy states. Cook, humane to his crews and Polynesians alike, was helped in mapping, collecting, exploring, by Americans, French, Spanish, with whom England was at war. Even during the Crimean War, Russian bands played the French anthem to celebrate the birth of an heir to their chief enemy, Napoleon III.

For the French Encyclopaedists, with correspondents in most capitals, knowledge and instruction would surely generate more reasonable society. They admired China, conceived as a rational society of responsible savants and Platonist emperors. Intelligent and assertive women too debated challenging issues, not of Soul, Sin, Grace, but of government, matter, liberty. Light and gases, physics and mechanics were being studied objectively from Berlin to Edinburgh. Little chauvinism disturbed the Royal Society, the Paris Academy of Science. Necker, a French Finance Minister, was a Swiss. Clarendon, Hume, Montesquieu, Boyle, Descartes, Harrington, Adam Smith, Pirenne, Dopsch, Voltaire, Locke, de Coulanges, related history and behaviour to genetics, climate, environment, psychology, economics. Newton and Locke were superbly popularized by Voltaire. Diderot explored the devious and irrational beneath politeness. The cool analysis of the Austrian Haugwitz, of North, Locke, Petty, Adam Smith, was creating a new technique, economics, virtually unknown to the Romans. Economists chastise each other, but do not ascribe social breakdown to the wrath of the gods or to conspiracy. Barrow and Newton, advanced mathematicians, shared more with Bentham, with Augustus, than with Luther and Cromwell. The British imagination was Cartesian without knowing it. 'I think therefore I am,' like Galileo's, 'Nevertheless, it does move,' made sufficient sense.

3

The typical pilgrimage was now the Grand Tour, 'glorified museum with bordello attached'.[64] Civil war had driven courtiers into involuntary travels, particularly in Italy, France, the Low

Countries. Here was a chance, not always taken, to quicken artistic and intellectual outlooks and areas of patronage.

The Tour was also part of a renewed classicism. Milton himself had visited Italy, making friends and correspondents, contacting survivals of Florentine humanism against pagan, medieval and renaissance backgrounds. English milords founded the Society of Dilettanti, 1732, which, from somewhat ribald beginnings, held serious studies of ancient architecture, topography, archaeology, in Turkish Greece. Like Goethe and Winkelmann, they were excited by a Greece more primitive than that revived by the Renaissance.

Only poverty and bandits restricted international travel. Save for Turkey and Russia, Europe generally existed without passports until 1914. Young British aristocrats, middle-class men of letters – Horace Walpole, Wordsworth, Smollett, Hazlitt – embarked. The Grand Tour, or bits of it, was a generous saunter through liberal studies, with a finishing-school in Italy. It might last for more than two years. Letters of introduction were as influential as purses. Gibbon was freely welcomed in Paris by Helvetius, d'Holbach, Madame Geoffrin; he conversed with the Encyclopaedists, watched Voltaire perform tragedies at Fernay and, though cool towards the 'stinking ditches' of Venice, was enthralled by Rome, where he did amateur archaeology, and decided his own imperial project.

Prodigies of opera, painting, pleasure were often preferred to those of nature, though in time cults arose, admiring bizarre solitudes, the stillness of lakes, the romance of peak and valley. 'Sometimes,' Firbank was to protest, 'I feel like *shaking* Switzerland!' International celebrities were permanently on view, keeping open house, table, frequently bed. The traveller could see Mary Shelley on the Rhine, surrounded by 'disgusting Germans'; Beckford at the Escurial, examining a three-foot feather dropped from Gabriel's wing; Hume, Lord Hertford, Sterne, or Wilkes, at Diderot's; Lady Mary Wortley Montague studying Turkish in Belgrade; Casanova everywhere . . . Hume again, at Mlle de Lespinasse's Paris salon, talking with Condorcet; Shelley and Byron at Geneva; Southey at Chamonix where Shelley reputedly signed his profession as 'atheist'; Madame de Stael at Coppet. One could discuss alchemy with Cagliostro at posting-stations; watch Frederick the Great at Potsdam avoiding Boswell; hear Rousseau exclaim to Boswell, 'I love the Scots, but you are irksome to me.' One could listen to Stendhal in Naples – 'Did ever a French admiral play so despicable a part as this Nelson?'; see Genoese galley-slaves, some of the million French serfs, Milanese opera-goers wearing hats so that they could doff them to royalty, Spanish garottings, the Chevalier de la

Barre tortured to death (1766) for not saluting 'a crowd of dirty monks'. One could have stood with Byron in Rome watching thieves guillotined, amongst masked priests and a half-naked executioner, 'very striking and chilling'. Peasants could be examined. 'In the Middle Ages Ovid was known throughout the European Courts and Universities as a subtle psychologist and a learned cosmologist; but then and thereafter the simple folk of Sulmo preferred to think of him as a formidable wizard, a memorable preacher or a powerful knight.'[65] Rich connoisseurs found unending treasures. Kent's palladian Holkham Hall (1734–59) houses Thomas Coke's great library, collected on his Tour, 1715. The painters most admired in Britain, Watteau, Fragonard, Tiepolo, were mostly gathered from abroad, particularly by Lord Hertford. British money, British tastes, Professor Haskell notes, helped to promote new forms of Italian landscape and portraiture. 'The picturesque', Salvador Rosa's bandits and mountains, and, in a debased Romanticism, the Gothic novel of lonely towers, mad priests, seducing poisoners and monstrous spectres, gained vogue, reinforced by the exhumation of Pompeii, which Shelley visited and Sir William Hamilton studied. Wedgewood introduced Pompeian designs into his pottery.

The English Milord abroad, fair game for satirist and gamin, amused yet impressed Europe, as the English Gentleman fascinated Henry James, Conrad, F. M. Ford : and Turgenev, who felt that continental landowners were developing intelligence and sensitivity but more crudely than the English, and at the expense of political liberalism. British prestige, military, intellectual, social and sporting was high in France. The English rich were at home in foreign capitals. Casanova, in Rome, was 'greatly surprised to see Lord Tallow, whom I met in Paris at his mother's, the Countess of Lismore, separated from her husband, and the kept mistress of M. de Saint Albin, Archbishop of Cambrai. He was a natural son of the Duc d'Orleans, Regent of France. Lord Tallow was a handsome young man full of wit and talent, but unbridled in his vices.'

4

The Milord retained his profitable alliances with commerce, investing in tobacco, cloth, timber, sugar, with concerns in Ireland, the Levant, Guinea, Hudson's Bay, India.

As Milord, as Gentleman, the English landowner, save in Ireland, was generally more socially conscious than his coevals abroad. At Harrow and Winchester he shared Spartan existence with classes other than his own. Bryant recalls that the Duke of Dorset was always beaten twice at Harrow : for his misdemeanour, and for being a Duke.

The Milord looked not to medieval England for excellence, nor to Potsdam, St Petersburg, nor to the cultivated Versailles noblesse with their sinecures, privileges, their peacock rituals and political futility, but to Cato, Regulus, Seneca, to whom privilege entailed responsibility and right action must accompany right culture. Much was superficial. The Republic was the ideal, the Public Good, not the hurly-burly of 'Wilkes and Liberty', though a Walter Scott could endure tribulation with a fortitude that Marcus Aurelius could have saluted. Dignified, dispassionate, pretending to be more indolent than he often was, indifferent to clerical notions that sex is not pleasure but social duty, the Milord, the Gentleman, could feel lofty compassion without compulsion to descend to the arena. Agnostic, adaptable, generally a trifle bored, seldom counting the cost, not always paying, easy with all – save Methodists, card-sharpers, sea-lawyers and moneylenders – yet intimate with few; urbane, loyal, yet at bottom, perhaps, chilled, he assumed, unlike Danton, Mirabeau, Washington, that correct behaviour or retorts existed for all situations. At worst, in *Vanity Fair*, as bilker, seducer, ignoramus, he degenerated with some style, carelessly assuming his own rights, ignoring those of others. More temperately, he was reliable in crisis, often wilfully tedious when out of it. With emotions concealed or ambiguous, motives distorted or cushioned by affluence, with unflinching physical courage, eccentricity rather than imagination, tolerance rather than profound convictions, he could mingle with the poorest at cricket-match or prize-fight yet remain inwardly exclusive, never far from his club. He was sporting, adventurous, patriotic, proud of what he could not always name, and agreeing with Lord Melbourne that nobody ever did anything foolish except from some strong principle.

The Gentleman – More, Philip Sidney, Burke, Scott, Buchan, Wavell – appealed to the British more than did Caesarism, Papalism, Jacobinism, Gandhism, the Superman and World Revolutionary. Distasteful to Blake, to Wells – to other Gentlemen, Byron, Shaw, Morris, Russell – he became by the mid-twentieth century, forgotten or despised, even by himself.

The rich provided more than free show. They sat in Parliament and on the Bench, built roads, canals, experimented with root crops, cross-breeding, steam-power, social reform, managed immense colonial territories as they might Berkshire, with Roman *gravitas* and the panache of the Edwardian amateur cricketer. Carrington's verdict on Sir Thomas Maitland, a governor of Malta, is apposite : 'a benevolent autocrat, tirelessly efficient, scrupulously honest, and somewhat contemptuous of the people he devotedly served.'

If few were original save in wit and repartee, many had enterprise. Taste is not all-important, nor is it negligible. Lord Westmoreland pioneered the Royal Academy of Music. Lord Burlington (1695–1735) published Palladio's and Inigo Jones's drawings, was patron of Giacomo Leoni, William Kent, Colin Campbell, building a calm architecture remote from Baroque fantasy, of measured unrhetorical authority too self-assured to require originality. For such men, Inigo Jones's pupil, John Webb, together with Wren, de Caus, Robert Adam, built the country houses. Handel's patron, the Duke of Chandos, erected the church at Little Stanmore with Handel as its official composer, and an organ-case designed by Grinling Gibbons. The Prince-Regent, employer of Nash, created the Royal Pavilion, bizarre imperial offshoot, of which Sydney Smith remarked that it was as though St Paul's had gone down to Brighton and pupped. Lord Byron, like Napoleon, Robespierre, Wilde, gave all Europe a multitude of selves. Sir William Hamilton was not only a famous cuckold but a soldier, friend of Wolfe, an MP, geologist, musician, antiquarian, gallant, sportsman, adroit diplomat – until his decline when he shared with Nelson the military fiasco of 1798 –, patron, connoisseur, member of the Dilettanti, to whom life was to be enjoyed but also enhanced. His discoveries, nucleus of the British Museum Department of Antiquities, showed a discrimination applauded by Reynolds; his Royal Society papers impressed Gibbon; his sumptuous antiquarian publications are still read; his classical vases influenced Wedgewood and Adam, revealing him as forerunner of J. D. Beazley of Oxford, whose knowledge of Greek vases was unsurpassed. He directed Emma's theatrical 'Attitudes', admired by Horace Walpole and Goethe. Amiable, magnanimous, perhaps a bit of an ass – in old age he referred to Nelson as 'the most virtuous, loyal and truly brave character I have ever met' – he observed the rules but refused to reduce life to a convention.[66]

Paragon of more static conventions was Lord Chesterfield, respected by Voltaire, though not by Dr Johnson who considered that his precepts taught the morals of a whore and the manners of a dancing-master. Laughter, like sharing a house with one's wife, Chesterfield considered ill-bred. Of love-making he observed that the pleasure was momentary, the position ridiculous and the expense damnable. His son, on the Grand Tour, must write to him in French, 'the language of confidences'. He adds.

I will not tell you what I think of the French, because I am very often taken for one. . . . I will only say that I am insolent; that

I talk a great deal, very loud, and in an assured manner; that I spend a vast amount on powder, feathers, white gloves and so on.

Singularity abounded. Sydney Smith taught his pigs to grunt the National Anthem. Beau Brummell never ate vegetables – 'No, that is not correct. I once ate a pea' –, withdrawing attention to a lady on discovering that she had once eaten cabbage. Wellington too was a mass of singularities. Today, his politics would be unacceptable, his military virtues unfashionable, yet he still presents a curiosity of achievement, wit, melancholy, stoicism, odd spurts of feeling rounded off in memorable anecdotes. As a young commander in India : 'Protect the inhabitants, do not oppress them. Behave like gentlemen.' In Spain, after a triumph : 'I felt the need of a voice behind me to remind me that I was a man.' On the battlefield : 'Lord Wellington does not approve the use of umbrellas during the enemy's firing.' As Tory leader, alarmed by the future and fearing that railways 'would encourage the lower classes to move about', he maintained of the unreformed Parliament that 'to improve it is beyond human wisdom.' As Iron Duke he remains like a tree, twisted, dry, difficult to climb, nevertheless giving shade.

In a last flush of colour before drab industrialism, the Ladies and Gentlemen in patches and powders, huge skirts and flamboyant wigs, seem perpetually in a minuet as 'mysterious' as much in the Newfoundlands.

By that date (1735) the variety of wigs was sporting in full profusion; there were the pigeon's wing, the cornet, the cauliflower, the royal bird, the staircase, the wild boar's back, the she-dragon, the rose, the snail back, the spinach seed. . . . But even amongst this medley, Lady Montague's son caused a certain furore when he arrived back from Paris, in 1751, with an iron wig spun out of the finest wire.

(David Piper, *The English Face*, Thames and Hudson, 1957)

5

Wealth crystallized in country houses – Chatsworth, Hatfield, Knole with its fifty-two staircases, seven acres of roof –, in Burgundian tapestries, Bernini statues, Sheraton and Chippendale furniture, the tribes of servants – Rowse mentions Lord Derby, even in 1590, using 140 for a family of five –, the prolonged dinners, with collar-boys waiting to drag the drunks from under the table. Labour quarrels about 'who does what?' were familiar.

British wealth and craftsmanship combined with European taste and skill to produce the luxurious, ornate, the beautifully practical, the charmingly useless. William III's accession created a vogue for Dutch parterres and water-gardens. At Chatsworth, ceilings are by the Englishman Thornhill, the Italian Verrio, the Frenchman Laguerre; there is sculpture by Watson and Cibber; paintings by Reynolds, Verrio, Rembrandt, Claude, Poussin, Carravagio; woodwork by Grinling Gibbons; French ironwork by Tijou; Mortlake tapestries. Harewood House, built by John Carr and Robert Adam, largely decorated by Joseph Rose, has panels painted by Goethe's and Marat's friend, Angelica Kauffmann. Boughton has Bühl furniture, Caffieri clocks, Van Dyck paintings. Harewood, Kedleston, Petworth are portrayed in dim, exotic swirls by Turner. Italianate work abounds at Longleat, home of Monmouth's friend, 'Tom o' Ten Thousand', not soldiers, but tenants and servants. French, Italian and English design, together with English craftsmanship, adorn Wilton, where Kent was probably the first to build furniture for the over-all plan of the house.

The façade of Sutton Scarsdale was designed by Smith of Warwickshire, decorated by the Venetians Astari and Bagutti. Palladio inspired Stourhead, also Chiswick House, planned by Burlington after his first Grand Tour, 1714, with internal work by William Kent. Venetian painters embellished Moor Park, and Kimbolton. Hever Castle, Anne Boleyn's old home, an English structure, is filled with German armour, French, Spanish, Italian and English paintings – Geerhardt's reddish nobleman stares from a foam of lace and jewel, a Holbein Henry VIII glitters. Caught by Mabuse, the bright eye of ageing, ascetic Henry VII is alert for all his realm's secrets. Perhaps the very tumult of English history is reined within the tolerable by such an eye. Titian's King Philip stands above baby clothes made, with whatever feelings, by Elizabeth, for her sister's baby, that never came. Also at Hever are English and French embroidery and tapestry, formal Italian gardens, statuary, topiary, an Italian bath and grotto. Hatfield, designed by Robert Lyminge (1607) glows with Martin de Vos's 'Four Seasons' tapestries, paintings by Zucharo, Reynolds, Wilkie, Romney. Hampton Court, enlarged by Wren, himself of polyglot genius, displays Raphael tapestries, Mantegna panels, decoration by Gibbons, Thornhill, Laguerre, Verrio; French ironwork, English gardens. Le Nôtre laid out the formalized gardens of Versailles, the Vatican, Kensington, St James's and, in Ireland, of Antrim Castle. The later fashion was for carefully designed impressions of wildness balanced by classical temples, grottoes and artificial ruins, in Poussin-like recollection of Arcadian harmonies seen and unseen.

Ham House has Dutch and French furniture, French costumes, English, French, Dutch and Italian tapestries, some influenced by Watteau and Pater; paintings from Spain, Venice, Holland and England – by Hilliard, Oliver and Cooper, whom David Piper assesses as 'one of the greatest British portraitists. As a face-painter I would claim that he has no rival in Europe in the seventeenth century.' Though Britain had Reynolds, Gainsborough, Lawrence, Bonnington, Morland, depicting most social classes and livelihoods, illustrating landscapes, sport, and, with Wright of Derby, new industries . . . not until Constable, Turner, Ruskin, did British art make much stir in Europe.

To many, the Country House, itself a court, must have seemed an offshot of Eden, pastoral yet controlled, even of heaven itself, hierarchical, static, blissful, eternal, inviolable, struck with planetary harmonies, enshrined with the best that imagination, rural but not rustic, could conceive. Devils of social anger might lurk, but even blackness was necessary, to emphasize the golden toxic splendours of God.

Neo-Gothic, romantic, sham-classical – like an arrested wave, castellated, turreted, moated, or formal as Racine, Haydn – some times with the dun hovering at the back door while Orpheus played soundlessly in the park, the Country House was weighed down with spoils from shores ever more fantastic : from China, Brazil, Polynesia, Jamaica, India, Egypt; heaped with exotic fruits and vegetables, with coins, crystals, gold leaf, oriental screens, tapestries, silks, lacquer, mirrors, musical instruments, leopards, humming-birds, pavilions, temples, pagodas. Within this ornate shimmer developed features so marked in English fiction : housekeeper, butler, valet, governess. Also, wider offshoots. The Haile Selassie University, at Addis Ababa, was modelled (1935) on Lord Buxton's Norfolk home.

Rich, damp, green landscapes, the pale calm of column and portico, at once Then and Now, did not axiomatically engender gracious lives for villager and tenant. Magistrates were ceasing to regulate prices and wages, and the 'free market' bore hardly on the poor. 'Liberty' could be more sung about than relied upon. Tenants might be evicted without redress, for game or sheep, sexual irregularity; even, and within living memory, for non-attendance at church. There were also more homely disciplines. At Preston (Suffolk), 1724, Sam Lygoe was paid five shillings annually for 'whiping of the dogs out of the Church on all Sundays and other days upon which there is Divine Service, also he is to prevent anyone Sleeping in the church by Waking them with a White Wand.'

Enclosures, by ending medieval strip-systems, increased rural

efficiency but depopulated hundreds of small farms, legally but
uncharitably. Mass evictions in the Highlands, like Goldsmith's
'Deserted Village', share the legendary cruelty of the game-laws.
While the Country House prospered, the yeoman farmer and
labourer went down, before new technology, the decline of cottage
industry, rising prices, new and harsher masters often enriched
by India or the Caribbean, who owned land but were not of the
land. Monmouth's rebels had been sold as slaves to the West Indies;
Scots children were abducted to New World plantations where
evicted Scots and Irish sold themselves as indented labour. An
occasional unexpected fact reminds us that village isolation or
security was seldom complete. A parish record at Blaydon,
Churchill's burial place, shows money paid, 1770, 'for the redemption of captives in the Empire of Fez and Morocco'.

Until World War II, the Big House was capable of despotic
enormity, with children edged out of education by squire and
parson, for ill-paid domestic service. Osbert Sitwell[67] relates a lady
meeting, in Belvoir Park, 'a country girl who would have been
exceptionally lovely save for the loss of a front tooth. "How did it
happen?" she enquired, "What a misfortune!" "Oh, the Duchess
had lost one of hers, so she forced me to have one of mine taken
out to replace it." '

Polite society in Edinburgh, Bath, London, was ignoring the
creative possibilities of the new, noisy, apparently unromantic
machines. London enjoyed the theatre of Congreve, Goldsmith
Dryden, Sheridan, Garrick, Keen, Siddons; much mock-Roman
drama, and versions of Shakespeare that gave even *King Lear* a
happy ending. There was music of Purcell, Boyce, Arne, Blow, J. C.
Bach, Haydn. Mozart, at eight, composed his first symphony in Lon-
don, where Handel had lived, of whom Beecham said that 'he wrote
Italian music better than any Italian, English better than any
Englishman, German better than all Germans save Bach.' The
London Philharmonic Society commissioned Beethoven's Ninth
Symphony. Two English performers were in the original cast of
The Marriage of Figaro.

Scotland, recovering from Knox, released prolix talent: Hume,
Scott, Macadam, Adam Smith, Robert Adam, Boswell, Burns,
Telford, 'Ossian', Allan Ramsay, Raeburn, Watt; its universities
influenced later American counterparts. Hume, temperate, sceptical,
was a historical materialist demolishing without fuss accepted notions
of human nature, to whom religion was the outcome of culture,
not of revelation or incarnation, and rooted in 'the incessant hopes
and fears that actuate the human mind'. Soul, self, ideas, were
reflexes of mind, of sense-impression, dying with the body, an

attitude reducing Divine Right to absurdity and stimulating not only the French Enlightenment but Thomas Jefferson.

'Ossian' and Scott enthralled all reading Europe, Napoleon carrying the former with him on campaign. Shaw, comparing his own mind to Shakespeare's, remarked that there was no other writer he more thoroughly despised, 'not even Sir Walter Scott'. Yet the Marxist critic, Lukacs, saw Scott as an epic novelist with profound grasp of History working through average decent people of mixed needs and make-up, neutral ground for the clash of extremes. Professor Trevor-Roper (BBC, August 1971) regards Scott not only as founder of the historical novel but a catalyst in the study of history itself through his effect on Macaulay, Von Ranke, Carlyle. 'He knew what History meant, that was his chief intellectual merit.' (Carlyle) Trevor-Roper suggests that professional historians are the adept technicians, but that the innovators have been amateurs : Machiavelli, Montesquieu, Herder, Marx – and Scott.

Middle-class affluence demanded the Portrait, and the Novel – Defoe, Fielding, Goldsmith, Scott, Jane Austen – which vied with sermons, executions, cruelty to animals and lunatics, travelling shows, royal and civic pageantry, creating illusions real as a turbine, more far-reaching than lunar travel, freely scattering vistas from angles hitherto unconsidered. Scott helped recharge the French novel.

Goethe was moved not only by Shakespeare, Milton, Pope, Swift, but particularly by Goldsmith's *The Vicar of Wakefield.* 'I felt in harmony with that ironical cast of mind which lifts itself above each object, above fortune and misfortune, good and evil, life and death, and thus masters a truly poetic world.'

The first German furore about Shakespeare was actually caused by a mediocre anthology from the Rev William Dodd, later hanged for forgery. An avid Shakespearian was Danton, himself capable of an authentic tragic phrase. 'They cannot stop our lips touching in the basket!'

Outside the parks and mansions, material change was incessantly at work. James Lind's discovery of fruit-juice as cure for scurvy (1753) rid sailors of an enemy more dangerous than storm. Amid the horrors of Asylums, the humane innovations of Maudsley and Tuke in England, Pinel in France, led to the treatment of inmates as patients not delinquents. Watt and Newcomen at home, Huygens, Papin, Savery abroad, were exploiting steam. Agriculture was stimulated by population increases, war needs, more scientific tillage and breeding, often from French and Dutch experiments. Towns swelled haphazardly as the Machine advanced, cottage industries declined, the peasant became proletariat. Unemployment, food

G

riots, machine-smashing, high prices, coercion were at hand and, 1779–81, Britain herself, fighting America, France, Spain, seemed ruined.

Meanwhile, the slave-trade was unrelenting. Boswell considered abolition would 'shut the gates of mercy on mankind'. Bishops preached the benefits of enforced Christianity. Nelson defended slavery. When 132 slaves were pitched overboard from the slave-ship, *Zong*, the subsequent court case, 1783, merely concerned itself with the compensation due for loss of property.

More blacks probably existed in Hanoverian England than in 1945. From 1672, the Royal Africa Company was empowered to import 'redwood, elephants' teeth, negroes, slaves, hides, wax, guinea grains, or other commodities'. The Solicitor-General, 1677, defined the negroes' status as 'goods and commodities within the Acts of Trade and Navigation'. This was given Common Law backing, 'Negroes being usually bought and sold among merchants, so merchandise.' For over a century, a succession of Acts and judgements confirmed this, despite the vigilance with which popular rights were so often debated.

> Black chattel slavery existed in England for two and a half centuries. But it was not the same as West Indian slavery, nor a development of medieval villeinage. It was fundamentally a colonial institution transplanted into England, where it was kept uneasily afloat by certain English traditions which were ill-designed to cope with the concept of property in human beings. In all this, English law played a crucial role.
>
> (Walvin)

Blacks joined Irish and Roman Catholics as alien scapegoats. Black immigration disturbed Augustan England, magnifying ancient superstitions: sexual, genetic, economic, cultural. Relatively few black women arrived. Blacks were usually, though not invariably, slaves owned by naval officers, retired merchants, officials, colonists. London had its black ghettoes, notably at Paddington. Mr Walvin finds that the American Revolution increased this, many pro-British blacks finding refuge here. They could be kept fettered; were often pugilists and entertainers. A few were accepted in Society. At least one black clergyman is known.

There were other forms of slavery. Streets were thick with thieves and prostitutes, many of them children, victims of a lop-sided society, reeking with pox. City life seen by Defoe, Swift, Johnson, Wilkes, was pushing and licentious: larceny and murder were commonplace, voters could be intimidated, children hanged for riot. A social conscience was private luxury, not national policy.

At Sadlers Wells, 1783, *The Deserter* was acted entirely by dogs trained by who knows what cruelties, cruelties endured also by actors, acrobats, clowns, castrated singers. Men and women were hanged in droves, debtors left to rot in prison. Gentlemen crossed the Channel to gloat over Damien, tortured on the wheel. Impersonating a Chelsea pensioner and associating with gypsies were capital crimes. A fourteen-year-old girl was sentenced to be burnt for forgery, 1771; a youth hanged for handling calico in a shop, 1777; a nine-year-old condemned for a theft worth 2½d. Rebecca Downing, fifteen, was burnt alive, 1782, for poisoning her employer.

Such sentences could be commuted, compassionate juries might refuse to convict – as JPs might emasculate the penal laws – but, in a society inadequately policed, retribution was often immoderate. Yet the Law never degenerated into rank despotism : just judgements, notably on slavery, could be extorted, sometimes reluctantly, from sodden, ill-tempered judges, with world-wide implications. To sentimentalize the era would, however, be difficult. As if from an unwholesome dream flicker the Newgate condemned, enduring the last sermon with their coffins beside them; the coming Pentonville 'silent system' with hooded prisoners confined in perpetual silence; the stench of child mortality and poverty, with Blake passionately smashing through politeness and humbug.

Is this a holy thing to see
In a rich and fruitful land,
Babes reduced to misery
Fed with cold and usurous hand?

A rough, common life always continued, not only with struggle and resentments, but ribaldry, gusto, occasional grace. Refined art had been withdrawn into theatre, palace, gallery, though links remained with the street through Hogarth and Gay, through the engraver's art, and music in the Public Gardens. The masses may have respected Dr Johnson as a 'character', they would have been unable to read him, though one might remember illiterates clubbing together to have a news-sheet read aloud, or ringing the church bells when 'Pamela' got married.[68]

Popular tastes were unacademic, while Tyburn, prize-fighting, whoring, drinking, racing, fairs, bull-baiting, cock-fighting, attracted all classes. Imagination fed copiously on the rowdy, the strange, the gruesome. Frazer suggests that human sacrifice in Beltane Fires existed in the eighteenth-century Highlands. Also,

By a fatal mischance a peasant and a girl were drowned on 14 January, 1675. They were found on 3 May the same year but

were buried again in the bog on the instructions of the coroner.
Twenty-nine years later an inquisitive peasant opened the double
grave and found the two bodies, quite fresh, with the skin unbroken and maintaining their original colour as if at the time
of death. After that the luckless couple were exhibited annually
at the local fair and the surviving relatives did not succeed until
1716 in putting a stop to this macabre display.

(P. V. Glob, *The Bog People*, Faber, 1969)

Throughout Europe, puppet theatres had helped sustain old
tales: Charlemagne, the Cid, Faust. The 'Seven Paladins of
Christendom', watched in Palermo by D. H. Lawrence, was in
essence the 'Seven Against Thebes'. Stuart and Hanoverian London
patronized puppetry. Jonson and Fielding wrote for puppets;
Johnson, like Goethe, admired them. *Macbeth* was in Rowe's
repertory until about 1800. Marlowe and Webster were played,
alongside the antics of Faust, Paul Pry, St George, the Witch of
Endor, the King of Spain, Dick Whittington, Solomon and Balkis,
Fair Rosamund, Jane Shore. George Speaight[69] mentions a London
puppetry, 1660, which included an aerial view of Norwich, also
songs, acrobats, a fight between Tamerlaine and Guise, the instiga-
tor of the St Bartholomew massacre. The puppets' quasi-magical
skills and wild humour perhaps toned down some social anger,
squaring the circle of existence so patently unjust, ludicrous, lust-
ful and tormented.

The Falstaff of the streets was Punch, anti-hero, thumbing nose
at the Chesterfields and Brummells, at nobility, authority, convention: libidinous, amoral, indecent, vindictive, cowardly, braggardly,
not eloquent but loquacious, free of Christian shame and guilt.
Speaight sees him as a specifically English twist to an Italian stock-
figure somewhat modified by French puppet masters. A low-life
comic, Pulchinello, with ancestry in Imperial Rome and Classical
Greece, joined the wandering Commedia del Arte with Pierrot,
Columbine, Harlequin, Doctor, a charade of wistful zanies, grand-
iloquent quacks, beauty with fading smiles, sinuous heroes, uproarious non-sequiturs, bouts of violence, still alive in Marx
Brothers movies. Pepys would confess preference for 'Polichinello' to
the theatre proper. A recent Punch text includes, without exaggerated respect, Winston Churchill.

On the eve of industrial excesses, standardization, longer working
hours, despite hulk, gibbet, workhouse, winter starvations, evictions,
pillories, transportations, pox and crime, popular life now seems
more vivid and enterprising than it might then have appeared.
Already cricket teams were open to talent rather than exclusively

to class. Poverty was still no absolute bar to merit : the sculptor,
Sir Francis Chantrey (1781–1841) began as a grocer's boy. Common
life had savour. Rules of a country inn included :

> No more than 5 persons in one bed. No Boots to be worn in bed.
> Tinkers and Razor Grinders not to be taken in. Organ-grinders
> and Bear-handlers to sleep in wash-house. Performing Bears to be
> securely chained in the barn at night.

A bell-ringers' drinking-cup at Hadleigh is inscribed as if for
Shallow, Silence and Mouldy :

> If ye love me due not lend me
> Use me often keep me clenly
> Fill me full or not at all
> And that with strong ale and not with small.

Such popular art maintained a certain well-finished style,
individual within the conventions. An epitaph at Sudbury (Gainsborough's birthplace, Dickens' Eatanswill), 1706, runs :

> Traveller, I will relate a wondrous thing. On the day that
> Thomas Carter breathed his last a Sudbury camel passed through
> the eye of a needle; if thou hast wealth, go and do likewise.
> Farewell.

If churches were sedate, conformist, snobbish, they could also
permit the singular. St Mary's, of Bromley-by-Bow, had an epitaph
for a sailor, William Dean :

> He now at Anchor lies amid the Fleet
> Awaiting orders – Admiral Christ to meet.

Vigour abounded. The British have never been tempted to emulate
the Jews who refused to defend themselves against Pompey on the
Sabbath, or those Red Indians whose religion forbade fire-arms,
even against the whites. They would cheer a lord, salute him on
militia service, yet bespatter him at an election. Against much
visible evidence, they knew themselves free-born. Medieval compulsory arms-bearing had engendered that self-respect both tough
and frivolous which, during the General Strike, 1926, allowed
strikers to play football with the police and, 1945, applaud the
aristocratic 'old bugger', then decisively vote against him.

Concern with Europe was the privilege of wealth and leisure.
Ordinary folk, vulgarly patriotic – though a ruthless press-gang

was needed to man the cruel old fleet, from which thousands
deserted even during the life-struggle with Napoleon – felt for the
foreigner contempt, ignorance, misgiving, or fear. Indisputably
mongrel, they stared at the outside world as if hung with immaculate
pedigree, from towns and villages named by long-forgotten foreign
invaders, and under a Teutonic monarch whose title 'Defender of
the Faith' was awarded by the hated Papacy whose faith was
forbidden the Crown and proscribed by the Penal Laws. Gillray's
cartoons of foreign rulers were visual equivalents of the later Wog,
Kraut, Hun, Froggie, Wop. A Smollett character refers to 'chat-
tering Frenchmen, an Italian ape, a German hog, a beastly Dutch-
man'. A story survives of villagers killing an ape, thinking it an
escaped French prisoner. Johnson rated France as low as Scotland.
In popular lore, the Spanish were perpetually torturing bulls and
roasting heretics, Germans were half-witted giants or titled
buffoons with squelchy names, Italians cowardly, treacherous,
operatic and absurd, Jews unwashed scoundrels, Russians childlike
but barely human, the French superstitious, vain, dirty, indecent.
All shared a grave fault, they were not English, and they preferred
despotism to liberty. Three centuries later E. M. Forster wrote of
Virginia Woolf :

> She was convinced that Society is man-made, that the chief
> occupations of man are the shedding of blood, the making of
> money, the giving of orders and the wearing of uniforms, and
> that none of these is admirable.

The majority in England could identify all but one of these as
specifically continental. They also suspected that 'fair play' is
untranslatable. An arrogant lack of curiosity or imagination was
long rife. Shaw was bored by Athens 'with its stupid classical
Acropolis and smashed pillars.' 'Do you suppose', demanded
William Morris, 'that I should see anything in Rome I can't see in
Whitechapel?' Morris did favour Iceland, until he actually saw it.
This attitude was to be briefly resolved in late Victorian 'Splendid
Isolation'. Even today, foreign travel, however picturesque, can
be spoiled by the prevalence of foreigners. A directive from Winston
Churchill, 23 April 1945, would have been perfectly recognized by
Johnson.

> I do not consider that names that have been familiar for
> generations in England should be altered to suit the whims of
> foreigners living in those parts. Constantinople should never be
> abandoned, though for stupid people Istanbul may be written
> after it. . . . If we do not make a stand we shall in a few weeks be

asked to call Leghorn Livorno and the BBC will be pronouncing Paris Paree. Foreign names were made for Englishmen, not Englishmen for foreign names. I date this minute from St George's Day.

An Essex tourist in Greece, 1974, maintained that stealing from 'a Dago' was not stealing!

Issues were reduced to personality and drama, the St Bartholomew slaughter detailed in story while the deliberations of the Council of Trent were scarcely known. Burnings, secret police, violations of safe-conducts, spoke more vividly than reasoned pamphlets. Later, the painful, early industrial underworld left smaller energy for the poor to contemplate Europe, though, save towards Ireland, public opinion could usually be roused for the weaker side. Popular caricatures freely attacked continental despotism. 'Foreign Atrocities' would bestir the mob, the suppressor of Hungary, Haynau – 'Hyena' – was beaten up by London draymen, while Palmerston, contemptuous of protocol, publically entertained the defeated Kossuth. British volunteered for Garibaldi as, seventy years later, they did for Republican Spain. Gandhi was always popular. Bulganin and Kruschev were rejected, not because they were Russian but because their record seemed cruel.

The Hanoverian succession, 1714, perhaps made German affairs more conspicuous, besides contributing a pool of German mercenaries, used, notoriously, against the Americans. Thoughtful opinion tended to admire Prussia – ally against Louis XV and Napoleon – until Wilhelm II, and the quickening of imperial rivalries. The Victorian Court was Germanic in culture, Victoria and Albert eager for German unity under Prussia. Lutheran hymns, genre paintings of blue-eyed peasants and simple homesteads, solid but robust music, libraries of profound unreadables, supported a British view of serious respectable, healthy-minded Germany, as against barbarous, tyrannical Russia and mercurial, untrustworthy France. For Carlyle, Germany was 'noble, patient, deep, pious and solid.' Mill, whose conceptions of liberty influenced several generations in all continents, supported Prussia in 1870. This respect revived after the Versailles Treaty, 1919, was not extinguished until well into the Nazi era. A present-day tendency is to hope that Britain and Germany may usefully counter France in the EEC.

6

Superficially, the *Ancien Régime* seems demure enough on the upper storey, Ladies and Gentlemen passing ritual lives in tune with Palladian strictness, ordered metres of Racine, controlled melodies of Haydn, the symmetries of Gibbon, the Cartesian belief that all was responsible to Reason.

God seemed not *Me* but *It*. The Temple of Philosophy at Rousseau's Ermenonville had columns to Rousseau, Voltaire, Descartes, Montesquieu, Newton and Penn. Yet trim façades, analytical thought had not eliminated the irrational which de Sade was to tabulate and the Terror confirm.

The Enlightenment was not only Encyclopaedia and Reason, Gibbon and Walpole, but 'Nature'. News-sheets, mechanics, electricity, cartography did not abolish the vague frontiers of the soul, any more than the weight of Johnson or wit of Sheridan could cut down the roughly-tender ballad, tragic drama in miniature which, with Percy's *Reliques* indeed revived.

Courtliness, science, machinery invited their opposites. The mind could follow rival courses. Newton postulated a determinist universe yet accepted biblical truths, a zealot might proclaim human brotherhood while sharpening his sword. Dr Johnson, publically so assertive, had a private and morbid obsession with Death and After-life. No less typical than Locke was Cagliostro, Friend of Humanity, Son of an Archangel, alchemist, magician, Freemason, client of the Prophet Elijah, dispensing an elixir ensuring 5,557 years of life, which he had already reached. The mystery-monger, Comte de Sainte-Germain, announced that he was two centuries old, alternately, that he had known Jesus.

Palaces attracted wandering Fausts, providing unchanging fetishes. The miraculous ikon, 'Mother of Smolensk', was paraded before the Russian army at Borodino, 1812, as, 1914, the Tsar's War Manifesto was delivered before the miraculous 'Virgin of Kazan' to whom Kutuzov had prayed. At Versailles, Mesmer's disciples experimented with hypnotism and astrology. At Grenoble, Casanova, by faking a girl's horoscope, launched her towards a royal bed; at Milan a witch made a waxen image of him; at Aix he persuaded Madame D'Urfé, anxious to be reborn as a man, to write to the moon, which replied by return. Daniel Dunglass Home (1833–86), Browning's 'Mr Sludge', fascinated Napoleon III's courtiers with seances and alleged levitation.

Discredited by seventeenth-century fanaticism, the Churches had lost vital currents. La Mettrie (1709–51) in *Man, a Machine,* praised the cool liberations of atheism, developed by d'Holbach into a mechanical materialism. Shelley presented the Bench of Bishops with *The Necessity of Atheism*, like Pelagius believing that the Will could be perfected. Modern insights into mythology, as social and political shorthand, to which Freud added psychological symbolism, were anticipated by Vico.

Orthodoxy now preferred piety to enthusiasm and revelation. 'The conversation of clergymen', said Dr Johnson, 'is infinitely disgusting.' That a Mr Collins was appointed by a wealthy patron scarcely encouraged radical churchmanship. (In 1972, out of some 11,000 parsons, 4,100 were still appointed by private patrons.) Owen Chadwick[70] finds, even in 1851, very few working-class Anglican communicants. Some connection between Protestantism and commercial contracts was unconsciously reflected in Bishop Wordsworth's hymn :

Whatever, Lord, we lend to thee,
    Repaid a thousand-fold will be;
Then gladly will we give to thee
    Who givest all.

Tennyson's father was shuffled into the Church not from vocation but through his parents' distrust of his abilities as a landowner. Religious houses abroad continued to be filled not only by the devout but by social failures and spinsters.

Cravings for Mystery, for Dionysus, were assuaged by new cults : the Illuminati, Knights of Light, Asiatic Brothers, Cabbalists, the Rosy Cross, the Grand Orient of Freemasonry, with rituals of dim renaissance, medieval or garbled Asiatic origins. The latter-day Golden Dawn, claiming descent from the Rosy Cross, enrolled Aleister Crowley, and W. B. Yeats who witnessed a vampire routed by a magician. Theosophy continues the eighteenth-century veneration of eastern sages, sometimes encountered after their ostensible deaths, with the Mystery promises of transformation by esoteric knowledge; also with claims that Francis Bacon was the reincarnation of a Himalayan Guru, that Sainte-Germain was in Russia during the Revolution. Annie Besant, 1926, announced that her protegé, Krishnamurti, had enjoyed thirty-one incarnations in 30,000 years.

Electricity was exploited by eighteenth-century charlatans. James Graham used electromagnetics in his 'Celestial Bed' which, exuding music and small delicious shocks, guaranteed ecstasies and was a universal panacea. Throughout Europe was a craze to prolong youth, make gold, solve all problems – in a political constitution, an alchemical formula. Vampire-mania replaced witch-mania, enthusing the Gothic novel, contributing to obsessions with death and suicide.

Methodism, through hymn, Bible, sermon, in apocalyptic fervour, distracted the poor both from Anglicanism and Jacobinism. John Wesley was an anthem in himself. Meanwhile, a vague pantheism lingered. Shelley, Keats, John Martin were soon seeking extreme ranges of spirit in landscapes of fantastic colours, evocations, demi-gods, that compensated industrial blight. European Romanticism fed on British literature, as on revolution and Napoleon.

Against restrictions of mind, custom, institution, Blake (1757–1827) praised the tempestuous vitality of naked body, naked soul, forever abused, yet forever emerging in indestructible images.

> Tho' thou art worshipped by the names divine
> Of Jesus and Jehovah, thou art still
> The son of Man in wearing Night's decline,
> The lost traveller's dream under the hill.

Disgusted by mechanistic philosophy and unnatural values, Blake saw 'Progress' as making life bloodless, exterminating individuality and lonely beauties. Standardized education would enslave opinions, root out old harmonies, insights, instincts, empathies. Art was Tree of Life, technocracy was Tree of Death. Like a Mystery adept, he passionately summoned the imagination, the impulsive, to illuminate, soar, reveal the commonplace as miraculous, the polite as a fraud, and prevent hard reason from sapping enthusiasm and flair. No encyclopaedia or academy could explain, even define, love, soul, beauty, wisdom, life. The very attempt soiled the spirit.

> Mock on, mock on, Voltaire, Rousseau,
> Mock on, mock on, 'tis all in vain!
> You throw the sand against the wind,
> And the wind blows it back again.

> And every sand becomes a gem
> Reflected in the beams divine;
> Blown back they blind the mocking eye
> But still in Israel's paths they lie.

7

Reacting from James II, the 1688 Settlement guaranteed the institutions, ensuring that government should be permanently diffused through propertied Interests, rather than through King and hand-picked Council. Completed more dramatically than in Holland and Switzerland, this constitutionalism impressed foreign reformers, particularly in France, where the Estates-General had not met for over a century. Voltaire, visiting England, though not Ireland, reflected (1764):

The English Constitution has in fact arrived at the point of excellence, in consequence of which all men are restored to those natural rights of which in nearly all monarchies they are deprived. These rights are, total liberty of person and property; freedom of the press; the right of trial in all criminal cases by an independent jury, the right of being tried only according to the strict letter of the law; and the right of each man to profess what religion he wants.

Imperfections were more obvious to a Blake, Wilkes, Baboeuf. Until 1832, 96 per cent of Englishmen, 98 per cent of Scots, lacked the vote. Parliament was oligarchical, unperturbed by demographic change, Gratton now only a wall, yet possessing two Members, busy Liverpool none. Whigs and Tories were not yet monolithic or homogenous : party membership could derive from accident, bribery, passion for office or status, from personal loyalty, domestic antipathies, as much as from settled convictions or naked class-interest. Some boldness would have been needed to tell Peel, Gladstone, Palmerston, Disraeli, the two Churchills that they were mechanically controlled by class or economics.

Until the end of the nineteenth-century, opposition was scarcely systematic and unremitting. To a Blanqui, Blanc, Marx, full-blooded revolutionaries, it was mere shadow-boxing. Whig and Tory, Liberal and Conservative, revered property, religion, institutions, private enterprise, only disputing about their management and interpretation. Whig and Tory, Disraeli remarked (1832), were two names with only one meaning, 'to delude you'. Palmerston could say (1852) : 'We who are Gentlemen on this side of the House should remember that we are dealing with Gentlemen on the other side.' Paul Bloomfield[71] counts fourteen interrelated Tory and Liberal premiers.

Neither party wanted economic equality. Under Victoria, each effected, or were forced to effect, reforms, not only to benefit the community but to dish the other, relatively painlessly. This is the weakness of the British system, it is also its strength.

The overthrow of constitutional order was never a serious possibility, though intellectual radicalism in Edinburgh, London, in Whig mansions, sympathized with European reformers and anti-clericalists. The American revolution, and Ireland, cut across party limits. Mere popular discontent could be resisted while the government could pay its troops and suspend Habeas Corpus – despite riot, the broadsides of Cobbett, the wide sympathies of Fox, the occasional furious eloquence of Byron. Only national bankruptcy – gambled on by Napoleon – could replace Westminster, Windsor,

Dublin Castle, by a Convention, from Luddites, Friends of the
People, Corresponding Society, United Irishmen. Wordsworth,
who supported the early French Revolution, lived to write:

> Forth rushed from Envy sprung and self-conceit
> A power misnamed the Spirit of Reform.

After 1688, instead of revolution or civil war, the Interests could
now defeat or replace a government. Cabinets were soon responsible
to Parliament, without the royal presence. A Prime Minister
evolved, chosen by the King, but enjoying powers and patronage
still expanding to this day. JPs continued to control the masses.
Parliament supervised the national income and foreign policy but,
by modern standards, was uninterested in the details of administration, including penal, electoral, industrial, educational and economic reform. Canning was representative in holding that government should remedy obvious practical grievances but not pursue
theoretical perfections. Men and interests should make their own
way and stark pressure was needed even to remedy obvious grievances though, in the midst of calamitous war, 1807, Parliament,
with a formidable combination of mixed motives, did abolish the
slave trade. The growth of the Civil Service, with its own language,
procedures, mystique and minor tyrannies, provided a new Estate
of the realm.

Following Waterloo, 1815, land and industry struggled for
parliamentary control and, from Reform, 1832, seeking an ever-
widening national vote, the Interests – Coal, Cotton, Railways,
Brewing, Steel, Banking, Shipping, Agriculture, Fishing, Tobacco,
Sugar, what Belloc called 'the wretched money-game at Westminster' – dominated, combined, overlapped, quarrelled, lost ground,
within or beyond party. Guided by Manchester as much as London,
they veered and tacked over reform, corn laws, Ireland, health,
social justice, South Africa, eventually joined by others, the most
powerful unions. In 1972, parliamentary Tories held 780 director-
ships; unions financed individual Labour Members, owned property
and investments. Parties were to unite against Wilhelm II and
Hitler – and against Edward VIII.

Before 1832, landowners controlled 'Pocket Boroughs'. Bribery
was commonplace. Relations between Member and constituents
could be informal. 'May God's curse light on you all, and may it
make your homes as open and free to the Revenue Officers as your
wives and daughters have always been to me while I have represented your rascally constituency.' (1714)

The system perhaps more approximated Rousseau's General Will, even Mussolini's corrupt State, than modern democracy. Unlike the French and Prussians, the British were less apt to codify. English literature has never felt need for an Academy : a printed Declaration of the Rights of Man was unlikely to emerge from Westminster; it might, however, be goaded to pass an India Act, impose an Income Tax, prosecute an exorbitant proconsul. Despite frictions, omissions, injustices, some might still feel that Britain was succeeding where the Greeks had failed and in what few others had attempted, the spreading of political democracy outwards from the City, relatively peacefully. Taxation, not another civil war, would assist a degree of economic democracy.

The Cabinets which lost America, stabilized India, magnified the national wealth, defeated Napoleon, now seem more gentlemanly than professional.

Windham would have agreed to participate in the government. Pitt was willing to include him, but Dundas, who was head of the Home Office, Minister of War, Secretary for Ireland, and Treasurer to the Navy, obstinately refused to reduce his extravagant pluralism. Dundas, however, merely held the title of Minister of War. Knowing nothing about the army he turned it over to Yonge, first secretary of the War Office, who was not a member of the Cabinet.

(George Lefevre, *The French Revolution. 1793–99*, Routledge, 1967)

Here was Dickens' Boodle-Coodle-Doodle, supplemented by Melbourne's famous, 'Stop a bit, what did we decide? Is it to lower the price of bread, or isn't it? It does not matter what we say, but, mind, we must all say the same.'

8

Parliament was one of several complementary institutions, not wholly caste-bound, scarcely democratic. Evolving from the Coffee House, the Club was prospering, less political and philosophical than in Paris. Church and school seem less energetic than in Tudor and Stuart days. The fee-paying Public Schools, violent and rampageous, theoretically held the Confucian ethic, that patristic institutions, traditions, wise seniors, promoted moral excellence : the renaissance belief in the virtues of Greco-Roman literature. Science, art, political economy, did not qualify. Evangelized, and somewhat more disciplined by Arnold and his successors, these schools fashioned proconsuls, soldiers, administrators, parsons more readily

than imaginative independents, though Byron, Shelley, Brummell
survived. Talleyrand, asked what were the best schools, replied,
'The English Public Schools, and they are dreadful.'

'What we look for is, first, religious and moral principle; secondly,
gentlemanly conduct; thirdly, intellectual ability.' Thomas Arnold's
question-begging synopsis, ridiculed by posterity, sounds less contemptible to those who discovered, in Gestapo, OGPU and
KGB, torturers of unquestioned intellectual ability and no moral
principle whatsoever.

Like Anglicanism, Trade Unionism and the Services, the Public
Schools changed slowly. Dickens spoke with two voices, neither
inapposite even in 1939.

> He had been eight years at a public school (Winchester) and
> had learnt, I understood, to make Latin verses of several sorts,
> in the most admirable manner. But I never heard that it had been
> anybody's business to find out what his natural bent was, or
> where his feelings lay, or to adapt any kind of teaching to him.
> He had been adapted to the verses, and had learnt the art of
> making them to such perfection that if he had remained at school
> until he was of age I suppose he could only have gone on making
> them over and over again, unless he had enlarged his education
> by forgetting how to do it. Still, although I have no doubt that
> they were very beautiful, and very improving, and very sufficient
> for a great many purposes of life, and always remained all through
> life, I did doubt whether Richard would not have profited by
> someone studying him a little, instead of him studying them quite
> so much.
>
> *(Bleak House)*

Nevertheless, the Public Schools had glamour, Dickens himself
sending a son to Eton, as did a socialist Minister in the 1960s
so that his boy could meet his social equals. Dickens (*Speeches*) also
confessed,

> I believe there is not in England any institution as socially liberal
> as a public school . . . so complete an absence of servility to
> mere rank, to mere position, to mere riches . . . a boy there is
> always what his abilities or his personal qualities make him. We
> may differ about the curriculum and other matters, but of the
> frank, free, manly, independent spirit preserved in our public
> schools I apprehend there can be no kind of question.

It was to be noticed that the Public School, emphasizing prefects,
Bloods, team spirit, conformity, leadership, military initiative, fear

of ridicule, in its by-products of social work and Christian missions, has affinities with muscular socialism, even communism. Field-Marshal Allenby, and Prime Minister Clement Attlee were both recognizably from Haileybury, originally the training-ground for East Indian Company officials. Examinations were revered less in England than in France and Prussia. Privilege, bribery, snobbery and luck outweighed expert selection, fair competition, academic distinction. Until the Gladstone era, church, universities, civil service and armed forces – one woman bought a full colonelcy – were officered by anything save Napoleonic meritocracy.

None of this went by uncriticized. Injustice, together with corn-laws, game-laws, inter-trade rivalries, tolls, taxes, high rents, unemployment, new machinery, extortionate prices, hunger, Irish immigration, enclosures, Methodism, aroused mass rallies or protests. Dr Sacheverell, Wilkes, Gordon, Porteous, Priestley are associated with famous riots. The poor were generally orderly and unvindictive. George Rudé warns against the indiscriminate and pejorative use of 'mob'. He supplies instructive figures, showing that strikes were frequent in France and England, particularly after 1780, together with window-smashing, rick-burning, house-burning, wrecking of looms and threshing-machines. Yet 'the mob' killed few; the militia killed forty-two marching miners, 1761, and wounded forty-eight. The Gloucester riots, 1766, entailed nine hangings and seven transportations, with further executions at Reading, Norwich, Salisbury, more sanguinary than the French grain riots, 1775. Manchester, 1753 and 1758, endured two remarkably 'modern' wages movements, the second arousing 10,000 militant strikers, forcing their more reluctant fellows to join them and pay levies. 285 Gordon rioters were killed, 1780, and twenty-five hanged. A miners' strike in the North-East threw 100,000 colliers and seamen out of work. Seven London coal-heavers were hanged after a riot, 1768. Unions being illegal, violence here was common, in general more so than in pre-revolutionary France. 'Machine-breaking was a recognized form of industrial action.' As in present-day Northern Ireland, the Gordon Riots saw religious hysteria and hooliganism sparked off by poverty, ignorance and perhaps criminal elements. None of this ceased with the new century, the era of the struggle for Reform, for legal unions, repeal of the Corn Laws, Chartism. 464 rioters were transported, 1831, 600 imprisoned, nine hanged.

Rudé finds that the well-organized Luddite riots under the Regency tied up a larger military force than Wellington used in Portugal, 1808. The Gordon Riots necessitated 10,000 soldiers, double the force which routed Monmouth at Sedgemoor. In London, 1848, 170,000 special constables – allegedly including the future Napoleon

208   *Worlds and Underworlds*

III – were enrolled against about 30,000 Chartists. In riots, 1736–1848, he estimates that the military shot 630, and 180 were hanged.

To many observers, revolution was to be expected in restless Britain, politically divided, and humiliated in America. Faced with continental revolutions and a hungry, discontented urban and rural proletariat, the choice seemed between adaptation and violence. Despite riots, risings, mob uproar, rising prices, angry radicalism and harsh squirearchy, the institutions were in fact to adapt, became indeed strengthened, not absolutely for the better, with complacency, inertia, injustice always latent. The organization and powers of the meritocratic Civil Service are currently being attacked as partisan, obstructive, over-independent, too much a Mystery. Workers' associations, after initial intimidation, were grudgingly allowed their place with evangelical dissent, outspoken press, obstinate juries. Corn Laws, franchise, factories, were reformed through the laborious apparatus of Parliament, committees, Blue Books, inspectors, education, variously rejected by Owen, Robespierre, Napoleon, Tolstoy, Kropotkin, Marx, Lenin, Schweitzer. To these, Parliamentary parties were identical, the institutions manned by what Dickens called 'the arrogant, the froward and the vain'. More was being offered in France.

> Plots, massacres, assassinations, seem
> to some people a trivial price for ob-
> taining a revolution. A cheap bloodless
> reformation, a guiltless liberty, appear
> flat and vapid to their taste.
>
> Burke
>
> It is the most sacred duty of a people
> whose rights are violated to rebel.
>
> Robespierre

I

European Enlightenment, though anti-clerical, anti-feudal, did not wish to destroy institutions, but to modernize them, like the Americans, adapt them, like the British, or centralize them more thoroughly, like Catherine, Frederick, Joseph. America had given impetus to European republicanism, much of it academic or senti-mental, but monarchy had silent roots as organic as any trumpeted in the Rights of Man. The withdrawal of God could increase the mystique not only of the State but of visible kings. The revolution-aries treated Louis with considerable forbearance, even respect, until his abortive flight to Varennes.

French royal and clerical institutions had long been in question, but not total question. Louis XVI was popular : Robespierre him-self estimated that, as a progressive, he would exceed Charlemagne and Henri IV. De Tocqueville wondered whether there was ever a more remarkable clergy than in the pre-revolutionary Church.[72] However, while rich in Mediterranean trade, France had lost two empires; industry lagged far behind Britain, the treasury was ex-hausted by assistance to America and by lax, inefficient management. Banks and farms were backward; internal customs barriers, disparate measurements, provincial rights, feudal privileges, a ludicrous taxa-tion eroded a nascent wealth. Despite arbitrary powers, and complete choice of Ministers, the Crown was less absolute than it seemed, obstructed by tradition, undermined by inflation, govern-ing a people of whom it knew little, through a nobility it had emasculated, a middle-class to whom it refused privileges, and

210 · Worlds and Underworlds

through armed forces defeated in three continents. The peasantry had as many grievances as they had children, which were many. A number of unpaid labour days were demanded, as of Africans on the roads and rivers of British Kenya during the 1930s. In 1789, peak of over fifty years of price rises, France, despite strikes, hardships, actual hunger, was not revolutionary, but middle-class professionals wanted more value for money. Paying more taxes than the pitiful contributions from the wealthy nobility and Church, it wanted, as Sieyès put it, 'to count for something', as in Britain and America it already did. With the State confessedly bankrupt, despite enormous assets, government should be more precisely defined, finances reorganized, feudal nonsense removed. These were not impossible objectives. Mirabeau knew English history as well as Roman, Lafayette was friend of Washington. Both had reason for optimism.

The horrors of the Revolution were spectacular but had long been preceded by the tortures, galley-slaving, evictions, arbitrary imprisonments which Voltaire, Diderot and Rousseau knew so well. Before 1789, French police methods were far more systematic than in Britain and penalties arguably more atrocious. Branding was still practised. In France there was

a noted Punishment so much in vogue abroad which is the greatest service to restrain such Hands: and that is, breaking upon the Wheel; by which the Criminals run through ten thousand of the most exquisite Agonies, as there are moments in the several hours during the inconceivable Torture of their bruised, broken and disjointed limbs to the last period. Or there is another way which could not but make the most daring spirit fearful of running into the danger of feeling the severity thereof; and that is (instead of dispatching them by a cord about their Neck, etc.) by twisting a little Cord about their Arms or Legs, which would probably affect the Nerves and Sinews and the more sensible Parts to produce the keenest Anguish; under which, as there would be some time before they expire, they will suffer the pain of many Deaths in one; with this if they were fixed on some Gibbet at some little distance of about ten or twenty Poles from those Roads where now are the usual places of Execution, that their Cries may not much disturb the common Passengers, and yet not so far off out of hearing, but that they may a little reach the Ears of their offending Brethren at their passing by, in Order to remind them of the dismal end they are likely to come unto.

(Malvin R. Zirker, Jr, *Fielding's Social Pamphlets*, University of California, 1970)

Other emotions gushed as the Century aged – man is apt to find a *fin de siècle* mysteriously significant. Rousseau, whose observation of human nature was not impeccable, was teaching that institutions inhibited or crushed humanity which, if freed from throne and altar, parliament and bank, would stream harmoniously towards justice, brotherhood, virtue, even perfection. The call from America that, by self-evident truths, all men were entitled to Life, Liberty and the Pursuit of Happiness, excited youth more than the less fluent views of human potential that governed Prussia or Britain. That Pitt had attacked the war against the American colonists as 'most accursed, wicked, barbarous, cruel, unjust and diabolical' passed unnoticed by those drunk on Rousseau, on Brutus and Cassius, and suspicious, or ignorant, of Legal Opposition. The Jacobins, not without reason, denounced Britain as a corrupt and grabbing oligarchy. Unadulterated idealism could not survive practical politics, war, treachery, but the Terror was not planned; it was a drastic improvisation in drastic circumstances which, like quarrels, drugs and bad manners, grew an inner, uncontrollable dynamic. The future regicides believed fervently that humane law could transform humanity, classical Virtue could restore civic conscience and fraternity. 'When all men are free they will be equal, and, when equal, just.' (Saint-Just) Yet none, save Baboeuf, began as an extremist. The Revolution was not against property, but for defending and expanding it in the interests of those who actually worked; it was not atheist but, mainly, Deist; not against Law, but against unjust laws and corruption; it wanted more order, not less. Patriotic, it was not at first nationalistic, yearning to free all men, even Jews – though in 1789 domestic servants were not enfranchised – offering its supreme command (1792) to that very Duke of Brunswick it defeated at Valmy, where Goethe reported the birth of a new world, and that cannon-balls 'made a strange noise, something between the humming of a top, the splash of water and the cry of a bird.' Marat was Spanish-Swiss. The Englishman, Tom Paine, was elected to the Convention and voted for the King's execution. David Williams helped plan the Constitution of 1793.

2

Like British magnates, the revolutionaries admired ancient Rome but discovered a different moral. The Public Good meant something more urgent than that leisurely discussed at Chatsworth, Stowe, Edinburgh salons. For Saint-Just, revolution should have no end but perfect happiness. The adjective is significant. Girondins and

Jacobins, some taking classical names – Gracchus, Anaxagorus –
were to see their own National Assembly as a swindling machine
to preserve the traditional, the traitorous, rich, over-fed and stupid.
Speaking, often at inordinate length, of reason and virtue, they
assumed that man in the mass could swiftly absorb both, on orders
from the Rousseau-ian State. Yet voices emerged speaking the language of neither. Examples are too many. During the September
Massacres, over 150 children of Bicêtre Reformatory were killed
and mutilated by mysteriously incited 'People's Courts' of ordinary
commoners, in the panic of Prussian invasion. While appealing to
the quixotic and progressive, revolutions give ample scope to the
voluntary stool-pidgeon, part-time policeman, vindictive informer,
false witness, spy, blackmailer, exhibitionist. France, Germany,
Russia, Spain show the same melancholy tale.

Almost all the most famous revolutionaries – not always the most
important – had the disposition of middle-class intellectuals to
dogmatize from inexperience. Belief in the kindly simplicity of
Nature, embraced by Rousseau and Robespierre, so appealing to
those suffocated by small print and stuffy drawing-rooms, could
have been dispelled by a glance at peasant Ireland, Spain, Poland,
Calabria. They were like the English gardener who spoke of Nature
to J. B. Priestley 'as if he had been a member of the small committee
that had appointed her.' Believing that laws would produce virtue,
they claimed that failure to do so did not invalidate the principle.
Failure was blamed not on error or mismanagement but treachery,
counter-revolution, wickedness – to be punished by death, prison,
exile, loss of civic rights. In war, confusion, under a hopeless King,
Mother Nature was quickly ousted by Kali, goddess of destruction.
In Terror, in Napoleonic blood-baths, 'Nature' issued punctilious
reminders of her independence. Individually attractive or inspiring,
many revolutionaries pandered to dangerous, irrational mobs. 'The
Crowd', said Mussolini, more professional, 'is like a woman who
likes strong men.' Many politicians were more eager to gain support
from the poor than to transform society in the interests of the poor,
while the genuine idealists were too impatient. The Government
was the People, the People could not vote against itself, therefore
opposition was treason. The Terror, 1794, was prophetic, government by headlines, not evidence. Cosy family men, ruthless killers,
the new Catos, found themselves shedding ideals, scruples, finally
common-sense, ending as bewildered and trapped as their victims.
General concepts and great conceit, Goethe said, are always breeding
dreadful calamities. Earnest, humourless, in a hurry for Utopia –
Binyon's 'Slowness is Beauty' would have repelled them –
they found temperament and circumstances forcing them into

inquisitorial short-cuts, self-deception, revenges. 'Liberty, Equality, Fraternity, or Death.' Only de Sade, more explicitly than Diderot, openly acknowledged, from within revolutionary prison and asylum, the attractions of pain, crime, torture, one's own as much as another's. 'Nature' was at best unreliable, like God : faced with good and evil, a man, highly trained, richly endowed, may, through boredom, caprice, malice or curiosity, choose evil. Republican institutions could be as pitiless as monarchical, Monarchy and Republic be identical. For them, society, life, needed movement : blood, destruction, were healthier than the neutral and torpid.

The revolutionary Convention, with superb effrontery, renamed 1793 as 'Year One'. Its phrases clanged and challenged, its slogans were generous and exciting. Robespierre's 'The French People decree the Liberty of the World' loses nothing beside Lord Melbourne's, 'I say, Archbishop, what do you think I would have done about this slavery business if I had my own way? I would have done nothing at all. It is all a pack of nonsense. There have always been slaves in the most civilized countries, the Greeks and the Romans. However, they *would* have their own way and we have abolished slavery. But it is all great folly.' For such a man, as for Talleyrand, former bishop, ex-revolutionary Minister, Robespierre's last years made sincerity disreputable. Robespierre, in power, preferred assertion to debate.

Europe saw the revolutionary Tribunate become revolutionary Tribunal, Throne replaced by despotic Committees, Christ by 'Supreme Being' in that compulsory state religion which Rousseau, never wholly consistent, had felt would enforce social cohesion. (Even Voltaire had built a church.) Only official candidates were permitted in Jacobin elections, in the name of the rights of man.

3

Like the Renaissance, the Revolution still provokes controversy. Efforts to interpret it periodically convulsed the nineteenth century. Where did it end? Has it ended? Did Napoleon fulfil or betray it? Soberly, it strengthened the executive by abolishing local 'freedoms' : it freed trade, industry, peasantry from restrictions; regularized taxation; standardized weights, measures, language, law; established schools, hospitals, academies; improved the lot of women and children – conditions favourable for liberal economic advance.

The redistribution of power transferred sovereignty from the king to the people. The redistribution of land transferred property from the aristocracy of church and state to the middle and lower classes. What had been the monopoly of one French-man in a hundred was now shared between twenty-five. The magic of property – of property freed from the old encumbrances, and guaranteed by new laws – was now within reach of any thrifty and hard-working citizen.

(Thompson)

This can be viewed more caustically. Harold Laski defined Liberalism, 'starting as a method of emancipating the middle-classes, changing after 1789 into a method of disciplining the work-ing class'. Free corporations and universities were prohibited, any-thing that intruded between citizen and State. This infected Marxism and Fascism, alike crushing independent trade unions, judges, schools. Napoleon crushed Caribbean independence as Marxist Russia was to crush Baltic and Hungarian.

Napoleon, lawgiver and conqueror, art-thief, author of a lush story, *The Earl of Essex*, was in many ways grossly unfit to rule. 'Everything big is good.' He is not to be imagined remarking, or even understanding 'Ripeness is all!' Even as warrior he remained unable to delegate, prone to bad human judgements, neglecting to create a genuine General Staff, a neglect that Prussian professionals were to notice.[73] In traditions of Roman Law, Convention and Empire reaffirmed the ascendancy of State, father, husband, teacher, businessman, the tyrannical, enclosed family, while Napoleon coldly exploited the mystique of Crowns. In place of revolutionary life and humanity, he developed his personal empire, fitting unimpres-sive relatives on thrones of Westphalia, Spain, Rome, Naples, Tus-cany and, vital to Britain, Holland. He would have appreciated Belloc's remark that, while intimately desiring a republic, most men are not republicans. His Empire swept away Inquisition, ghetto, obsolete laws and frontiers; stimulated, for better or worse, German and Italian nationalism; encouraged talent, so that an inn keeper's son could become King of Naples. In exchange were 300,000 French cannon, conscription, twenty years of war. The Dreyfus Case, eighty years after Mirabeau and Danton, made it difficult to believe that revolution had ever occurred.

For Freud, Napoleon's career was the indulgence of puberty fantasies. A lonely man can cause explosions, and his view of others made him permanently lonely. The stars shone for him alone. He did not enjoy people, like a Palmerston, a Danton, but used them : disliking variety in people, he wanted to grow them out of flower-pots. At best, they were untrustworthy machines. His vanity repels, extracting the worst in his followers. 'Your Majesty's presence plunges them into a frenzy of self-oblivion,' a character remarks,

in Prokofiev's opera, *War and Peace*. His discipline was not that of
the artist, batsman, wise judge, but of an underfed policeman. He
was concerned with the duties of people, but not with their rights –
the rights of women, children, young males, workers, negro slaves,
foreigners. Like most dictators he had to hurry, unable to rely on
traditional loyalties and institutions. Talleyrand remarked that the
Emperor's watch was fast, while the rest of humanity had normal
time. Power, said Napoleon, is never ridiculous. He may have
been wrong.

Nevertheless, people tend to love defeated generals. Napoleon
survived, as Tragic Hero, inciting romantic egos passionate for the
top, at whatever cost. Such romanticism painted and laureated the
French sufferings in Russia, without demanding why they had
occurred.

> By the bivouacs
> One saw the picket dying at his post,
> Still standing in his saddle, white with frost,
> The stone lips frozen to the bugle's mouth.
>
> (Robert Lowell, Imitations,
after Hugo's Russia. 1812, Faber, 1962)

He had started the new century with a bang, determined to hurl
it into new shapes, many of them emancipating, until leaking away
into overambition and the apparently irresistible dynamics of conquest. His glory had a permanent effect on Churchill, Mussolini, de
Gaulle – as Marie Antoinette, an image of flawed beauty defaced
by venomous reality, troubled countless dreaming adolescents. His
rule signally opposed the Balance of Power, an international order
imperfect, unromantic, yet susceptible to diplomacy, arbitration,
bribery – history without too much zeal. Napoleon himself, a 'classical anti-Gentleman' (Freud), was uneasy in the international
culture of Goethe, Lermontov, Pushkin, Haydn, Schiller, Sheridan,
Maria Theresa, Talleyrand, Metternich, Melbourne, preferring to
soar with 'Ossian' than submit, clumsily, to the minuet. He yet could
be seen, not only by himself, as the vital force needed to shatter a
tired century. Byron wrote :

> Extreme in all things ! had'st thou been betwixt,
> Thy throne had still been thine, or never been;
> For daring made thy rise and fall, thou seekst
> Even now to re-assume the imperial mien
> And shake the world, the thunderer of the scene.

Hazlitt   admired   him   to   the   end.   Henry   James,   whose conversation with the Emperor is unimaginable, seems, when dying, to have sunk himself into Napoleon. Mussolini's rhetorical play about Napoleon was produced in London, 1927.

4

Jean Monnet, an architect of the European Coal and Steel Community, belated reconciliator of France and Germany, remarked (1950) that Britain prefers to make decisions not from principles but from facts, continentals the reverse.

Industrial, imperial Britain, in what had appeared the most savage threat in her history, had to examine with unprecedented severity her attitude towards the outside world. Momentarily it seemed that America, with her mammoth commercial potential, would drift into the power of her benefactor, vengeful and triumphant revolutionary France. Much good-will was extended to the early Revolution, seen both as overdue reform, the useful weakening of old enemy and American ally, the retort to repressive British plutocracy, pompous unimaginative profiteers. The Whig Leader, Fox, applauded it. To Paine, Bentham; the atheists Shelley and Godwin; Hunt, Southey, Wordsworth, Wilberforce, Priestley, Byron, Place; to the Regenerators, to the Corresponding Society, Constitutional Society, United Irishmen; to agitators for universal suffrage, for Free Ireland, even for a republic, the fall of the Bastille represented the ascent of man. Enchanted by Mirabeau, Lafayette, Brissot, Robespierre, they would regard British indignation against France, 1792, as contemporary liberals do Russian intervention in Budapest and Prague, and indeed the latter is in strict European tradition, papal, monarchical, imperialistic or socialistic. Louis XVI would have welcomed foreign royalist troops; Louis XVIII was escorted home by Allied armies; Russia crushed Hungarian rebels for the Habsburgs, 1849; France invaded Spain against Spanish rebels, 1823, and fought for Italian nationalists against Austria, 1859. The international Left and Right fought each other in Spain, 1936–9.

For many British, the Napoleonic Plebiscite was the democratic answer to stagnant, unrepresentative Westminster. Others, Pitt, Burke, Castlereagh – like Jefferson, like Henry Adams – kept their heads about human nature, neither dazzled by its potential nor appalled by its lapses. Burke had supported the Americans as reformers, opposed slavery as vehemently as any revolutionary. He defended imperfect institutions that worked and, recognizing that destruction is easier than creation, disliked universal solutions generous but impractical. Subsequently, the integrity and social realism of Peel, of Gladstone, had nothing to learn from Robespierre, Barras, Louis Philippe, not much from Napoleon. Something perhaps from Talleyrand, who knew from experience Shaw's definition of a fanatic as one who doubles his efforts when losing sight of his objectives.

Tone of voice can be as significant as sentiment. Guillotine, Red and White Terror, political hysteria, military aggression, dissipated much of the revolutionary promise. Fox and Byron were not obvious associates of Hébert, Fouché, Marat, even Napoleon. Robespierre's 'There must be one Will and one Will only' had no recognizable counterpart in British political philosophy save in Hobbes. The Republic became mistrusted, even amongst the poor, not because it was wrong, not only because it was French, but because, like the Puritan major-generals and preachers, it was verbose, self-righteous and apparently aggressive. The tangled emotions of English patriotism, like song or drugs transcending ugly social facts, were roused by the French invasion of the rich Netherlands and Mediterranean, by momentary landings in Ireland and Wales, and, not least, by French tariffs to foster new and rival industries and banking. British sensibility, leisure, liberties, ultimately depended on round incomes and square meals, on exports. In twenty years of blockade, counter-blockade, invasion, defeats and victory, the City financed anti-French coalitions involving Russia, Austria, Sweden, Spain, Portugal, Holland, Naples, Sardinia, Prussia; and Westminster acquired, if not a better world, at least a dominantly British world. Napoleon despised the British as amateur militarists but overlooked the solid artillery innovations of Shrapnel, Mercier, Robins (Fuller), and could not prevent the adroit capture of Spanish American markets, Ceylon, Trinidad, the Cape, Malta – a British sea-power and credit unrivalled for a century – the final occupation of Paris itself by British, Russians, Prussians. It was the end of 'You Fire First', wars of rules and seasons and mercenaries as downright, conscript armies marched to all ends of Europe, conscription, save in Britain until 1916, becoming a permanent factor of civilized life.

At home, the cost was dismaying. Profits throve, not only in trade but in food and rents. Protest again disclosed that blacker side of British government never quite redeemed by songs of liberty, and peeresses giving kisses wholesale at elections. Gibbets were uncovered, Habeas Corpus revoked, Gagging Acts and Combination Acts forbade organized radicalism and unions. Irish 'troubles' renewed hatreds. 'Peterloo' still reverberates. Scared of Jacobinism, the Pitt government had used spies, informers, perhaps provocateurs.

Victorious Britain at once revised her conception of the Balance of Power, requiring a strong, though constitutional France to offset her late allies. Steel, coal, cotton, cloth needed all available markets, and British economists were inclining away from mono-polistic colonialism, towards Free Trade. The problems would be to assess the role of the Empire, to reconcile profits with conscience, to decide whether the post-Revolution masses should be trusted or coerced, how they should be fed and worked. Also, France, even Europe, might again be wrenched askew by Napoleonic glamour which glowed like a banner or waited with appetizing nostalgia, among the mounting statistics of industrial casualties.

The Revolution repeated to British parliamentary democracy the lessons long ago experienced by Rome. That humanity is endlessly susceptible to dictators, who usually prove paranoic; that neither public opinion nor the informer is a satisfactory instrument of government; that greed for status, privilege, profiteering are not changed overnight by legislation; that constant appeals to the streets endanger society; that monopolistic tendencies are perhaps endemic but are also resistible; that power is a drug, potent and unpredictable; that idealism, venality and violence are not indig-enous to particular classes, religions, races; that a revolution which uses secret police, censorship and terror ceases to be a revolution.

In short, the unconscious proved itself the first internationale. To overthrow a Church was not to escape religion, the hankerings after incarnation, hierarchy, miracles, last judgement, immortality, predestination, apartheid. Robespierre came to see himself as messiah of the Supreme Being, Napoleon went one stage higher; the Jacobins degenerated into a dedicated priesthood. Similar visions affected their successors. Stalin, educated to be a priest, never ceased to be one. Terror made the Enlightenment distressingly unreal, medieval assumptions of 'the powers of darkness' discon-certingly modern. Like 'Napoleon', the 'Revolution' could become not a reasoned programme, but an anthem, with tunes powerful enough to distract from the words.

Part Four

Part Four

An Englishman never respects you until you stand up to him.
Then he begins to like you. He is afraid of nothing physical,
but he is very mortally afraid of his own conscience if you
ever appeal to it and show him to be in the wrong. He does
not like to be rebuked for wrong-doing at first but he will
think it over and it will get hold of him and hurt him till
he does something to put it right.

Mahatma Gandhi

Provided they can sell you a piece of calico, what do they
care if they plunge a nation into calamity?

Chateaubriand

I

Like the peacemakers of 1919, the aristocrats at the Congress of
Vienna, 1815, had a chance, exaggerated by hindsight, of assisting
an un-Napoleonic but international liberal constitutionalism. But
two decades of slaughter scarcely attracted Metternich and his
royal overlords towards further experiment. The old order was
largely restored, though on sufferance. International solidarity
was monarchical, claiming to maintain civilization and Christianity
against revolution. The dignified Austrian Empire had replaced
the ancient Holy Roman Empire, still holding down multi-racial
possessions, while permitting relative freedoms not enjoyed today
in its successor states. Russia remained ' the gendarme of Europe',
repressing liberal nationalism on demand, or without it. The Papacy
was in its last decades of temporal power. Some 300 German states
were reduced to thirty-seven, potentially on the move, under Austria
or Prussia.

Economic self-interest largely, but seldom entirely, dictated British
foreign and colonial policy. Following the American Revolution,
the African Association was founded, 1788, to explore and map the
African hinterland for commerce, science and geographical research.
Evangelists campaigned against slavery including traffic in eunuchs,
supplied by Ashanti and Hausa kings, and Arab middlemen. Few
British premiers were devotees of imperial expansion; Gladstone

and Disraeli both began as Little Englanders, but the criss-cross of tensions and opportunities ensured that, under each, the Empire increased. Heavy industry, railways, bridges, cables, turbines, guns – particularly in Africa and India – would demand greater control of finance, defence, cheap labour, finally of government.

Secure in India and the West Indies, and in all oceans, victorious over Napoleonic France, British manufacturers could assault the world. That ancient economic bridgehead, Belgium, independent of Holland by 1830, must be guaranteed, particularly from reviving France, still intriguing for it with Prussia in 1866. Taking gross advantage of her war-gains, and the shortages, dislocations and reconstructions abroad, Britain, repressive at home and in Ireland, was soon aiding Latin Americans against moribund Spain. 'South America free,' Canning said, adding with the cynicism of strength, 'and, if possible, British.' Britain supported liberal nationalism in Germany, Belgium, Italy, Hungary, the Balkans, helped Greek independence from Turkey. Grateful nations would be capital investments and allies against Russia or France. The affections and prejudices of individual statesmen still trained in classical lore and values could also have had some part, as indeed did public opinion. People could see, erroneously, the Greeks as the descendants of Periclean Athens, as heroes of Thermopolae resisting barbarians: many Italian nationalist ruffians were haloed with ancient Roman associations. Mussolini – himself more a typical *risorgimento* figure than many Italian liberals care to admit – was to gamble, unwisely, on his people being literal heirs of the Roman Empire.

Without formal political pacts, Britain showered Europe and the world with bridges, roads, cables, coaling-stations, harbours, steamships, railways, cotton, pottery, transmuting the everyday and, in the area of interest-rate, unconcerned with imaginary pasts. The engineer, Isambard Kingdom Brunel – the name is redolent of his own magnificent struggles – moulding sea and land for new life-lines of wheel, turbine, steam, was almost the God of Genesis and remains sanctified on a stained-glass window at Westminster Abbey.

Simultaneously, the invisible exports of banking, insurance, freight-carriage, technical expertise, garnered huge and ever-increasing royalties.

'Properly speaking,' Disraeli declared, 'Manchester is as great a human exploit as Athens.' Nor is it fanciful to compare Brunel – or Gladstone and Disraeli, with their many books and interests – to Renaissance Man, versatile, active, knowledgeable, and indeed with a wider social conscience. Starting as gardener's lad, Paxton, who designed the Crystal Palace, four times the size of St Peter's and for purposes at least as humanitarian, was engineer, botanist, railway director, Member of Parliament, head gardener at Chatsworth, newspaper promoter : he imported the Monkey Tree, laid out public parks in Glasgow, Halifax, Liverpool. General Sir Richard Strachey was explorer, mathematician, engineer, painter, contributing powerfully to Indian botany, geology, geography, railways, tunnels, canals, forestry, public works, currency, financial and administrative decentralization.[74] Stamford Raffles was archaeologist, botanist, historian, explorer, as well as an imperialist ruler.

British engineers built Lima railway station, that mass of polished mahogany, the first European railways, railways in Argentina, Sudan, Canada, India, Australia; they exported steam-engines to France, Austria, Russia; they sank oil wells in Mexico, cut Burmese teak, extracted Bilbao iron, supplied electricity to France, irrigation to Egypt; erected Austrian factories, Italian banks. Sheffield sold Europe electro-plating, South Wales and the North despatched coal dug with locally-invented machines and transported by British steam and coal to France and Belgium. British-built machines were exported to British-built factories financed by London or Manchester for foreign firms, many of whose shareholders were British. British steam, gas, steel, chloroform, vaccination, created unprecedented comfort and security. The Great Exhibition, 1851, industrial and commercial, was a congress as significant as that of Vienna, steam, coal, banking enthroning London above Amsterdam, Marseilles, Hamburg. British fleets were unprecedented in size and range. London, until 1914, was flamboyant with luxuries – Balls, gold plate, ornate dinners, rare flowers and scents, uniformed servants, distinguished manners supported by a 3 per cent interest rate. The British helped organize the Swiss hotel industry. D'Oyly Carte was to pioneer new hotel grandeur, importing French and Swiss managers, inducing a fashion for dining out and for hygiene, installing at the Savoy not only Cesar Ritz as chef but seventy bathrooms. 'What, are your guests going to swim?' he was asked. One long-term guest at the Savoy was Monet. Italian opera still predominated but concerned only fashionable London, and that not very seriously. A visitor to Covent Garden noticed 'the impudence of the women in the corridors'.

Exports were not solely economic. Tuscany adopted a British-inspired constitution more liberal than the Jacobin or Napoleonic. Cavour quoted Erskine May in Piedmont's parliament. Louis Napoleon, granting certain union rights, was aware of British precedents. 'The history of England', Macaulay pronounced, 1835, 'is emphatically the history of progress.'

Europe was not consistently grateful or admiring. Napoleon had particularly resented the selfish British commercial and banking monopolists. Delacroix could not understand how Shakespeare and love of liberty emerged from a land where 'aristocratic pride and class-distinctions are carried to a point I find infinitely shocking.'[75] Such defects certainly inspired generations of British novelists, humorists, sociologists. George Orwell was to be described as 'lower-upper-middle class'. British high moral tone must have seemed as intolerably complacent and hypocritical to continentals as to Dickens. Flogging and homosexuality were regarded as specifically British, a race cruel, rapacious, warlike, narrow and insensitive.

The vaunted British 'Freedom of the Seas' meant British naval supremacy, seen at home as guardian of world peace but, abroad, as guarantee of British wealth. Britain had forced the Vienna Congress to forbid the slave-trade, vainly, until 1840, so that Britain was able to enforce presumptuous blockades and Right of Search – and gain plenty of prize-money – particularly galling to Spain, Portugal, France and the United States who were aware that, endowed by slavery, Britain rejected it only when it was ceasing to be profitable for herself. From aggressive slave-imperialism, she had changed to the imperialism of aggressive slave-prevention. Fulminating at Russian cruelty in Poland and Neapolitan atrocities, Britain forgot Ireland; the 100,000 transported convicts, the lash and gibbet at Norfolk Island, the sadists' paradise. Germany, imperial or Nazi, was particularly resentful of what Wilhelm II called 'the first World Empire since the Roman', described in a music-hall song as 'the Envy of the World', an empire obstructing 'legitimate' German expansion. Palmerston, contemptuous of foreigners, appeared, even to many British Liberals, a bullying Knight without chivalry, leaving much of Europe glad of the ascent of Bismarck. South African Wars reinforced British unpopularity. British grandiloquence about justice and peace, following several score colonial wars, sounded nauseating to newer nations conscious of lacking not justice and peace but empires. Humbug was an expression both novel and apt. Hitler was disgusted that Britain should protest about German policy towards Poland and Czechoslovakia when he was not overtly interfering in British India and Palestine. When the 1941 South Rhodesian Land Apportioning Act gave half the best land to the 5 per cent white population, foreigners could feel the British were now operating Nazi ideals, only, typically, more slyly.

2

Napoleon called the British a nation of shopkeepers. but they were not shopkeepers alone. Palmerston, Russell, Gladstone, Disraeli, Salisbury were not puppets dominated by the rapacious City. Their values were wide, sometimes contradictory, only slowly shedding the slow, barely organized, vaguely principled Augustan system. (In the same casual mode, the Victorian cricketer, William Midwinter, played for both England and Australia!) They considered themselves good Europeans though, like the Puritans, discovering without embarrassment that selected idealistic targets were compatible with prosperity and power. For most of the century, bound by no formal alliances, Britain acted as she felt fit. With generosity as well as foresight, she, with Napoleon III, repaid the debt to Italy, helping to free her from Habsburg, Pope and Bourbon, Palmerston and Russell sending secret service funds to Garibaldi. Subsequent British foreign policy was gradually and ineptly to dismember Anglo-Italian good-will.

Utilitarian capitalists and nationalists were not uniformly extortionist. While believing unrestricted marketing to be a law of nature irrefutable as Puritan Grace, Darwin's Natural Selection, Marx's Class War, they saw it too as a Law of Progress, led by those of proved will and capacity to survive. For Mazzini, even for Napoleon III, nationalism would extend the range not only of governments but of civilization, bettering human nature itself. With Non-Conformist self-belief and moral passion, the Liberal messiahs, Cobden and Bright, crusaded for Free Trade. Its advantages for eager, *laissez-faire* manufacturers exporting to ambitious, still underdeveloped nations − with the corollary of cheaper food and goods for their employees and perhaps a rise in real wages − seemed obvious. But Free Trade could also be an instrument not only for profits but for peaceful international intercourse, cultural and political, with ancient feuds forgotten. It affected particularly Britain's relations with Napoleon III's France, an unaccustomed ally with whom to fight the Crimean War, briefly intervene in China, 1860, and even more briefly, in Mexico, 1862.

Avatarism is a historical determinant as pronounced as any reasoned manifesto. France, since Waterloo, had had two unsensational monarchies and in 1848 a new republic. Prolonged caution and common-sense have been unacceptable to Frenchmen since 1789. Napoleon still strode through peoples' dreams. 'France needs a Napoleon! I cannot yet see him,' Wellington said, 1849, 'where is he?' Actually he was in England, the Duke had met him. Shortly,

H

he was President of France, later Emperor Napoleon III, installed by popular acclaim not through the persuasiveness of his books, adventures, personality, but by that mass-hallucination, or magic, that saw in each twitch of his huge moustaches a possible Marengo. Mingling dynastic obstinacy, self-interest, liberal idealism, Napoleon III, devious and untrustworthy, was one whom Marx considered grotesque and mediocre, of whom Bismarck remarked that at a distance he was something – close at hand, nothing. Yet he was a creature of ideas, though these interlocked, if at all, in unexpected places. Indifferent to art, he usefully inaugurated a Salon des Refusés; dreaming unrealistically of International Peace Assemblies and European Banks, actually establishing an elementary banking EEC between France, Belgium, Italy and Switzerland, his vision was morally superior to Bismarck's, more generous than Marx's. An amateur emperor, general, economist, historian, he ruled France longer than any other since 1789; in his attitude to foreigners, industry, labour, he was more a man of the future than his uncle.

Napoleon III ('Count Florestan' in a Disraeli novel) had lived in England, travelled in America. He wished to encourage and reconcile one traditional French enemy, Prussia. His acumen convinced him of the need to reverse Bonapartism and, while unfreezing the Vienna settlements, establish Anglo-French entente. He abolished passports between Britain and France. 'Other countries are my mistresses,' he said, in a typical phrase, 'England is my wife.' On his brilliant but unsteady throne, grappling with unending shifts of French loyalty, he must also have envied the British institutions, unglamorous but stable, that his own sensational regime so lacked, institutions that could rebuff Chartism but spread franchise, secret ballot, social reform.

Anglo-French Free Trade, 1860, due largely to Cobden and Napoleon, would, it was hoped, inaugurate an international understanding based on capital, machines, free exchange, leading to universal freedoms, and protected in the interim by British navy, French arms. It cost the Emperor popularity amongst less well-intentioned French industrialists, and the rapid Prussian expansion removed Napoleon himself, 1870, gratifying the British, who, making little effort to avert the war, felt that extravagant, boastful, restless France again needed taming, though the arrival in England of the ex-Emperor in new, humiliating exile brought him a good-will not granted during his power. The death of his heir, apparently in disgraceful circumstances, serving with the British in Zululand, 1879, convinced many Frenchmen of yet another treachery from Albion.

Britain, 1840–1932, maintained Free Trade policies, with profits after 1870 increasingly vitiated by the refusal of client-nations to remain static, and by the startling rise of foreign protectionism, though Cobden in 1968 could still enthuse an English writer.

Cobden was a man of the proudest civic allegiance
But also of a truly international benevolence.
His pacific and mercantile spirit always opposed
The ranting and vulgar belligerency of Lord Palmerston.
And though he had worked a life-time to establish new markets
(He sold cotton cloth to hottentot and sultan)
Yet he always refused to support that gunboat diplomacy
Which forced our British goods on the world at the cannon's
mouth.
True-blue? Yes, he was a true-blue Englishman
Far more that damned aristocratic mountebank.
For Cobden was the true elder brother of all who work
Soberly in mill and office; affectionate fathers,
Reasonably pious sons; all who have made England
Renowned for a (self-confessed) civic honesty,
Domestic virtue(we like to believe), and yet no less
For a zestful spirit of enterprise in far places.

(Philip Toynbee, *A View from the Lake*, Chatto and Windus,
1968)

3

Riches', asserted Dr Johnson, 'do not gain hearty respects; they only procure external attention.' Victorian wealth today procures attention by its crushing of the once-independent poor – yeoman, craftsman, artisan shopkeeper, cottage-manufacturer – now de-graded into unemployment or into vast, anonymous, reeking populations of factory, iron-works, mine. Actual misery prevailed amongst workers, still barely organized and already under-cut by Irish and European immigrants, frequently jobless, kept hungry by Corn Laws and Game Laws, even though real wages seem to have risen, 1780–1850.[76] The French Revolution itself, while ordaining many exemplary social services, forbade strikes, even begging. (Thompson) Similar severity was claimed to have safeguarded Britain from the 1849 revolutions.

Machines, progress itself, were easily correlated with pain, smearing the pages of Dickens, Mrs Gaskell, Kingsley, Mayhew, with appalling narrations and grisly images. South Wales, the North coalesced into murderous, polluted Coketown, with deformity,

waste, drunkenness, crime. Lancashire, 1842, had one public park
and a multitude of gibbets. Railways provided cheap fares fo
hangings. New mines and mills gashed the countryside, invaded
organic, balanced country towns, spread acres of disease-ridden
shanties, choked the air, grass, trees and water with the ruthlessnes
of a modern motorway smashing homes, sports-grounds, churches
20,000 British died of cholera, 1854: 18,000 Londoners, 1849. In
Eastern France, copper-smelting fumes helped deforest 7,000 acres
Woodlands were pillaged for wood-pulp – 'The hum of the news
papers turning forests into lies.' (Auden) Animals were exterminated
for Fashion: whales slaughtered for oil and corsets, elephants fo
ivory; bears' grease was advertised to restore men's hair. Natura
dependencies were ignored, in the race for the future.

Politics, technology, morals were confusingly entangled. Explora
tion, alliances, conquests were needed for zinc, tungsten, bauxite
opium, nitrates, rubber, tin, manganese, gold, chromite: palm-oi
to grease crank and wheel; indentured labour to replace slavery.

The Puritan ethos continued. Authority demanded that employee
devote themselves to the job, not to frivolity, particularly female
frivolity. An obsession with women's virginity matched an obsession
with outward respectability, facts, and fear of the imagination
though, in a pre-penicillin age, virginity had a significance scarcely
absurd. An early Victorian workhouse at Andover forced unmarried
mothers to wear a yellow stripe. The body, still refusing to respond
like a machine, was often mistrusted: nakedness was seldom per
missible, prudery was common. A Victorian house-agent's brochure
referred to the lavatory as 'the first place of general interest on
leaving the hall'. An editor emended Shakespeare's 'Under th
Greenwood tree, Who loves to lie with me?' into 'Who loves to
work with me?' At late-Victorian seasides, though male nakednes
might be allowed on distant beaches, the sexes could be forbidden
to swim within twenty yards of each other. A reviewer castigated
Anne Brontë's *The Tenant of Wildfell Hall* for its 'profane ex
pressions, inconceivably coarse language, and revolting scenes'
Generations later, violent dismay greeted Freud's sexual conclu
sions, his follower, Ernest Jones, being dismissed from his job
1908.

Like the Aztecs, the Victorian masters governed a pleasure-loving
people. The English had for centuries been addicted to song, jocu
larity, drink, sport, leisurely work. Now, as under Cromwell, the
arts of popular life were being reduced to rules, draining or dis
torting many instinctive juices. They have never been totally
extinguished.

Counter-attack, less from the depressed classes than on their behalf, was delayed. Revolution and Napoleon, Tsarist absolutism, Napoleon III's December Massacre (1851), even legends of Stuart and Catholic tyranny, alike reinforced Britain's distrust of State interference. Quasi-scientific laws of political economy and natural selection were added to puritan notions of self-help and labour rewarded. Cobden and Bright, for all their ameliorative Liberal zeal, found it hard to believe that a powerful State could afford compromises and restraints. Nor were the uneducated, ill-housed, enigmatic men of the streets easier to trust. For another Liberal, Macaulay, universal suffrage was 'utterly incompatible with the existence of civilization'. Direct popular rule appealed no more to Mill than to Dickens. Mill, though occasionally impatient with the apparent stagnation and philistinism of British institutions, feared the heavy State as he did the heavy father or husband. 'Public opinion', if over-encouraged, could create lynch-law, anarchy, hatred of reasoned debate – as seen today in the average Western film.

A crude determinism temporarily inhibited legislative fervour. Malthus, a clergyman, held that war, disease, famine were checks, presumably divine, on over-population. Darwin and Spencer agreed, against evidence, that war eliminated the unfit and encouraged self-sacrifice, courage, co-operation, views still trumpeted by Mussolini 1922. After the failure of bourgeois revolution, Marx saw violence as a vital class-weapon. Schopenhauer opposed vaccination, as preserving the unhealthy. Carlyle suggested that anaesthetics removed the moral qualities of suffering – reminiscent of medieval males welcoming women's labour-pains as punishment for Eve's sin.

A certain fatalism was current. Opposing the Public Health Act, 1848, the *Economist* wrote :

> Suffering and evil are Nature's admonitions : they cannot be got rid off : and the impatient attempts to banish them from the world by legislation . . . have always been productive of more evil than good.

A generation later, Lord Lansdowne was objecting to the Old Age Pensions Bill as more expensive than war, and more injurious to the moral fibre. Adam Smith believed that purposeful self-interest, by natural law simultaneously benefited all society. Here were old Puritan values: starvation as evidence of sin, culpable failure, Divine disfavour – discontent anti-social, perhaps damnable. Westminster successfully opposed Treasury relief during the Irish Famine, not only as useless but as inimical both to Private

Enterprise and the Will of God. Major Wainwright was rebuked from Whitehall for giving free food to those starving in Galway.[77]

Parliamentary interference with business and landlords' heartlessness was granted unwillingly, so that with apparent incongruity Liberalism, largely the industrial Interest, could be less concerned with urban reform, while Tories opposed rural reform and long defended the Corn Laws, which manufacturers attacked, partly from humanity, partly to reduce their own costs. In general, interest for reform could be ambiguous. Even Las Casas had favoured black slavery to protect the American Indian from Spanish mines and estates. Abolition of female mine-labour was advocated by English colliery owners against the Scots, who employed more women. Certain slave-abolitionists wished to injure foreign competitors by impairing their labour supply.

Cobden and Bright opposed the Ten Hour Bill. Shaftesbury and Wilberforce opposed political reform, agrarian reform, emancipation of the Jews. Laws of supply and demand seemed irrefutable, therefore divine. A million and a half Irish died of hunger, cholera, starvation, 1846–51, yet rents were extracted more conscientiously than relief was given. There were exceptions, eventually more direct action, but the British intervention popularly remembered is the actual removal of food from Ireland under military escort, 1847, when a starving cat was found gnawing a dead baby and bodies lay half-eaten by vermin. Mrs Woodham Smith quotes Jowett on Nassau Senior, economic adviser to the Government:

> I have always felt a certain horror of political economists since I heard one of them say that he feared the famine of 1848 in Ireland would not kill more than a million people, and that would scarcely be enough to do much good.

4

Even barbarous communities are not exclusively savage. In Victorian Britain there were never lacking such public-spirited Anglo-Irish landlords as Richard Lovell Edgeworth, father of the novelist, Maria; nor philanthropic Victorian families and individuals. The political and the charitable could conflict in one breast, urging on Marx the conviction that the magnificent but selective charity of Shaftesbury and Dickens only prolonged the very system whose products so shocked them; that private humanity was kindly bestowing what was a public right.

As in most ages, contrasts were drastic. *Hints on Etiquette*

(1834) might have been known to bourgeois Marx and his aristocratic wife, but not to those whose lives he wished to redeem.

Never *use your knife to convey* your food to your mouth, *under any circumstances*; it is unnecessary, and glaringly vulgar. Feed yourself with a *fork* or *spoon, nothing else* – a knife is only to used for cutting.

Fish does not require a knife, but should be divided by the aid of a piece of bread. The application of a knife is likely to destroy the delicacy of its flavour; besides which, fish sauces are often acidulated; acids corrode steel, and draw from it a disagreeable taste. In the North, where lemon or vinegar is very generally used for salmon and many other kinds of fish, the objection becomes more apparent.

Nothing indicates a well-bred man more than a proper mode of eating his dinner. A man may pass muster by *dressing well*, and may sustain himself tolerably in conversation; but if he be not perfectly *au fait, dinner* will betray him.

Ladies should never dine with their gloves on – unless their hands are not fit to be seen.

Finger glasses, filled with warm water come on with the dessert. Wet a corner of your knapkin, and wipe your mouth, then rinse your fingers; but do not practice the *filthy* custom of gargling your mouth at table, albeit the usage prevails amongst a few, who think *because* it is a foreign habit, it cannot be disgusting.

Never allow any person above the rank of a shopman to leave the room without your ringing the bell for the street door to be opened. Thousands have been irremediably offended by having been suffered to quit a room unattended, and to 'let themselves out'. This deserves particular notice, as it is a very common omission with persons, who, having amassed a little wealth and set up for '*somebodies*', would be exceedingly annoyed to have it whispered that they could be guilty of such gross ill breeding.

The first half of the nineteenth century was notorious for failure to adapt or invent institutions for novel developments in production, labour, housing, population. Mass unemployment and violence in the 1840s evoked shootings. The Machine, signal chance to enlarge passions and skills, was contracting them, was feared like present-day technology which threatens to computerize relationships. Dr Arnold noticed that 'people' were becoming 'hands' like Roman slaves, or machines themselves, merely for use. 'The soul', deep, subtle, unconscious, was treated as a minority attribute. A 'Just Sufficient' attitude was common : just sufficient bread, leisure, charity, education, to keep the wheels moving.

To relieve rate-payers and hapless parents, the orphanages, poor-houses, asylums, domestic hovels were ransacked for children, from three upwards, to work in factory, mine, mill. Shaftesbury suggested to Parliament that when 'the House in its wisdom and mercy' decided that forty-five hours a week were sufficient for an adult negro, sixty-nine hours a week were rather too much for British children.

Children died in country house chimneys, were ripped by machines; dragged, naked, trucks with two hundredweight of coal through darkness where babies pushed rats from miners' food and half-stripped women, many pregnant, struggled for coal alongside men for twelve or more hours a day. 'It's only horse work that ruins the women,' a survivor said. 'It crushes their haunches, bends their ankles, and makes them old women at forty.'

William Kershaw, at eight, was working (about 1799) a twelve-hour day in a mill for 2s 6d a week.

Yes, I have been ill-treated myself; and I have seen others that have been a good deal worse used. There is a difference in the disposition of the slubber or person under whom the child is placed; some have more humanity, and rather wish to encourage the children to attention, than to punish them for negligence. Some of them who are kind have some rewards, such as some fruit, and say that those who have the fewest number of ends in a given time shall have this fruit; and others will keep beating the children, whether they are in fault or not. I have been beat with a billy-roller (a roller running along the top of the machine, perhaps 2 or 3 yards long and 4 or 5 inches in circumference) towards night, when I have been particularly drowsy, till I repeatedly vomited blood. . . . I entreated my mother not to make a complaint, lest I should be further beaten. The next morning after I went to work, she followed me, and came to the slubber that had used me in that way, and gave him a sharp lecture; and when she had done she retired into the engine-feeder's house, and left me to my work : and as soon as she was gone, he beat me severely again for telling.

Alexander Dean, in a Dundee flaxmill, was, at twelve, working not less than seventeen hours a day, beaten very often.

At the time I was in the mill there was a young woman who had been kept seven months in the gaol at Dundee for deserting this mill; and she was brought back, after having been in the gaol for seven months, to make up for her lost time and the expenses incurred. One day I was alarmed by her cries. She was lying on the floor, and the master had her by the hair of her head, and was kicking her in the face till the blood was running down.

Subsequently deserting again, unable to find a job, ringed by magistrates of the employing class, 'she became a prostitute. She was tried at the circuit of Perth for stealing, and transported to Van Dieman's land.'[78] An eight-year-old girl, working a twelve-hour day : 'I have heard of Jesus many a time. I don't know why he came to earth, I'm sure, and I don't know why he died, but he had stones for his head to rest on. I would like to be at school far better than in the pit.'

Victorian conscience could not swiftly transform this. To pass acts was easier than to implement them. Tennyson, Laureate of the trophies and hopes of the Industrial Exhibition, could still write, 1886 :

Is it well that while we range with Science, glorying in the Time,
City children soak and blacken soul and sense in city slime?
There among the glowing alleys Progress halts on palsied feet,
Crime and hunger cast our maidens by the thousand on the street.
There the master scrimps his haggard sempstress of her daily
                                                        bread,
There a sordid attic holds the living and the dead.
There the smouldering fire of fever creeps across the rotted floor,
And the crowded couch of incest in the warrens of the poor.

('Locksley Hall Sixty Years After')

Certain of Doré's illustrations of Dante's *Inferno* and of London's East End are interchangeable. In the high days of Palmerston and Disraeli, of Kings Cotton, Coal, Steam, 50 per cent of slum children could be exterminated by rickets, typhus, cholera, tuberculosis, malnutrition. Of the huge urban dung-heaps that Dickens featured in *Our Mutual Friend*, one at Greenock towered twelve feet high. Bradlaugh, prosecuted, 1877, with Annie Besant, for publishing a birth-control pamphlet, quoted Dr Lankaster's statement that, in 1866, 16,000 women had murdered their babies. Thirty-seven million articles were pawned in London, 1870 : the weasel could be popped weekly, redeemed on pay-day: 'We had rather face a civil war than another such century of suffering,' Shaw said, in the 'eighties.

I rushed from the room like a madman
And flew to the workhouse gate,
Crying 'Food for a dying woman,'
And the answer came 'Too late.'

They drove me away with curses;
Then I fought with a dog in the street,
And tore from the mongrel's clutches
A crust he was trying to eat.

(G. Sims, 'Christmas Day in the Workhouse', 1903)

Even in the new century, with a big drop in real wages, 1896–1914, one adult in four was dying on public relief.[79] In 1907, a London woman card-illustrator was paying five shillings weekly rent, from an income of eight.

Statistics are often more suggestive than conclusive. It can be baldly said that at Victoria's death 2 per cent owned two-thirds of the national wealth. One can add further, that in 1961, the richest 1 per cent in Britain owned 38 per cent, by 1972, 30 per cent. In 1970, 10 per cent owned 72 per cent.[80] So that despite reform, super-tax, death-duty, the gap between rich and poor, champagne and wallop, narrowed, but at a pace not headlong. In 1936, four and a half millions spent less than four shillings weekly for food. (Hampden Jackson) Even in 1970, two millions were estimated to live in exceptional poverty. On Christmas Eve, 1972, an old woman was found two months dead, choked with cardboard. This was not wholly exceptional. With society becoming more sophisticated and respectable, the individual can be left in tragic loneliness and private grief.

Victorian middle-class virtues could include smugness:

'Tis proper, Sophy, to be sure,
To pity and relieve the poor :
But do not waste your pity here,
Work is not hard to her, my dear,
It makes her healthy, strong and gay,
And is as pleasant as your play.

In Coketown, the body was stunted, maimed, deprived of colour and vitamins; died too soon, and sought consolation in an after-life handed down from above. Frustrated artists, would-be saviours, discontented wives, the poor and diseased, slumped into gin, beer, opium-tinctured laudanum, chlorine, morphia, and 'humanity's third scourge', cocaine. Malnutrition was the creeping scourge of a quarter of the nation, one relatively late victim being Charles Chaplin's mother. Beneath late Victorian and Edwardian opulence were the rank doss-houses and brothels that lured thousands of underpaid servants, shop-assistants, and children. Virgins could be hired for defloration, under sedatives.

Women's legal rights were negligible, at least until the Married Women's Property Act, 1882. A Mr Threthewey sold his wife for 4d, at St Austell Market, 1835, a custom still extant in the West some years later, and a reminder of Hardy's *Mayor of Casterbridge* – and of the African Masai, with whom eight cows will buy a wife.

Gloom and savagery can, of course, be exaggerated. The Victorian century did not lack dynamic women: Hester Stanhope, Mary Kingsley, Victoria herself, and her daughter, the Empress Frederick; Florence Nightingale, Mill's friend and collaborator, Harriet Taylor, Annie Besant, Olive Schreiner, Eleanor Marx, Frances Mary Buss, Dr Elizabeth Garrett Anderson, Dr Barry. However, Mill, Ruskin, Dickens, Morris, Carlyle, Gladstone, Disraeli – like Bismarck, Wagner, Freud – had scant enthusiasm for women leaving home, discarding their suppliant beauty for higher education, politics, the professions. The 'New Woman' of Ibsen, Shaw, Wells, vying with men professionally, sexually, intellectually, is still not wholly accepted.

In the villages and country towns, on the estates, even in the City of Dreadful Night, much popular gaiety continued, cherished since the junketings of the Middle Ages, since the exuberance of Tudor cottagers preferring the May-day rites of Robin Hood to a celebrated visiting preacher. When Palmerston in old age fathered an illegitimate child, Disraeli feared the excess of popularity that this might bring him. Personalities were ripe. The bullying joviality of a Palmerston, a W. G. Grace provoked as much affection as resentment and made the virtues, sensitivity and intelligence, of Prince Albert seem pale and humourless. People still living recall the fairs, harvest festivals, race meetings, sporting Derbies, civic pageants, comings of age, gin-palaces, crowded, noisy, tolerant, disgusting those who demanded swifter reform and relentless class war. Through the travail of slum, unemployment, battlefield, humour made tolerable the intolerable. 400 London music-halls made a last link with the bawdy, knockabout Shakespearian theatre, powerfully moving such disparate figures as Dickens, Max Beerbohm, T. S. Eliot, Maurice Chevalier. They provided a salve, transmuting the vicious to laughter. 'My wife's so ugly that it's easier to take her out than to kiss her goodbye,' Max Miller was to confide. Of the rich, Will Fyffe demanded, 'What do they do? I'll tell you what they do. They do *us*!' Song sublimated poverty, violence, old age. 'I'm one of the Ruins that Cromwell knocked about a bit.' It made rumbustious social comment, ribald, perky, suggestive allusions. Tunes were hummed, whistled, parodied, amongst all classes.

As fierce a race of savages as ever I did see –
In the wild wild West of London.

or

Charlie Dilke
Upset the milk
While taking it home to Chelsea.

Despite associations with disrespect and prostitution, the Music
Hall would find a staunch defender in Winston Churchill, when
Home Secretary.

Pre-1914 Britain did not suffer from jaded emotions or moral
fatigue. 'A little of wot yer fancies does yer good,' sang the raucous,
drunken, magnetic Marie Lloyd. People voted heartily, imitated and
mocked the grand, touched forelocks while often believing politics,
religion, fine manners to be sanctimonious frauds. Though art was
regarded as less essential than gardens, often totally inessential,
people forgot that gardening, pursued everywhere by all classes, was
itself an art. Stefan Zweig, an assiduous Herr Doktor, visiting
England, 1906, actually considered that, with their gardens, art
collections, schools, the English were nearer the ancient Greeks than
any other contemporary people. A further Greek touch was supplied
by the love of sport. Alpine mountaineering and competitive ski-ing
were pioneered from Britain, Whymper climbing the Matterhorn,
1865. Rackets, rugby football and later squash, were formulated in
Britain, which exported golf, lawn tennis and Association Football
throughout the world, and cricket to the white Dominions, to
Holland, Denmark, Argentina, Corfu, Hong Kong, Fiji, Papua, New
Guinea, East Africa, North America and, most notably, India.
Britain organized the rules of modern yacht racing, athletics,
hockey, bowls and croquet.

5

Social protest came from within and, at times, from outside the
Institutions. Chartism itself, though its appeal was wide, wanted to
democratize, not destroy Parliament. This was at odds with French
and Russian reformers, where political progress was being increasingly identified with violence : with anarchic, or authoritarian
socialism.

Prince Albert experimented with housing design for the poor.
Carlyle lashed at cruel *laissez-faire*, industrial Bastilles, Mammon-
worship. Disraeli's temper, in *Sybil* (1845), was not surpassed by
Marx and Engels as, in a famous passage, he described the 'two
nations', the rich and poor :

Between them there is no intercourse and no sympathy; who are ignorant of each other's habits, thoughts and feelings, as if they were dwellers in different zones, or inhabitants of different planets; who are formed by different breeding, are fed by different food, are ordered by different manners and are not governed by the same laws.

Zola's *Germinal* (1885) portrayed the same, in mid-century France.

Lord Shaftesbury (1801–85) provided Prince Albert with evidence for the effect of bad environment on bad morals. He did not question Capitalism, only a particular stage of Capitalism. He feared Socialism and unions, 'strikes, intimidation, strong language'. Chairman of the Lord's Day Observance Society, he vehemently upheld the grim Victorian Sunday, so repellent to Dickens, de Quincey, and to foreigners. He never looked beyond Parliament, though it manfully obstructed his demands for Early Closing and the Saturday half-day; his Ten Hour Bill and Factory Acts; his work to transform evil lunatic asylums into public hospitals; his establishment of Ragged Schools for child pimps, whores, thieves, derelicts, drunks; the erection of model housing estates. A biographer compares him to Tolstoy.

> Both were aristocrats, born to wealth and privilege. Both turned in religion from doctrine and ritual to the simple teachings of Christ. . . . Shaftesbury's conscience, though strict enough, had not that terrifying consistency of Tolstoy's. English in its illogicality, it permitted contradictory ideas to lie side by side in his mind. Thus he could believe literally in the words of Christ without feeling it was necessary to deprive his wife and family of all comfort and amusement. Thus he could condemn the opium trade but defend his country's act when the trade brought on a war. Tolstoy and Shaftesbury were both prophets of the way of love . . . to them both the life of the mind was nothing compared to the life of the soul. But of what these two men set out to do by the light of their religion Shaftesbury did more than Tolstoy. The weakness of Tolstoy was spiritual pride. Shaftesbury's strength was humility.

(Barbara Blackburn, *Noble Lord*, Home and Van Thal, 1949)

Robert Owen (1771–1858), godchild of Godwin and the Enlightenment, eschewed humility, striving, without party, union or violence, 'to emancipate the human race from ignorance, division, sin and misery'. His experiments recalled the Civil War co-operatives, partially anticipated Quaker model-factories, contemporary communes, progressive schools. His New Lanark factory showed that order need not be coercion; that real production should and could benefit the participants' total lives, not the investments of absentee shareholders. For Owen as for the young Jacobins, Carlyle, Ruskin, Bradlaugh, Morris, Kropotkin, society should be cemented not by cash but self-fulfilment through satisfying work, with mind and senses quickened for leisure, art, freedom, new apprehensions dispelling ugliness, cant, ignorance, frustration, spiritual dry rot. Fullness of life outsoared fullness of purse. Man was more than he realized, charged with unused powers : released from drudgery by co-operative enterprise he would open like shutters. 'There is no wealth but life. . . . Life without work is robbery. Work without art is brutality.' Thus Ruskin, whose *Unto This Last* kept Gandhi sleepless in admiration and desire to emulate. Owen, though a practical manager, was convinced that happiness and play, shorter hours and good-will actually improved work and that monolithic hierarchies improved industry as little as they did society. Cheaper goods would produce higher wages. Crime, drugs, vindictiveness were the products, not cause of social rot. Machines were not per-verse, anti-romantic corrupters of life but superb creative potential. New Lanark proved these even to such visitors as the Tsar, though larger schemes in Britain and America eventually failed.

More than an isolated Owen was needed if hopelessness or violence were not to prevail. Dickens (1812–70), no revolutionary but an observant, unremitting critic, found the London streets quarries as deep as libraries.

I came to the great steps of St Martin's Church as the clock was striking three. Suddenly, a thing that in a moment more I should have trodden upon without seeing, rose up at my feet with a cry of loneliness and houselessness, struck out of it by the bell, the like of which I never heard. We then stood face to face looking at one another, frightened by one another. The creature was like a beetle-browed hare-lipped youth of twenty, and it had a loose bundle of rags on, which it held together with one of its hands. It shivered from head to foot, and its teeth chattered, and, as it stared at me – persecutor, devil, ghost, whatever it thought me – it made with its whining mouth as if it were snapping at me, like a worried dog. Intending to give this ugly object money, I put out my hand to stay it – for it recoiled as it whined and snapped – and laid my hand upon its shoulder. Instantly it twisted out of its garment, like the young man in the New Testament, and left me standing alone with its rags in my hands.

(Night Walks)

This apparition, commonplace in the London of Chaucer, Shake-speare, Johnson, was surely inappropriate to that of Bentham, Mill, the Marylebone Cricket Club. In response, Dickens remains youthful and contemporary. 'My faith in the people governing is, on the whole, infinitesimal; my faith in the people governed is, on the whole, illimitable.' He demonstrated, before Freud and Huizinga, that childhood should be fed not with repression, silence, utility, but with drama, fantasy, mirth. A Pelagian spirit, he demanded personal responsibility. Man willed himself good, evil, or both at once. Dynamic mixture of vituperation and geniality, insight and myopia, fun and harshness, extraversion and brooding, he knew, as much as de Sade, the havoc of duality: an amusing man may be a monster, a first-class degree disguise a quack, piety conceal hypocrisy, appalling scaffolds exercise theatrical glamour, a respectable choir-master be a murderous drug-addict, the marvellous hero a cold seducer. He was riven by psychic conflicts. No one did more to abolish public hangings, no one was more assiduous in attending them. He describes floggings with more relish than he does sexual orthodoxy. His own interior world convinced him that Newgate had attractions potent as coaching-inns and village greens. He hated the degradation of man by calloused traditions, fine old families gone vicious; equally he feared the mob. Revolution might arouse the best in the few, it certainly lashed up the worst in the many. He supported Governor Eyre of Jamaica. Bastilles may be less frightful than they appear; revolution ends not with abolition but exchange of Privilege. His judgements on American democracy are harsh. He finds gentility often more despicable than vulgarity. He urged that immediate attention to the suffering had priority over missionaries, empire, technology, women's suffrage. He was sceptical of institutions – Parliament, unions, Church Law, civil dignitaries, civil servants, armed forces and Napoleon III – knowing how swiftly the spirit gets frozen into office-furniture. The Law could be an Ass; personal regeneration was more promising than change of law or ruler, though a personal raid on actual injustices was always applaudable. Justice, then as now, could be a matter of paying. He could explore a Report as thoroughly as most: as Parliamentary journalist he had early surveyed the official arenas, and his delineation of class, bureaucracy, self-interest is as powerful as Marx's and more subtle. For Wittgenstein he was 'the poet of the common people'. He affected Tolstoy, Dostoevsky, Strindberg, Kafka, Brecht, Proust, Conrad . . . was Hogarth in words. As inescapably as Tolstoy, Shaftesbury, Gandhi, Schweitzer, he saw society suffering not from lack of masterpieces, ideas, economists, philosophers, evangelists, engineers, plausible despots and reasonable statesmen but lack of good people. He did not ignore politics but believed that boards, committees, government departments were soulless and obscurantist, and that the dedicated individual could accomplish more. He saw the absolute need to preserve human relations in an era of mechanization, rapid population growth, social divisions. More participation was needed, less officialdom; not a Platonic utopia but better behaviour. Imprecise, unsystematic in his analysis – he jeered at many of the greatest Victorian social achievements – he pointed to all classes treating their children abominably. He denounced public life as a sham, inventing lavish language and character in his indictment of diseased slums, brutalized youth, indifferent old, the horrible respectable in that urban pall confirmed by Mayhew, Disraeli, Engels and, later, Rowntree. His black comedy and imageries are never archaic : Chancery, Gradgrind, Coketown, Bumbledom, the Circumlocution Office which undeniably 'may ultimately shipwreck everybody and everything, still, that will probably not be in our time – and it's a school for gentlemen.' Oliver Twist trembling in the darkness, seeing coffin-boards 'like high-shouldered ghosts with their hands in their pockets'. Mr Merdle, the swindling millionaire, before suicide, staring into his own hat 'as if it were a well some twenty feet deep'. Mr Dombey, 'who could have been hung up for sale at a Russian fair as an example of a frozen gentleman'. Lady Tippins, 'with an immense, obtuse, drab, oblong face, like a face in a table-spoon'. Mrs Pipchin, whose teaching was not to encourage the mind to develop and expand like a flower, 'but to open it by force, like an oyster'. His genius had flaws, could be unfair, ill-informed, sentimental – a man, said Wilde, must have a heart of stone not to howl with laughter at the death of Little Nell – but his initiative, generous, angry, concentrated, never slackened.

General change, however, was not to be left to poets and visionaries, mocking the political parties, and receptive to Wilde's view that those who wish to lead the people only do so by following the mob. Socialism preferred two alternatives. 1789 and 1848 had, in the main, wanted relative social extension of franchise, and British Chartism followed this, while Karl Marx continued with grim relish the doctrine of the rule of the Elect. Workers had gained little from the Revolution. Equality under the Law was a shoddy palliative without equality of income and property. The evil present must be shocked into the just future. Marx was no pacifist. He saw Man as conditioned by class and the past, credulous, needing rescue by the Elect, predestined to victorious world-revolution, though he admitted (1872) that revolution was not inevitable in Britain and Holland. He and Engels had founded the Communist

League in London, 1847, their theories indebted not only to Hegel but to the British political economists Smith and, more notably, Malthus and Ricardo.

A personal irony intruded. Marx, in a household of poverty, debt, malnutrition, child-death, had political insights far keener than Dickens's yet, had he been treated in a Dickens novel, the author, himself reproached for domestic cruelty, might have contrasted Marx's schemes for total human brotherhood with his total and venomous party hatreds and rivalries, and his rejection of his illegitimate son fathered on the family housekeeper. Engels, in many ways an attractive figure, was himself an industrialist, far more authoritarian than Owen, holding that managers' orders should always be obeyed 'instantly and without question', like those of a ship's captain.

Later Victorian London, besides being enlarged by East End immigration from Poland, Russia, Germany, was an intellectual power-house. Carlyle, Ruskin, Mill, George Eliot, Morris, Herzen, Mazzini, Darwin, Louis Blanc – Marxism, Spencerism, Positivism, Anarchism, Revisionism, competing like early Christian sects. Bernard Shaw was absorbed not only with Wagner and Ibsen, but with fellow Londoners, Marx, Morris, Kropotkin, and the Russian nihilist, Stepnick-Kravchanski. Monet and Pissaro fled to London, 1870, Monet re-exploring on Thames-side the endless subtle variation of light on water, sky, buildings, with which Impressionism had enlarged the discoveries of Constable and Turner. He found a dimension in fog that countered Dickens's in *Bleak House*. 'Without the fog', Monet said, 'it could not be a beautiful city. It is the fog that gives it its magnificent amplitude.' The process continued. In 1946 there settled in England the scientific and democratic philosopher Karl Popper, 'incomparably the greatest philosopher of science that has ever been'. (Medawar)

More percipient about Britain than Marx was Eduard Bernstein, later German Social Democratic leader who finally, like Shaw, found Marxism more a stimulant than a final solution. Research into Cromwellian rebels reinforced his growing interest in Parliamentarianism, as against Marx's dictatorial Old Testament vengefulness. Bertrand Russell's first book, on German socialism, 1894, owed much to Bernstein.[81]

Blatchford, Morris, Hyndman, Cunningham-Grahame, led in adapting socialism to British constitutional pragmatism, joined, more methodically, by the Fabians. Here the trust was less in human nature than in the power of expert, teacher, intellectual aristocrat. Like the old paternalists, Fabianism prefers granting to sharing.

Despite a John Ball, Shelley, Morris the panacea was never a

British preoccupation. Bentham's 'What use is it?' was more typical.
Class enemies were less evil than unfair, inefficient, unnecessary.
Statistics outbid futurism. British socialism demanded goals limited
but practical – as tiny Gibraltar, Malta, Suez, could be vital hinges
of Empire, though H. G. Wells, with imagination as lively as
Dickens's, tried to penetrate far beyond and behind institutions
with exuberant scientific optimism, tempered by apocalyptic
warnings. Socialism itself, with its parliamentary Labour Party,
encountered dilemmas still unresolved : the need to reconcile old
liberties with State control, the exaggeration of working-class
solidarity and of working-class disparagement of bourgeois habits,
snobberies, private property; the conflict of Interests within its own
movement.

Victorian Britain was never static – the pace might indeed seem
headlong to those exclusively informed by the great Victorian
novelists. Real wages recovered for some years, around 1860. The
pillory was abolished 1816, the hulks 1858, the last convict ship
1867, public executions, 1869. Capital crimes were reduced from
over 200 to six. Parliamentary reform began, 1832; modern local
government through County Councils, 1888. The Corn Laws were
repealed, 1846. Chadwick's Sanitary Report appeared in 1842, together with the searing First Report of the Children's Employment
Committee, followed by the Factory Acts and the 1848 Public
Health Act. Hopkins made the world vitamin-conscious, Ross
discovered the cure for malaria that had weakened the Roman
Empire; Lady Mary Wortley Montague's daughter was the first
European to accept Jenner's vaccination; Florence Nightingale
forced sanitation and medical reform onto the British and Indian
armies, drains and water onto Calcutta. Though rickets and malnutrition were rife, plague had vanished; ague, smallpox, typhus,
cholera, tuberculosis were being overcome by 1880, Pasteur's work
on microbes was influencing Lister. Trade unionism, beginning in
Britain, not as in Australia with State help but against violent
parliamentary opposition, was increasingly emancipated from 1824,
ultimately becoming, until 1971, virtually free of legal interference.
Secret Parliamentary Ballot was enacted, 1872, replacing the public
hustings, State Schools prescribed, 1870, Compulsory Education,
1876, the beginnings of State Insurance and Welfare, from 1906.
(Dates, protested the Regency whore, Harriet Wilson, make ladies
nervous, and stories dry.) All this was far from Melbourne's insistence that the sole duty of government was to prevent crime and
preserve contracts.

Reform, though, was not presented to colonial labour. South
African and Rhodesian miners, cotton workers in Bombay, jute

hands in Calcutta, could be treated as callously as those formally enslaved. One attraction of Empire was that of cheap labour. As late as 1972, a wage study (by the South African Productivity and Wages Association for the United Kingdom South African Trade Association) revealed that almost 80 per cent of Africans employed by British and European companies were receiving wages 'below subsistence levels'.

At home, administrative delays, omissions, laziness, chilliness and inexperience warranted anger from Marx, Shaw, Morris. Social legislation was, indeed, lagging behind that of Bismarck. Poverty and squalor could erupt in strike and conspiracy, 'unlawful assembly', and would increasingly disturb middle-class men of conscience, such as Clement Attlee, to whom resolute human sympathies were more important than profound economic understanding. A Londoner was killed, on Bloody Sunday, 1887. 'But lo, this dead man, knocking at the gate.' (Morris) Burnings and assassinations continued in Ireland, though Britain kept free of the mass-killings, mass-arson, barricades, foreign occupation endured by Paris (1871), the massacre suffered in St Petersburg (1905), the suppression of strikers by soldiers, in Russia, Spain, France and America.

Continuing British hardships, particularly after 1918, produced lengthy strikes, occasional confrontations with troops, police horse and baton charges, sporadic class venom; but for years the impression was more of smouldering suspicion and denunciation than of conspiracy.

6

Other, and prophetic changes were looming. Though the populace could be moved by Hungarian, Neapolitan and Bulgarian atrocities, they could be equally enflamed at home by Irish, East European, oriental and colonial immigration, with renewed fervour after 1870. Earlier, the West Indian Interest had agitated against abolition, playing on popular fears of the wholesale immigration of over-sexed and voracious ex-slaves, accompanied by higher taxation. Unimpressed by Queen Elizabeth's failure, politicians renewed their demands for black repatriation, after the Sierra Leone black settlement project, 1787. Racial riots were to shake English cities in 1910, and again in 1919. An anti-immigration act was passed, 1905.

A new alarm was summarized in the Kaiser's phrase, 'the Yellow Peril'. Chinese servants had been known since the eighteenth century, but *Cassell's Family Magazine*, on threats of a Chinese labour overflow, commented, 1877 :

There are grave and pressing social difficulties in our own midst, which an ample supply of very cheap labour would do much to solve; yet, on the other hand, it is certain that we, in our crowded community, could even less than America afford to tolerate a horde of people whose habitual vices cast ancient Corinth into the shadow.

More obvious changes were at hand. The unparalleled British free-trade prosperity had been due more to others' temporary backwardness than to permanent British superiority and hard work. By 1870, ebullient European and American nationalism was lunging outwards. Between 1879 and 1890, Germany, Russia, France, Austria, Italy, the United States went Protectionist, increasing the importance of British colonial markets. The new German Empire, seizing the mines and plant of Alsace-Lorraine (1871), began rapid exploitation of steam, mechanics, finance, manufacture, education, and, like New Zealand, like Uruguay, of social-democratic, non-collectivist Welfare. By 1879, a prolonged British trade and agriculture decline set in. American and German steel were over-taking Sheffield. 'Made in Germany' increasingly queried the advantages of Free Trade. Foreign oil and cheap electricity were menacing British coal and steam. The Dominions were exporting cheap meat in cold storage. America was turning from western expansion towards world affairs, and would in a few years be competing with Britain for Latin American oil and nitrates, a struggle which underlay a number of the constant South American wars. Britain herself had begun to feel complacent, a portly master of the house, hitherto unchallenged, digesting comfortably yet ignoring the changing attitudes not only of neighbours, clients, but also of his own servants. After 1880 British industry loitered, so evident before both World Wars. By 1900 Britain had lost her high command, though remaining chief exporter, customer, financer, even in 1972 being the third largest trading nation.

Commercial and naval rivalry with thrusting, noisy Wilhelmine Germany particularly menaced British profits, forcing London away from 'Splendid Isolation' towards understanding with Russia, Italy and France. The entente with France was one of convenience, not affection, Middle Eastern oil rivalry eventually to replace territorial rivalry in Africa, where the late arrival of Germany, Italy and Leopold II, the Belgian King, hastened direct, uninvited and amateurish white partitions and hatreds. 'The colonial powers had partitioned Africa as an insurance against the future, not because they had any present plans for its exploitation. Thenceforward their main concern was that the annual premium should not be too high.' (Oliver and Fage)

Russia's defeats by Japan, 1894 and 1904, and Italy's by Ethiopia, the first major white defeats, were welcomed in Asia, particularly in India. For complacent Britain, a rapid Japanese ascent seemed a useful counter to Russia; Japanese surprise attack on Port Arthur – like Drake's on Cadiz, Nelson's on Copenhagen – was acclaimed as 'high honour', and 'gallant', terms not used over Pearl Harbor.

A response to violent and unpopular Western entry into Far Eastern markets, the new industrial-military imperialism, 'brave little Japan' and its flamboyant destruction of the wicked Tsar's fleet, was happily applauded by a public that relished the dainty fantasy and rollicking pastiche of *The Mikado*.

> The Tsu Shima victory is the outcome of Bushido, of the whole training of the Japanese people in the great fundamental principle of human conduct. That training is not a veneer which can be put on for a given purpose. It is a thing which must begin with the cradle, and which must be universal in a nation which hopes to come through the last ordeal as the Japanese have now come. Which thing may well give this nation pause, and set it considering whether there are not greater ideals than buying in the cheapest market and obtaining the greatest average return upon capital.
>
> *(The Times, 2 June 1905)*

The British nation might indeed have paused, could it have foreseen the Japanese assault on Singapore, the building of the Burma Road on British slave labour, the destruction of four centuries of British sea-power and, by 1965, a hard, industrial competition from a revived Japan.

Meanwhile, in 1900, British and European progressives, so hopeful of the new political, commercial and national freedoms, were largely prepared to give good, as well as extract goods, even from colonial empires. They were unready to accept that science, finance, industry might superannuate national sovereignty, and demand new institutions that required decades to formulate, and, through pain and war, are scarcely secured yet.

Ever since the world's far-off lands
were discovered, what has been the
conduct of the whites to the
coloureds? What is the meaning of the
simple fact that this and that people
has died out, that others are dying
out, and that the condition of others
is getting worse as the result of their
discovery by those professing to follow Jesus? Who can describe the
injustices and cruelties that, through
the centuries, they have suffered from
Europeans? Who can measure the
misery produced among them by strong
drink and hideous disease that we
have taken to them?

Albert Schweitzer

I

Imperialism remains a word of international loathing, stuffed with
partisan generalizations, romantic misunderstandings. The three
million Empire casualties in World War I have been exploited as
boast, as reproach. Colonialism diverted or sublimated some violence
at home by sending young males abroad, but also involved subject
races in inter-white savagery. Indians suffered on the Marne,
Africans on the Somme, Maoris at El Alamein. Automatically the
stalwart enormities flicker past: Europeans sacking the Pekin
Summer Palace, 1860; Wilhelm II, 1900, exhorting Western forces
in China to 'behave like Huns', barbarous as medieval priests
promising salvation to murderers of Jews; Stanley's guns delivering the Southern Congo to Leopold; opium wars; Amritsar; the
extermination of Tasmanian, Bushman, Carib; French torture in
Algeria; Leopold's hand-cuttings and crucifixions for Congo
rubber; the British Arano Company beating, mutilating, killing
for Peruvian rubber; German genocide amongst African Hereros;
Indian village crafts and cotton and silk industries sacrificed to
Lancashire; the 60,000 Boer deaths in Kitchener's Camps; British
cocoa and chocolate imported from Portuguese slave-plantations
in Angola; Mussolini's son finding it 'most entertaining' to set fire

246

to Ethiopian villagers from the air; Gladstone's Royal Commission reporting that Ireland had been over-taxed £300 million in fifty years; Gold War, Diamond War; Rhodes swindling Lobengula, Sir Garnet betraying the Ashanti; Lugard collaring Uganda, ignoring its chiefs, its people and Whitehall; destruction of Zulus and Matabele; questionable seizure of Cyprus, the Sudan; warfare against Maoris for green stone.

Imperial premises can be interpreted as contempt of one man for another, despite incidental benefits; Romans and British building fine roads, to facilitate troop movements. Wellesley, assiduous, efficient, considered his Indian subjects 'vulgar, ignorant, rude, familiar and stupid'. Of the machine gun, the School of Musketry Report, 1894, stated, 'a very useful gun for fighting a crowd of savages though a somewhat puzzling addition to the machinery of the battle-line in a civilized war'. After the Mutiny, music-hall comics sang gaily of 'Hunting the Pandie with sterling British steel'. An ex-governor of Burma, Sir Reginald Dorman-Smith, confessed, 1941, that he could see nothing that the British had done for Burma. Churches, barracks, debtors' prisons had frequent priority over schools and hospitals. Leonard Woolf, district magistrate in Ceylon, when nearly five million square miles was added to the British Empire in twenty-five years, considered that in Africa European civilization despite 'considerable benefits' was totally vitiated by 'horrible cruelty, exploitation and injustice'.

Students of atrocities have found much data from the bullets and bayonets in Alexandria, 1882, and can doubtless compare them with the Russian communists' tanks in present-day Budapest and Prague. Britain's protests to Russia must have sounded cynical, not only in the aftermath of the Suez bombardment, 1956, but to those who remembered Britain's cavalier treatment of King Farouk of Egypt (1941–3) and, with Russian co-operation, of the Shah of Persia (1941).

Economic aggression had, perforce, political correlations. In 1863, following the murder by Japanese of an Englishman at Kagoshima, Britain demanded and received £100,000, following this with bombardment and burnings.

Egypt remains a painful example of a 'special relationship'. The guardianship of the Canal and the route to India, the lure of investments, were sufficiently tempting for Britain and France to capitalize on Egyptian financial incompetence. After intrigue, coercion, breaches of faith, contrived crises, the two nations virtually took over the country immediately after Britain had, with five other Great Powers, signed a promise forgoing territorial and commercial advantages and exclusive privileges. France, with growling ill-will, eventually transferred her interests to Algeria and Morocco.

The ensuing benefits for Egypt – solvency, order, drug reduction, hygiene, granted by aloof British officials, has still not assuaged the ache of violated nationalism.

There was more. British money was lent at high rates to pay for exorbitant public works which enriched the foreigner as much as the pashas. In 1877, two-thirds of the country's revenue was going to Western bondholders.

> When one thinks of the poverty-stricken, over-driven, underfed fellaheen in their miserable hovels, working late and early to fill the pockets of the creditor, the punctual payment of the coupon ceases to be wholly a matter of gratification.
>
> (*The Times*, 21 July 1877)

Even during a catastrophic famine, punctual payment was insisted upon by the City. *The Times* was continuing, March 31 1879 that :

> People are dying by the roadside, that great tracts of the country are uncultivated, because of the fiscal burdens, and that the farmers have sold their cattle and the women their finery, and that the usurers are filling the mortgage office with their bonds and the court with their suits of foreclosure.

Elsewhere, concern for native rights could be insouciant. Lord Salisbury stated, 'We need not discuss the principles developed in this despatch. They amount to this : if a merchant differs from a native chief as to their respective rights, the native chief is to be deported.'[82] In 1844 the British had fewer troops in India than in Ireland where, alone in nineteenth-century Europe, the population declined, perhaps one and a half million fleeing to America, establishing persistent anti-British bases. Whites of goodwill could be hideously unaware of the role of the dead, of magic, of mana : that to evict a tribe entailed its abandoning cherished ancestral spirits; that 'superstition' could sustain vital morale and sometimes more. Macaulay, enlightened admirer of British institutions, totally rejected Indian culture, though ignorant of it, envisaging India as a potential imitation Britain.

Simultaneously, imperialism elicited nostalgia, love, mystique. 'Land of Hope and Glory, Mother of the Free' ends with 'God who made thee mighty, make thee mightier yet.' Imperialism revoked strict Party lines. Liberals – Churchill, Grey, Haldane, Ruskin – believed in Empire, as did Sydney Webb, one of those whom Woolf described as Socialist at home but elsewhere a common or garden Conservative. Liberals were heavily divided over the Boer War, as indeed were Socialists. Shaw and many Fabians supported Britain, who was denounced by their working-class colleagues. Other Liberals who condemned Britain for crushing Boer freedom lived to condemn that freedom as Hitlerite. Gladstone's Liberal government occupied Egypt. Cobden, Bright, Adam Smith opposed colonies. Rhodes would have agreed with John Buchan[83] that imperialism 'is a spirit, an attitude of mind, an unconquerable hope. You can phrase it a thousand ways without exhausting its content. It is a sense of the destiny of England. It is the wider patriotism which conceives our people as a race and not as a chance community.' For Lord Curzon, the British Empire was 'the greatest institution for good the world has ever seen.' For Joseph Chamberlain, 'The British race is the greatest of governing races that the world has ever seen.'

More vulgarly, Music Halls sang 'The Great White Mother', 'The Miner's Dream of Home', 'God Bless the Dublin Fusiliers', 'We'll Bring back the Flag to Majuba'.

Here's another little Baby Queen Victoria has got,
Whatever will she do with little Cyprus?

'British' must be broken down into company agents, civil servants, soldiers, missionaries, adventurers, hunters and plain ruffians. Some saw a chance to spread moral light as well as gather treasure. Livingstone was explorer, anti-slaver, doctor, evangelist, and commercial traveller. 'Philanthropy plus five per cent,' Rhodes said. Ironies were considerable. All Britain seethed, 1866, over Governor Eyre, who had shown in Australasia unusual black sympathies. In Jamaica he suppressed a black rising with executions that led to his prosecution, British opinion as divided as it was to be over Dyer of Amritsar, with Dickens, Ruskin, Spencer, Carlyle, Mill, Huxley, Kingsley passionately defending or reviling him.

Gandhi himself, revered as a traditional Indian saint, for whom to enjoy Mozart was sin, enjoyed a reputation fostered by British sympathies as well as by nationalist fervour, as in that signal vignette of him, 1922, receiving a sentence of six years' gaol for sedition, pronounced with regret, acknowledged with a smile, the prosecutor hastening to shake hands with the prisoner who had invited the judge to be converted to non-violence and Indian freedom. 'Either resign your post, or inflict on me the severest penalty.' He pleaded guilty in terms that left him strangely masterful, the British judge, in memorable language, praising his moral character and renown.

Verdicts remain provisional, 'I discovered', the young Gandhi announced, proposing a loyal toast, 'that there were certain ideals of the British Empire with which I had fallen in love.' 'Governments are best which govern least, and the British govern least of all.' He valued many British benefits but came to feel that their imposition by force cancelled their virtues. The 1,200 wounded, 379 dead at Amritsar, 1919, thereafter forced him to condemn Britain for rendering India more helpless, less self-assured, less productive, in an unnatural relationship designed for foreign profits. 'A crime against humanity, perhaps unequalled in history.' Such events established guilt-feelings amongst the British themselves, that allowed many to support the slave states of Stalin and Hitler, sometimes both simultaneously, in rejection of imperialism and monopoly capitalism.

Apologists refer to the creation of Singapore, Madras, Accra, Hong Kong . . . Rhodesian copper-belt, Malta docks, Russell Pasha battling against Egyptian narcotics as Sleeman did against Indian Thugs; Cromer's financial and medical reforms in Egypt; DDT effecting revolutions that would have amazed Voltaire and Mirabeau; Sun Yat Sen training in western medicine, Nehru educated at a British public school and university; the rigidly paternalist Curzon admiring and exploring Indian culture; Allan Hume founding the Indian Congress Party; Niolle almost eliminating North African trachoma; Marshal Lyautey showing a flair for paternalistic government and sympathetic comprehension of Islam; Cypriot malaria reduced from 90 per cent to 3 per cent; the British, despite two discreditable wars, modernizing the Imperial Chinese Customs Service from 1863; 'Chinese' Gordon, succeeding an American, suppressing the bloody Taiping rebellion, William Bowman saving the Emperor's eyesight; rubber established in Malaya, cocoa in West Africa. The Indian Civil Service, though monopolized at the summit by British, had Pepysian qualities of honesty, industry, efficiency and has been largely retained by independent India. In 1821 British direct rule was established on the Gold Coast to enforce anti-slavery policies, though later, and typically, extended more variously. Ethiopia, whose colonial period was short, does not, in terms of freedom and welfare, compare too well with countries once ruled by Britain and France.

British rule in Africa, outside the Union, as against her commercial and diplomatic movement, endured less than a century, and in an Africa much of which would have shocked Rousseau or Tolstoy. A Zanzibar sultan kept a beach strewn with dead slaves; the Denim king was still sacrificing humans, 1890; the Ashanti King Kaffee kept the Sacred Stool fertile with human blood

(1874). Arab slaves throve in Uganda, 1880, where King Mwange burnt or beat to death African Christians, adults and children; Bantus joined with whites in exterminating Botswana Bushmen. The segregation of Indian Untouchables evolved without European encouragement. Scores of Ashanti slaves were killed at the funerals of notables, live blood animating dead bones – one recalls the European Countess Bathory, allegedly rejuvenating herself by bathing in the blood of eighty strangled peasant girls. The League of Nations accused black Liberia (1930) of behaviour 'scarcely distinguishable from slave-trading and slave-raiding'. Despite analogies and myths fascinating to anthropologists, much African religion was squalid, bloody and terrifying. Schweitzer[84] records West African 'Leopard Men', secret society terrorists, disguised as leopards, severing their victim's carotid artery as leopards do, recruiting by forms of magical cannibal hypnosis. The imperialist was often tempted into the profitable opportunities caused by native dissension, poverty, misrule. The Zulus were as aggressive as the whites. The British took Ceylon mostly by sharp practice but ruled less corruptly, cruelly, arbitrarily than the Kings of Kandy. Despite Ashanti wars, numerous 'expeditions', and Rhodes's slaughter of Matabeles, the African populations increased under British rule, arbitrary and customary killings decreasing, medicine and hygiene being introduced, if never quite swiftly enough. The Lawrences' Punjabi reforms preserved and increased life; while opposing wholesale westernization, they forbade the burning of lepers and widows, the killing of female infants, and mitigated some sickness and poverty. Many Dyaks, Malays, Chinese, saw Brooke of Sarawak more as protector than conqueror. More sadly, Asia and Africa also produced countless living replicas of what P. G. Wodehouse has described as 'a small china figure of delicate workmanship. It represented a warrior of pre-khaki days advancing with a spear on some adversary who, judging from the contented expression on the warrior's face, was smaller than himself.'

Many considered the African as feckless, lazy, dangerous, though Graham Greene (1935) found only gentleness, kindness, honesty, amongst Liberians of the interior.

I seldom saw a crying child, except at the sight of a white face, and never saw one beaten, they were tender towards each other in a gentle muffled way; they didn't scream or 'rag'; they never revealed the rasped nerves of the European poor in shrill speech or sudden blows. One was aware the whole time of a standard of courtesy to which it was one's responsibility to conform.

Too few did thus conform, or even read Kipling with understanding.

> Ye who tread the Narrow Way
> By Tophet-flare to Judgement Day,
> Be gentle when the heathen pray
> To Buddha at Kamakura.

The wise doctor is he who induces the patient to cure himself.
The Westerner, punctual, legalistic, literal, dedicated to methodical
administration or to profits from soap-oils or diamonds, from Indian
opium and salt, from Nigerian cocoa, ground-nuts, cotton, oil, could
not easily agree with T. E. Lawrence (1921):

> We have to be prepared to see them [Arabs] doing things by
> methods quite unlike our own: but, on principle, it is better
> that they half-do it than that we do it perfectly for them.

White disdain developed much native duplicity and malice,
resented as poor exchange for irrigation, elimination of infanticide,
head-hunting, erosion. Lord Wavell, penultimate Viceroy, held that
the Empire was lost, not by tyranny or exploitation, but by 'the bad
manners of the British overseas', so vivid in Kipling and Forster.
Even money, even sex, can be valued lower than self-respect. 'The
new Imperialists strutted like owners rather than administered as
trustees.' (H. G. Wells) Here was repetition of Carrington's belief
that the American colonists had been infuriated not by British
tyranny but by neglect and because 'London Society was unwilling
to believe that Washington could be a gentleman or that Franklin
would not be patronized.' Even Orwell, once an imperial policeman,
came to hate the 'yellow grinning faces' of his Burmese. Imagination was often lacking. In sixty-three years of rule, Victoria spent
only one month on visiting Ireland.

Christianity's record was variable. Kerala, India, now a Marxist
stronghold, benefited in education, medicine, printing, from
Christian teachers. The Roman Church kept silent about the Congo
atrocities, the ruthless Bishop Augouard tyrannizing over blacks
as delegate not of Christ but of Leopold, hounding out the humane
explorer and administrator, Brazza.[85] Nkrumah taught in a
Catholic Gold Coast school. From French priests at Hara, Haile
Selassie received his own education and recognition of the importance of education for others. Mother Theresa is the saint of today's
Calcutta. Missionaries fought against crippling Asiatic narcotics,
though these helped the Raj's finances until 1913; against New

Zealand slavery, cannibalism, tribal wars; against West Indian
slavery, despite the Church's slave-holdings. Two-thirds of Zaire's
schools were still Catholic, 1972. Proselytizing Catholic-Protestant
rivalries caused bloodshed in Uganda during the 1890s, as amongst
the Red Indians. Lobbying for native rights, missionaries could
also be ignorant and intolerant. Doctrines of hell and moral
exclusiveness, even when accompanied by penicillin, are unsatisfactory ripostes to indigenous magic. It is an old story. Historians
have claimed that, by forbidding the traditional, hygienic, pagan
Egyptian burial rites, Christianity spread the sixth-century plague
that so ravaged Egypt. Post-war Kenyan Mau Mau, secret societies
nationalist obscurantists, killing 20,000 blacks and whites, had been
encouraged by tribal decline due to the foisting of foreign religion,
foreign land-laws on peoples whose traditional rites were simultaneously forbidden as barbarous, heathen and cruel.

2

Popular audiences might bawl 'What we Have we Hold,' but
Bentinck, Ripon, Dalhousie, Lytton, Lugard, the Nicolsons,
Lawrences and Livingstones were not common plunderers. Mary
Kingsley was shrewd, rational, humane. The anonymous, devoted,
paternalist District Officer was not invented by Kipling, any more
than the hard tax-collector, acquisitive narrow settler, grasping
Gold and Diamond Kings, were by Lenin. Even in the West Indies
there was little stagnation : fitfully supine or aggressive the bureaucracy could be manipulated by Interests, was ponderous, unimaginative, but reasonably honest. Forced labour could be for a hospital as
well as for a military railway, taxes for revenue as well as for
dividends.

Learning from their American losses, British proconsuls could
be more far-seeing, or shrewd, than the Ottoman, Portuguese,
Roman.

When the improvement of the natives reaches such a pitch
that it is impossible for a foreign nation to maintain government,
then we must go – and take the glory of the achievement as our
reward.

Thus Lord Elphinstone, Bombay 1823. To his contemporary, Lord
Stanley :

If ever the Canadas separate from this country, some day or
other in the ordinary course of things, it is in our power to
retain their friendship.

Macaulay – of whom Sydney Smith said he had occasional flashes of silence which made his conversation perfectly delightful – serving in India 1834–9, later helping draft its Criminal Code, recognized that 'no nation can be perfectly well governed till it is competent to govern itself,' (1833) though 'the proudest day in British history would be when India voluntarily demanded British institutions.'

British Imperial policy was pragmatic, variable, inconsistent, a response not to central directives but local needs and opportunities, local assets, man-power, circumstances, environment. It was never quite agreed whether British institutions should be exported to the Empire, or whether native institutions should be purged but retained. Compromises were inevitable, and much of the better traditions could be carelessly, or deliberately impaired. Corrosion of the ancient, self-contained, self-governing Indian village council was one sad feature of British rule. The Empire, containing 400 million by 1900, was never a legal, political or economic unity. In much of it, economic or political *laissez-faire* long operated, with results and actual profits still disputed. The Interests and their shareholders may have benefited far more than the British people as a whole. After World War I, dividends were declining. After 1918, wider political concepts developed, sometimes influenced by the League of Nations and its 'mandates'. Expensive promotion of education, hygiene, scientific agriculture, policing, civil service, however inadequate, required growing native skills, with important political consequences.

Only a few further details can be noted here. Several British and European wars were fought with China, enforcing by 'the Unequal Treaties' monopolistic rights in the opium trade, and immunity from native laws in Chinese parts. The British thus acquired Hong Kong, 1842. In West Africa, native lands, institutions, laws were largely preserved, constitutional advance encouraged; in East Africa the reverse. Safeguarding trade, investment, route to India, the Suez Canal was one motive in the occupation of Egypt, German expansion a factor in Britain taking over Uganda, Kenya, Bechuanaland. A real or imagined Russian threat to India impelled or excused further annexations in India, Malaysia. An appetite for teak whetted by royal incompetence, Burmese anarchy and a desire to forestall the French precipitated the conquest of Burma, 1885. After 1918, attempts to establish a British oil-empire in the Middle East barely survived World War II.

Proposals for Empire Free Trade or 'Imperial Preference' failed to unite the Empire, emotionally or economically; British navy and finance were stronger bonds but dangerously vulnerable. The

British Asiatic Empire proved to command little spontaneous loyalty against the Japanese, whose destruction of British capital ships, and easy capture of Singapore (1941) promised its end. Everywhere, the financial, physical, moral effort against Hitler quickened movements for colonial independence. Suez, 1956, finally taught Britain the brute realities of her world and imperial situation.

3

The ending of Empire, of the Crown's writ, was outstanding, but not dominating, for post–1945 Britain. Only over India, oldest and largest 'possession', were emotions genuinely roused. After the Mutiny, the Viceroy, Council, a few thousand British civil servants, some 90,000 white officers, ruled over 100 million peoples, their diverse castes, religions, loyalties. Mutiny terror – and the white counter-terror deplored by Queen Victoria – worsened racial relations, though the conciliatory and reforming policies of the Governor-General won from British opinion the disapproving nickname, 'Clemency'. Friendliness, curiosity, inter-marriage declined. The Suez Canal is often blamed, facilitating the arrival of white wives. The Club became synonymous with colour-bar, snobbery, arrogance. Village poverty, mass-illiteracy, religious hatreds, taxation, periodic famine could seem the only result of imperialism, a view propagated by Japanese and Nationalists. The light of impeccable civil servants shone before men who showed increasing inclination to extinguish it. Political discontent, constitutional wranglings, led by new Indian middle-classes, was enflamed by the two wars. British policy of increased Indian provincial self-government and representation, however well-meant, could be spoilt by maladroit timing, blandness, unimaginative presentation, too blatant an appearance of reluctant concessions. Dilemmas seemed insoluble. Even to attack Caste would insult Indian religion, to recognize it would condone inhumanity. Gandhi opposed viceregal attempts for Moslem-Hindu friendship while blaming Britain for their hostility; denying the rights of others he insisted that only Congress could represent India. A pacifist – 'real manliness consists in not retaliating even under a shower of bullet' – he could advocate policies that could only provoke mob-violence, or even support violence in Kashmir. The surge of British India's revenue and trade, gratifying Nehru, horrified Gandhi, to whom railways, hospitals, law-courts, machines, money were materialist traps or inessentials, endangering the soul of Mother India, despite the slums of Bombay and Calcutta.

By 1942, nationalists were disunited, British Cabinets preoccupied with war, with many voices, frequently American, interfering from bastions of ignorance or prejudice. Few of the loudest noises came from the best informed, though a former viceroy, Lord Linlithgow, contrasted Indian stupidity with British dishonesty. Wavell felt that Winston Churchill 'hates India and everything to do with it and, as Amery said in a note he pushed across to me, "knows as much about the Indian problem as George III did of the American colonies."' (27 July 1943). By 25 October 1944, the Viceroy was writing to Churchill,

> I am bound to say that after a year's experience in my present office I feel that the vital problems of India are being treated by His Majesty's Government with neglect, sometimes with hostility and neglect.

> (See Penderel Moon (ed.), *Wavell: The Viceroy's Journal*, Oxford, 1973)

The circumstances of the British withdrawal – partition, 600,000 dead in the Punjab, fourteen million homeless – are too well-known to recapitulate. A contemporary British historian can add a graphic word. In August, 1947,

> Gandhi again did his best to reduce violence, moving through the riot-torn areas with his customary disregard for personal safety. But he did not spend much time in the Punjab; he too believed that the worst trouble would be in Bengal. There he was to be outstandingly successful. There he showed his real greatness. Not Gandhi the reformer, not Gandhi the Hindu politician, but the Gandhi behind them both, the man who hated suffering and violence. Though, by his past actions, he had contributed as much as anyone to the communal divisions which now resulted in bloodshed, he went out to face that bloodshed when it came, and by doing so saved thousands of lives.

In September he decided on a fast to the death, to end 'only if and when sanity returns to Calcutta'. The entire police force of north Calcutta, Europeans included, undertook a twenty-four hour fast in sympathy, while continuing with their duties.

> In this and what followed, the unique Indian-ness of India emerges. Nowhere else in the world could an ugly little man of 77 years of age, growing steadily weaker because he refused to eat, have such an effect. On the basis of this episode alone, so alien to western understanding, it becomes almost possible to sympathize with the ignorance and incomprehension of India

displayed by the British Government and Lord Mountbatten. After four days, Gandhi received a pledge from Hindu, Muslim and Sikh leaders to keep the peace in their own area, and broke his fast. The city became quiet almost overnight.

(Michael Edwardes, *The Last Years of British India*, New English Library, 1967)

The British Empire can perhaps be held more humane than the Assyrian, Aztec, Carthaginian and Iberian; more multifarious than the Persian; more dynamic than the Egyptian and Chinese; more flexible than the Roman. Yet mistakes were grievous and unnecessary. Carelessly-drawn boundaries between competing imperialists accentuated new violence between black states emerging after 1945, year of the Manchester Pan-African Congress. The unprecedented British solution of Dominion Status, granting political independence, recognizing Commonwealth republics, shedding responsibilities while retaining emotional and constitutional links, could itself disappoint. While Lugard himself, overlord of Uganda, wanted a British Africa trained for this, he grandly overlooked the probability that many young Africans through schools, travel, war-service, would desire more, indignantly rejecting the paternalism of a Lugard, even a Schweitzer. British-indented Asiatic labour would leave behind friendless minorities. Kenyan territory was offered to the Jews, 1903, with no African consulted. British indirect rule appealed more to old-fashioned chiefs than to those who demanded the rewards not of docility but of self-respect and power. British Central Africa produced few trained Africans to manage after independence: white trade-unions had kept Africans from the most appetizing jobs. New rulers had to cope with dislocated tribalism, semi-urbanization, ill-balanced economies, inorganic law, neo-imperialist intrigues. White and black States alike were, 1972, practising one-party rule, coercion, genocide, expulsion, dictatorship, censorship, aggression, following massacres in the Congo, in Zanzibar, megalomania in Ghana, civil war in Nigeria. In Uganda, public executions, forbidden by the British, were restored, 1973. Similarly, in independent, rebellious white Rhodesia, Habeas Corpus has long been suspended, one African lying in prison for fourteen years without having been charged (1973). In return for previous and uninvited white colonial intrusions, mass black and brown emigration to Britain, from the 1950s, evoked a response comparable to that once shown towards the Flemings and Huguenots.

Sardonic tribute to imperialism was paid, nevertheless, by the

I

most pretentious and loudest anti-imperialist powers, America and Russia. Roosevelt almost seemed to compare the British Empire unfavourably to the Nazi, and to rate Stalin more trustworthy than Churchill. America has invaded Latin America forty-one times, annexed Texas and, through trade monopolies, long secured virtual economic control over Cuba, Haiti, San Domingo, Nicaragua, Columbia, Panama. Improving on Tsarist Asiatic imperialism, Red Russia, between 1918–40, twice invaded Finland; invaded Georgia, 1922, coercing and destroying; suppressed national minorities and churches – Jewish, Orthodox, Islamic, amongst Byelo-Russians, Armenians, Caucasians, Cossacks, Ukranians, Siberians, Turkestanies; annexed Latvia, Lithuania, Estonia; dominated, sometimes bloodily, Poland, Hungary, Czechoslovakia, the Balkans. That General Eisenhower could write[86] that America and Russia were free from the stigma of colonial empire-building by force, was an irritating absurdity. Perhaps the loss of empire may at least be reducing American and European suspicions of Britain.

We repudiated all versions of the
doctrine of original sin, of there being
insane and irrational springs of wickedness in most men. We were not aware
that civilization is a thin and precarious crust erected by the will and
personality and only maintained by
rules and conventions skilfully put
across and guilefully maintained.

J. M. Keynes

Money is indeed the most important
thing in the world; and all sound and
successful personal and national morality should have this fact as its basis.
Each teacher and twaddler who denies
it or suppresses it, is an enemy of life.
Money controls morality.

G. B. Shaw

True National Socialism is instinct,
not knowledge.

Joseph Goebbels

I

1900–1914 has been mourned as a Golden Age, as mellow twilight.
Cities were indeed stung with vital controversies, dazzling hopes,
prodigious challenges, abysmal griefs. Many could await the
marvellous telegram, 'You've won.' By the 1880s Nietzsche had
proclaimed 'the death of God', freeing man to exploit the gods
within himself. The authority of the old and traditional was crumb-
ling. Tsarism was in decay. Napoleon III, with his plebiscites,
censorship, sensationalism, was surely the last dictator. Inventions
and trade surpluses could assuage poverty, despite apocalyptic
Marxist warnings. Marx and Freud appeared to offer scientific and
total understanding of man and society. Religion, ceasing to be
a battle-cry, was more a symbol of historical relativity, psychic possibility, personal consolation or stimulus. European rather than
national, trends seemed thrilling, audacious, outrageous. Liberal
Europe had hopes of the Tsar's foundation of the Hague Inter-

national Peace Tribunal. Socialists dismissed this last as a hypocritical red herring, but were resolving to refuse war credits and
to strike if war came, certain that wars, like religion and traditional
morality, were capitalist devices to raise taxes, profits and cannon-
fodder for over-weight scoundrels.

The Paris Commune had not been forgotten. Gerard Manley
Hopkins could refer to 'Loafers, Tramps, Corner Boys, Roughs,
Socialists and other pests of Society,' but the Second International
was a serious candidate for the Nobel Peace Prize, 1913.

Humanitarian teachings were being fostered by Rolland, Karolyi,
Rathenau, Nansen, Jaurès, Chekhov, Montessori, Schweitzer. Europe
seemed seeking a conscience. Talent and insights were prodigious :
Unamuno, Gasset, Brandes, Kraus, Gorky, Croce, Verhaeren,
Plekhanov. There were Marconi, Rilke, Apollinaire, Hesse, Gris,
Picasso, Matisse . . . Stravinsky, Satie, von Hofmannsthal, Strauss,
Cocteau, Valery . . .

Angell's *The Great Illusion* proved war economically unviable.
Truculent British, French, Belgian imperialisms were accepting
co-existence. An international culture seemed a fact. Queen Victoria,
though no intellectual, as a matter of course knew four modern
languages; her daughter, Empress of Germany, studied Marx together with Darwin and Mill. Though Churchill already saw
nationalism overtaking religion as man's most potent drive, the
procession of European leaders headed by the Kaiser – plumed and
dazzling – at Victoria's funeral, suggested a unity more than superficial.

In Britain, the Grand Tour itself had entered a more democratic
lap, with the one-time garden boy, printer and missionary, Thomas
Cook (1808–92) and his tourist organization. This was not
only for pleasure : he arranged Moslem pilgrimages, also trans-
ports for imperial war-casualties, and for the troops to relieve
Gordon.

In Britain, as in Germany, France, Italy, organized Labour had
joined the parliamentary Interests, as indeed had the press. European feelings everywhere condemned rubber atrocities, British
South African 'concentration camps', Tsarist shootings, German
militarism. Though Grey, British Foreign Secretary considered
that the hangings, floggings and imprisonments at Denshawi, Egypt
– the hangings conducted in front of the victim's families – 'were
admirable, and reflect great credit on all concerned,' Western
opinion was shocked. Leonard Woolf wrote :

It seemed that human beings might really be on the point of
becoming civilized. . . . the forces of reaction and barbarism were

still there, but they were in retreat. They had suffered a tremendous defeat in the Dreyfus Case. In the Zabern incident and in the Denshawi incident a new note began to be heard in what may be called world opinion. It seemed at last to be generally agreed that for a German officer to beat up an Alsatian cobbler was an outrage against law and order and decency and civilization. When at Denshawi a British court passed savage sentences upon Egyptian villagers for killing a British officer who insisted on killing the villagers' pigeons, a cry went up, not against the villagers but against the insolence of the officers and the vindictiveness and savagery of the judges. For the first time in the history of the world the rights of Jews, cobblers, coloured men, not to be beaten, hanged or judicially murdered by officers, junkers, or white men was publicly admitted; and it looked for a moment as if militarism, imperialism, and anti-semitism were on the run.

(Leonard Woolf, *Beginning Again*, Hogarth, 1969)

Jefferson, Owen, Saint-Simon, Spencer, Bentham, Darwin, Shaftesbury, Marx, Prince Albert, Matthew Arnold, Napoleon III, Kropotkin, Bakunin, Bismarck, Wells, Shaw, the Webbs, Chekhov, Jaurès, Lloyd-George, Clemenceau, Churchill, Attlee, Smuts, MacDonald, Lenin, believed in progress, were unhampered by Freudian doubts. Unlike Buddha, Jesus, the Caesars, Luther, they believed not only that poverty could be cured but that it should be cured. Their absolute convictions sometimes indeed bordered on mysticism. Lukacs was to maintain that Marxism would remain valid even were all Marx's facts and prophecies totally disproved, somewhat in the spirit of Robespiere's statement that belief in God and the Immortal Soul was humanity's finest achievement, even if totally untrue.

In the age of the microscope and camera, Verne, Kipling, Wells revealed for mass audiences the beauties and promises of science and technology. For a Geddes, a Howard, the Garden City, factory, could be new, exciting, social units, of work and play, health and intercourse, rehabilitated man living amongst flowers in clean, clear architecture.

Such optimism invited scepticism, dissent, malice. Darwin, Marx, Freud gave no very reassuring news about freedom, peace, civilization itself. Science, Tolstoy declared, is a bar of gold made by a charlatan alchemist. Sorel, Bergson, Dostoevsky, saw science as irrelevant to the real problems of soul, morality, motive, love, sin. For Dostoevsky parallel lines met, the dead could be literally resurrected. Carlyle, Melville, Nietzsche, Tolstoy, Yeats, Gandhi, heirs of Blake, were repelled by the identification of progress with state-power, mass-literacy, superficial information, technology, parliaments, unions, bureaucracies that alike impaired peasant or elemental vigours, piety, devotion, individual choice, direct human relations. That a factory could be superior to a farm was visible, pernicious nonsense. For Spengler, 'All world-improvers and world-citizens stand for fellaheen ideals, whether they know it or not. Their success means the historical abdication of the nation in favour not of everlasting peace but of another nation.' He considered war a natural device to revive moribund cultures and institutions; for Neo-Malthusians it relieved communal tensions, strengthened the breed by inter-racial matings, preserved the balance of Nature. Hegel diagnosed war as purifier of peoples, the State as 'the absolutely supreme phenomenal form of the spirit'. White-gloved, ornate officers strode, conforming to arrogant inhuman codes, contemptuous of civilians. Tuchachevsky, Tsarist General, Soviet Marshal, executed by Stalin, 1937, wrote:

> Seriously, it would be good for humanity were all books burned, so that we would bathe in the fresh spring of ignorance. I even think that it is the sole means of preventing humanity from becoming sterile.

Nietzsche, who attracted the young Shaw and Yeats, watched imperial mediocrity setting in like rot, liberalism and socialism proving drearily philistine, to be redeemed not by plutocracy, herd values and gutless Christianity, or by votes of hordes emasculated by foolish education, barren homes and work, but by individual genius and aristocracy. 'When the ends are great, humanity employs other standards and no longer judges crime as such, even if it resorts to the most frightful means.'

2

Like the anthropologists, Malinowsky and Frazer, like post-Impressionist art, Vienna psychology was deriving strange evidence from dreams, behaviour, illness, primitives, mythology, suggesting a human unity more fundamental than any empire, expressing clinically the intimations of Shakespeare, Blake, Goethe, Dickens, Rimbaud, Dostoevsky: of the Mysteries. When Aristotle, himself a Mystery initiate, declared (*Ethics*) that political students must know the facts of the soul, he recognized that the dark, irrational, magical and unknown could offset the light, reasonable, proved. In the lure of contradictions,

All beings that one loves
Are cups of acid to be drunk, eyes shut;
And the heart, pierced through, drawn on by sorrow,
Dies daily, blessing the arrow.

(Baudelaire)

Schopenhauer had been powerfully concerned with Buddhist beliefs, that culture, religion, human goodness were illusions, protections against intolerable reality. Feuerbach had considered 'dreaming is the key to the mysteries of religion.' Fourier, whose comments on human motives excited Dostoevsky, not only listed forty-nine varieties of cuckold but warned against repression of vital instincts.

Freudianism reached conclusions enthralling, disconcerting or incredible. Strangers in dreams were revealed as oneself; Christianity could be diagnosed as castration-complex; Jews suffered unconscious guilt from killing Moses; anti-semitism was assisted by terrors aroused by circumcision; drunkenness could be sublimated homosexuality. Actions apparently trivial revealed fundamental, revolutionary clues to personality. Novel or overlooked perspectives appeared. Jung treated three young girls :

When they were approaching puberty they confessed shamefacedly to each other that for years they had had horrible dreams of their mother. They dreamt of her as a witch or a dangerous animal and they couldn't understand it at all, since mother was so lovely and utterly devoted to them. Years later the mother became insane and in her insanity she went about on all fours and imitated the grunting of a swine, the barking of dogs, the growling of bears.

(Frieda Fordham, *An Introduction to Jung's Psychology*, Penguin, 1953)

Theories of the death-wish, the unconscious, the primal horde, hatred of fathers, obsession with mothers . . . tore down old superstitions, sometimes established new ones, with all the flair, insight, excesses of intellectual realignment. The body shed its last renaissance glamour but was identified with powers coarser but as vital as those of the soul, itself explained away in terms of infantile fantasy, suppressed desires, archetypal dreams. From headlong generalizations one learnt of the role of anal fixation in the Reformation, of sexual frustration and paternal complexes in war and that we hate most in others traits we unconsciously secrete in ourselves. Omnipotence of the libido was elevated to dogma, Freud wishing to excommunicate those followers who rejected it – though the careers of Alfred, Peter the Great, Voltaire, Cook, Napoleon, Louis XIV, Pitt, none of them sexually deprived, might seem to dispute it. Man does not live by bed alone. Anna and Vronsky ultimately required more than sexual passion.

Explicit diagnosis of motive could – like violence – solve private neurosis, but signally failed to affect public problems. The new psychology was ignored by generals, statesmen, rulers. Karl Kraus mocked Freudian analysis as 'the disease of which it pretends to be the cure'. But positive gains could be claimed : an understanding that the apparently accidental might be an unconscious warning, reproach, hope; further recognition of the importance of dream, fantasy, play : of memories long submerged but still active; of infantile experience; of the irrational in domestic and social life; of the psychosomatic causes of illness. The pathologist J. G. Halliday estimated that in pre-1939 Britain, not the most hysterical nation, 33 per cent of industrial sickness was neurotic in origin. Medieval demons had reappeared under other names. In 1972, more than half the hospital patients of Britain's Welfare State were suffering from mental illness, a disappointing comment on the relativity of progress.

3

Façades of Court and Chancellory were less substantial than they seemed. Poverty, prostitution, discontent, were still massive, female virginity still treated as real-estate. Bureaucracies held down Poles, Czechs – and indeed the Nazi death-camps have often been identified as godchildren of dulled, anonymous functionaries, of Circumlocution Office and Kafka's Castle, where humans become ciphers rendered interesting by the magic not of personality but of numbers and patterns. Over-rapid industrialization, nervous sensitivity of new states, a menacing arms-race presided over by erratic, incompetent or aggressive rulers, troubled the early twentieth century. Anarchism promoted political violence in Europe and America, assassinating a French President, 1894, the Austrian Empress, 1898, the King of Italy, 1900, the American President, 1901.

Nominally subordinate to the government, General Staffs, particularly in Germany, Austro-Hungary, Japan, seemed at times to be conducting independent foreign policies. Posterity saw more clearly the power of supra-national Interests . . . oil, metal, banking, chemicals . . . Krupps, Standard Oil, Electric Boat, General Motors, Schneider-Creusot, United Fruit, I. G. Farben, Vickers Armstrong . . . secretly linked and with finances superior to many national budgets and intimately associated with national policy. Rhodes was a diamond and mining millionaire, also a prime minister, Leopold a rubber tycoon, also a king. Zaharoff, chairman of Vickers, directing its foreign affairs 1900–14, owned newspapers, banks, railways, mines, shipyards, factories, held 298 decorations from thirty-one countries, was knighted by George V, endowed a Sorbonne Chair, had pronounced influence on Joseph Chamberlain, and on Lloyd George, particularly over the disastrous Turco-Greek War, 1922. The Mitsui Cartel earned more than the Japanese State; I. G. Farben more than all Scandinavia, with global sales of plastics, chemicals, rubber, steel, aspirin, fibres, synthetic fats, soaps, fuels, dyes, cotton, petroleum, soil-producing plants, by-products of coal. In Middle Eastern oil conflicts, British Shell would influence Britain and Greece, French-American Standard Oil would back Turkey. Such powers were in descent from the Lombards, Templars and the Fuggers. Between 1870 and 1945 the energies of international steel and explosives, documented by League of Nations research, transformed history into melodrama. Krupps, covertly allied to American Standard Oil and Japanese Zaibatsu, with close relations with the Hohenzollerns, subsequently with Hitler, had unpublicized control of important sections of the press, armed both sides at Sadowa. Germans in China, 1900, faced Krupps guns as, 1896, Italians met Italian artillery used by the victorious Ethiopians. Krupps sold Vickers a formula for shrapnel fuses, used 1914–18, subsequently demanding 123 million shillings in royalties. Though condemned after World War II for mass-slavery, starvation, torture, beatings,

Ten years after his reoccupation of the main plant on 4 March, 1953, he [Alfred Krupp] had octupled his pay-roll. In the Bundesrepublik alone he commanded more men than the Duke of Wellington led at Waterloo, Lee at Gettysburg, Moltke at Könnigratz (Sadowa) or Napoleon III at Sedan. In Asia, Arabia and Africa there were natives who had never heard of Eisenhower, Macmillan or de Gaulle, yet who nodded vigorously at the mention of Alfred's name.

(William Manchester, *The Arms of Krupp 1587–1968*, Michael Joseph, 1970)

Zaharoff armed Boer and British, 1899–1901, and all armies in the Balkan Wars. British-made guns used against the British at the Dardanelles were delivered by Zaharoff. He and the French Schneider-Creusot cartel seem to have interfered with military strategy, 1914–18, enforcing the refusal to bombard the German-exploited Brieuy industrial basin, admitted in the French Parliament, 24 January 1919. Of Zaharoff, Donald McCormick writes:

> In 1913–14, the British Foreign Office actually considered it part of their work to ensure that Vickers and Armstrong secured munition orders from foreign countries and that the British bankers, Rothschild and Cassell, made similar conditions when they granted loans to foreign governments. Thus, with government blessing through the Foreign Office the power of the armament-makers was paramount. Schneider-Creusot actually regarded the nomination of the Minister of Marine in France as their own perquisite, and the firm dominated the Army Commission of the French Chamber of Deputies, while in Russia the military hierarchy had been systematically demoralized by the bribes and threats from arms agents from all over Europe.

During the 1927 Naval Conference, three US shipping corporations employed a Mr Shearer to make propaganda against naval arms reductions, and were sued by him, 1929, for a quarter of a million dollars. The Italian arms firm, Ansaldo, joined electrical combines, bankers, industrialists, landowners, even Freemasons in financing Mussolini, 1919–21, in return for strike-breaking and anti-Red violence. British firms, 1932–39, were supplying direct military aid to Nazi Germany, advertizing in Nazi papers. 70 per cent of Japanese war-material was of Anglo-US supply. Within a week of war the *News Chronicle* reported,

> Huge German orders for rubber and copper were executed in London yesterday, regardless of cost. The buying of nearly 3,000 tons of copper sent the prices rocketing. . . . Germany has bought over 10,000 tons this month.

The prosecution at Nuremburg, 1946, of Farben for war crimes and slavery at Auschwitz, revealed the millions spent on subversive political and military conspiracies in Norway, Poland, Czechoslovakia, Luxembourg, Austria, Alsace-Lorraine; the monies paid to Franco, and to one-third of the members of the Chinese National Assembly. It exposed, also, intrigues against British and American military supplies prior to Pearl Harbor; political and economic powers in Latin America; the provision of special gases for Auschwitz, plans for Tabun, an irresistible corrosive gas, and Sarin, a gas inducing mass-madness within seconds.

Today the quasi-independent role of military and civilian government departments is fitfully questioned, critics maintaining that the archives of the Pentagon, and the Russian KGB would reveal unpublicized influences on national policy. Innocuous names can mislead. The Central Intelligence Agency helped involve Kennedy in the Bay of Pigs fiasco against Cuba. Congress was informed, 20 March 1973, that the International Telephone and Telegraph Corporation, backed by the CIA, organized direct opposition against the Marxist government of Chile. The FBI is accused of secret involvements with UNO. The phenomenon of supra-national cartels, quasi-independent combines, is intensifying the problems of taxation, labour relations, with concentration of power in secretive, distant, unapproachable offices.

4

The British imagination in the early twentieth century was less insular than it may have thought, though less adventurous than perhaps it should have been. For the educated, but not highbrow, it was still stacked with heroes and dream-figures known throughout Europe, often more closely related than they seemed. Odysseus, Falstaff, Quasimodo, Pickwick, Satan, Solomon, Adam and Eve, Don Quixote, Anna Karenina, Robin Hood, Werther, Apollo, St Joan, the Little Mermaid, d'Artagnan, Hamlet, Balder, King Arthur, Raskolnikov, Professor Higgins, Sherlock Holmes, Faust, Mimi.

Arts and sciences were without national limits. Drama meant the Greeks, Molière, Shakespeare, Ibsen, Shaw, Hauptmann, Chekhov, Reinhardt, Stanislavsky, Bernhardt, Duse, Irving; music, the Germans, Stravinsky, Chopin, Scriabin, Berlioz; the novel, Dickens, Tolstoy, Dostoevsky, Turgenev, Flaubert, the Manns, Henry James, Proust; sculpture, the Greeks, Michelangelo, Rodin; painting, Rembrandt, Leonardo, Rubens, Vermeer, Watteau, Van Gogh; philosophy, the Greeks and Romans, Germans, French, perhaps Bertrand Russell. Ballet meant the Russians and French; poetry, Homer, Shakespeare, Villon, Dante, Hugo; opera, Monteverdi, Mozart, Wagner, Verdi, Puccini; medicine, Pasteur, the Curies, Lister, Jenner, Ross, Paul Ehrlich, Walter Reed, Robert Koch, Elie Metchnikoff, Emile Roux; psychology, Freud, Jung; history, Gibbon, Hume, Taine, Von Ranke; anthropology, Frazer and Malinowsky; physics, Rutherford, Clark Maxwell, Einstein.

Wagner's influence on British intellectuals was far-reaching. If Italian cultural impact had diminished, French, Russian and German had increased. French insistence on poetic and visual truth uncluttered by sentimentality and decorative comment entered British painting through Sickert, British poetry through Symons and the Americans Eliot and Pound. Courbet, Corot, the Pissaros,

Cézanne; Baudelaire, Rimbaud, Laforgue, cut away from the generalized and rhetorical. An art was promised that collected images and allusions from all nations, all times : from the primitive and futuristic, from dream and waking, the commonplace and the abstruse, appealing to an Anglo-European-American cultural aristocracy.

Similarly, professional nomenclature derived from many European cultures. Doric, Ionic, Gothic, Faustian, Machiavellian, Wagnerian, Proustian, Dickensian, Newtonian, Napoleonic, democratic, Marxist; concerto, sonnet, sestina, elegy, nocturne, counterpoint, terza rima; genre, picaresque, hieroglyphic; rotunda, clerestory, apse, chancel; voltage, galvanize; oligarch, dictator, plutocrat; Bessemer, Daimler, Zeppelin.

Disraeli's mind had been cosmopolitan. Gladstone, a Homeric scholar, considered, 'we are part of the community of Europe, and we must do our duty as such.' Rosebery was a historian, author of a study of Napoleon, Balfour a philosopher, Haldane a serious student of German thought. Asquith was at home in Greek. Churchill, waywardly patriotic, boorish in foreign tongues, was yet at ease in old patrician Europe. Carlyle, Buckle, Spencer, Winwood Read, Wells, Russell, strove to make Britain think internationally. Blériot's cross-channel flight, revoking dimensions of time and space more or less constant since the Wheel, suggested an achievement more momentous than Waterloo. Racial mixtures increased cultural ranges. Marx's daughter, Eleanor, translated *Madame Bovary* and, with Shaw, acted in the first, and amateur, performance of *The Doll's House*. Her husband, Aveling, probably the original of Shaw's Dubedat, translated *Das Kapital*, wrote *The Wickedness of God*. Moore, Russell, Whitehead, Tawney . . . Ruskin, Shaw, Wells, Lawrence, Kipling . . . reached beyond the English-speaking world, interacting with Rolland, Bergson, Proust, Croce . . .

The effect was meagre. Lloyd George, at the Versailles peacemaking, allegedly could not find key places on the map. Grey spoke no French. Neither Baldwin nor Neville Chamberlain had knowledge or instincts of Europe superior to those of their predecessors. Despite a rare Noel-Baker, Hugh Cecil, Arthur Henderson, British liberals and Socialists have been obstinately insular. In 1974, the Labour Party, from motives reasoned as well as obstructive and timid, remains largely indifferent, or hostile, to the European congresses at Brussels and Strasbourg, having neglected (1945–51) to encourage or lead the economic foundations of European unity.

Ruskin ignored his French contemporaries. The 1910 London post-Impressionist exhibition made Virginia Woolf exclaim that human nature had changed, but public opinion reckoned that this was for the worse. Rank outcry against Cézanne's distortions was repeated after 1918, when the Sitwell brothers exhibited Derain, Picasso, Modigliani, Vlaminck. In 1947, the Picasso-Matisse exhibition angered Londoners as vehemently as had Hitler, Freud, Stravinsky . . . none could honourably assist the British way of life.

Pre-1914 rulers were unconcerned with new science, art, psychology. Bismarck's Empire was fashioned more for the driver than the train, the constitution depending too much on the Emperor. The premature death of Victoria's son-in-law, the liberal Frederick III, wrecked Albert's hopes of Anglo-German understanding. Under the philistine, shallow Wilhelm II, an expensive and unnecessary naval rivalry was sharpened, after Berlin's rejection of a tentative British offer of a defensive alliance, 1898.

The majestical, poignant Franz-Josef of Austro-Hungary, beset with internal national hatreds, survived too long, simultaneously maintaining his Empire and keeping it too inflexible. Cabinets and General Staffs, more proficient at intrigue than statesmanship, postured beneath royal houses of inadequate mental ballast, moral fibre, even authority. 'Gentlemen,' said Wilhelm II, signing for world war, 'you will rue the day when you made me do this.' Of other royalty, Chancellor Bülow, an obsequious, well-mannered nonentity, wrote in his memoirs :

The Queen-mother was already a passionate Italian patriot . . . what she most regretted about the War was that events would have made it very difficult for German princes and princesses to marry their equals in France and Russia. A second disagreeable result of the War, the Queen suggested, was the possible danger to a serious spread of democracy.

President Wilson's peacemaking in Paris, 1919 – one visitor to that Paris was an anachronistic reminder of the past, Eugénie, Napoleon III's widow – tried vainly to suppress secret diplomacy. In 1898, Britain and Germany had conspired to partition Portuguese Africa. Largely rebuffed in Africa, Germany and Italy intrigued in the Baltic and Middle East. Secret pre-1914 treaties involved Britain, Italy, Russia, Germany, Portugal in schemes to dispose of other people's colonies. To involve Italy in the War, 1915, detaching her from her pledged allies, Britain and France promised her slices of independent Ethiopia and Libya. Grey, apparently on his own, suggested Russia take Constantinople. Publication of such negotiations assisted post-war cynicism, without discontinuing the process. Britain, 3 March 1938, secretly offered Hitler a colonial deal; Sir George Gater, Permanent Colonial

Under-Secretary, confided to the head of the Foreign Office (July 1943): 'Out of fear of Germany we were prepared to hand over large tracts of colonial empire to Germany, without consulting the wishes of the inhabitants.' (Public Record Office) This plan, covering French, Belgian, Portuguese Africa, was unknown to these governments.

In the French Revolutionary and the two World Wars, Britain's enemies, misled by experts, assumed that she was too preoccupied internally to fight. Her pre-1914 foreign policy was perhaps too indeterminate, neglecting positive policies towards Vienna, neglecting to back Anglo-French loans to Russia with more positive demands for reform. She seemed more anxious to preserve than to initiate. Churchill wrote (1911):

> We have got all we want in territory, and our claim to be left in the unmolested enjoyment of vast and splendid territories, mainly acquired by violence, largely maintained by force, often seems less reasonable to others than to us.

Britain's entry into World War I, formally on behalf of Belgium's treaty rights, diminished little of the continental impressions of Albion.

Periodic economic depressions, over-production, unemployment, monopoly-capitalism overlooking the facts of malnutrition and bad housing, the competition for markets and raw materials . . . such factors certainly helped cause the World Wars, they are less obviously the cause of war itself. Political causes were obvious in 1914, perhaps too obvious. The French urge to retrieve Alsace-Lorraine, the Slavonic and Magyar threats to the Habsburgs, Russian dynastic insecurity, the unpopularity of Tsarism and Prussianism, the arms race. . . . Less accessible, barely acknowledged by Lenin, Jaurès, Wells, are those stirrings against convention, drudgery, discipline, the desire to break not only the injustices but what seemed to be the enervations of peace, the wish to love paternalist states and armies, the appeal of 'national destiny', finally, created by slum, doss-house, private failure, the growth of brutal spectacles, hatreds, gambler's fantasies, yearning for deliverance at any cost.

Since Waterloo, free from all but localized wars, many, seeking the colour, vitalities, throb of life, were finding it in violence and vicarious power. Stefan Zweig, pacific internationalist, remembered his exhilaration at the outbreak of war, how hundreds of thousands felt 'what they should have felt in peace, that they belonged together.' Rilke, Freud, had similar feelings. German socialists found that their own aggressiveness was excused by the chance to overthrow Tsarism. In *Mein Kampf* Hitler confessed :

> For me these hours came as a deliverance from the distress that had weighed upon me during my youth. I am not ashamed to admit that I was swept away by the current enthusiasm and sank onto my knees and thanked God from the fullness of my heart for the favour of being allowed to exist at such a time.

Freud once revealed that an intimate friend and a hated enemy were indispensable to his emotional life. It is not abnormal. Nations too demand, or were made to demand, these opposites, if opposites they were. Posing as the friend, a press-lord, politician, king, general noisily indicated the enemy but could himself be friend and enemy in one.

Progress itself entailed drastic contrasts and penalties. Both Ebenezer Howard and Heinrich Himmler grieved over the continuing pollution of earth, water, forest, man himself. In cities, the air could seem worn out. Poverty assisted the lure of uniforms. People alive today can recall boys barking in the field, from hunger. Ronald Blythe, in his Suffolk study, *Akenfield*,[87] shows how fine rural craftsmanship was too frequently the effort of a hungry people, goitrous from pond water, seeking perfection only as defence against despair, before volunteering for war as an escape from the hated land. Within a village of roses, thatch and lace curtains, the old could be shoved into dark corners and, in death, want their veins cut, as precaution against being buried alive by the careless and indifferent. Coffins, not only in Suffolk, have revealed bodies with finger-nails ground down, as if from desperate clawing.

With personal immortality no longer unquestioned, more hurry ensued for earthly rewards. These were being enhanced by inventions but were unevenly distributed. Politics, sport, alcohol, adultery, conspiracy, hooliganism, war, could be devices for people to prove that they actually existed.

Nazi fanaticism made Hitler appear a unique demonic enchantment. More soberly, he was a drastic twist to lengthy historical development. Pan-Teutonism, cravings for a leader, State-worship, doctrines of a Nordic racialism and the German civilizing mission, had been promulgated since the medieval Emperors, quickening with the Napoleonic invasions, becoming strident after the intoxicating German victory over Napoleon III, 1870. Wagner, like the Frenchman, Gobineau, hailed the white race as incontestably the noblest, to be preserved intact. Gobineau and the Englishman, H. S. Chamberlain, Wagner's son-in-law, believed in the German 'master-race'. Racial exclusiveness was in biblical tradition. Austrian Catholicism contained much anti-Semitism. Long before Hitler, Bismarck wrote to Disraeli, 'As soon as the Army should have been brought to such a condition as to inspire respect, I shall seize the best pretext to declare war on Austria.' The speeches of Wilhelm II, vainglorious, militaristic, chauvinistic and banal, could, if published anonymously, be attributed to more than one leader, German, European or Asiatic.

The Pan-German League, before 1914, wished to incorporate all Germans into a Greater Reich. Proto-Nazi ideas can be found in French, British, Russian and American publicists, though at their most voluminous in Germany : Curtius, Mommsen, Hegel, Fichte, Hart, Nietzsche, Liszt, Jahn, Wilser, Rohrbach, Lang, Wagner, Treitshke, Lambrecht, Perty, Herden, Duncher.

German foreign policy, 1914–18, wanted Russia and France permanently reduced, the forced removal of whole Slav populations, the establishment of Baltic satellites, a huge German navy and African empire.[88]

In all countries, war revoked party lines. Russian Liberals were blatantly annexionist. Kerensky himself wanted Constantinople. War patriotism usually wrecks intelligent sympathies. Prince Albert's daughter, as Crown Princess of Prussia, fiercely anti-Bismarck, could describe Prussia's defeat of Austria as 'the victory of all the Good, the Great and the Noble, for which the German people have been striving for years.' Mao Tse Tung has said that 'armed struggle is the highest form of conscious activity.'

World War I toppled the Tsar, two Kaisers, the Sultan, emancipated Poles, Czechs, Southern Slavs and, though in terrorism and civil war, the Irish Catholics. It strengthened America, Japan and ultimately Russia; weakened France, impaired Britain's foreign investments, particularly in America, and British naval hegemony; established the League of Nations on bases more broad and liberal than those of the Holy Alliance but remaining an association of victors and lacking America. The terms of Sèvres, Trianon, Versailles, though less vindictive than those imposed by Imperial Germany on Russia, greedily neglected to reconcile the defeated, and saddled new, potentially peaceful regimes with total war-guilt, reparations, territorial losses. Lloyd George and Clemenceau were no economists. Woodrow Wilson, though a historian, was ignorant of Europe and combined lofty moral tone with the ineptitudes of unworldliness. His insistence on eliminating long-established Teutonic monarchies for republics theoretically democratic but lacking organic emotional roots was a gamble. Churchill, referring to World War II (8 April 1945) wrote :

This war would never have come unless, under American and modernizing pressure, we had driven the Habsburgs out of Austria and Hungary, and the Hohenzollerns out of Germany. By making these vacuums, we gave the opening for the Hitlerite monster to crawl out of the sewer onto the vacant thrones. No doubt these views are very unfashionable.

They were, though perhaps some recognition of them underlay the controversial American retention of the Japanese Emperor after Hiroshima.

All statesmen in 1919 needed votes from those needing revenge. Millions of deaths – 57,000 British casualties on the Somme in one day, 1916 – vitiated calm judgement, mutual trust. Churchill considered Versailles financial exactions as 'malignant and silly'. Vienna, 1816, had settled the peace in dynastic terms, Versailles, 1919, in national. Neither was sufficient.

The League, like its prophet, Wilson, promised more than it achieved, despite a fair record in rehabilitating ruined cities, war-prisoners, settling smaller disputes, reducing narcotics and prostitution. Britain and France drew apart in recriminations, muddled objectives, lack of conviction in policies, often opposing, towards Germany, Russia, the Middle East, Disarmament, the League.

Nine million battle deaths had transformed earlier idealism into traumas of horror and cynicism. Survivors came

> home to old lies and new infamy;
> usury age-old and age-thick
> and liars in public places

(Ezra Pound)

The songs from the trenches reiterated the scalding bitterness of Sassoon and Owen.

> If you want to find the Old Battalion,
>   I know where they are –
> They're hanging on the old barbed wire.

> I wore a tunic, a dirty khaki tunic,
> And you wore civilian clothes,
> We fought and bled at Loos while you were on the booze,
> The booze that no one here knows.
> Oh, you were with the wenches while we were in the trenches
> A-facing our German foe,
> Oh, you were a-slacking while we were attacking
> Down on the Menin Road.

Anger and apathy bred on reports of profiteering, of unjust military executions, financial and political scandals, conviction that the slaughter had been unnecessarily prolonged, then on unemployment, embittered labour relations, inflation. Guilt throve over old colonial wars, Versailles, non-intervention in Spain, talk of British concentration camps in Deoli and the Andaman Islands, a half-hearted allied intervention against Bolshevik Russia. Fear, of Communism, of renewed casualties, dried or warped the will. The dispossessed, the despairing, the frustrated could dream of power, destruction, the sensational, while leaders attempted to appease dictators, allowed Anglo-Italian amity to moult, neglected German anti-Nazi overtures, 1937–9. Struggles for markets increased during the 1930's. Degeneration seemed neither unrelieved, nor inevitable but, to constitutional Left and Right, it was undeniable. 'The Locust Years,' Churchill said. For W. H. Auden, 'History seems to have struck a bad patch.' Others spoke more violently. Press and radio, replacing pulpit, town crier, broadsheet and gentleman's journal, offered devastating powers to those who discovered how to use them.

5

Beneath institutions, Interests, flamboyant or furtive power-policies, patient men and women had throughout been discovering radium, analysing poverty, cancer, violence, the mind, exercising magnanimity. Yet history tends to be made by those who do not read Spinoza, Hegel, Marx, Freud, though they may breathe a climate that these have helped make. While science abolished distance, the irrational always remained, a Puck, gleefully unpredictable, disreputable, malign or helpful, forcing consideration of Schopenhauer's belief in thought not as the master, but the slave of life.

In 'modern' Europe, crowns, uniforms, swords, crosses, ritual, numbers, names, titles, were still key symbols. Socialist rationalists over-estimated the economic and environmental, overlooked the psychic, the hereditary and unknown. Religious pronouncements often assumed attitudes unchanged for five millenia. For Cardinal Newman,

The Catholic Church holds that it were better for sun and moon to drop from heaven, for the earth to fail, and for all the many millions who are upon it to die of starvation in extremest agony as far as temporal affliction goes, than that one soul, I will not not say should be lost but should even commit one venial sin, should tell one wilful untruth.

Years afterwards, on the atomic bomb, Archbishop Fisher of Canterbury reflected,

> The very worst it could do would be sweep a vast number of people at one moment from this world into the other and more vital world, into which anyhow they must all pass at some time.

Varied, sometimes conflicting facets of mind jostled man and society. Wagner's 'music of the future' also recapitulated Mystery heroes redeeming lands, overcoming monsters and gods with enchanted metal : guarded by nymphs, elves, dragons, gold is the means to world-power; gods die in fire to renew a guilty universe. Shaw translated this as an attack on Capital, Economic Man: audiences may have accepted it more literally.

Rasputin (1871–1916), a Black magician for many – like Paganini – with powers of second-sight and tactile healing, helped discredit the Russian monarchy. The French disasters of 1870 and 1940 were in some quarters explained as divine retribution. 'We must suffer and suffer again, for we have not yet paid for all our sins.' (Marshal Pétain, 1941) Satanist cults survived in most pre-1914 capitals.

Ernest Jones recounts Freud himself performing unconscious magic actions : smashing a marble Venus when his daughter was in danger of death, breaking a beautiful figurine to avert the collapse of a friendship. More overtly, W. B. Yeats spoke of encountering spirits in Paris, expelling one through a window. He claimed that poetry could reach him or his wife by automatic writing dictated from the spirit world. Of the literary partnership of Edith Somerville and Violet Martin of Ross, Miss Martin died first, the survivor continuing to publish jointly, maintaining that Violet's spirit was still collaborating. At a seance, she described, from the beyond, herself seated on Tennyson's knee and calling him Alf![89]

Academics seldom ventured into street, stadium, field, clinic, to see how little Europe had been significantly altered by print, automobile, school. Louis Blanc, in Victorian England, had reported that fortune-tellers, readers of cards, rural and urban astrologers, sorcerers and prophets of both sexes could be counted by the thousand, doing excellent business. The Theosophical Society was founded 1879 by a former spiritualist, Madame Blavatsky, reincarnation of Paracelsus. A clairvoyant was invited to help trace Jack the Ripper, still today a potent dream-figure. French soldiers were convinced that Joan of Arc was encouraging them from the Marne sky; a belief was popular that the air-hero, Guynemer, had flown from Verdun directly into Paradise. To avert universal

destruction, Santander Spaniards sacrificed a baby, 1926. 1930
Serbian peasants killed black cocks and lambs to cure barren women.
Pius XII saw the Virgin on three successive days, 1950, and her
visitations have latterly been accepted at Fatima and La Sallette.
Poland still celebrates the Virgin's leadership against the Russians,
1921. Baltic refugees in Bucholzberg, Germany, 1948, destroyed all
their possessions, believing in imminent world-destruction, and were
arrested when about to sacrifice their children. A London clairvoyant was helping Teeside police in a murder hunt, 1970; the
Dutch clairvoyant, Gerard Croisset, was consulted by Norfolk CID,
1969, about a missing girl. Civilization, like love, is provisional, the
past may strike without warning. At Tenerife, 1972, a German
sectarian and his son killed his wife and daughter, beating 'evil
spirits' from them, before cutting out their hearts. Addressing
the Royal Commonwealth Society, June 1970, the Secretary-General
of the United Nations reported that he received a surprising amount
of appeals from those who thought themselves bewitched. The
Archbishop of Wales, 5 June 1973, wished his clergy to investigate
the extent of Black Magic practised by church vandals.

Much was merely picturesque, husks of old knowledge. John
Holloway[90] recalls his parents, vigorous, practical, yet convinced
of the validity of Christ's thumb-mark on every haddock. Compton
Mackenzie[91] remembers chimney-sweeps on May Morning dancing
in leaf-covered wicker cages, 'Jacks in the Green with centuries
behind them to remind us that there was once a Maypole in the
Strand.'

Horse-magic was still practised until the tractor was finally
supreme. George Ewart Evans told British Association anthropologists (September 1971) that he had found remnants of an East
Anglian secret Horse-Society with initiations held by a stream under
the full moon, performing with a dismembered toad or frog. Much
country lore abounded, certainly until 1939. To cure warts, meat
should be buried under the full moon, the warts falling off as the
moon waned. Corn-dollies placated fertility-spirits. In Yorkshire the
magpie was still unlucky, for having refused to enter the Ark.
'Science', says Blyth, of his Suffolk villager, 'is a footnote to what he
really believes.' Irish 'Hungry Grass', sprouting where starvation
occurred during the Famine, could ambush travellers with sudden
hunger. Around Lincoln, people would not cut an elder without
a prayer to 'the old lady'. In remotest Norfolk, when a villager dies,
the others still tie black cotton round their trees to prevent their
deaths. Old resentments linger. At grim Glencoe, April 1969, a hotel
manager, a Macdonald, was still barring any Campbell. A Scottish
children's game song can yet be heard :

Escape from the Small Thing,
Escape from the Big Thing, Escape from the Death King.
Escape from the Grave King, Escape I will from thee,
And, if I can, stay free.

Games and dances had once had sympathetic magic to assist
harvest, solar energy, the dead. Funeral games, like those held by
Achilles, invigorated the departing soul; sacrificial blood, races,
dances, mimes quickened ghosts into semblance of life. Suggestive
marriage-games survived until today : blocking and unblocking of
chimneys and the like. People beat boys at Rogation, shot at the
winter sun. Of 'Hopscotch' Olivia Robertson (*Tribune*, 12 December, 1946) writes :

There are various theories held as to the origin of this game,
including one involving the solar system, but the following
explanation appears in the Folklore Dictionary : in the Minoan
Age warriors were initiated stage by stage in the labyrinth, and
this may have been taken over by the children as a game. Their
sign for a 'start' is not as one would expect, a 1 (one), but a
symbol like a circle and a seven. Several of these games are
scratched on the pavement of the Roman Forum, and 'round
hopscotch', radiating stages in a circle, is almost identical with
the one described by Pliny. Christians then converted the pagan
idea to Christian allegory, using the Basilican plan, divided into
stages, the Basilica being the forerunner of the early Christian
church. This game was divided into seven stages, as heaven was
believed to be divided, with the inner sanctum, Paradise, in
the place of the altar; the seventh stage in the game was usually
named Paradise, Crown or Glory. . . . Two games, 'Oranges and
Lemons' and 'London Bridge', are universal and actually bridge
the gap between the nursery children and the street children.
I remember I used to hate being caught by the 'arch' in 'Oranges
and Lemons'; this capture is said to recall the habit of our
forebears in seizing the first four or eight comers to a new
gate and burying them alive under the posts. 'London Bridge',
a popular game in the most respectable middle-class nurseries,
is a miming play recalling the fact that in the old days an
aperture was left in a new bridge in which a prisoner was buried
alive : the foundations were bespattered with children's blood.

Mass compulsory schooling was a novel form of education – Jane
Austen left school at nine. Early hopes were often disappointed.
Schools could be barracks, hard little knots of authority, dogma,
prejudice, with teachers intolerant of criticism and minorities,
talking too much about too little. Montaigne, scornful of the
terrifying visage and the armful of rods, remains pertinent. 'The

usual way is to bawl into a pupil's ears as if one were pouring water
into a funnel, and the boy's business is simply to repeat what he is
told.' Few reformers and progressives have yet surpassed the work
of Vittorino da Feltre.

Belief in patent remedies against impotence, baldness, old age,
bad luck, against evidence, had replaced holy relics. Boer War
soldiers sang perhaps more seriously than they realized,

> When I was a Private I took Beecham's Pills,
> Now I'm a Sergeant-Major.

Dream-figures were not displaced but strengthened by books and
films. If saint and prophet faded there were film stars and fictional
heroes. *The Cape Town Times*, 15 July, 1896, announced that
Sherlock Holmes and Dr Watson had landed in South Africa. H.
B. McNicol[92] found, 1946, army recruits associating Rasputin with
the Reformation, identifying the Scarlet Pimpernel as a historical
revolutionary, estimating the population of Stuart England at 300
millions. Of 20,000 questioned, 1969, by Mass Observation, one in
eight considered James Bond actually existed, one in four Sherlock
Holmes. In a Glasgow survey, 1971, 48 per cent did not know where
the heart was, 80 per cent could not precisely locate the stomach.
The Director of the Cambridge House Literacy Scheme (5 May
1966) estimated a minimum two and a half million illiterates.

With such ill-trained equipment, much remains speculative.
Whether racial antipathies are primarily economic, or whether they
owe something to irrational, fairy-tale colour-associations, remains
unanswered, not always asked. The Nazis did not necessarily receive strongest support from where there was a large Jewish minority,
but often from where Jews scarcely existed. People may secretly
desire their hero's eclipse : this, with more candid Party antipathies,
may have contributed to Churchill's downfall on the morrow of
his war triumph, 1945. When the Liberals with apparent reason,
1909, posed 'the Lords versus the People' they actually lost a large
slice of the popular vote. Happiness is not an automatic response
to agreeable conditions. Furthermore, Barbara Tuchmann,[93] dis-
cussing the Liberal victory of 1906, aptly cites the deliberately
fostered rumour that the British, having imported cheap Chinese
Labour into the South African mines, and treated them savagely,
had grosser plans. 'Pigtail' resounded everywhere.

Working-class audiences were told the Tories would introduce
Chinese Labour into England if they won, and pictures of a pig-
tailed coolie in a straw hat were labelled 'Tory British Working

Man'. Thrown on a London screen at political meetings, the pictures, reported Graham Wallas, a Liberal sympathiser, aroused 'an instantaneous howl of indignation against Mr Balfour'. The audience could not have told whether it howled from humanitarian indignation or fear of the competition of cheap labour. Underlying both these sentiments Wallas thought he detected a fear of the alien symbolized by the alien pigtail. The hideous yellow face aroused 'an immediate hatred of the Mongoloid racial type and this hatred was transferred to the Conservative Party'. In the howl of the audience he heard the force of the irrational in public affairs.

The body was emerging from nineteenth-century puritanism in cults of pleasure, sport, walking, nudism, idolatory. A slave, Euripides said, is he who cannot express himself. Europe, 1900–70, has wildly experimented in self-expression and mob-expression in convulsive spasms. Barbarism can still appear healthier than cultures gone sour, than cities squalid and impoverished. Bloodshed had made civilization visibly short of breath. For the post-1918 generations, much of the tyrannical and conventional past must be ditched, and this seemed easier than it proved. Whitman had already written :

Come, Muse, migrate from Greece and Ionia,
Cross out please those immensely overpaid accounts,
That matter of Troy and Achilles' wrath
And Aeneas', Odysseus' wanderings.
Place 'Removed' and 'To Let' on the rocks
Of your snowy Parnassus.

When Odysseus re-appeared it was in Joyce's cuckolded, unheroic, thoughtful Dublin Jew and in Ezra Pound's sharp-edged fascistic epic of blood, beauty, economics and considerations of orderly government.

African rhythms entered dance music with clamour bacchic or revivalist, an escape for many inarticulately fleeing the standardized, desiccated, mechanical. More individual notes also sounded, some, like Spengler's, interpreting Europe as more senile, boring, hopeless than it really was. Yet the earth was visibly being stifled by the shoddy, mass-produced, unspontaneous, and by concrete. Even before the Great War, for G. M. Hopkins :

What would the world be, once bereft
Of wet and wildness? Let them be left,
O let them be left, wildness and wet.
Long live the weeds and the wilderness yet.

Nijinski, first flying by plane, 'cried without knowing why : I had the impression that it would destroy the birds.' (*Journal*) D. H. Lawrence sought an ideal society of sun, wine, glowing birds, panthers, snakes, sacramental religion of Dionysus or Quetzalcoatl : not of herd violence but of surging individualism, of passionate males and gasping, submissive women. 'Give us Gods, oh give them to us. We are so tired of men and motor-power.'

W. B. Yeats wrote, tellingly, of 'the boredom of the desk or of the spade,' some day to be redeemed when

> . . . we shall get up before the dawn
> And find our ancient hounds before the door,
> And wide awake know that the hunt is on;
> Stumbling upon the blood-dark track once more,
> Then stumbling to the kill beside the shore;
> Then cleaning out and bandaging of wounds,
> And chants of victory amid the encircling hounds.

The exotic or simple could easily become vicious, or ludicrous. Yeats confessed to preferring the violent expression of error to the reasonable expression of truth. One could momentarily sympathize with Hitler demanding, however cloudily, a national and human personality assessed by other than cash-values, a 'natural' exchange of goods for goods, not money.

The moral of the destruction of Berlin, 1945, was not absolutely accepted. At an Acton by-election, 1969, 'Mr Fountaine, a simple-minded Norfolk forester, who confessed once to a faith in Nordic folk-destiny and sun-gods' gained half as many votes as the Liberal candidate in 'a level-headed London suburb'. (*Guardian*)

6

To give orders, goes the Sicilian proverb, is better than making love. Most rulers and teachers seem not only to relish power but believe in it. Intelligence, impatient with the slow majority, may seek limitless authority. Religion and State often sanctify criminal behaviour, by proscribing the damned and heretical. Dictators could rely on considerable support from Christian Churches.

An unexpected exception to this love of power was Peter the Great, who admonished his nobles for over-docility and shirking of responsibility, warning them that his successors would thus claim too much power, and invite terrible reaction. Few dictators had such qualms. They saw themselves as indispensable, though some perhaps secreted feelings of inferiority; like Robespierre, they might be physically mediocre, with unsatisfactory fathers. Some, with blood on their hands, must have noted a human craving to be victimized, easier to analyse than to eradicate.

Since classical times, dictators have emerged as temporary expedients in crisis. Sulla, Cromwell, Danton, Cavaignac, Louis Napoleon. 'Dictator' was enveloped in the open-air glamour of Garibaldi, the efficiency of Caesar, even Napoleon. They had the primitive appeal of monarchy, without the stuffiness. In modern times they were usually military nationalists, restoring order and modernizing society, often after defeat. Such were Kemal, and Pilsudski who saved Poland and perhaps Germany from the Russians, 1921

The fallacy was that an expedient seeks to become an institution. Even a Cromwell comes to enjoy prospects of a crown. Few men can stand the strains of power. Some do not wish to. Others, when there is no crisis, skilfully invent one.

Throughout traditional, popular drama had stalked the charlatan 'Doctor', dispensing elaborate hocus-pocus. The larger, political theatre can produce a Hitler, exploiting the failure of institutions, and also unemployment, inflation, slums, boredom – 'the stampede of suburbia.' He assures the masses that they are sick, betrayed by devils of wealth, race, class, and that he alone can avert further catastrophe. His secret is that he wishes to prolong the sickness or panic, and does not shrink from catastrophe. He believes, as it were, in progress backwards, diluting the programmatic with the mythical and supernatural.

An age of science, 1870–1945, revealed itself worm-eaten with superstition, and with ambitious or timid scientists seeking orders from mediocrities. The business-man in *The Magic Mountain*, also, is instantly recognizable, 'a confirmed anti-semite, out of conviction and the sporting spirit.'

All eras seem those of transition. Here, God was no longer counting the hairs of one's head nor attending to the fall of a sparrow but, throughout Europe, children were still being trained to rely on his existence. Whoever replaced him would be the Hero, denouncing or abolishing feeble churches, bourgeois law and banks, cowardly general staffs, corrupt press, the 'market' that left millions unfed, 'the system' that ran the world for the few.

The Hero would tap the primal instincts, restore tree and horse, plough and blood, sword and flag, racial aristocracy, trumpets and processions, instincts still heard in the banging vagueness of the Francoist hymn, 'Face the Sun'. Scapegoats, mediators, fate, omnipotent gods, giants, fathers were very much alive. Liberals were slow to recognize the continuing needs for totem, ritual, heroism, while the authoritarian soldiers, Tuchachevsky, and Ludendorff who hated Jesus as a wily oriental shaman, were dreaming of restoring literal paganism.

The appeal was religious, with translucent promises handed down from an aching height. In a Germany of social and economic chaos and rampant, ineffective intellectualism, Speer's teacher, the anti-Nazi Professor Tessenov, was brooding, 'Someone will have to come along who thinks very simply. Thinking today has become too complicated. An uncultured man, a peasant, so to speak, would solve everything very much more easily merely because he would still be unspoilt. He would also have the strength to carry out his simple ideas.'

Loyalties flowed more vigorously towards ministers than towards ministries, though at times – it is a democratic virtue – a solid institution may transcend the minister, as at the Abdication, 1936. But all Germany listened to Hess, 1934 : 'Do not seek Adolf Hitler with your brains : you will all find him in the strength of your hearts. Adolf Hitler is Germany, and Germany is Adolf Hitler. Germany is our God on earth.'

For many, Darwin, Marx, Freud had given encouragement only to elites. That man was basically animal dismayed rather than fascinated. That his mind, his class, his nation were being controlled as implacably by unchanging instincts and unalterable economic forces as by the 'sin' taught by Augustine, Luther, Calvin, Knox, was intolerable. Not soft education but the individual Will must develop a tough resourcefulness, able to face ruthless solutions. In his novel, *Michael* (1929), Goebbels, influenced by Dostoevsky, wrote that intellect endangers the formation of character.

More genial teachers were not always the more reassuring. Shaw appealed to the authority of the Life Force, and envisaged rule by ancient, disembodied intelligences; Wells anticipated the rule of scientific samurai; Russell required the average man to use his brains. A Mussolini, a Lenin, suggested measures more tangible to whoever had lost faith, or had too inordinate faith, in himself. The onus of self-discipline and the often discouraging search for truth is revoked by despotism. 'One was relieved of having to think, particularly of unpleasant facts.' (Speer). Like the Inquisition, the Party was offering the paradox that in total slavery was total freedom. Democracy, in contrast, entails the obligation to think, and act upon one's thought. The strain at times becomes too painful.

Galvanizing the spirit, Hitler restored the Napoleonic promise to men and, while despising women, attracted them. Contemptuous of the masses, he flattered them by boasts of the master race and destiny. Dictatorship can give both order and the romance of chaos, easy access to revenge, not rest but glory, a magical helter-skelter of the exalted and commonplace, practical and bizarre. It is the opposite of Leonardo's 'short-cuts injure knowledge and love.'

Here was a messianic escape for those stupefied by an excess of culture and ideas and needing air, sunlight, peasant earthiness. Even to certain Jews, the Nazis seemed exciting expressions of youth, song, adventure, mountain aura. Though nonsense, it was not complete nonsense for nervy, unemployed youngsters and the disappointed resentful middle-aged survivors of military defeat and the end of Empire. Rehabilitation was possible, a rigorous identity, determined not by wealth or genetics but by thrilling choice, courage, sacrifice. Furthermore, by exploiting the Napoleonic plebiscite, dictatorship could actually claim to be more democratic than the parliamentry plutocracy condemned by Lenin and Hitler alike; by Shaw, Belloc, Yeats, Wyndham Lewis, Mosley.

Lenin, ruthless, tyrannical, had set himself to find rational solutions to tangible problems of housing, food, electrification, schooling, industry. Hitler and Mussolini increasingly offered the chimerical. They were the waste-products of a dispiriting decade; degrading the myths by which men lived. But all dictatorships, by their nature, stimulated the search for panaceas. Whether one was Left or Right was often a matter of timing, gamble, or chance. 'It is almost immaterial what we believe, so long as we believe in something.' (Goebbels) Communists and Nazis could collaborate, as in the huge Berlin strikes, 1931 and 1932. Beside this tribal valour, Anglo-French and American diplomats, leaders and rationalists seemed yawns in striped trousers and discredited hats, without souls.

Germans were increasingly reminded that defeat – as inflicted by Napoleon, 1807, or suffered under Frederick the Great – could actually restore purpose, then achieve victory. Amongst forgotten ex-soldiers, declassed bourgeois, anxious small tradesmen, intellectuals seeking a name, angry nationalists, the jobless smarting at monopoly and cartel, the constitutional could be futile and ignoble. Street-corner demagogues everywhere exhorted them to chalk their mark on the wall. Wonders and hopes were extravagant, loneliness was to be banished. 'No one', Hitler assured them, 1933, 'will be able to say that at any time of his life he was left to himself.'

Here were moods similar to that of the Cornish blacksmith, Michael Joseph, executed for rebellion, 1479, but rejoicing that he 'should have a name perpetual and a fame permanent and immortal.'

Zealots always imagine themselves starting new orders, but

revolutions in France, Spain, Mexico, China, Russia, Germany, Austria, Hungary, 1793–1933, made no break with history, the 'Left' no more than the 'Right'. Capitalist tyranny was exchanged for party tyranny, all ideologies failed through lack of generosity. Though Marxism did not see itself as bleakly determinist – Engels wrote in *Anti-Dühring* that freedom was in 'the control over ourselves and over external nature' – Marxist societies have in practice eschewed freedom in any sense beyond that of freedom from foreign capitalists.

In Russia, rulers had for centuries been secretive, xenophobist, expansionist, bureaucratic. Behind blasts about human brotherhood, the Leninist State has maintained executions, censorship, goose-stepping troops, deification of public officials, anti-Semitism. 'You must', Lenin ordered, quite vainly, 'protect the people from the state bureaucracy.' The Tsarist secret police force was imitated by Dzerzhinsky, under Lenin, and used against strikes, sabotage, treason : it swiftly controlled society at large, arresting independently, responsible to no parliament, no jury, remaining virtually unchanged throughout the shootings of successive chiefs, on fantastic charges. It supervises slave-labour camps, has spies in farms, tenements, industry, armed forces.[94]

Lenin may have under-estimated the difficulties of imposing collectivism on a vast and perplexing mixture of peoples. Socialist faith, and an impressive army of martyrs, were inadequate. Within Russian imperialism, and in China and Cuba, if private profiteering was forbidden, so were strikes, permitted and even subsidized by the despised social democracies in Britain, Scandinavia, France, Italy and West Germany. In Europe, alone but for France, Spain and Turkey, the Soviet bloc openly retains capital punishment, in Russia for those over sixteen.

Lenin's early death left important questions that remain unanswered. His successor, Stalin, was vouched for in Britain by the Webbs and Shaw, stuck in statistics and moral vapours, accepting Russian proposals and the 1936 Constitution as accomplished facts, and in whose presence the secret police remained secret. Shaw airily described Stalin as only a secretary, subject to instant dismissal at ten minutes' notice if he did not give satisfaction.[95] Fabians, and Stafford Cripps, imagined the Russian State and foreign policy controlled by 'workers', for equality, fraternity and superior efficiency. John Strachey, co-director of the influential Left Book Club, hailed Stalin's Russia as 'the Kingdom of Freedom'.

More humble folk, until the Stalin-Hitler pact, 1939, sincerely believed that, in Russia, a planned, equitable society was at last in being, though Gide, hitherto sympathetic, shocked them after his

visit in 1936. He found cruelty, conformity, enthusiasm for applaud-
ing one's own sufferings. 'The slightest protest, the least criticism,
exposes one to direct penalties and is extinguished at once. And I
doubt that in any country today, even in Hitler's Germany, the
spirit is less free, more cowed, more terrorized, more enslaved.'
Bertrand Russell reported the same.

Russian killings and deportations involved many millions, before
and after World War II. Accusation of massacres of Polish officers
at Katyn and Starobielsk have not been convincingly refuted. Until
Stalin's death in 1953, his police chief, Beria, had a reputation for
secret killings and torture that made socialism, like fascism, a word
at which to shudder.

One can dispute whether such figures are manic aberrations, or
a predictable result of too much reliance on the State. The facts
themselves do not seem in dispute. The widow of one of Stalin's
victims, Osip Mandelstam, sadly recounts in her memoirs[96] that,
under Stalin, save in the camps, the word 'conscience' was dropped,
in literature, journalism, schools, social life, in favour of 'class-
feeling', and 'the good of the State'.

'Politics is not a science, as many professors seem to imagine.
Whether you like to call it that or not, it is an art. It cannot be
taught, one has to be born to it.' Bismarck may have been right,
but the operatic appeal of untaught political mountebanks was
shown by Mussolini, braying of Roman legions, popularizing
'totalitarian', describing himself as 'the most intelligent animal that
ever existed on the face of the earth', and whom Noel Coward saw
in 1938, 'like an over-ripe tomato plum squeezed into a white
uniform.'

Leading a Fascist regime of political hooliganism and vivid,
rhetorical journalism, destroying inept and corrupt parliament
and unions, Mussolini could see himself as a Caesar. He was more
of a Nero than a Julius, though Nero too had talents. Eventually,
the Duce's confused policies, and Anglo-French political fumblings,
drove him fatally towards Italy's old enemy, Germany, and his
own natural rival, Hitler. In Britain he was for many years admired,
for his police, his respect for private property, his assumed strength.
Belloc rated him 'disinterested, and lacking in personal ambition'.
For Alec Douglas-Home he was 'in many ways a very attractive
man'. 'That he is a great man I do not deny,' Churchill broadcast,
on Italy's furtive entry into the World War, 1949, before turning
to abuse 'the criminal that wrought the deed, folly and shame.'
But a Mussolini is timeless, gesticulating at the crowd in ornate
charades: as though long-dead soldiers are delivering violent
soliloquies, and the living lie inert under tombs of heroic pattern.

He is hard to imagine alone; he has less a job to do than a performance. He believes in his mission with Bonapartist fervour that
makes the horoscope as significant as the market. He is the Knight
back in power, heroic statuary unfreezing. Self-assertion is an overall
guarantee, Bismarck's ability to strategically withdraw is impermis-
sible, existence of objective truth hooted at. Humour is outlawed.
Even Nicholas I, the Iron Tsar, appreciated Gogol's pointed
The Government Inspector, but laughter from Stalin and Hitler
must, at best, have sounded uncanny, and from Mussolini too
aggressive.

The Führer had no great intelligence but a mass of half-
knowledge. More important, he had intuition, oddity : he had aura.
Also, as Orwell suggested, pathos. For the present writer, a sight
of Hitler always made him feel vaguely guilty.

Like Napoleon III, Mussolini, the ageing Pilsudski, like Ludendorff, Hitler had occult fantasies, oscillating between mental
extremes. He could use the language of Black Magic, black opera,
political surrealism. 'The masses need something that will give them
a thrill of horror.' His SA and SS were legalized Mafia. His outcries
echoed the mad Roman emperors. 'A new age of magical interpretation of the world is at hand, of interpretation in terms of the
will and not of the intelligence.' It showed a certain prescience, a
recognition of the nature of crowds. It also allowed him to avoid
systematic hard work. For the crowd, he appeared to fulfil the
need for certainty : a few slogans summarized society, the very
universe.

His followers eagerly supported government by rhetoric. 'Lies',
proclaimed Joseph Goebbels, crippled product of a pious and
loving Catholic home, 'are a Jewish invention.' Rosenberg, official
Nazi philosopher, classified Jews as 'rats'. Here was a howling
dynamic foreign to the British and French; Daladier, Reynaud,
Blum, MacDonald, Henderson and Baldwin, to the prosperous
capitalists and civil servants in the British government, the wishful
thinkers in opposition. Poets and psychologists might have been
more profitably invited and have attended the conferences that
littered the inter-war years. Winston Churchill himself, though
saturated with conventional history, did not condescend to psychological studies. Eventually recognizing Hitler as a 'bloodthirsty
guttersnipe', he had for a few years seen him as an undersized Bismarck, upholding traditional institutions against Bolshevism. Misled
by books, he diagnosed him as Prussia incarnate, a country with
which Hitler had little in common, though Bismarck's famous
dictum must have impressed him – also Lenin and Marx. 'The
great contemporary events are not decided by the speeches and

resolutions of majorities – that was the mistake of 1848 and 1849 – but by blood and iron.'

For Hitler, the League of Nations, pacts to outlaw war, to build reconciliation, were poisonous wedges driven between man and nature, Germany and destiny, by Jewish and plutocratic scoundrels. As early as 1920 he was explicit, if neither well-informed about foreign nations, nor master of any craft or disciplines. Early failures and rebuffs had given him harsh dreams of power and conquest, with perhaps yearnings to inflict and receive pain in ways grotesquely at odds with the sexual and financial peccadilloes of a Lloyd George, the doggy womanising, and alcohol of an Asquith. He had emerged from an underworld of failure, and a defeated army, into an arena in which the ex-war-lord, Ludendorff, was blaming the Sarajevo murders and the 1918 collapse on Jews, Jesuits, Freemasons, a world conspiracy of those who broke 'race-consciousness, the national pride and the masculine will of men, and makes them artificial Jews – the tool of the Jews that has no will of its own.'

Hitler's convictions, however shoddy and unoriginal, were in his bones. Narrow to the point of dementia, he had peasant shrewdness – the shrewdness of Hollywood movie-bosses who gave *Anna Karenina* a happy ending for country audiences, a sad one for town. His assessment even of the master race was pessimistic.

> The masses' receptive powers are very restricted . . . on the other hand they quickly forget. Thus, all effective propaganda must be kept to a few bare essentials and expressed as far as possible in clichés . . . (and) must show only whatsoever of the truth favours its own side.

The Nazis had an astrological view of history, a grossly subjective conception of race. That the Australian blackfellows were probably the 'purest' of races would not have gratified Hitler. From Indian scriptures, Himmler deduced that the Führer, like Buddha, had returned to earth from previous lives. The future SS chief refutes any view that Hitlerism appealed only to the criminal, the outcast, the mad. Puritan, herbalist, of feeble physique, frustrated soldier, civilian failure, young Himmler was familiar enough : an enthusiastic yet disappointed joiner of clubs – ex-soldiers, marksmen, mountaineers, sportsmen, debaters, politicians. For him, as for thousands, the Nazi regime, purging sin, fear, despair, loneliness, was as if a Mystery had burst free of secrecy in wild assurance, orgiastic yet disciplined, of initiation, blood-brotherhood, blood-sacrifice, a new world of revenge upon old gold, bankers, aliens,

Jews, Slavs. In SS barracks, Nazi palaces, even in ghettoes and camps, fantastic quasi-royal pageants and rituals parodied antique chivalry. 'In Auschwitz', stated Commandant Hoess, 'I truly had no reason to complain that I was bored.' The titanic Hitler-Speer plans for a new Berlin complemented the Bonapartes' grandiose new Paris. 'If it's big, it's good.'

Post-1918 Europe was crowded with small men, barbarian youth clubs, occultism – the swastika itself had immemorial magical associations. With dreams of being taken seriously, men were willing to risk all to prove it. The dictators seemed to be extending life though, politically, artistically, sexually, they were limiting, often ending it. Or perhaps there were no dictators, only victims: Macbeth and Coriolanus manipulated by the unconscious and half-remembered, by human duality and the madness of crowds; government more a matter of nerves than a matter of course.

The European Left reacted with curious unconcern or like a certain type of tennis player more impelled to upset his partner than to beat the opponents. Shaw approved of Stalin, Mussolini and, with reservations, of Hitler. Sartre ignored the Fascist dictators. Simone de Beauvoir recalled: 'I avoided all problems posed by Hitler's political activities and regarded the rest of the world with an indifferent eye.'[97]

The collapse of the New York stock market, October 1929, convulsed the world. Trade and employment shrank overnight and by 1933, Hitler's triumphant year, world trade was down by two-thirds.[98] Britain dithered between obligations to neighbours, ex-enemies, empire; between disarmament and re-armament, League or bombers. She achieved a half-hearted invasion of Russia, 1918, that rankled for years, irresolution towards German re-armament and aggressions, an 'appeasement' that appeased no one and whetted appetites, a meaningless guarantee to Poland. Labour won a by-election, 1933, with its leader, the saintly George Lansbury, desiring to 'disband the army and disarm the air-force'. With menacing problems of hunger, poverty, housing, unemployment, Irish and Indian unrest, there was disposition to trust to luck in Europe, avoiding alliance with militarily despised, politically disreputable Russia. 'Collective security' at times seemed a clumsy bluff. The Nazis learnt more from French and British military experts – de Gaulle, Liddell Hart, Fuller – than did the Western war-offices.

Few English read *Mein Kampf*. Hitler's oratory was big noise from a small man of vulgar appearance, vicious background, a horrible buffoon of suspect intelligence. They were unaware of the slower movements that persist within the fastest music, not yet apprehending that a coronation, Nazi rally, General Strike, war crisis, state funeral, murder trial were theatrical rituals closely related; that man is helpless against tunes: Marseillaise, Internationale, Horst Wessell.

Leaders were culpably complacent. 'I have only to raise a finger, and the whole of Europe is changed,' Neville Chamberlain announced, August 1937. Archbishop Lang praised Hitler for 'the immense, undoubted, and on the whole beneficial awakening which had come to Germany.' (1934) Lloyd George reassured, as war approached, 'I have studied the whole thing . . . . I don't think Hitler is a fool – he is not going to challenge the British Empire again,' though on the map, the Empire, sprawling in boastful red, looked more cohesive than it was. At home certain key appointments were designed to leave Chamberlain, ill-educated in European history and psychology, too free a hand. At the Foreign Office, Lord Halifax stated that 'if we have to choose between Poland and Russia, Poland would give the better value.' At the British Embassy, Berlin, Sir Neville Henderson reported that Goering was ' a charming fellow', that Hitler was an apostle of peace and 'a constructive genius'. To counter the German Foreign Minister, Ribbentrop, in Moscow, Britain despatched a minor Foreign Office official. To Churchill, Eden, Robert Vansittart, Boothby, the Premier preferred Sir Horace Wilson. In the outcome Britain was to find herself fighting for almost a year, alone in a Nazi-occupied Europe, sheltering the legal governments of Poland, Norway, Holland, Belgium, Luxembourg, Greece, Yugoslavia; and Haile Selassie and de Gaulle. East London burned and in the West End J. B. Priestley saw the rich dragged out of a bombed night-club and laid out in Coventry Street, covered with sawdust, like broken dolls. Parliament rejected the application of the death-penalty for looting.

The subsequent involvement of Russia, Japan, America is familiar. The rival dictatorships reached a shuddering and blood-drenching climax at Stalingrad, where the surrender of a German field-marshal in the presence of half a million corpses, 1943, awed the world. Familiar too are the Nazi appetites, in the spirit of that SS brochure which describes the Slav as 'totally different and a frightful creature, a caricature of a man with features similar to those of a human being but intellectually and morally lower than any animal'. Mass-burning at Oradour, mass-shootings at Lidice, at Babi Yar, the gassings, have become stereotypes. Murderers emerged from all classes, races, sects, educations, some adept at distinguishing the particular aura of Urbino, Florence, Milan, Naples, Ferrara, Venice, Mantua; at quoting Goethe, translating Shakespeare, criticizing Mozart. Franz Stangl remembered (1971) :

K

Treblinka that day was the most awful thing I saw all during the Third Reich. It was Dante's *Inferno*. When I got out of the car on the Sortierungsplatz I stepped knee-deep into money. I didn't know which way to turn, where to go. I waded in paper notes, currency, precious stones, jewellery and clothes. They were everywhere, strewn all over the square. The smell was indescribable: the hundreds, no, thousands of bodies everywhere, putrefying, decomposing. Across the square in the woods, just a few hundred yards away on the other side of the barbed-wire fence, there were tents and open fires with groups of Ukrainian guards and girls – whores from Warsaw I found out later – drunk, dancing, singing, playing music.

(Daily Telegraph)

Like the Jacobins and Napoleon, by cruelties and extortions, the Nazis transformed potential allies into implacable enemies. They were extravagantly inefficient: Party leaders were amateurish, corrupt, seeing each other – with Hitler's encouragement – not as colleagues but rivals, jostling for favour. This seems endemic in dictatorships. The SD security wing of the SS was typical, infuriating Ribbentrop by acting as an alternative Foreign Ministry and clandestinely influencing Hitler. Goering hated and feared Bormann, all mistrusted Goebbels. War-time industry and the army suffered when crude racial theories eliminated thousands of Slavonic recruits, volunteers, slaves. Hitler himself condemned nuclear research as 'Jewish thought'. Too late, the ruined Nazis, like Napoleon in 1813, tried to win over their Western enemies against 'barbarous Asiatic Russia'.

Like priest-kings, the Führer and the Duce kept themselves insulated from bad news. Like earlier dictators, they relied on luck, stars, destiny, fitful or wilful bursts of activity. Systematic planning, comprehensive research, organizational symmetry, personal responsibility amongst subordinates, did not flourish. Party infiltrations and disastrous political appointments in technical departments – notably Goering's – vitiated cohesion. Authority could be diluted, corrupted, even ignored. German war-time industrial mobilization was never as total as that of Britain and America.

Too often trapped by a romantic or successful national past, some leaders, Napoleon III and Pilsudski, had failed to modernize their armies. As for Stalin, Mussolini and Hitler, their regimes encouraged flunkeyism, fear of truth, black markets, slovenly thought, vacuous education and moral torpor.

Nazi defeat cemented little European unity. At Yalta, 1944, the continent was divided into Western and Russian spheres, the latter including Poland, for whom Britain and France had ostensibly declared war. 100 million were swept under Stalin's direct or indirect control. Churchill demanded Polish national independence and ballot rights but without American support could win only vague and fruitless Russian promises. 'Uncle Joe's' assurance that Russia would respect other countries' internal affairs seems, briefly, to have been trusted.

Moral indignation without armed force was to prove continuously futile, even after the establishment of the United Nations, on remnants of the League, with right of veto allowed to America, Russia, Britain, France, and Nationalist China. Only one of these consistently used it.

17   New Perspectives

I said 'We shall need peculiar strength,
Unusual assiduity, to live through this
ice-age of the human spirit.'
'Rubbish!' he said, 'Like everybody
else,
We'll build our igloos and survive dis-
gracefully.'

Philip Toynbee

I

In a hurrying world – Hiroshima, emergence of Black Africa,
Maoist China, Korean War, moon landings, artificial insemination,
obduracy of cancer, inflation, racial and political apartheids –
Britain could no longer ordain and finance a Balance of Power. In
grim 1940, Churchill had offered Anglo-French union, and Jean
Monnet – later the first president of the European Coal and Steel
Community – proposed joint Anglo-French citizenship. Their efforts
were premature. Britain could, 1945, have led the movement towards European unity, but, preoccupied with Indian independence,
social reform, Balance of Payments, Labour rejected Britain's
joining the European Coal and Steel Community, 1950. Churchill
had stumped for a Council of Europe (1946) but, regaining power,
he lost interest. His Foreign Secretary, Eden, had no over-riding
concern for European economic unity though, alarmed by Russia,
he showed initiative in securing Germany and Italy for NATO
and the Western European Union. Labour, mistrustful of capitalist
bureaucracy, has never shown as much intensity over European
federalism, or workers' internationalism, as over the fortunes of its
own unions, though both Parties broadly agreed to join with France
in accepting Marshal Aid, in the Berlin Airlift, 1948, and in sup-
porting Western Germany almost regardless of expense. For many
years foreign policy preferred American markets and World Bank
loans to economic experiment nearer home. Public opinion probably
distrusted Europe as cruel and unreliable. The blood-drenched
Spanish Civil War, the millions officially killed by Russia and
Germany, Italy's ignoble war-time policies, experience of French

alliance in two world wars, the repeated Russian veto at UNO, post-imperial economic rivalries, and the resumption of discredited French political procedures following the first departure of de Gaulle, extremist take-overs in many countries – all these obstructed Britain's whole-hearted acceptance of Europe, scarcely assisted by the Anglo-French entente over Suez, 1956. Yet, in tradition, political suspicions did not prevent human feelings. As much enthusiasm greeted the first Russian sputnik as England's winning the World Football Cup. Possibly, the surge of tourism, secular pilgrimage not for relics but sun, may, together with the mobility of the young, have slowly broken some of the old narrowness.

2

It was soon clear that, if institutions alter, man does not. Though the ancient Franco-German bloodshed was stilled, deeper struggles persisted. Crisis in Berlin, violence in Korea, subsequent war and massacre in Indo-China, the Middle East, Africa . . . revealed disheartening evidence of those who, in Louis Macneice's poem, shoot straight in the cause of crooked thought. War continued under various names, shifting from proclaimed national wars to 'confrontations', unopposable 'liberating' invasions, 'volunteer' crusades, downright political and economic repression. Not exceptional was the fate of 53,000 German refugees, hired by UNO for the Brazilian rubber plantations : by July 1947, 31,000 had died from beatings, overwork and execution, the remainder left in Amazonian jungles, disease-ridden, debt-ridden, impotent. Torture was used by France in Algeria. Prominent Jews were shot in Russia, 1952. League virtues and flaws re-appeared in UNO : auxiliary offices of health, labour, education worked well, but Great Power feuds, emerging from sources expertly disputed, prevented effective co-operation for peace. 'Left' and 'Right' proved equally susceptible to bigotry, greed and cruelty : a trade union could be as intolerant and lacking in benevolence as old church or chapel. Old-style capitalists had held that purposeful self-interest necessarily benefited all; the socialist felt similarly about State control, often with as gloomy results. Huge organizations to handle increasing populations and complicated technology have – like Church and Monarchy – inner impulses tending towards the thoughtless and cruel. 'Shelley was talking nonsense. The only "unacknowledged legislators" are the secret police.' (Auden, 1965) Yet secret police are not a party monopoly, and 'Third Degree' is a 'democratic phrase'. The century was enjoying arguably less poverty but more torture. Ideology continued to be subordinate to the need for military bases and cash : capitalist

Catholic Italy would sell tankers to Russia to supply Castro's Cuba
with oil; South African trade unionists support apartheid. . . . Huge
take-overs and appropriations operated without prime reference to
consumer needs.

3

Britain, no longer a decisive world power, had to commit herself to
military alliances, in the Dunkirk, Brussels and North Atlantic
Treaties, in which she could no longer dominate.

Symbolically, imperial aloofness ended at Churchill's funeral. To
thousands gathered on raw February streets, the deep bells, the
uniforms, titles, noble words, the dipping cranes, saluted not only
an exhausted old man but an exhausted national style.

Extravagant, humorous, melancholy, egotistical, sentimental,
demanding, born in a palace, master of a country house, romantic,
cynical, hedonistic, largely self-educated despite expensive school
bills, wry, courageous, fiercely, sometimes ludicrously British and
imperialist yet with unexpected moods of internationalism, Winston
Churchill must have died disappointed. The Empire was dismantled,
Britain's pretensions ridiculed at Suez, Anglo-French accord once
again fractured. Poland was a Russian satellite, parliament losing
prestige, personal leadership mocked, History itself questioned as a
relevant study. Last of the Milords, he has left a name but, it is
said, no message. For a society of CND, pupil power, black power,
disc jockey culture, and clashes between unimaginative manage-
ments and cumbersome unions, the departure of so archaic a monument perhaps cleared the air.

Britain's post-war history has seen a search for new definitions,
new adjustments. There is doubt as to whether Parliament can
control multi-national Interests and government departments, even
whether it can continue to command respect. That 'minister' means
'helper' is too often a sour joke. The masses, with political rights
long assured, are using them to demand economic and social rights
though, by 1974, in education and housing, Disraeli's 'two nations'
are not yet anachronistic.

Changes in industrial and political management, the needs of
Celtic minorities, the role of private enterprise, property, the
family, of rewards and incentive, debate over the nature of education, the emotional need for more varied work-patterns, the
challenges of immigration, population growth, the acidulation of
party politics, the British entry of the EEC, January 1973 . . .
should offer sufficient momentum to prevent broodings over the
lost imperial past. The growth of bureaucracy remains constant, not

least within the EEC organizations. Europe has a traditional tendency to accumulate desk-work. When Britain employed 16,000 civil servants, Bagehot found Napoleon III employing 800,000.

Britain's assets remain considerable. World trade brought her £20,000 million in 1971. London remains a centre of banking and world insurance. Science, engineering, ship-building, invention are impeded not by loss of skill but by labour relations. Her problems are common to all societies, communist or capitalist. Pollution, drugs; reaction against authority and institutions; the need to link increased leisure with increased responsibility, greater pleasure with greater profundity; the complexities of cities, better planned but claustrophic, with movement seemingly paralysed by the conventions of the middle-aged; the unremitting spread of inflation.

There is no proof that identical situations produce identical societies, no proof of anything very much. The marvellous and tiresome fact of humanity is that there are usually innumerable and valid points of view. Government, industry, education are not arts or sciences but, like marriage, like diplomacy, need insights from both, leavened by humour. Education, by developing subtlety and skills, can develop wickedness and frustration. Unpredictable genetic processes, it seems, cannot be wholly displaced by environment and equitable legislation. People may be trained to expect more than menial work, but without discovering outstanding personal talents. Loss of innocence can be dangerous, in discovering that one has, after all, no genius. Here is the root of so many agitators and propaganda ministers who discover, with bitterness or hatred, that education may develop, but cannot invent, genius.

Society ties discordant values and interests into political knots, of their nature uneasy, sometimes unworkable. There are fears of a new priesthood, the technocrats, which prompted Arnold Toynbee's assertion (1969) that the Third World War has already started, in the revolt against man's exchanging 'a harsh master, Nature, for a harsher, conscienceless Technology'. Swollen populations, dwindling sources of energy, new and jealous countries, Great Power arrogance and wealth, may impose novel if indirect tyrannies. Computer-banks are said to be threatening individual freedom; one notes the use of bio-chemistry and dietetics in modifying behaviour – pupils, in Omaha, 1972, given drugs to increase discipline and intellectual receptivity, an extension of Dr Arnold's view, probably unpopular, that education should form character. Expensive moon-landings, for many, are irrelevant to life, liberty and the pursuit of happiness.

In such a context, the sensibilities of the Free Spirit may be more in demand than those of Luther or Loyola, Mill or de

Tocqueville, Russell or Popper. Asked to choose between saving a cat or a Prime Minister, a contemporary might well choose the cat. To him, politics are futile or stodgy. He applauds Blake's view, that it is better to strangle an infant in its cradle than to nurse an unacted desire.

Such a rebel can claim much justification. Not only the idealistic, the intolerant, the young felt it unseemly that, on a January day, 1972, when unemployment climbed to one million, dealers on the Stock Exchange were cheering the *Financial Times* Ordinary Share Index, for passing the 500 points mark. Few could have been enthusiastic when a widespread fall in American shares followed immediately on the announcement of peace in Vietnam. That, years after Hiroshima and Auschwitz, an American general can declaim, 'We will bomb them back into the Stone Age,' is dispiriting. The blandness of governments infuriates : for years the American troops in Vietnam were 'advisers', as Jacobin, communist and fascist invaders were 'liberators'. Despite the Russian tanks and bullets in Warsaw, East Berlin, Prague and Budapest, the Russian premier, Kosygin, could state (April 1968) that the Soviet State 'makes its invariable principle in international policy the strict observance of equality, national independence, and non-interference in the internal affairs of other states and other peoples.' Years after Orwell denounced the pollution of language, millions were still being killed in 'land reform', burnt alive for 'freedom'. Americans massacred civilians at My Lai; the Viet Cong at Hue and Dag Son. That Britain, 1973, was still earning £100 million annually from arms sales can be defended, it can scarcely be boasted about. In a rich era, meat and milk are still unavailable for five-sixths of the world, and UNO calculated (1973) that 30 per cent of children in 'developing countries' die before they reach five.

Demands for more direct human relations and simpler lives can underlie strikes, thought-killing stimulants, sexual experiments in public, howling music. 'Mysteries', in pop-festivals and drug parties, even witchcraft orgies, promise speedy transformation of vision and personality. Sport enables millions to identify with teams, heroes, bruisers, as they once did with gods. Hunters' instincts are set to work in managerial rivalry, industrial competition, take-overs, office intrigue, union rivalries, sexual piracy, personal publicity – and against waste and muddle.

Elaborate research investigates the validity, no longer of the soul, the magic of numbers and sacred shapes, but of IQ: analyses the causes of poverty, crime, and the reality, if any, of 'entropy', the moral fatigue of mature civilizations. Man's animal inheritance is no longer considered shameful : animal mutual aid, property and sexual customs, rituals to mitigate violence, animal language and relations with environment and community, are yearly becoming more suggestive. (Konrad Lorenz reported, 1969, that in wide habitats baboons submit to an elderly senate that rules by disapproving frowns but, if space contracts, the senate is displaced by the young and violent.)

In human affairs, the pace of change, and continuous stimulation of tensions allow vast hopes and dreams, and colossal disappointments. Tribal totems are destroyed, but can be replaced, human relations deepened or acerbated. Moral confusions can create a new or exciting ethic, or reinforce aggression and bewilderment. Standardization and advertising may draw peoples closer, or send them mad with boredom and threaten the integrity of language – its gifts of precision, allusion, continuity.

Every day brings startling evidence for good or ill. People in Britain now seem healthier, taller, better-looking, better-dressed, more articulate, more widely travelled and wealthier than they have ever been. This allows one to rejoice, but never to relax. On 3 July 1973, the government had to set up an inquiry into, of all things, widespread wife-beating! Two newspaper reports, from October 1972, made this pen momentarily pause : the National Union of Teachers advising members to 'remain aloof from pupils, avoiding physical contacts and never being alone with them.' This seems far from Montaigne, Commenius and Thomas More. Then, the Institution of Civil Engineers being advised to consider more seriously the construction of bomb-proof public buildings. This might have surprised Gladstone or Cobden, is an ironic footnote to the generous hopes of the Enlightenment. But they are only symptoms, with ample precedents, warning but not dictating.

These pages have recalled energies, the black and the white. There is no conclusive evidence that such energies are incapable of withstanding the future. Human life has continually transformed defeats into assets, as a faded love-affair can open up wiser attempts elsewhere. This may not be the point of life, it is at least the art of life. The past, with its splendours, grotesqueness, wickedness cannot be escaped, but it can be used, like a novelist exploiting his childhood. Perhaps it is not human good or evil that can be finally trusted, but human curiosity. It will need to discover social forms that induce good-fellowship without officialdom, good management without bad temper, good work without drudgery and good works without condescension or bullying. The problem remains, of how to love the unlovable and, occasionally, the unspeakable.

References in the Text

1   Marc Bloch, *The Royal Touch* (Routledge and Kegan Paul, 1972).
2   Robert Graves, *Greek Myths* (Penguin, 1955).
3   J. M. Allegro, *The Sacred Mushroom and the Cross* (Hodder and Stoughton, 1970).
4   Translated Reynold A. Nicholson (Allen and Unwin, 1950).
5   *Letters to Anais Nin* (Peter Owen, 1965).
6   *The Court and the Castle* (Macmillan, 1958).
7   See K. K. Doberer, *The Goldmakers* (Nicholson and Watson, 1948), and C. J. Jung, *The Secret of the Golden Flower* (Routledge and Kegan Paul, 1931).
8   *The Crowning Privilege* (Cassell, 1955).
9   Mary Williams (ed.), *Glastonbury, A Study in Patterns*, (Research into Lost Knowledge Organization, 1969).
10 Richard Coe, *Samuel Beckett* (Oliver and Boyd, 1964).
11 *The Ancient Civilization of the Celts and Gallo-Romans* (Barrie and Jenkins, 1970).
12 See David Talbot-Rice (ed.), *The Dark Ages* (Thames and Hudson, 1965).
13 Arnold Toynbee, *Man's Concern with Death* (Hodder and Stoughton, 1968).
14 *The Poems of Catullus*. trans. Peter Wigham (Penguin, 1966).
15 See Geoffrey Grigson, *The Shell Country Book* (Phoenix House, 1962), and George Every, *Christian Mythology* (Hamlyn, 1970).
16 Trans. Philip Vellecott (Penguin, 1954).
17 See Marcello Craveri, *The Life of Jesus* (Secker and Warburg, 1967).
18 See also the *Cambridge Medieval History*.
19 See Alan Lloyd, *The Year of the Conqueror* (Longmans, 1966).
20 In *The Origins of English Place-names* (Routledge and Kegan Paul 1960).
21 *The Quest of Three Abbots* (Murray, 1968).
22 G. M. Young, *Today and Yesterday* (Hart-Davis, 1948).
23 See Richard Barber, *The Knight and Chivalry* (Longmans, 1970); Charles T. Wood, *The Age of Chivalry* (Weidenfeld and Nicolson, 1970); Jonathan Riley-Smith, *The Knights of St John in Jerusalem and Cyprus* (Macmillan, 1967).
24 See Johannes Nöhl, *The Black Death* (Allen and Unwin, 1926); Norman Cohn, *The Pursuit of the Millennium* (Secker and Warburg, 1957).
25 See D. Stafford Clark, *Psychiatry Today* (Penguin, 1952).
26 *Dictionary of Angels* (Collier–Macmillan, 1967).
27 See Frederick W. Cartwright, *Disease and History* (Hart–Davis, 1972).
28 *The Eagle and the Dove* (Michael Joseph, 1969).
29 J. Huizinga, *The Waning of the Middle Ages* (Leiden, 1924).
30 See Helen Waddell, *The Wandering Scholars* (Constable, 1927).
31 *Memories* (Allen and Unwin, 1970).
32 *The Name's Phelan* (Sidgwick and Jackson, 1948).
33 *Sigena* (Harvey Miller and Medcalf, 1972).

34 In Joan Evans (ed.), *The Flowering of the Middle Ages* (Thames and Hudson, 1966).
35 *Gothic Europe* (Weidenfeld and Nicolson, 1969).
36 George Rudé, *The Crowd in History* (Wiley, 1965).
37 In *Verdict in Dispute* (Wingate, 1947).
38 Trans, Brian Stone, *Medieval English Verse* (Penguin, 1964).
39 *Black and White* (Allen Lane, The Penguin Press, 1973).
40 Alan Macfarlane, *Witchcraft in Tudor and Stuart England* (Routledge and Kegan Paul, 1970).
41 In *The Cambridge Medieval History*.
42 See Jean Randier, *Men and Ships Around Cape Horn, 1616–1939* (Barker, 1969).
43 See Roland Oliver and J. D. Fage, *A Short History of Africa* (Penguin, 1962); Margaret Shinnie, *Ancient African Kingdoms* (Arnold, 1965).
44 See Jacquetta Hawkes, *Dawn of the Gods* (Chatto and Windus, 1968).
45 See C. A. Burland, *The Gods of Mexico* (Eyre and Spottiswoode, 1967).
46 *Brown Men and Red Sand* (Phoenix House, 1951).
47 See Fernando Henriques, *Love in Action* (Panther, 1970).
48 *Journey Without Maps* (Heinemann, 1936).
49 Leonard Woolf, *Downhill All the Way* (Hogarth Press, 1967).
50 Jerry Rubin, *Do It* (Cape, 1971).
51 A. L. Rowse, *The Elizabethan Renaissance* (Macmillan, 1972).
52 See Denys Hay (ed.), *The Age of the Renaissance* (Thames and Hudson, 1967).
53 See Kenneth Clark, *Civilization* (John Murray, 1969); E. Sichell, *The Renaissance* (Butterworth, 1914).
54 In *The Age of the Renaissance*.
55 Delio Cantimori in *The Age of the Renaissance*.
56 *Pagan Mysteries of the Renaissance* (Faber, 1958).
57 Trans. J. M. Cohen (Penguin, 1958).
58 A. L. Rowse, *The England of Elizabeth* (Macmillan, 1950).
59 *Survivors of the Armada* (Constable, 1966).
60 *Oliver Cromwell* (Duckworth, 1973).
61 *The Evolution of Man and Society* (Allen and Unwin, 1969).
62 Alan Moorhead, *The Fatal Impact* (Hamilton, 1966).
63 Keith Feiling, *Warren Hastings* (Macmillan, 1967).
64 Anthony Burgess and Francis Haskell, *The Age of the Grand Tour* (Elek, 1967).
65 Gilbert Highet, *Poems in a Landscape* (Hamilton, 1957).
66 See Oliver Warner, *Emma Hamilton and Sir William* (Chatto and Windus, 1960).
67 *Left Hand, Right Hand* (Macmillan, 1946).
68 See F. R. and Q. D. Leavis, *Dickens the Novelist* (Chatto and Windus, 1970).
69 *Punch and Judy* (Studio Vista, 1970).
70 *The Victorian Church* (Black, 1966–70).
71 *Uncommon People* (Hamish Hamilton, 1955).
72 See J. M. Thompson, *The French Revolution* (Blackwell, 1944).
73 See J. F. C. Fuller, *Decisive Battles of the Western World* (Eyre and Spottiswoode, 1954).
74 See Michael Holroyd, *Lytton Strachey* (Heinemann, 1967).
75 *Selected Letters 1813–1863* (Eyre and Spottiswoode, 1971).

76 Arthur Seldon (ed.), *The Long Debate on Poverty* (Institute of Economic Affairs, 1972).
77 C. Woodham Smith, *The Great Hunger* (Hamish Hamilton, 1962).
78 E. Royston Pike (ed.), *Human Documents of the Industrial Revolution* (Allen and Unwin, 1966).
79 Simon Nowell-Smith (ed.), *Edwardian England* (Oxford, 1964).
80 *Social Trends* No 3 (HMSO, 1972).
81 James W. Hulse, *Revolutionaries in London* (Oxford, 1970).
82 See Naomi Mitchison, *African Heroes* (Bodley Head, 1968); Leonard Barnes, *Empire or Democracy* (Gollancz, 1939).
83 *A Lodge in the Wilderness* (Blackwood, 1907).
84 *More from the Primeval Forest* (A. and C. Black, 1931).
85 See Richard West, *Brazza of the Congo* (Cape, 1972).
86 *Crusade in Europe* (Heinemann, 1948).
87 Allen Lane, The Penguin Press, 1969.
88 Fritz Fischer, *Germany's Aims in the First World War* (Chatto and Windus, 1967).
89 See Maurice Collis, *Sommerville and Ross* (Faber, 1968).
90 *A London Childhood* (Routledge and Kegan Paul, 1966).
91 *Octave Nine* (Chatto and Windus, 1970).
92 *History, Heritage and Environment* (Faber, 1946).
93 *The Proud Tower* (Hamish Hamilton, 1966).
94 Boris Levytsky, *The Soviet Secret Service 1917–1970* (Sidgwick and Jackson, 1972).
95 David Caute, *The Fellow Travellers* (Weidenfeld and Nicolson, 1973).
96 Nadezhda Mandelstam, *Hope Against Hope* (Collins–Harvill, 1967).
97 *The Prime of Life* (Deutsch and Weidenfeld and Nicolson, 1965).
98 Charles P. Kindleberger, *The World in Depression* (Allen Lane, The Penguin Press, 1972).

Bibliography

In a generalized survey, one is at best reminding readers of what they already know. My sources are those easily to hand for readers of normal range and curiosity. Besides the books mentioned in the text itself, and the standard works of Pollard, Trevelyan, Collingwood, Coulton, Rowse, Power, Namier, the Hammonds, I am adding below books which may interest readers desiring to confirm, refute, follow up remarks in my text. C. E. Carrington and J. Hampden Jackson were both masters at my own school. Their *History of England* remains, in my opinion, amongst the very best of its kind.

P.V.

Abse, Dannie, *Medicine on Trial* (Aldus, 1967).

Acton, Lord, *Lectures on Modern History* (Macmillan, 1906).

Ashe, Geoffrey, *From Caesar to Arthur* (Collins, 1960).

Auden, W. H., *Selected Essays* (Faber, 1964).

Bedford, Sybille, *A Legacy* (Weidenfeld and Nicolson, 1956).*

Blake, Robert, *Disraeli* (Eyre and Spottiswoode, 1966).

Blumenberg, Werner, *Karl Marx*, trans. Douglas Scott (NLB, 1972).

Branston, Brian, *The Lost Gods of England* (Thames and Hudson, 1957).

Brett, Henry, *English Legends* (Batsford, 1950).

Brewer, S. M., *Design for a Gentleman* (Chapman and Hall, 1963). (The education of Philip Stanhope.)

Briggs, Asa, (ed.), *The Nineteenth Century* (Thames and Hudson, 1964).

Bullock, Alan, *Hitler, A Study in Tyranny* (Odhams, 1964).

Camus, Albert, *The Rebel* (Hamish Hamilton, 1953).

Carrington, C. E. and Jackson, J. Hampden, *History of England* (Cambridge, 1932).

Cecil, Lord David, *The Young Melbourne* (Constable, 1939).

Cobban, Alfred, *France Since the Revolution* (Cape, 1970).

Cranston, Maurice, *Sartre* (Oliver and Boyd, 1962).

Dickson, Lovat, *H. G. Wells* (Macmillan, 1969).

Dubois, Josiah E., *Generals in Grey Suits* (Bodley Head, 1953). (The conspiracy and trial of the I. G. Farben Directors at Nuremburg.)

Evans, George Ewart, *The Pattern Under the Plough* (Faber, 1966).

First, Ruth, Steele, Jonathan and Gurney, Christabel, *The South African Connection* (Temple Smith, 1972).

Forster, E. M., *Two Cheers for Democracy* (Penguin, 1965).

Frazer, J. G., *The Golden Bough* (Macmillan, 1890).

Glendinning, Victoria, *A Suppressed Cry* (Routledge, 1969). (Late Victorian middle-class family life, with emphasis on the difficulties of the ambitious girl)

Hanson, R. P. C., *Saint Patrick* (Oxford, 1968).

Heiber, Helmut, *Goebbels* (Hale, 1973).

Höhne, Heinz, *The Order of the Death's Head* (Secker and Warburg, 1969).

Hole, Christina, *English Folk Heroes* (Batsford, 1948).

Howe, Ellic, *Urania's Children* (Kimber, 1967).

Hughes, Pennethorne, *Witchcraft* (Longmans, 1952).

Huizinga, Johan, *Homo Ludens* (Routledge, 1949).

Hunter, Antony, *The Last Days* (Blond, 1958).

Huxley, Aldous, *Ends and Means* (Chatto and Windus, 1937).

——, ——, *Grey Eminence* (Chatto and Windus, 1941).

Jackson, J. Hampden, *England Since the Industrial Revolution* (Gollancz, 1936).

——, ——, *Europe Since the War* (Gollancz, 1939).

Jahoda, Gustav, *The Psychology of Superstition* (Allen Lane, The Penguin Press, 1962).

James, Robert Rhodes, *Churchill, A Study in Failure* (Weidenfeld and Nicolson, 1970).

Jones, Ernest, *Sigmund Freud, His Life and Works* (Hogarth, 1962).

Kellet, E. E., *A Short History of Religions* (Gollancz, 1948).

Kochan, Lionel, *The Russian Revolution* (Hart-Davis, 1970).

Latey, Maurice, *Tyranny, A Study in the Abuse of Power* (Macmillan, 1969).

Letwin, Shirley Robin, *The Pursuit of Certainty* (Cambridge, 1965).

Letwin, William, *The Origins of Scientific Economics* (Methuen, 1963).

Lindsay, Jack, *Arthur and his Times* (Muller, 1958).

Lord, Robert, *Dostoevsky: Essays and Perspectives* (Chatto and Windus, 1971).

Mackenzie, Norman (ed.), *Secret Societies* (Aldus, 1967).

McCormick, Donald, *Pedlar of Death* (Macdonald, 1965). (Sir Basil Zaharoff)

Mack Smith, D. (ed.), *The Making of Italy 1796–1866* (Macmillan, 1968).

Madaule, Jacques, *The Albigensian Crusade* (Burns and Oates, 1968).

Magee, Bryan, *Popper* (Fontana, 1973).

Magnus, Philip, *Gladstone* (Murray, 1954).

Mann, Thomas, *The Magic Mountain* (Secker and Warburg, 1928).*

Markham, S. F., *Climate and the Energy of Nations* (Oxford, 1947).

Martin, E. R., *Where London Ends* (Phoenix House, 1958). (English provincial life since 1700)

Martindale, Andrew, *Man and the Renaissance* (Hamlyn, 1966).

Middlemas, Keith, *Diplomacy and Illusion* (Weidenfeld and Nicolson, 1972).

Minogue, K. R., *The Liberal Mind* (Methuen, 1963).

——, ——, *Nationalism* (Batsford, 1967).

Nassauer, Rudolf, *The Hooligan* (Peter Owen, 1960).*

Neill, A. S., *The Free Child* (Jenkins, 1953).

Neuman, Robert, *Zaharoff the Armaments King* (Allen and Unwin, 1938).

Noel-Baker, Philip, *Challenge to Death* (Constable, 1934).

Oakeshott, Michael, *Rationalism in Politics* (Methuen, 1962).

Osborn, R., *Freud and Marx* (Gollancz, 1937).

Paz, Octavio, *The Labyrinth of Solitude* (Allen Lane, The Penguin Press, 1967).

Plumb, J. H., *Men and Places* (Cresset, 1963).

Price, M. Philips, *My Three Revolutions* (Allen and Unwin, 1970).

Priestley, J. B., *English Journey* (Heinemann, 1938).

Raglan, Lord, *The Hero* (Methuen, 1936).

Rattray Taylor, G., *Sea and History* (Thames and Hudson, 1959).

Rees, David, *The Age of Containment* (Macmillan, 1967).

Reid, Margaret J. C., *The Arthurian Legend* (Oliver and Boyd, 1938).

Reynolds, E. E., *Nansen* (Penguin, 1948).

Reynolds, Reginald and Stock, A. G., *Prison Anthology* (Jarrolds, 1938).

Saurat, Denis, *A History of Religions* (Cape, 1934).

Scott, J. D., *Vickers, a History* (Weidenfeld and Nicolson, 1963).

Silone, Ignazio, *The Story of a Humble Christian*, trans. William Weaver, (Gollancz, 1970). (Celestine V)

Slocombe, George, *William the Conqueror* (Hutchinson, 1959).

Smith, Janet Adam, *John Buchan* (Hart-Davis, 1965).

Soustelle, Jacques, *Mexico* (Barrie, 1969).

Speer, Albert, *Inside the Third Reich* (Weidenfeld and Nicolson, 1970).

Spilka, Mark, *Dickens and Kafka* (Dobson, 1963).

Talmon, J. L., *The Origins of Totalitarian Democracy* (Secker and Warburg, 1952).

Taylor, A. J. P., *The Course of German History since 1815* (Hamish Hamilton, 1945).

——, ——, *The Origins of the Second World War* (Hamish Hamilton, 1961).

Tennyson, Julian, *Suffolk Scene* (Blackie, 1939).

Trevor-Roper, H., *The Last Days of Hitler* (Macmillan, 1947).

——, ——, *Historical Essays* (Macmillan, 1957).

Vansittart, Peter, *Dictators* (Studio Vista, 1974).

——, ——, *The Lost Lands* (Macmillan, 1964).* (The fall of the Templars, the rise of the Brothers and Sisters of the Free Spirit)

——, ——, *Vladivostock: Figures in Laughter* (Covent Garden Press, 1972).

——, ——, *The Dark Tower* (Macdonald, 1965). (English folk tales)

——, ——, *The Shadow Land* (Macdonald, 1967). (English folk tales)

Wells, H. G., *The Work, Wealth and Happiness of Mankind*, (Heinemann, 1932).

Wheeler-Bennett, Sir John, *Nemesis of Power, the German Army in Politics, 1918–1945* (Macmillan, 1964).

——, ——, *King George VI* (Macmillan, 1958).

White, Patrick, *Riders in the Chariot* (Eyre and Spottiswoode, 1961).*

Williams, Raymond, *Culture and Society, 1780–1950* (Chatto and Windus, 1958).

Wilson, Angus, *No Laughing Matter* (Secker and Warburg, 1967).*

——, ——, *The World of Charles Dickens* (Secker and Warburg, 1970).

Young, G. M., *Today and Yesterday* (Hart-Davis, 1948).

* novels

Index